THE BOOK OF POLITICS

Asia-Pacific: Culture, Politics, and Society

Editors: Rey Chow, Michael Dutton,
H. D. Harootunian, and Rosalind C. Morris

The Book of Politics
China in Theory

MICHAEL DUTTON

DUKE UNIVERSITY PRESS
Durham and London
2024

Printed in the United States of America on acid-free paper ∞
Project Editor: Michael Trudeau
Typeset in Minion Pro, Univers LT Std, and Source Han Serif
by Westchester Publishing Services

Library of Congress Cataloging-in-Publication Data
Names: Dutton, Michael Robert, author.
Title: The book of politics : China in theory / Michael Dutton.
Other titles: Asia-Pacific.
Description: Durham : Duke University Press, 2024. | Series:
Asia-Pacific: Culture, Politics, and Society. | Includes bibliographical
references and index.
Identifiers: LCCN 2023052346 (print)
LCCN 2023052347 (ebook)
ISBN 9781478030195 (paperback)
ISBN 9781478025948 (hardcover)
ISBN 9781478059189 (ebook)
Subjects: LCSH: Affect (Psychology)—Political aspects—China. |
Power (Social sciences)—China—21st century. | Ethnology—Study
and teaching—China. | China—Politics and government—2002– |
China—Social conditions—2000– | BISAC: SOCIAL SCIENCE /
Ethnic Studies / Asian Studies | POLITICAL SCIENCE / History
& Theory
Classification: LCC DS779.46 .D88 2024 (print) | LCC DS779.46
(ebook) | DDC 320.01—DC23/ENG/20240220
LC record available at https://lccn.loc.gov/2023052346
LC ebook record available at https://lccn.loc.gov/2023052347

Cover art: Cai Guo-Qiang, *Head On*, 2006. Installation view
at Guggenheim Museum Bilbao. Photo by I-Hua Lee,
courtesy of Cai Studio.

TO DEBORAH

CONTENTS

PART 3. RECONSTRUCTIONS

PART 4. BECOMING MODERN

PART 5. BECOMING POLITICAL

ILLUSTRATIONS

FORE*WORD*

Let's cut to the chase and recognize that the things being critiqued in this book—such as the market—aren't going away anytime soon. At the same time, let's recognize that neither are the problems. Let's also begin by recognizing that some of the arguments I present may prove hard to swallow. Nevertheless, every book has multiple potential readings and therefore multiple potential readerships, and while this book is no exception, its wide-ranging critique of the political and its amoral stance in relation to Mao and the Chinese revolution are likely to irritate, vex, and possibly anger some. Hopefully, however, it might also lead to rethinking across a broad range of readers from a variety of disciplines. Let me try to narrow down the most likely readership for a work such as this.

I'm hoping scholars of area studies will recognize this work as an implicit critique of their field, inspired, in no small part, by what in some circles might be thought of as a postcolonial turn. Here, however, the postcolonial turn is not designed to unveil or unearth an authentic "other" or simply to add non-Western theory and "stir." Rather, pushing theory beyond the Western frameworks in which I and every other Western scholar have been trained is to recognize that the concept of the political is global. This is painful because it involves digging into unconscious attitudes as one might pick at a scab. However, this is not to dismiss Western theory or even to suggest a "provincialism" about it but instead to try to reexamine what undergirds its assumptions and operations. For me, the binary form seems quite central to this form of thinking.

For the China specialist, this work offers a new and novel reading of the early Maoist revolution as well as its postrevolutionary aftermath. In highlighting the connection of the former to the concept of the *jianghu* and the latter to a theory of the gift, not to mention the possibility of treating the economic reform period as a metaphor of the Crystal Palace, this work is hopefully registered as a novel way of writing "area" studies. To gain such insights, we need a change of direction in the flow of theory and a recognition that theory sometimes manifests not as a textual articulation but as a set of material practices. Adopting just such an approach enables me to channel thoughts away from the geographically solid ground of "area" and toward a recognition of practices as being, in themselves, forms of theory. Moving from solids to fluids and from texts to materiality opens a new way of understanding, contextualizing and interpolating the Maoist revolution into the conceptual realm. This is an understanding based less on a set of ideas or texts and more on the unique form of lived, untheorized, and habituated "theory" that was building up beneath the feet of Chinese Marxism-Leninism. This "theory," in catching history in its wings, helped propel Mao and the revolution to victory. Propelled by the idea of "China" less as place and more as a theoretical turn produces a very different account of, and role for, area studies; but this only makes sense if, in embarking on this journey, we set aside the version of Maoism that is encountered in the West as a moral stain on humanity and instead approach it as an inadequately developed, often untheorized, set of technologies and machinery. The advantages of this are that, back-engineered all the way to the Crystal Palace, this work might help cast new light on some of the more intractable contemporary dilemmas that have been thrown up with the growth of modernity. If such amorality does not stick in the throat of Western writers who have built their careers exposing the ills of China or lead the largely Western readership that have swallowed that approach to vomit, then it is possible that this book might produce its own kind of "affective rechanneling."

Such affective rechanneling is political. But to understand it as such involves rechanneling conventions around the gold standard of scientificity within the discipline of political science. In place of science, I have turned not just to China but also to art and the humanities for guidance and inspiration. As a result, both the content and the form of this book are arranged slightly differently to most texts concerned with things political. In this regard, while still only a small step, the novelty of this approach is that it opens new ways of thinking about the concept of the political.

If the book begins with a context section rather than an introduction, it is because context is everything and there can be no understanding outside of it. Moreover, the context in which I am writing and in which we all currently live carries within it tasks of such political urgency as to require us all to rethink and decolonize the politics in which we live. I have attempted to trace the political as a flow of affective but vital energy, and that has not only returned me to China for inspiration but also drawn me toward politics as a field of artistic channeling. Such a simple move involved rethinking the relationship between art and politics and that meant rethinking not just the content but also the form of the book. Hence from its almost aphoristic beginnings right through to its employment of images that go beyond mere illustration at the end, this book attempts to rearticulate a theory of the political through a rearrangement of both form and content. Such grandiosity, however, has been "downscaled" by organizing the work around the flow of vital affective energy as it moved in relation to the concept of the political in the era of modernity. Yet, despite the centrality of affective energy flows within this work, I have said very little throughout this work about figures who have helped me channel my thoughts about the flow of affective energy and who have been instrumental in helping me rethink key areas of the book. The acknowledgments are but a small attempt to rectify that, but before I name names, let me also acknowledge the help of a number of institutions, for this question of institutional help bears on some of the issues that concern me in this book. Four institutions—Griffith University, Goldsmiths College, Tsinghua University, and Beijing Capital Normal University—have supported this work in a variety of ways, but collectively they are part of a problem I want to address in the book. As part of a modern global academic scene, I am effectively writing within but also against such institutions. In some ways then, I am biting the hand of those who have fed me. Thus, while my thanks to them are sincere, they are thanks tempered with the recognition that, as institutions, they are not only tied to but also productive of the system of market veridiction I am railing against. In other words, the academy is part of the problem. Collectively, such institutions are supportive of intellectual work, but that support always comes at a cost. Increasingly drawn into the world of market veridiction and indeed teaching and promoting it, they invariably impose such impossible demands and burdens on academics that the work being produced often ends up resembling versions of products coming off a Fordist assembly line. For a somewhat bespoke work like this, which has taken decades to piece together, such a demanding timeline could not and did not work. The anxiety-inducing results of timelines or ever-increasing demands to write with relevance are replaced by demands to fulfill what are effectively work quotas. While I understand the need for accountability, I also see the systems introduced to bring it about destroying the very work they hope to create. In this respect, therefore, this really is something of a retirement book in that it could have been written only by someone near the end of an academic career who no longer cares about tenure or career advancement and therefore someone for whom the constraints of institutional assessments matter less and less. Freed from such endless anxiety creating yet transitory and superficial concerns and pressures, this book has operated as a space of critique of an academy hell-bent on global expansion, on judging the quality of work only on the basis of grants gained, assessing "usefulness" in administratively conjured-up taxonomies, and applying management techniques learned from the very university teachers who are now oppressed by them. Universities, having long taught systems of market veridiction, now find themselves being devoured by the very systems they created or propounded. And what is the discipline at the heart of that training in administration if not the modern discipline of politics? In leaving behind this Charlie Chaplin factory of modern university times, I feel increasingly drawn to the sentiment expressed by Stefano Harney and Fred Moten when they insist that "the only possible relationship [to the modern university] . . . is a criminal one."[1] The challenge for the university and teachers within it is to prove that logic wrong.

1 Harney and Moten, *The Undercommons*, 26.

ACKNOWLEDGMENTS

For well over a decade, indeed nigh on two, this book has been a journey that has followed the flow of ideas. Following this flow has taken me from Melbourne to London and on to Beijing and from a political science department into a theory positing an art of the political. It is a journey nourished by the gifts of others and it has left debts that seem almost impossible to repay. After all, every twist and turn of this argument, right down to image choice and placement, has been fueled by the friendship and generosity of others. These brief acknowledgments do no justice to the debts I owe, because I can include only a small fraction of those very special people who have left their mark on me and this work.

Some influences are ongoing and easily remembered, and, for me, one of the main ones would have to be the remarkable Harry Harootunian. Harry has been friend and mentor and has always offered his support alongside rigorous critique. Harry, more than many, has pushed me to get this book out because, like me, he believed it has some important things to say. I might long ago have abandoned this entire project were it not for his ongoing encouragement, patience, and occasional impatience. On the topic of patience, Judy Farquhar deserves special mention. As another source of inspiration she generously guided me through a field she is a master in and also showed enormous patience when faced with my carelessness and stupidity. Indeed, only she can answer this riddle: How many versions of the same text can a person read before they simply say, enough already?

To Haiyan Lee, Viren Murthy, and the anonymous readers commissioned by Duke, I can only offer my sincerest and heartfelt thanks for their erudite readings, their understanding, and their willingness to embark on this journey with me. Patience was also a virtue that my editor, Ken Wissoker, has displayed. Along with Ryan Kendall, Ken has shown an appreciation of this book project as being something more than words on a page. The sympathetic understanding of the approach shown by Ken and Ryan, not to mention the rigorous reading and textual corrections of Michael Trudeau, stand in sharp contrast to that of many contemporary publishers who seem to have adopted, or been driven into, a factory model of production.

Throughout this lengthy period of writing and thinking, I've been honored by the friendship of some of China's leading intellectuals and thinkers. Wang Min'an, Xu Zhangrun, and Wang Hui, as well as the curator Huang Du, stand out in this regard. They have helped in too many ways to recount. Former students, both in China and in the West, have been simply amazing. Huang Gang, Suhail Nazir, and Elaine Jefferys are worthy of special mention, as is my former tutor, Wang Yanqiu. Thanks must also go to my current PhD student, Wang Cheng, for the last-minute help he gave. I should also mention my brilliant former research assistant, Sharon Baggio (Li Shaorong), who made my last Duke book so erudite and also started me on the road to this one. I cannot (and probably didn't) thank her enough. Indeed, this book was in many ways meant to be the theory behind the last one but ended up taking on a life of its own. As it did, interlocutors have been plentiful, but John Cash and Scott Lash stand out. Old mentors, like Stephan Feuchtwang, offered stimulating discussion on parts of this work, while friends like Francisco Carballo offered insightful commentary and support on earlier versions. My dear friend Pal Ahluwalia is deserving of a special mention as he stayed with me throughout this journey, not only offering intellectual support but also giving me the gift of unwavering friendship. Other old friends from Adelaide, like Greg McCarthy, also contributed to me thinking through problems in this book, as did friends from my Brisbane days, such as Sue Travaskas and Sang Ye, who not only offered generous support and help but also supplied some of the materials I've used here. Don Miller, Rob McQueen, Zhou Tao, and Zhao Fengshan have always been there for me, while others, Rajyashree Pandey, Sanjay Seth, David Martin, Zhu Jianfei, Borge Bakken, and Phillip Darby, have traveled at least part of this long and forked road. To all of them, whether still with me or not, I offer heartfelt thanks. This journey to completion was peppered with theological discussions on biblical evidence (Allen Kerkeslager), unforgettable exchanges on Maoism (Nick Knight), fabulous comments on and debates about Carl Schmitt (Peter Fenves), not to mention erudite advice on triads and printing (Berend Ter Haar), on bandits and place (Hans Steinmuller), and on the city, place, and the human (Abdou Maliq Simone). And, speaking of place and the human, fieldwork at various sites mentioned was facilitated by support, insights, or contacts from Alf Ludtke in Göttingen, Huang Du in Anren, and Don Gasper in Hong Kong, while much of the writing took place either at home in London or in a small, ancient, and beautiful little *pingfang* my generous and dear friend, the amazing Laura Trombetta Panigadi, allowed me to use as she headed off to Tibet to milk the yaks. I have indeed been blessed with some remarkable and gifted friends. Most of the artwork used in this book has been facilitated through discussions with artists Cai Guoqiang, Joe Fig, Long Taicheng, and Zhao Shudong. Like the aftereffects of moxibustion, discussions with a practice-based traditional Chinese healer, Rey Tiquia, have also left their mark just as the affective energy of my family has been harnessed and carried this work to its penultimate form. My son's wife, Amanda Khairunnisa, proved herself to be the Sherlock Holmes of the internet when she found half-remembered source materials online, while her cousin, the gifted designer, Bunga Larascaesara, helped produce a final prototype of this book that expressed, in form, something that words alone could not. Meanwhile, my son, Tavan, worked tirelessly and selflessly, tracing permissions, checking translations, and pushing me ever onward. He not only ensured that this book saw the light of day but also made sure that I survived this process by guiding me through one of the darkest periods of my life. To him and to his in-laws, I offer both love and thanks.

Finally, there are three people who stand out as having both helped and inspired me and who ended up being woven into the very fabric of this book. They are Stacy Lo, John Reardon, and Deborah Kessler. Without the brilliance of Stacy Lo, who accompanied me on large parts of this journey, I might never have joined the dots between my own past work and the flowing rivers and pooling lakes of the Chinese *jianghu*; nor could I have interpreted, much less used, some rather complex and ancient Chinese works on vital energy. She has been, and continues to be, a wonderful friend, supporter, and interlocutor. It is because of her that the *jianghu* spirit became more than merely a bookish and abstract concept. With her, it gained embodiment. The artist John Reardon is a force of nature with whom I have been through every imaginable season and from whom I have learned much. In some crucial ways, he has "rewired" my thinking. Without his hectoring, I would never have learned to think beyond the bookish textualism the academy encourages, paid attention to the way images themselves "speak," or learned how to weave images into and through textual argument to enhance both. Lastly, and more than ever lately, I realize that without Deborah Kessler, to whom this book is dedicated, none of this would have even been possible. I simply could and would not have continued this work without her. She not only carried out detailed research into the Crystal Palace, spending weeks in the British Library on my behalf, but she also read and approved every sentence and corrected every error. She was the one who helped me bring all these thoughts, images, and experiences together into a form that, hopefully, will excite the reader as much as it has excited me. If you, the reader, decide to go beyond these few words of thanks, my hope is that this book might help you as it has helped me to rethink our world, by rethinking the concept of the political.

Context

Some of the greatest achievements in philosophy could only be compared with taking up some books which seemed to belong together and putting them in different shelves.
Ludwig Wittgenstein[1]

We are entering dangerous times politically and doing so at a moment when the intellectual discipline charged with the task of thinking through the question of politics has little "out of the box" to offer, having become so intellectually embedded in the very system it purports to "objectively" analyze. The system that has imposed these limits is called *market veridiction*.[2] The

1 Wittgenstein, *The Blue and Brown Books*, 44–45.

2 As Wendy Brown writes, "Market principles frame every sphere and activity, from mothering to mating, from learning to criminality, from planning one's family to planning one's death." Brown, *Undoing the Demos*, 67.

framework through which it developed was the nation-state and the impetus for it comes out of modernity's encounter with the telluric. With the environmental crisis, however, our very existence is now threatened because of our inattentiveness to the soil, the nation-state, and, most of all, the modern market. If market veridiction continues to lead to unsustainable growth, the nation-state that has led us into competitive monads will continue to produce conditions that fuel feverish growth. Growth might be killing us, but it is also keeping our dreams alive.

Growth has long been regarded as a key precondition for dreams of democracy, freedom, justice, and the material good life. With such dreams, political science all too often thinks through the same sorts of frameworks and uses the same kinds of analytics as those that guide market calculations and growth predictions.[3] It is a benchmarked, fantasy-inducing world, underpinning a system of market veridiction that, as an a priori, thinks "good" and "growth" are synonymous.

To rethink the question of the political, therefore, involves breaking with the limitation imposed by a field such as political science, which is mired in the rationality of market veridiction. It means moving toward something more akin to an art, rather than a science, of the political. Briefly stated, an art of the political works with fluids rather than solids, focuses on affect and energy rather than on the pragmatic and purely rational and, rather than centering on an understanding of humans as "individual rational utility maximizers," is concerned with the agglutination and dissipation of affective energy flows.[4] It is concerned with the agglutination and dissipation of such flows as they take on a particular "political" form, even when that form may appear to be nonpolitical.

3 The contemporary market has been important to (principally) the US discipline of political science in two ways. First, in terms of an underlying theory, market growth was often central to ethical claims, as was the case with, say, modernization theory. Second, in terms of political calculation, rational choice theory would draw heavily on the methods of econometricians, thereby ensuring that the logic of market-based forms of calculation became the principal method of political calculation. For the former approach, see Gilman, *Mandarins of the Future*. For the latter approach, which grew into rational choice theory, see Amadae, *Rationalizing Capitalist Democracy*.

4 "Individual rational utility maximizers" is an expression used in a short review and critique of rational choice theory. See Brogan, "A Mirror of Enlightenment," 795.

This approach, therefore, draws away from the conventional view of politics centering on concrete institutions, regulations, laws, and policy. It shies away from such an approach, not because these things are unimportant but because their overt functions—be they institutional, legal, or policy based—tend to overshadow and even mask their collective and essentially collaborative role in guiding and harnessing affective energy flows. Recognition of this energy-channeling function of institutions, laws, and policies is not to deny the importance of their manifest functions. Parliaments do make laws and bureaucracies do codify regulations, just as markets will distribute resources, and stadiums will house sporting and entertainment events. At the same time, parliamentarism also arguably reduces the cycles of political violence by de-intensifying debate, stadium sports do focus the emotional intensity of the roar of the crowd onto the game, and, most important, markets do transform affective energy into material desire. Collectively, then, these institutions are essential for any understanding of the political because they all play key roles in directing and channeling the flow of affective energy away from or toward moments of political intensity.[5] Irrespective of whether such machines drive this energy away from or toward political intensity, however, this economy of flows and its relationship to the formation of the modern political is of interest in this book. This art of the political focuses on "machinery," big and small, that is used to channel this vital energy. This book examines how this process develops or is augmented, how manifest functions work with latent channeling functions, and how, why, and where such machinery "leaks." As politics enters more dangerous and unpredictable times, we need to follow this channeling of currents and undercurrents more carefully, despite their unpredictability, instability, and incalculability. How we collectively channel these energy flows, after all, might well determine our collective fate.

With an environmental crisis threatening our very existence, the spread of a pandemic showing the limitations of the nation-state to solve global problems, and intermittent financial crises exposing not just corruption and greed but also the myopic underpinnings of the "science" informing the intellectual discipline guiding decision-making, is it time to face the real possibility that at least some of the intellectual forces unleashed under the modernist code of positivist rationality, the nation-state, and market veridiction have

5 For a study that shares a similar concern with this form of fluid affectivity but takes it in a different direction, see Ahmed, "Affective Economies."

begun to show their age and their limitations? In one way or another, these problems are all symptoms flagging the possibility of global catastrophe. The problem, however, is that the modernist regime of market veridiction has so corrupted critical thought, that any capacity to think beyond its horizon has narrowed in the extreme.

The stranglehold the modern market has achieved is not just over our consumer and working lives, but also over our critical thinking. It has resulted not only in the instrumentalization of reason and bureaucratic stultification but also in the emergence of a particular style of modern thought that is little other than a mimetic reformulation of the commodity process itself. Just as the commodity economy requires an endless material production and reproduction of difference to mask the perpetuation of an always-the-same form (i.e., the commodity), so, too, the cognitive mode of veridiction that accompanied the commodity form does much the same to knowledge but via a somewhat different route.

Underpinning the logic of the "knowledge economy" is the rationality of market veridiction, for to call "knowledge" an "economy" necessarily draws it into marketlike understandings and calculations. Take the modern university and its disciplines. The global university ranking systems employ the techniques of market veridiction to establish status and fee rates, just as the grant system, coupled with the internal operation of managerialism, directs academic agenda-setting. The net result is that the disciplines are made market ready as they are parceled into "use-values." In a field like political studies, this means that critical reflection invariably gives way to policy training, for this is where the discipline's market value increasingly lies. Moreover, there seems to be little ability or encouragement to think outside this style of thought because every potential break is either dismissed or immediately interpellated back into market assessments as a new intellectual trend or fashion, which, in terms of the knowledge economy, leads to more book sales, more grants, more web "hits," more scholarly citations, and, institutionally, a higher university ranking. Market veridiction thereby becomes this key nodal point in a never-ending cycle of potential growth. In this process of endless expansion, the markets might send affective energy flows and potential intensities spiraling in all directions but they are always guided by the profit motive.

Channeled by this money economy into tributaries and eddies, momentary material and immaterial desires can all be seen as symptoms of this larger process of energy redirection or dissipation. The channeling of this energy is, therefore, profoundly political even when it appears to be otherwise. The politicalness of systems of market veridiction, therefore, operates less through the manifest intensification of antagonisms than through the latent but profitable "dissipation" and transformation of energy, and it is in this process that the culture industry comes to play a pivotal role. More than any other domain, the culture industry can channel potential political intensities into energy forms that fuel the roar of the crowd in the stadium or that become romantic songs and gifts that "stand in" for feelings of love in the shopping mall.

In other words, the modern market is a crucial technology of political domestication that transforms affective energy flows into monetizable desires that simultaneously direct them away from thoughts or intentions that might otherwise (and sometimes do) agglutinate into political intensities. This ability of market circuits to pull in virtually all forms of affective energy flows therefore creates the conditions for their (political) dissipation, dispersal, and transformation into desire. In this land of market veridiction, even the manifesto-like arguments of oppositional flows—whether Marxist, post-Marxist, or postmodern—end up as versions strengthening the underlying rational presuppositions of the modern market economy. Yet, just at the very moment when the market regime appears all conquering, just when it reveals no outside, leakages from within begin to pool into signs of potential reenergization.

Past political reenergizations have challenged the process of market-energy dissipation with a politics of "agglutination." Centered on manifestos, party platforms, or even personality cults, agglutinations rely on the imposition of both a unified understanding and a method of action, and these, in turn, rely upon a revivification of political intensity. Such processes, while still in evidence in some quarters, are challenged by other forms today. Today, we face the specter of a new challenge brought on by a dispersed form of subjectivity that is political but not political in the "unified" ways created by past political movements. Far from being unified, the newly emerging social subject is not tied to any program, platform, or manifesto but, instead, takes on a form that Giorgio Agamben once called the "whatever singularities" of the coming community.

"The coming being is whatever being," writes Agamben, and this whatever being, he adds, is whatever entity is one, true, good, and perfect (*quodlibet ens est unum, verum, bonum seu perfectum*).[6] If this Latin phrase catches

6 Agamben, *The Coming Community*, 1.

Agamben's imagination, the events in Beijing's Tian'anmen Square in 1989 make him shudder and turn his imagination into something more concrete and political. Under banners proclaiming the desire for freedom and democracy, Agamben suggests that there was, paradoxically, a "relative absence of determinate content in [the Chinese protesters'] demands."[7] Instead of creating specific, pragmatic agglutinating demands, the Chinese student protesters of 1989 offered abstractions ("freedom and democracy") that enabled the movement of the one, the true, the good, and the perfect, to develop a sense of righteous intensity in the absence of any concrete, unifying manifesto, program, or organization.[8]

A Latin phrase, a Chinese street scene, a dead European language bursting with life, and a set of Chinese characters spelling out the words "democracy and freedom" that were alive to the political but dead to any deductive or concrete meaning. Here was a Chinese protest in which two words—democracy and freedom—flag nothing: nothing that is, other than the fact that "everything" was up for grabs. The Party, the system, their own lives: everything . . . except, perhaps, the nation-state form itself. Here was a movement in which demands were held together and intensified, not by detailed positive affirmations of who or what they were or what they stood for (a manifesto-based politics) or by a tightly disciplined organizational form (a party-based politics) but by a scattered mass of heterogeneous thoughts, fractured into fears,

7 Agamben, *The Coming Community*, 84–85.

8 There were quite pragmatic grounds for the "hollowness" of slogans in Tian'anmen Square in 1989. Over the course of this three-month occupation, the crowd (which was, by definition, always self-selecting) constantly changed. As Beijing students retreated in exhaustion, new energy came to the protests through provincial students coming to Beijing to join what was perceived at the time to be a new revolution. The crowd was made up of an ever-changing, ever-flowing supply of itinerant student protesters. Consequently, the critiques being offered, and values being espoused, while always critical of the regime, were, within that broad framework, also always changing. The leadership of the students could never speak for the student body any more than they could weave the thoughts of any particular moment of the crowd into a manifesto that could bind them all. Instead, unity was maintained because very few words were used to unify them, and those words were open to various possible meanings. In other words, the degree of abstraction enabled unity.

hopes, loves, hates, rumors, desires, and aspirations that gained a unity of sorts in what they stood against rather than what they stood for.[9]

Could this movement not flag the beginnings of a form that other contemporary social movements, be they Occupy, Anonymous, or Extinction Rebellion, then develop? At the level of the subject, did this movement not reinforce an existentially felt sense of righteousness and abjection that would, at the very least, flow into the formation of contemporary Western identity politics? Yet here, too, when this coin is flipped, and these calls for democracy and freedom spill into that other 1989 Tian'anmen mantra of "saving China," did they now also reflect a commitment to a telluric-based patriotism that, in a very different way, inspired Breitbart, Brexit, the alt-right, and an antiestablishment xenophobia? These movements of the populist right might be tied back to a telluric-based ethnonationalism and have antithetical notions of the collective good or individual liberty, but they were still anchored to slogans and ideals that proclaimed their struggle was for democracy, freedom, and justice. With the alt-right, however, this struggle is based on conspiracy narratives, "fake news," and "alternative facts."

No matter whether it manifests as progressive or otherwise, flows will always flow, just as leakages and contradictions, inequalities and injustices will always potentially devolve into challenges to this cognitive regime of market veridiction. What is now being witnessed is the global spread of this "non-form" as it emerges as, or in, a series of movements and disturbances. These movements and disturbances each develop their own forms and their own points of intensity, and these are so culturally, socially, and politically embedded that the very idea of any unifying political manifesto is either an absurdity or a total abstraction. Democracy and freedom might still be their rallying cry, but in the bifurcated world of "alternative facts" and "fake news," these words mean very different things.

The spectacular rise of Donald Trump with his simple slogan "Make America Great Again" or, across the pond, the call to "Get Brexit Done" both demonstrate the "relative absence of determinate content," while still

9 This opposition is not unified into a single "enemy" figure for, as Gloria Davies notes, the students' rather theatrical reenactment of petitioning the emperor suggests a very different form to that of state and civil society, much less a friend/enemy divide. On the petition and its role in 1989, see Davies, "Homo Dissensum Significans."

producing a clustering and intensification around telluric patriotism.[10] This is not, however, the only political form this telluric element can take—think, for instance, of past left-wing national liberation movements—nor is patriotism the only way intensity can be generated. The success of this form of contemporary telluric populism, however, has tended to eclipse those smaller, more fragile progressive movements that are channeling energy and lighting "prairie fires" across continents in seemingly unconnected and quite random, often localized, ways.

Less a "movement" than a trend, less a trend than a telltale sign of a potential future political taking shape, these sparks sometimes appear as quickly as they disappear; sometimes they appear only as minor triggers, while at other times they become fully formed social movements. They range from overt political waves of destabilization like the Arab Spring, through to the trigger mechanisms generating new cultural norms such as the #MeToo movement and Black Lives Matter. They also include those forms dismissed as "purely criminal," like the 2011 London "riots" as well as those political "platforms" increasingly criminalized, such as Anonymous, WikiLeaks, and LulzSec. Herein lie certain facets of whatever subjectivity, revealing themselves as part of a new "glocal," political refusenik culture.

Enough is enough, but what is not enough has not yet been decided. Even the formation and rise and fall of some recent European political parties and coalitions, be they on the left, the right, or simply the edge of confusion (for example, Greece's SYRIZA, Spain's Podemos, Britain's UK Independence Party, France's National Front, and Italy's Five Star Movement), speak to this informal refusenik culture. Manifesting as antiestablishment and antiglobalization, both the left and right are responding to the alienation that the market-based dissipation of energy has produced. In these movements, the whistleblower is the newfound hero, while new technology (whether made up of tweets, Instagram memes, or TikTok videos) is the newfound

10 The telluric is an important concept in this work. The word itself comes from the Latin *tellus*, meaning "earth," or *terra*, but it is (strangely) tied to flow. Most often referred to in relation to a "telluric current," it signals the natural electric current flowing near the earth's surface. Here, however, I want to add to this fluidity something of the spirit of Carl Schmitt's usage by referring to practices that relate to the earth itself or to those culturally and spatially grounded and embedded practices that are tied to the earth. For Schmitt's usage, see Schmitt, *The Theory of the Partisan*.

means of communication and "organization." As new technologies reduce the complexity and size of the message being communicated, the dominant mode of understanding also begins to shift. A simplification and reduction of "variables" is one effect, but more positively, there has been a change in the very mode of political thought. A "this, this, and this, but not that" definitional logic is gradually being replaced with a new, and growing, politico-knowledge sensibility that says "not this, not even this, and definitely not that." Here, then, is a negative politics that, paradoxically, still displays a vibrant political positivity. A politics of "whatever" that was first spotted by Agamben on the streets of Beijing during the events of Tian'anmen Square back in 1989[11] has now gone "viral" and turned "glocal." If market veridiction helped produce this particular "whatever" sensibility, it was through new social media that it went viral. New social media could do this because it was a market that both government and business could exploit. In China, "supply-side" disciplinary technology proved highly effective in preventing the spread of COVID in its early stages but, in the West, it was read as simply another sign of China's rising authoritarianism. This system, which requires the mass scraping and extraction of personal online information, had already been "stress tested" in China with earlier attempts to turn credit-card systems into a disciplinary mechanism,[12] by using a series of techniques that were first developed in the West. In the United States, data extraction would be combined with psychological profiling and machine-driven algorithms to tap into, target, and influence consumer desire. The results might have been mixed but they nevertheless proved highly profitable when employed in relation to the sale of product. Drawn from the world of push-marketing, such techniques would also enter the political realm as technologies that could help influence voter behavior. The election of Donald Trump highlighted the power of business techniques in politics and, more than ever before, opened onto the virtual world. In the United States, the clustering of left-leaning elements around groups, like Extinction Rebellion, might still be attacking the "establishment," but Trump's assault on the "establishment" was from the right. Business, not politics, should rule, and competition and growth as well as draining the swamp combined in his ethnonationalistic "America First" campaign.

11 Agamben, *The Coming Community*, 85.

12 It is important to note that, at the time of writing, this system was still not unified nor is it clear that it ever will be. See Matsakis, "How the West Got China's Social Credit System Wrong."

Trump's inflammatory tweeting, his hyperbole, not to mention his claims about "the establishment" and "fake news" all played to an alt-right songbook but did so through an update of techniques familiar to any Barnum and Bailey circus act. Most important, the techniques were suited to a digital age of consumption—the constant and quick surfing of the net, picking up on viral iconoclastic trends while simultaneously turning away from those that were regarded as passé or uninteresting. Sensationalism dominated as this mode of knowledge consumption increasingly turned anything and everything into bite-sized commentaries. Meanwhile, viral trends emerged like fashion fads alongside "alternative facts." In this way, the unified, disciplined organizational forms of more "grounded" politics were being forced to adapt to this new, often unpredictable, rhizomic form that mimicked and resembled the virtual and viral world and gave these new forms of organization protean life.

One does not have to be wedded to the vitalist tektology of Alexander Bogdanov[13] to realize that the question of organization is also a question of cognition. Modes of production leading to forms of organization producing different styles of thought are increasingly changing the way we interact with the world around us. Cyberspace leads from ground to air, from static to mobile, and from the mechanical, linear, and hierarchical to the rhizomic and virtual. Cyberspace induces a mode of cognition that is not only transforming traditional organizational forms and practices, such as mainstream political parties, but, more importantly, also changing the way in which the political manifests as a crowd and, once again, it is in Beijing that the first signs of things to come would be witnessed.

Ten years after the crushing of the "whatever" politics of Tian'anmen Square, one of the world's most successful mass-based grassroots political organizations, the Chinese Communist Party, once again faced a political threat from the streets. This time, however, there would be no warning signs, only the shock of a crowd's appearance. As if by some magical conjuring trick, followers of the heterodox spiritualist cult known as Falungong suddenly appeared before the leadership compound in Beijing in numbers too big to ignore.[14] What was significant about this crowd, however, was not just their

13 For details on Bogdanov's vitalism, see Bogdanov, *Essays in Tektology*, chap. 4.

14 For details and conspiracy stories surrounding this, see Palmer, *Qigong Fever*, 270–71.

numbers, but their stealth. Here was a mass protest that totally blindsided the so-called omnipotent Mao-era mass-line surveillance system.[15] Suddenly, one morning, in front of the Beijing leadership compound, Zhongnanhai, an estimated ten thousand silent protesters gathered in prayer. One text message, and the crowds appeared, avoiding every one of state security's "eyes and ears."[16] Pioneering the use of text messaging as a means of discreetly organizing mass gatherings, Falungong opened a new and parallel political frontier outside the purview of the then "grounded" and mass-based street-level surveillance system. In so doing, Falungong began to "morph" the telluric guerrilla-style tactics of the Mao-era partisan into something it could use to outfox the Maoist mass-line security system. Falungong pioneered the use of the text message as a protest weapon in 1999 but, by the time of the Arab Spring of 2011, the use of text messaging had become part of a myriad of web-based tactics that would interweave the new social movements into the new social media and feed into claims that this technology signaled the dawning of a new era of democracy.[17]

The 1999 Falungong protests shocked the Chinese Communist Party establishment just as the 2011 Blackberry-texting rioters in London and other British cities frightened the British establishment, and just as internet-savvy protest groups, whistleblowers, and hackers have unnerved the US establishment. If Falungong offered a small glimpse of the new, virtual mass-line guerrilla technology of future mass movements, the Chinese government's

15 While one cannot say that the Chinese government changed tack as a result of this blindsiding, it is clear that they have indeed changed. By 2014, James A. Lewis, a computer security expert at the Center for Strategic and International Studies in Washington, even went so far as to claim that "China does more in terms of cyberespionage than all other countries put together." See Sanger and Perlroth, "NSA Breached Chinese Servers Seen as Security Threat."

16 In effect, the eyes and ears (*zhi'an ermu*) that the Chinese police had used for years failed them. "Eyes and ears" is an expression used by the Chinese public security forces to describe their street-level informants. Falungong's protest totally outflanked this system that had ensured "stability" even in the most difficult of times under Mao and into the reform years. Indeed, even when protests erupted in 1976, and again in 1989, they were both well flagged. What was surprising about the Falungong protest in front of Zhongnanhai on April 25, 1999, was that it took the Chinese state totally by surprise. For a leadership so used to mass control, this must have come as both a shock and a threat.

17 Hempel, "Social Media Made the Arab Spring."

post-Falungong response revealed the state's growing realization that these tactics opened a new frontier of politics. From facial-recognition technology to the social credit system, the Chinese government has, since this time, invested heavily in high-tech experimentation. The Falungong protest didn't just force the Communist Party to become internet savvy, it also led them to address this issue in a way that helps shine a light on the process of (re)channeling (potential) political intensity. This, at least, could be one conclusion drawn from the findings of Gary King and his research team, who examined the post-Falungong but pre–Xi Jinping internet censorship strategies of the Chinese government.[18]

Censorship in China, the King studies show, was not so much designed to silence all dissent but "to muzzle those outside government who attempt to spur the creation of crowds for any purpose—in opposition to, in support of, or unrelated to the government."[19] In other words, Chinese government internet censors were less concerned with dissent than with rechanneling any signs of potential political intensity into forms of political quietism.[20] So-called internet spikes—that is, sites that went viral, attracting large numbers of clicks—were the sites focused on, not because of any political position they held or principles they espoused but based on their potential to generate intensities that could lead from the virtual world back to the streets. If a spike could potentially turn into street-level action, then the goal became to flatten it. That was attempted in many ways, but one may well have involved the use of the so-called 50 Cent Army, which was said to rechannel traffic away from potentially dangerous spikes with the allure of clickbait.[21] Harmonious

18 Gary King, Jennifer Pan, and Margaret E. Roberts demonstrate the way Chinese government censors employed a three-pronged approach, involving (1) building a virtual wall, (2) key-blocking banned words or phrases, and (3) manually reading and removing text. King's quantitative big-data studies focused on the latter and covered over 11 million social media posts from almost 1,400 Chinese websites. See King, Pan, and Roberts, "How Censorship in China Allows Government Criticism," 326.

19 King, Pan, and Roberts, "Reverse-Engineering Censorship in China," 891.

20 This approach excludes the Chinese government's total ban on internet pornography. See King et al., "How Censorship in China Allows Government Criticism," 326.

21 In his 2012 Distinguished Lecture to the UC Davis Institute of Social Science, King also points out that the infamous pro-government 50 Cent Army, *Wumaodang*,

society (*hexie shehui*), it seems, involved ensuring that the virtual crowd did not turn into a street crowd. This kind of manipulation, channeling, and redirection of internet flows, in order to redirect affect away from political intensity, is not confined to China but where China's concerns are to ensure a politically "harmonious society," in the West, it is (once again) used to enshrine profit as the principal goal.

Shoshana Zuboff describes how a financial crisis that engulfed the search engine company Google started a process that rather quickly developed into what she has called "surveillance capitalism."[22] In the late 1990s, Google had technologically sophisticated software, a user-friendly interface, and the biggest index of any of the search engines.[23] What it didn't have was any idea about how to monetize these factors. Then, notes Zuboff, they discovered advertising. In particular, they discovered how data being scraped from their search engine—the extraneous material that had, up until that point, been treated as "data exhaust"—could actually be gold dust to advertisers. The data that was being scraped enabled mass consumer profiling that could more accurately, timely, and cost-effectively produce targeted advertising. As Zuboff notes, "Google had discovered a way to translate its nonmarket interactions with users into surplus raw material for the fabrication of products aimed at genuine market transactions with real customers: advertisers."[24] While Google was first, others quickly followed. Aided by the surveillance-friendly regulatory regime of post-9/11 America,[25] Microsoft, Amazon, and Facebook, along with many other companies, explored different routes and

---

if it is dispatched at all, is used not to bombard sites with pro-government propaganda and thereby raise the degree of political intensity, but to lure internet traffic away from such sites and concerns, by producing bursts on other sites that are likely to distract. In other words, Chinese censorship is built around halting the eruption of political intensities, not stamping out all criticism. See G. King, "How Censorship in China Allows Government Criticism but Silences Collective Expression," Fung Institute for Engineering Leadership, accessed July 17, 2015, https://www.youtube.com/watch?v=hybtm4Fp1jc.

22 See Zuboff, *The Age of Surveillance*.

23 In 1999, Google had the biggest index, having indexed fifty million pages. See J. Mitchell, "How Google Search Really Works."

24 Zuboff, *The Age of Surveillance*, 93.

25 Zuboff, *The Age of Surveillance*, 9.

different methods of scraping data for profit, creating what Zuboff has called "a behavioral futures market."[26] In this context, she says, goods and services became mere supply routes for data. "It's not the car; it's the behavioral data from the car. It's not the map; it's the behavioral data from interacting with the map," she concludes.[27]

"Big data" was now big business, and that business was knowing consumer moods, ideally in real time and ahead of the consumers themselves. From the analysis of the spikes of collective internet activity through to the individual likes and dislikes from emoticons, data would be extracted and "crunched" in order to produce the appearance of a predictive ability that advertisers could exploit. From cookies that tracked millions of virtual links and Google maps that tracked millions of terrestrial journeys, people's documented habits, interests, temptations, and tastes became the raw material that, through predictive analytic modeling, channeled affective energy into material desire, thereby helping reinforce political quietism. In this respect, the behavioral futures market of which Zuboff writes is, like any contemporary market, a political machine that dissipates and transforms affective energy. While this makes it intrinsically political, it was, surprisingly, never really treated as such until the Facebook scandal of 2018. That was when this technology and methodology was directly applied to politics.

The ensuing scandal revolved around the company Cambridge Analytica (CA), which used megadata scraped from Facebook accounts to find "trigger emotions." From the data analysis, CA was able to produce targeted political advertisements that were specifically designed to tap into a person's unconscious fears and hopes.[28] While such overtly dark political arts, designed to push voter sentiment through unconscious triggers, was thought scandalous, as a business model, it had gone virtually unnoticed. Hence, once the scandal passed, so, too, did much of the public anxiety and anger about the data-scraping industry. Aided by "free product" and a mass media that both sensationalizes but quickly forgets, data scraping once again became a simple "business model," albeit one that exponentially expanded the market by extending it into cyberspace. Paradoxically, perhaps, the sensationalism en-

26 Zuboff, *The Age of Surveillance*, 96.

27 Zuboff, *The Age of Surveillance*, 131.

28 See Cadwalladr and Graham-Harrison, "How Cambridge Analytica Turned Facebook 'Likes' into a Lucrative Political Tool."

couraged by this system can also lead to small and seemingly inconsequential things upsetting the apple cart and triggering re-intensifications. The protests that took place in Hong Kong in 2019 exemplified this.

Sparked by a proposed bill that would have allowed the extradition of suspected criminals from Hong Kong to Mainland China, the 2019 protests saw unprecedented numbers of Hong Kong residents taking to the streets in a series of protests that quickly intensified into a mass movement.[29] The Chinese Communist Party regarded this as yet another challenge to its sovereignty over the territory, and it forced the bill through the Hong Kong legislature, leading to more demonstrations that became larger and more violent. Yet the violence and this challenge to Chinese sovereignty over the territory are not what is of interest here. Rather, just like the 1989 Tian'anmen and 1999 Falungong protests examined earlier, it is the tactics and technologies employed by these 2019 Hong Kong protesters and the forms of subjectivity they reveal that are of interest here, for these shed light on key facets of a new political. Where the Tian'anmen Square protests of 1989 announced the arrival of a new form of subjectivity—the "whatever singularities" of the Tian'anmen Square protesters—and the Falungong protests of 1999 highlighted the creative, disruptive potential of new social media, what the Hong Kong protests of 2019 shed light on was the "fluidity" lying at the heart of questions of the political.

Drawing on techniques from the 2011 Occupy movement in New York, and from their own 2014 Central Occupy movement, the 2019 protesters in Hong Kong showed a penchant for sign language; employed a dispersed, leaderless "non-structure"; and used the iconicity of popular culture to promote their cause.[30] Hong Kong's Sino-hybridic "mash-up" culture provided the resources drawn on by protesters that enabled them to "fit in" as they stood up and stood out. They would "fit in" by wearing the oft-used face mask to hamper state-run facial-recognition technology. This led the authorities at the time of COVID to ban the wearing of face masks. Protesters would stand

29 The reason for the proposed bill appears to be driven by the Mainland's desire to further assert Chinese sovereignty over the territory. The issue of extradition arose after a nineteen-year-old Hong Kong man was alleged to have murdered his twenty-year-old pregnant girlfriend while holidaying in Taiwan. Taiwan wanted him extradited but had no treaty. It was then that the Chinese government realized neither did they. For details, see Li, "Hong Kong-China Extradition Plans Explained."

30 Li and Ives, "Fueling the Hong Kong Protests."

out by putting East Asian cool to work, creating propaganda videos that used Japanese anime techniques to get their message across. Hollywood iconicity was also enlisted, with one poster of a Quentin Tarantino film showing the face of the then chief minister of Hong Kong, Carrie Lam, in place of the actor Uma Thurman's, but still carrying the poster's original message: "Kill Bill." The biggest icon of all for this movement, however, was their own homegrown martial arts hero, Bruce Lee. It was from Bruce Lee that they would draw their orientation, inspiration, and form.

"Be water, my friend," Lee once said and, in the hothouse atmosphere of Hong Kong in 2019, these words sent shock waves across the territory and led millions to the streets. A sensibility drawn straight from Taoist scriptures[31] yet proving so powerful it even influenced the Legalism of Guanzi,[32] now became a statement of defiance, protest, and action.

"Be water" meant being anonymous, spontaneous, flexible, and evasive;[33] it meant flash mobs, guerrilla protests, spontaneous roadblocks, and the circling of buildings.[34] Where Occupy occupied, the Hong Kong movement moved. Moreover, new technology enabled the protesters to move with stealth and agility while the new social media gave them their platform. This was activism working in tandem with new social media formats that were themselves fluid and expanding. At the same time, it also pointed to a tradition, culture, and language through which to "speak" of the fluidity within the political.

The return to a classical Taoist understanding of flow furnished the Hong Kong protests with a language of political fluidity, and this same source furnishes this book with the resources it needs to think the political in a more fluid way, albeit in a radically different way from the Hong Kong protesters.

31 This quotation was drawn from a short video clip of an interview with Bruce Lee that had already attracted 2.5 million views since it was posted in 2013. The clip captures that part of the interview where Lee says, "Empty your mind, be formless; shapeless, like water. If you put water into a cup, it becomes the cup. You put water into a bottle and it becomes the bottle. You put it in a teapot, it becomes the teapot. Now, water can flow or it can crash. Be water, my friend." See Lee, "Bruce Lee Be as Water My Friend."

32 For Guanzi's unique take on this question of water and life, see Guanzi, "Water and Earth."

33 Zhou and Wong, "Be Water," l.

34 Atkin, "Hong Kong Protests Embrace Bruce Lee."

Like the Hong Kong protesters, the references back to Taoism are made here only in order to shed light, not on the past, but on our present political predicament. The importance of fluidity in this book is marked not just by content, but also by "form." The chapters offer a series of ever-extending, ever-developing vignettes. An initial glance might suggest that these vignettes are random and unconnected, yet these seemingly inconsequential stories trickle toward ideas that pool into illustrations, exemplifications, and arguments about various facets of the political. The appearance of the political in the everyday, its binary quality, and its formation across cultures, not to mention its visibility as it intensifies, form some of the conceptual issues that travel through the pages of this work and lead us toward two modes of being political in the modern era.

One leads us into examples drawn from Mao-era China, where the state itself became the vehicle carrying a series of experimental technologies through which affective energy would be channeled, harnessed, and transformed into political intensities. The other mode, developed in the West, but also very much a part of China's economic reform, channels energy in a very different way. The Crystal Palace was an early progenitor of this new type of technology, designed to dissipate, diffuse, and transform affective energy and turn it into material desire. It was a prototype that would transform affective energy into a form that proved productive both of profit and of political quietism. It flagged the early signs of a division of labor that would ultimately carve divisions into life itself as it attempted to make the human subject ever more calculable and knowable, even when human eruptions, abnormalities, contradictions, and paradoxes pointed to incalculability. It is at this point that we come to recognize that the modern technologies designed to effect moods, feelings, and emotions have a longer history than the internet era. With this new era, however, the sheer magnitude of change has produced a qualitative change. The tectonic plates of the political are, therefore, shifting and as they move, they require a more fluid understanding of this history. To begin to develop this understanding, let us start with the seemingly least political of material objects, the domestic home appliance.

PART 1

Beginnings

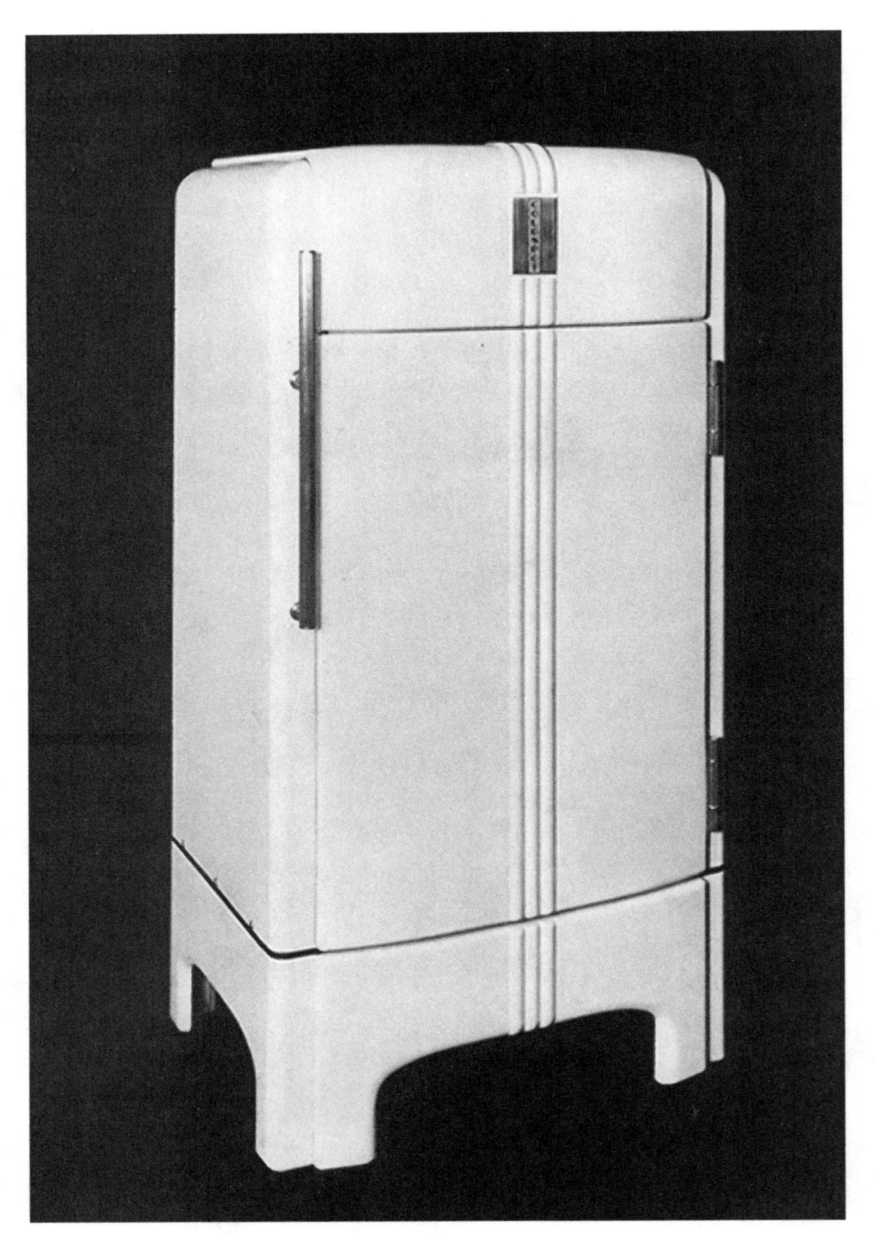

Figure 1.1. The Coldspot refrigerator, 1934. Image courtesy of Sears.

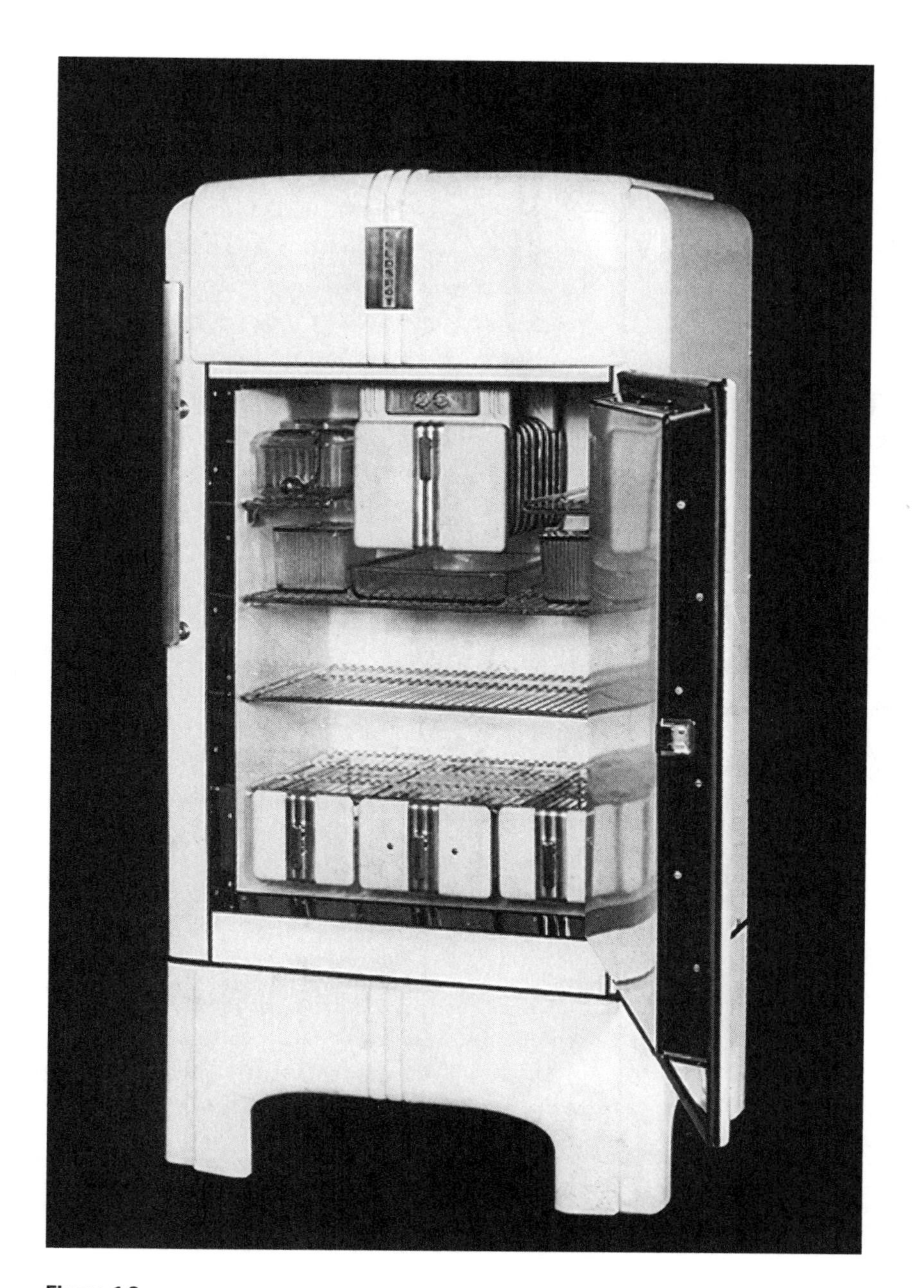

Figure 1.2.

1

Almost Aphoristic

Small Things

In his book *Domestic Spaces in Post-Mao China: On Electronic Household Appliances*, Wang Min'an looks at some of the little things in life: the washing machines, refrigerators, radios, television sets, mobile phones, computers, and electric lighting that are all designed to make life in the modern world feel easier and more comfortable (for examples, see figures 1.1 and 1.2). The introduction of these appliances into the household has had side effects and not just in terms of domestic female labor. Not only have these devices led to changes in the design and spatial ordering of households but, more importantly and quite unconsciously, they have reframed the ethical comportment of contemporary family members. In any understanding of family ethics, Wang tells us, the design of domestic space has always been important, even though it has largely been thought of as no more than a container holding in place a series of important kinship relations. Not anymore.[1]

In the contemporary world, Wang tells us, domestic space is no longer an auxiliary framework for family ethics.[2] This relationship has been overturned as the domestic space was redesigned to cater to an array of domestic electronic devices. With the introduction of these devices, domestic space, and the family relations within it, is altered profoundly. Wang doesn't explain how this transformation took place, nor does he focus on the obviously gendered nature of these changes. Instead, he focuses on the devices themselves and how they produce an array of spatial, cognitive, and sensory changes through the interlacing of domestic life and domestic appliances. He tells of how television sets create a particular spatial relation within the home between the viewer, the television set, and the couch and how radio, unlike television, doesn't produce visual relations but instead creates a very precise acoustic relationship between the ear and the sound. He notes, too, how washing machines enforce a domestic rhythm just as the existence of the refrigerator changes the ways we shop, cook, eat, and choose what we are able to eat.

Collectively, these appliances have established new household rhythms; built very particular relationships between light, sound, object, and subject; and encouraged a series of habituated patterns of behavior that have gradually come to change our relationship with nature. Household devices open onto a very different set of experiences between humans and the world around them. One might say, more in the language of Michel Foucault than Wang Min'an, that the domestic space has become a training ground of a new and modern form of biopolitical subject. This technical training and habituation, in establishing very different relationships between people and things, has led to an entirely new and different relationship developing between humans and the natural world. Moreover, the ethical regimes of traditional families, forged on the basis of a telluric embedded sensibility, have given way to a very different way of seeing, living, and being in the world.

1 Wang, *Domestic Spaces in Post-Mao China*, 82.

2 Near the end of his book on domestic appliances, Wang reflects on the rapid changes they have produced in China. The "auxiliary framework" (*fushu kuangjia*) of family ethics is the architecture and design of the household space, which underwent a dramatic change in urban China in the 1990s. For the West, of course, the effects were slower and occurred much earlier in history. See Wang, *Domestic Spaces in Post-Mao China*, 83.

The idea that small, seemingly insignificant machines have the ability not only to rearrange the domestic spatial order but to actually tilt life ontologically away from its telluric sensibilities into a machine-driven age is of help not just in detailing the operations of biopolitics in the modern domestic sphere, but, more generally, in helping us rethink the ontological and epistemological dimensions of modern public, political life through "devices." It is at this point, however, to steal a word from Sara Ahmed's work on affective economies, that things begin to get "sticky."[3]

For Ahmed, objects that accumulate "affective value" are those that become "sticky."[4] In her textual analysis, however, "stickiness" moves from white hate speech through to the masking of shame by public statements of regret. Through such examples she shows how affective value is an accumulated investment of emotions in objects of fear, pain, hate, shame, and disgust.[5] Emotions, she writes, being both performative and relational, involve "(re) actions or relations of 'towardness' or 'awayness' in relation to such objects."[6] Emotions, she continues, work to "generate the distinction between inside

3 "Sticky" is how Sara Ahmed refers to a particular agglutination of energy within what she calls *affective economies*. In her argument, affective energy circulates and flows, sliding sideways and backward, becoming "sticky" as energy attaches itself to certain things and people and is thereby charged. See Ahmed, "Affective Economies," 120. Stickiness, in Ahmed's account, generally tends toward the negative. Thus, while I have drawn this term from Ahmed, I have employed it slightly differently. For Ahmed, stickiness is a device by which to examine "how emotions can attach us to the very conditions of our subordination" whereas this approach regards "stickiness" as being far more promiscuous and tied neither to subordination nor to liberation but to context. See Ahmed, *The Cultural Politics of Emotion*, 12.

4 Ahmed, *The Cultural Politics of Emotion*, 11.

5 In this respect, Ahmed's work shares something of a family resemblance with the works of Judith Butler and Wendy Brown, who draw on contemporary feminist and queer theory as well as continental philosophy and psychoanalysis to trace questions of the political through particular emotional expressions—be they shame, grief, hate, or pain—which in their very performativity take the arguments back toward a closer encounter with identity politics. See Brown, *States of Injury*, and Butler, *Gender Trouble*.

6 Ahmed, *The Cultural Politics of Emotion*, 8.

and outside" through a process of differentiation and "othering."[7] Here, however, we are interested less in the interplay of emotions that produce "stickiness" and identity through othering than the general process of channeling affective flows through various "devices" toward or away from (political) intensities. Yet, in moving away from the private, agonal, domestic space of Wang's devices into the more symbolic public spaces—public squares, statues, monuments, or palaces of government—do we not also simultaneously move a step closer to objects of overt political "stickiness"? After all, the monumental public spaces of the state all desire stickiness and aim to produce it through symbolic references to things like "the people," the race, the nation, or the father- or motherland. Because the raison d'être of such state-sponsored machinery is to help forge a communal sense of oneness, public political machinery is therefore "geared" in a radically different fashion than the electronic appliances of the domestic biosphere described by Wang.

Everyday household appliances may well impose a discipline on the domestic subject and transform their ethical comportment and ontological orientation, but they do so only as side effects of their primary function. That function is invariably tied to their use-value in the household production process (dishwashers are there to wash dishes, refrigerators are designed to preserve food, and so on).[8] This is not the case with the public monument. The monument is designed to edify a particular ethical comportment. That is its raison d'être. This difference leads monuments to have very different degrees, forms, and expressions of stickiness and it is for this reason that a comparison shines a light on the question of the political. While Wang's biopolitical devices are no less sticky than public monuments, their stickiness comes not from political intensity, but from the market's ability to tap into affective energy flows, work out trigger emotions, and transform these devices into something more than just a use-value. Their stickiness, then, lies in the phantasmagoric element of the commodity form. Wang's everyday devices

7 Ahmed, *The Cultural Politics of Emotion*, 194.

8 This puts into a different perspective Graham Harman's claim that Latour's actor-network theory "like the ancient Megarians" suggests that "no one is a house builder unless they are currently building a house." Here, in the habituated household space, the dishwasher is always a dishwasher, irrespective of whether it is in use or not. This controversy between Latourian ANT (actor-network theory) and OOO (object-oriented ontology), however, is beyond the scope of this work. For details of Harman's critique, see Harman, *Immaterialism*, 10.

are, therefore, still political, just as many overtly political devices are also habituated into the everyday.

Whether we turn to the Hitler salute, which entered the everyday political realm as an attempt to turn fascism into an habitualized gesture,[9] or think of the Lenin badge as Vladislav Todorov does, as the "smallest unit of communism,"[10] the political can clearly enter the most private of spheres. These sorts of micro-level "devices," as they enter the everyday lifeworld, take us beyond the monumental, beyond any public/private divide, and as they become habituated, even beyond the belief systems in which they are embedded. As part of the habits of the everyday, they come from, and go into, "the lower depths, in the most diversified zone of life."[11] They are the machines and devices that push the political into the everyday political and attempt to habituate political ideas as lived everyday values, gestures, and comportments.

What the fascist salute and the communist badge share is neither a look nor an outlook. What they share is a use-value within what Ahmed refers to as affective economies.[12] Within such an affective economy, both the Hitler salute and the Lenin badge operate as part of an ensemble of devices and machines—some trivial and minuscule, others monumental and massive—that work in tandem to channel affective energy flows toward specific expressions of political intensity. Despite the manifest differences between fascism and socialism, the use-value given to their devices reveals their role and meaning within their distinctive systems. This is not to suggest communism and fascism are the same, only that their mode of operation differs significantly from market-based political systems that, in the main, use the commodity form to dissipate and transform intensity into material desire and desire into profit. It is, therefore, not that market economies are less

9 In becoming an everyday gesture, Tilman Allert says, it thereby provides "the most information about how people communicate, where they draw their boundaries and what they choose to disclose and conceal." Allert, *The Hitler Salute*, 3.

10 Todorov, *Red Square, Black Square*, 40.

11 Writing about the small Lenin badges worn on the lapels of Soviet Party members, Vladislav Todorov wrote that "badges impregnate the microstructures of everyday consciousness and expand the circuit of the 'universal connection' of communism down in the lower depths, in the most diversified zone of life." Todorov, *Red Square, Black Square*, 40.

12 See Ahmed, "Affective Economies."

political than the manifestly political nation-states and/or states of Being, it is just that their "machinery" is designed to channel affective energy in a radically different direction to regimes that have geared their machinery to the production of political intensity.

Think of Wang's household appliances and the disparate array of ontological effects they produced. These effects "shatter" the subject into an array of routines, comportments, actions, and desires. Devices that lead to a dissipation of energy and its transformation into material desire are poles apart from the overt political machinery that attempts to (re)assemble and unify the subject through a process of channeling affective energy into a single intense political cause. These radically different functions are not a matter of scale or a distinction between public and private realms. Instead, they should be thought of as being different modes of being political. These two modes of being political are not necessarily or ever fully discrete but are rendered in this study more as ideal types to show the way in which, in radically different ways, there is a circling of energy around that fundamental question of the political: the friend/enemy distinction. To ask about the "towardness" or "awayness" of an emotion in relation to the political is, therefore, to be drawn back to the distinction Carl Schmitt once made between friend and enemy.

The Political

> A definition of the political can be obtained only by discovering and defining the specifically political categories. . . . The political must therefore rest on its own ultimate distinctions, to which all action with a specifically political meaning can be traced. . . . The question then is whether there is also a special distinction which can serve as a simple criterion of the political and of what it consists. . . . The specific political distinction to which political actions and motives can be reduced is that between friend and enemy. This provides a definition in the sense of a criterion and not as an exhaustive definition or one indicative of substantial content.[13]

In circling around binaries of distinction, we cannot avoid Carl Schmitt's concept of the political, with its focus on the friend/enemy distinction. This focus does not, however, lead to a spotlight being shone on the friend, as Jacques Derrida's work does, any more than it requires following Leo Strauss's pre-

13 Schmitt, *The Concept of the Political*, 26.

scription and putting weight on the enemy.[14] It does not veer toward the exception (Giorgio Agamben) or attempt an agonistic incision between antagonistic pairs (Chantal Mouffe).[15] Instead, it will begin with the process whereby, for Schmitt, the political gains its authoritativeness.[16]

This authoritativeness of the friend/enemy distinction stems from the existential possibility of death that is carried in its most intense and extreme moment of eruption.[17] In other words, the greater the degree of intensity the political can muster, the more authoritative it becomes. This is because a high degree of political intensity opens onto a capacity within us not just to kill, but to kill without personal hate. It is this capacity that Schmitt insists differentiates political violence from actions he deems to be apolitical, private, and agonal.[18] Given that the authoritativeness of the political rests on the release of such intensity, is it any wonder that Schmitt would later gravitate toward the view that the political was, in the words of Jan-Werner Müller, "purely a matter of intensity"? In Müller's reading, "any antithesis, if it was strong enough, could become political," and his conclusion was, therefore, that "it was not the substance of enmity that mattered, but the intensity of an existential threat."[19]

14 Derrida, *Politics of Friendship*; L. Strauss, "Notes on Carl Schmitt." See Schmitt, *Concept of the Political*, 81–108.

15 Agamben, *Homo Sacer*; Mouffe, *Return of the Political*.

16 "The political entity is by its very nature the decisive entity, regardless of the sources from which it derives its last psychic motives. It exists or does not exist. If it exists, it is the supreme, that is, in the decisive case, the authoritative entity." Schmitt, *Concept of the Political*, 43–44.

17 Schmitt says that "the friend, enemy and combatant concepts receive their real meaning precisely because they refer to the real possibility of physical killing. War follows from enmity. War is the existential negation of the enemy." Jan-Werner Müller uses this quote to argue that herein lies the link between his concept of the political, constitutional theory and state unity. Here, it could be added, in anticipation of what is about to be argued, it tied his theory to solids and not to fluidity. On the Schmitt quote and Müller's use of it, see Müller, *A Dangerous Mind*, 33.

18 This possibility of killing without personal hate founds Schmitt's idea of a public enemy and it is the "publicness" of the enemy that separates political violence from that associated with personal, private, or agonal vendettas. Meier, *The Lesson of Carl Schmitt*, 28–29.

19 Müller, *A Dangerous Mind*, 32.

It was the possibility of this high degree of intensity that also enabled the political to cut across all domains and issue forth a "material power which mere 'ideas,' 'rational ends,' or 'normativities' lack."[20] Such intensity congeals, according to Heinrich Meier, into a "fluid, aggregate state" that leads, in Schmitt's case, to a "battle of faith."[21] Meier's focus on political theology leads him back to Schmitt's Catholicism and to highlight the biblical origin of Schmitt's understanding of the political.[22] Schmitt's faith, however, is not our concern; political intensity is. What can be said of Schmitt is that if it was his Catholicism that led him to recognize the importance of the intense revelatory quality of the political, it was his training as a jurist that pushed him away from the affective and ephemeral qualities of revelation toward a solid base built on a more concrete and intelligible conceptual form, namely, the friend/enemy grouping. The absolutism of such a binary division finds an echo in the work of Leo Strauss.

Strauss's Cities

The basis of Western civilization and progress, writes Leo Strauss, lies in the unresolvable conflict[23] and fundamental tension[24] between two cities—Athens and Jerusalem.[25] For Strauss, this tension would propel, and continues to propel, the Western subject into a modern future. Being in tension, but not at war, Athens and Jerusalem offer a somewhat different perspective on the power of the antagonistic binary form. For Strauss, the tension

20 Meier, *The Lesson of Carl Schmitt*, 31.

21 "The political is freed from its fixed reference to the community and, as it were, made fluid," Meier, *The Lesson of Carl Schmitt*, 61.

22 And for Schmitt, it begins with gender and Genesis 3:15 ("I will put enmity between thy seed and her seed") and manifests concretely between brothers (the brotherly enmity of Cain and Abel). This is the biblical foundation of his political theory. On gender and Genesis, see Meier, *The Lesson of Carl Schmitt*, 13; on Cain and Abel, see Ex Captivitate Salus, 89–90, quoted in Müller, *A Dangerous Mind*, 55.

23 "It seems to me that this unresolved conflict is the secret of the vitality of Western civilization." L. Strauss, "Progress or Return?," 44.

24 "The very life of Western civilization is the life between two codes, a fundamental tension." L. Strauss, "Progress or Return?," 44.

25 L. Strauss, "Jerusalem and Athens," 147.

between these two cities propelled Western civilization forward because Athens and Jerusalem were more than merely cities: they were symbols of the tensions that lie between reason and revelation.[26] With reason and revelation, one faces a twin question of the singular and the universal because revelation is never shared any more than reason can ever be singular. This binary tension between the singular and the universal takes us to the heart of democratic politics, for, as Derrida notes, democracy requires both absolute singularity and a universal community of friends. For him, it is from this "tragically irreconcilable" pair that political desire is born.[27] Both the dyadic and static nature of pairing proves problematic, for both point to culturally inflected norms universalized. First, let us address the question of stasis.

While the ancient Greek dictum *panta rhei* (everything flows) may have encapsulated the Heraclitan doctrine of universal flux, it has been Aristotelian "substance ontology" that has come to mark the Western conceptual mind.[28] Static things rather than processes have come to dominate thought, leading to the "thing-concept."[29] As the "thing-concept" came to dominate, it produced what Johanna Seibt has called a "myth of substance."[30] Through this myth, "objects" or "substances" become foundational static entities,

26 L. Strauss, "Progress or Return?," 33.

27 According to Jacques Derrida, there is no democracy without respect for "irreducible singularities," but also no democracy without the "community of friends." Derrida, *Politics of Friendship*, 22.

28 Although the scientific revolution is often thought of as a rejection of Aristotelian thought, it was never a rejection of his substantialism. See Dupré and Nicholson, "A Manifesto for a Processual Philosophy of Biology," 6.

29 For process ontologists John Dupré and Daniel Nicholson, this type of thinking should be reversed: "Instead of thinking of processes as belonging to things, we should think of things as being derived from processes. This does not mean that things do not exist, even less that thing-concepts cannot be extremely useful or illuminating. What it does imply is that things cannot be regarded as the basic building blocks of reality. What we identify as things are no more than transient patterns of stability in the surrounding flux, temporary eddies in the continuous flow of process." Dupré and Nicholson, "A Manifesto for a Processual Philosophy of Biology," 13.

30 Johanna Seibt says, "The myth of substance consists in a network of presuppositions which, in combination, engender the belief that the traditional category dualism

and the antagonistic dyadic form, "the most 'natural' way to describe the structure of the world."[31] Strauss's Athens and Jerusalem, being fixed points on a map, are two such thing-concepts. As such, they are part of the myth of substance presenting the tension of reason and revelation in a form that cannot explain that tension. This is because tension is caused by friction and friction requires movement.

If Schmitt's friend/enemy binary division of the political presupposed a degree of fluidity that could only be registered once it reached a high degree of intensity, then the tension created between Strauss's two cities presupposed a high degree of fluidity between these two fixed points. Moving our understanding of the political away from the static thingness of concepts and focusing instead on their fluidity means shining a spotlight not just on tensions and intensities but on the overall management of energy flows as they are channeled to produce multiple political effects across any spectrum. To understand such flow means turning to the often dispersed, unnamed, mislabeled, and misrecognized technologies, devices, machine-assemblages, and thoughts that collectively manage, direct, and harness potentially political, affective, libidinal, rational, and irrational energy flows for political ends. To begin to think in this more fluid way means leaving the cities of Athens and Jerusalem and heading east to a city where energy flows constituted the city's life blood. That city is old Peking.

The City of Flow

On the surface, Peking's grid-like design, coupled with its cosmological claims, appears to combine the geometric power of Athenian "reason" with the revelatory qualities of Jerusalem. Yet Old Peking was not built on this foundation; it was built upon a Confucian philosophical basis. But given the static, hierarchical nature of traditional Confucian society that was reflected in the design and spatial layout of Old Peking, it might appear no closer to a city of flow than either Athens or Jerusalem.[32] Nevertheless, the syncretic nature of the understanding of the cosmos that underpins this largely Con-

---

of substance and attribute provides the most 'natural' articulation of the ontological commitments of everyday discourse." Seibt, "The Myth of Substance," 121.

31 Seibt, "Ontological Tools," 113.

32 Gao Wei, *Random Notes on Beijing City*, 170.

fucian design helps explain this. Indeed, even the Confucian elements in the city's design, such as the "oneness with multiplicity" that forms a series of hierarchized concentric circles (multiplicities) surrounded by the emperor (oneness),[33] tends to reflect this.[34] More than anything, however, it is the syncretic nature of the city's design and especially the influence of the Yin-Yang School that lead to a recognition that along with its comprehensive, hierarchical, multifaceted, process-based understanding of the cosmos, there was also a recognition of the need for it to channel vital energy, or what the Chinese call *qi*.[35] The ancient city of Peking was then, in part, built on this understanding.

Like the city itself, *qi* has a oneness that is also a multiplicity.[36] Vital energy takes multiple forms and includes the complementary pairings *yin* and *yang* and the five phases known as *wuxing*.[37] In all cases, these are not thing-concepts but rather expressions of transient characteristics. *Yin* and *yang* are not oppositional but interrelated and mutually transformative, while the names given to the five phases—water (*shui*), fire (*huo*), wood (*mu*), metal (*jin*), and earth (*tu*)—do not indicate an actual substance or a natural quality but describe, instead, the nature of a transitional state. Water trickles downward in contrast to fire, which produces flames that flare upward; wood would bend and straighten while metal was said to conform and change. Earth,

33 See Zhu Jianfei, *Chinese Spatial Strategies*, 92, for the idea of oneness and multiplicity.

34 Zhu's idea of concentric circles surrounding the emperor is reminiscent of Fei Xiaotong's famous analogy of *guanxi*, or personal networks and connections, being structured like "the concentric circles formed when a stone is thrown into a lake." Fei Xiaotong, *From the Soil*, 63.

35 See Zhu Jianfei, *Chinese Spatial Strategies*, 91–92.

36 The multiplicities within *qi* can be seen in the way it is integrated into all numerical schemes of quantity in traditional China: "The *yin* and *yang* (two), the elements (five) [or what I refer to in this text as phases], the biggest *yang* number (nine), the temporal order (twelve), the hexagrams in the *Book of Changes* (sixty-four)." See Li Shiqiao, *Understanding the Chinese City*, 18.

37 One example of this comes from the neo-Confucian scholar Zhu Xi (1130–1200), who, as Zhu Jianfei points out, thought "active principles inform active material flow which creates *Yang*, while passive principles inform passive flow which creates *Yin*. *Yin* and *Yang* interact and create the five Agencies [phases] which in turn produce ten thousand things." See Zhu Jianfei, *Chinese Spatial Strategies*, 40.

forever the telluric element, would accept seeds and give forth crops,[38] but it was never the root form.[39] Contrapuntal by nature, and fluid in form, these conceptual categories could only ever be understood in the context of the cyclical processes within which they operated. Under such conditions, everything was impermanent, in flight and in flux. Hence, just as a male could be *yang* when young and *yin* in old age, so, too, the five phases were linked into a changing cyclical motion. Western attempts to pin these concepts down have been numerous.

From Matteo Ricci's linking of *wuxing* to the Greek four elements, right through to contemporary demotic depictions of *yin/yang* as being equivalent to male/female, there has been a constant attempt to "solidify" these fluid forms as "qualities" rather than treat them as phases within a process.[40] Understood better by their functionality than by any inherent qualities,[41] these concepts may have shared a kinship in fluidity with certain fragmentary and marginal pre-Socratic Greek philosophic trends, but the similarities end there. Chinese perspectives cast this fluidity in a vastly different light and as part of a far more comprehensive understanding of the cosmos than the Greek perspective did. Moreover, far from being marginal, this way of thinking became an extremely important element within the syncretic tradition of Chinese philosophy[42] and it is ancient Peking that opens its city gates onto this other way of seeing.

38 Sivin, *Traditional Medicine in Contemporary China*, 71.

39 Sivin, *Traditional Medicine in Contemporary China*, 73.

40 According to Sivin, the confusion between the Chinese five phases and the European four elements begins with Matteo Ricci in the first Jesuit treatise on cosmology (1608). Sivin, *Traditional Medicine in Contemporary China*, 73–74.

41 Sivin, *Traditional Medicine in Contemporary China*, 48.

42 As briefly mentioned earlier, the pre-Socratic thinker Heraclitus appears to come closest to Chinese thinking when he suggested that *πάντα ῥεῖ* (*panta rhei*), "everything flows," but, as Sivin notes, this was "far from the main trend in Greek speculation" and clearly far less developed than the highly elaborate theories of flow that came out of the Chinese Taoist tradition. See Sivin, *Traditional Medicine in Contemporary China*, 45.

Structured like text, the city layout was said to be a "voicing" of an ancient classic, the *Zhouli*,[43] and while this might be slightly exaggerated, the city, nevertheless, conforms to its overall pattern.[44] According to this ancient work, the flow of vital energy connected heaven and the earth.[45] Vital energy was generated at the point where heaven and the earth met, where there was a changeover of seasons, where wind and rain combined, and where *yin* and *yang* joined forces.[46] The mountains surrounding Peking were said to be vibrant with *qi*;[47] with the mountains as its body and rivers as its mother, the capital received its vital energy from the water that, as Guanzi reminds us, "is complete in its virtue."[48] If the location of the capital was, in this regard, said to be propitious, the spatial organization of the city was designed to take advantage of this propitiousness.[49] The spatial layout of the city and the seat of the emperor within it—that is, the Forbidden City, or Gugong—were designed

43 Yi Ding, Yu Lu, and Hong Yong, *Geomancy and Selections from the Built Environment*, 160, 173.

44 Zhu Jianfei has suggested that rather than using precise, metrical, numerical and positional geometry, which would suggest the city isn't like the *Zhouli*, if one instead focuses on the "abstract and relational pattern of disposition and configuration" then a pattern emerges. His conclusion is that "intentional configuration, the square-ness, the numerical series based on the number three, the orthogonal structure in relation to the four cardinal points, the implied domination of the north-south over the east-west orientation, the relative positioning regarding front and back, left and right, the importance of the southern front for the emperor's position, the implied axes, the suggested but not specific center, are the basic elements of an abstract pattern of this model." Differences exist, he concludes, but they are not central to this model, leading him to conclude that "Beijing, although not following all the specific descriptions, does follow the abstract and relational; configuration of the model." Zhu Jianfei, *Chinese Spatial Strategies*, 33–34.

45 The *Zhouli* states, "*Qi* (or vital energy) connects heaven and earth. *Qi* is the principle of *feng shui* (or geomancy)." Wang Zilin, *The Geomancy of the Imperial City*, 110.

46 Wang Zilin, *The Geomancy of the Imperial City*, 123.

47 Wang Zilin, *The Geomancy of the Imperial City*, 96.

48 Wang Zilin, *The Geomancy of the Imperial City*, 76. The quotation from Guanzi is from Guanzi, "Water and Earth," 101.

49 Stephan Feuchtwang details the considerations and technologies that go into *fengshui* determinations:

to channel and harness vital energy.[50] The city was built along a central meridian that was said to be in accord with the celestial bodies, most of which pointed to the Big Dipper.[51] With the Temple of Heaven to its south, the Temple of Earth to the north, the Moon Altar to the west, and the Sun Altar to the east, Peking embodied the cosmos. Vital energy coursed from south to north, running from the (circular) shape and (blue) color of (the Temple of) Heaven through to modular, square shapes and red and golden colors that flagged earthly celestial governance in the form of the Forbidden City.

> They delineate the auspicious and the inauspicious combinations of points in the configuration of the walls and rooms of a dwelling or the alignment of a burial site, according to combinations of *yin* and *yang*, the 24 points of the compass, the five agents (often wrongly called "elements") in their orders of mutual destruction and production, their analogies with the five directions (centre and four quarters), five colours and much more, and a number of other systems of alignment. The forms to be found for the ideal site consist of a dominant mountain behind and a gathering of water in front with, to the sides, protective lower ranges, the eastward higher than the westward. Each of these forms have the names of the creatures of the four quarters, or more detailed designations of stars, trigrams from the *Book of Changes* and positions of the horizon traced through the year by the moonrise. Every one of these sets of signs indicates quite well specified gains or losses of fortune in wealth, fame and health for the two kinds of human soul, the one bound to earth, the other meant at death to rise toward Tian, the celestial canopy. The most extensive of the five classics, the Water Dragon Classic, provides illustrations of sites in different root and branch flows of water and their gathering in pools, explained in terms of the same systems of signs. This is landscape as schematic cartography. Later manuals for site selectors include cartographic diagrams of actual sites as examples. (Feuchtwang, "François Jullien's Landscape, Site, Selection, and Pattern Recognition," 118)

50 The *Kaogongji* from the *Zhouli* outlines the spatial order that flows from this cosmogony. This forms the basis of the theory and mode of ancient Chinese cities from which Peking would draw. This ancient text states, "The city is square. Each side should be nine *li*. Three gates on each wall. North-south roads are nine *gui*. To the left of the palace is the temple for ancestral worship, to the right is the Hall for the Earth God and God of Five Grains. At the front there is the imperial court and administration and at the back the market and common residences." Yi Ding et al., *Geomancy and Selections from the Built Environment*, 158.

51 Yi Ding et al., *Geomancy and Selections from the Built Environment*, 182.

While this is but a cursory glance at the cosmogony underpinning the design of old Peking, it is sufficient to enable us to understand that, more than the metaphoric and symbolic meaning attributed to Athens or Jerusalem, Peking was quite concretely a city of flow.[52] The city was, in fact, a functioning device or machine designed to contour the flow of vital energy toward good governance. From the syncretic form of prevailing Confucian order came a strand of thought that offered evidence of a fluid, functional, and essential cosmological understanding that goes well beyond a city plan. The city was a technology tying heaven to the earth, the earth to nature, and nature back to the celestial order. While each realm of government, be it of the body, the household, or of the state, had its own specificities, all were still part of a program of intervention and manipulation that ensured vital energy was balanced and channeled toward harmony.

From the government of the body to the medicines of the state, harmony was sought and balance created by channeling the flow of vital energy. While we are not suggesting that this is a "stand-in" for, or replica of, affective energy flows as they form into political intensities, it does at least function to shatter the stasis of the Straussian cities, not to mention any static understandings of friend/enemy. It does not make the concerns of the Straussian cities disappear but reimagines them in a very different and more fluid fashion. Yet Strauss's cities, in highlighting the need for tension over harmony and suggesting the production of that tension through the binary friction of two ideals, also focus our attention more powerfully on the function of the binary division in the Schmittian concept of the political. No longer simply a binary division producing tension, our focus on flow opens onto the relatively autonomous quality of this ternary, liquid element in relation to the friend/enemy dyad. The either/or quality of the tension built into the binary is now complicated by the introduction of this third fluid element. Through old Peking, we come to understand tensions as a crossing of cur-

52 Indeed, these concerns with flow even play into contemporary city discourse through health care and discourses on longevity. For a fascinating account of how this philosophy has continued to inform Beijing's life practices, see Judith Farquhar and Qicheng Zhang's work. Despite the more "self-health" body-based contemporary discursive form they describe, they nevertheless also argue that the Maoist notion of "the people" has left an indelible mark on the city, which is now seen as being "really nothing other than its people." See Farquhar and Zhang, *Ten Thousand Things*, 99.

rents whereby flows, channels, breaches, and breaks are all directed toward a particular political constellation that emphasizes harmony. It is as a machining of flow that ancient Peking draws our attention to an important omission within contemporary political thought. This omission casts a light beyond this city, beyond the Chinese state, and back to our understanding of the political. As the Chinese philosopher Zhuangzi once noted, *qi* gives rise to spirit,[53] and this, in turn, points to an affective element in this cosmological understanding.[54] Affect is, after all, the experiential state that involves an active discharge of emotion, leading to an augmentation or diminution of one's bodily capacity to act.[55] With *qi*, however, it spreads beyond the affective and corporeal, for it has the ability to affect all things.

City gates would open and close to the cycle of *qi*; *qi* organizes space and helps fashion the land with the geomancy of *fengshui* being one of the methods plotting its flow. Vital energy would guide the design of the city just as it would guide the brush in the hand of the calligrapher, the word in the head of the poet, or the needle in the hand of the acupuncturist.[56] *Qi* reached for balance in bodily functions, in city life, and in an enlightened celestial empire. It was the fluid telluricism of this rendition of nature, not reason or revelation,[57] not friend and enemy but *yin-yang*.[58] It was, therefore,

53 Zheng Li, *On Zhuangzi's Aesthetics*, 120.

54 "In the relation between form and spirit, form [*xing*] deals with materiality and spirit is categorized as affective [*xin*] and it is this form that envelops the spiritual [*xingti baoshen*], forming an inseparable union or unity. *Qi* in its movement at the level of both form and affect, turns humans into the carriers of the completeness of spirit [*shenquan*] and is bound together in a living form. Hence, *qi* must be involved between form and spirit." Zheng Li, *On Zhuangzi's Aesthetics*, 119.

55 This understanding of affect is drawn largely from the work of Gilles Deleuze and Félix Guattari, who refer to it as a discharge of emotion and as a weapon that alters a bodily capacity to act. See Deleuze and Guattari, *A Thousand Plateaus*, 441.

56 On the city, see Yi Ding et al., *Geomancy and Selections from the Built Environment*. On calligraphy, see Zheng Li, *On Zhuangzi's Aesthetics*.

57 On the origins of Western civilization as a tension between these two forms, see L. Strauss, "Jerusalem and Athens," 147.

58 In the *Dao De Jing*, how the way (or the Tao) is formed is explained. "The Tao originates in One. One produces Two [*yin* and *yang*]. Two produces Three. Three

many miles from the (Schmittian) political,[59] yet it was close enough for it to still recognize the possibility of disharmony and violence. Sometimes *yin* and *yang* were not in alignment, leading to flows being blocked and becoming floods that could sometimes even build into tidal bores. *Qi* could, therefore, also be heteropathic, or *xieqi*. Yet even here, *qi* is attributed no inherent quality but takes form only in relation to "what it relates to or what it does." In other words, context and function, not any inherent qualities, lead to its definition.[60] If *qi* is out of balance and becomes blocked, then, for the human body, this spells sickness while, for the state, it flags calamity. For the body, there is *xiefa*, whereby the insertion of a needle in a vital bodily point draws a strong reaction so as to release the torrent that has been building up within.[61] For the ancient Chinese state, something more than a needle was sometimes required.

---

produces ten thousand things [all things]. All things depart from *yin* and gradually embrace *yang*. They are harmonized while developing" (*daosheng yi, yisheng er, ersheng san, sanshengwanwu. Wanwu fuyin er baoyang, chongqi yiwei he*). In his discussion of Zhuangzi's philosophy, Zheng Shigeng also points out that "*yin and yang* are the largest structure that can be demonstrated by *qi*." In other words, *yin* and *yang* are the highest range of *qi*. Zheng Shigeng, *Zhuangzi's Theory of Qi*, 90.

59 In terms of Carl Schmitt's work, this then appears to constitute something of a disqualification in terms of the concept of the political, because, as he points out, "the specific political distinction to which political actions and motives can be reduced is that between friend and enemy." This is the closest Carl Schmitt gets to a definition of the political but even here he quickly adds, "This provides a definition in the sense of a criterion and not as an exhaustive definition or one indicative of substantial content." Schmitt, *The Concept of the Political*, 26.

60 Sivin, *Traditional Medicine in Contemporary China*, 49.

61 In traditional Chinese medicine, *xieqi*, or the heteropathic *qi*, is translated as a pathogen that stands in opposition to *zhengqi*, or orthopathic *qi*. For the body, the treatment is *xiefa*. *Xiefa*, meaning "torrent method," is a term drawn from acupuncture and is a needle technique designed to draw a strong reaction so as to release the torrent that has been building up. It was a method first mentioned in the classic *Neijing* but also found its way into the new methods that (Maoist) traditional Chinese medicine developed in acupuncture. For classic references to this, see Cui Xiaoli, *Huangdi Neijing*. For references within the Maoist canon, see *A Compilation of Materials*. For an examination of heteropathic *qi*, see Porkett, *The Theoretical Foundations of Chinese Medicine*, 54.

Figure 1.3. Straight Arrow Lane street sign, Hangzhou, China, circa 1999. Photo by the author.

Straight Arrow Lane

Among the labyrinth of tiny gray alleyways that once made up large parts of the city of Hangzhou, there is a small contemporary sign, flagging an ancient style of thought. Attached to an old, socialist-era apartment block, a blue street sign reads "Straight Arrow Lane" (*Zhijian Daogang*; see figure 1.3). Bisected by the leakage from a rusty bolt, the shabby appearance of the street sign belies its importance as a cosmological marker referring to a mystical time when the question of flow still worlded the world.

This inconspicuous, rusting blue street sign opens onto events that took place over one thousand years ago, reminding us of the power of flow, not just in setting the limits of government thinking in the ancient Chinese world, but also in setting the stage for a way of thought to be carried unconsciously into more modern and revolutionary times. Straight Arrow Lane takes us back to a time when spirit and energy flows ruled the waves. In the Five Dynasties and Ten Kingdoms period, King Qian Liu (852–932) ruled this land. It was a land threatened by raging torrents that were eroding the shoreline of his kingdom. The king needed a reprieve from the power of these sea spirits long enough to enable his engineers to build sea walls that would deflect the tidal flow and turn it away from his land. Chinese hydraulic engineering was employed to rechannel the flow of surplus energy, but the engineers' work was in constant need of repair.[62] Even as late as the Ming dynasty, imperial

62 See Elvin and Su, "Man against the Sea."

reports would stress the need to give alms in the hope of turning the surplus vital energy away from the dykes that Qian Liu had built to protect his land.[63]

The dykes would be Qian Liu's long-term legacy, for they were a material technology that could redirect and rechannel the immaterial surplus vital energy away from an aqueous intensity. To enable these dykes to be built, however, the king first needed to produce conditions allowing an abatement of the ferocious tidal bore. To do this, the king would not so much declare war on the sea spirits as apply the government of the body to the management of the (water) flow. In the eighth month, when tides were high and flooding made construction work impossible, the king outlined a plan borne as much of needles as of engineering. Similar to the *xiefa* method, his plan was designed to release pent-up flow. Where the traditional Chinese doctor would use needles, King Qian Liu used archers and arrows. Needless to say, the point was the same.

"When *qi* enters the human body," acupuncturists tell us, "it is formless."[64] Its presence is recorded only through the symptoms it displays. Symptoms, such as color, odor, taste, and sensations of hot and cold, erupt on the surface of the body, indicating the presence of *qi* but only as the needle touches key pressure points. It was through the needle touching these pressure points that these "external" symptoms revealed the presence of *qi*.[65]

63 Elvin and Su quote a 1733 work, *Haining Xianzhi* (Gazetteer of Haining County), in which it was written that "the surplus vital energy (*qih* 氣) in the roots of the mountains would seem to resemble the drawn-out fibers of silk floss, so that when the tides pass the sediment accumulates. It may happen at times that there is a passage through, but it will subsequently become blocked again. Thus, if the water does not go south, it goes north. If it goes south there are, however, Mount Kua and Mount Chang (常山, presumably for 長山) to defend against it. If it goes north, there is only the line of sea-walls, and it is easy in the extreme for the water to break in and flood." Elvin and Su, "Man against the Sea," 24. In their romanization, the character *qi* is written *qih*, while the romanization method that I employ throughout this manuscript is pinyin, which would spell vital spirit as *qi*. The Chinese characters used here are called "full form," having more strokes than the abbreviated version used throughout this manuscript. The meaning, however, remains the same, irrespective of the romanization or whether the character is abbreviated or in full form.

64 This formless state of *qi* belongs to the realm of *yang* and only when it is evident through taste or smell does it become *yin*. See Cui Xiaoli, *Huangdi Neijing*, 20.

65 Cui Xiaoli, *Huangdi Neijing*, 36.

Almost untraceable, *qi* is heard but never captured, directed but never stopped. This flow of *qi* through the human body, when described in the *Neijing*, is central to its "theory of acupuncture":

> When you insert the needle, observe the arrival of "vital energies" [*qi*]. This arrival is formless, it is heralded by no signal and is almost untraceable. It is like a flock of birds passing. When there is an abundance of *qi* it is as rich as a field of grain. When *qi* passes, it is as if the bird's wings have fluttered yet no one is left to capture the form. So, when using the needle, if the feel suggests that *qi* has not yet fully arrived, the needle must remain in place to await its arrival. It is like an arrow on a bow waiting for the archer to stretch it to its optimal position and then, when *qi* arrives, pulling out the needle immediately just as one would release the arrow from the bow.[66]

Six times Qian Liu's archers released their arrows from the bow as the surging tidal bore roared past them. On their sixth volley they succeeded and the tidal bore abated. Qian Liu's "needle work" had achieved its aim, and dyke construction could begin. Like the insertion and removal of the acupuncture needle, it was the flow of *qi* that governed the flight of the arrows just as it governed the use of the needle on the human body. Thus, while *qi* itself remained formless, it would be made "visible" through symptoms brought to the surface by a series of techniques specifically designed to give a sign of, if not a form to, vital energy.

Registering the presence of *qi* is an essential precondition for any act of redirecting or releasing its flow. For example, the corporeal technologies that led to the production of color, odor, or sensations of hot and cold on the surface of the skin all worked to manifest the presence and nature of vital energy (*qi*) within the body, as well as its expulsion. Can one not begin to think of the "political" as being akin to needle work? And if the political is tied to flow, is it not the multiple devices—from formal institutions to abstract ideas and on to entertainment and finances—that are like meridians? Do they not regulate and channel energy, such that the political takes on a particular form? Like the arrows the king had fired and the dykes the king had built, the political, too, gives rise to regimes and machines for the regulation of flow. In China, this linking of fluidity and the political can also be traced linguistically.

66 Cui Xiaoli, *Huangdi Neijing*, 95.

This is the approach of the "New Sinologist"[67] Geremie R. Barmé, who linguistically surfs this tidal bore of the Qiantang River in search of meanings and understandings that tie the story of the dykes to the tale of the political. Barmé makes links to the political through the linguistic continuity he finds between Qian Liu's firing of arrows to halt the tidal bore and the later Chinese modernist appropriation of the word "tidal" in the tidal waves of revolution. The language of the tidal bore in Qian Liu's firing of arrows would be remembered in 1903, Barmé tells us, when it was put to work on the masthead of the anti-Qing newspaper, the *Tide of Zhejiang* (*Zhejiang Chao*).[68] From sea currents to political currents, this term, *chao* or *tide*, would jump from the masthead of a newspaper into the ocean of revolution.

From Sun Yatsen's metaphor of revolution as a tidal wave through to the "high tides" or *gaochao*, of Mao Zedong's socialist campaigning, Barme's linguistic trail reveals the word as symptom. This politics of language points to the political but, like *qi*, is formless until it suddenly gains "color," "odor," or "heat," or triggers some other sensation. As the word *chao* snakes its way from being a sea spirit into being a political intensity, one catches a sense of the fluttering formlessness of this energy flow. This linguistic link Barmé establishes helps reveal the connection between such energy and political forms. In a political landscape of "continuous revolution"(*jixu geming*), and high tides of socialism, as China was under Mao, the tidal rhythm of intensity seems driven by currents that break the banks of reason and revelation to travel down the channel created by friend and enemy. It is through this flow of words linked to energy flows that this connection with the political comes to the surface.

Chinese Curios

The oft-referred-to opening gambit of Michel Foucault's *Order of Things* was all about words: words that created laughter, laughter that was then shattered. Laughter erupted when Foucault introduced—via the work of Jorge Luis Borges—a taxonomy drawn from "a certain Chinese Encyclopedia."[69] Within

67 On New Sinology, see Barmé, "Toward a New Sinology." For a critique, see Fitzgerald, "The New Sinology."

68 Barmé, "The Tide of Revolution," 6.

69 Foucault, *The Order of Things*, xv.

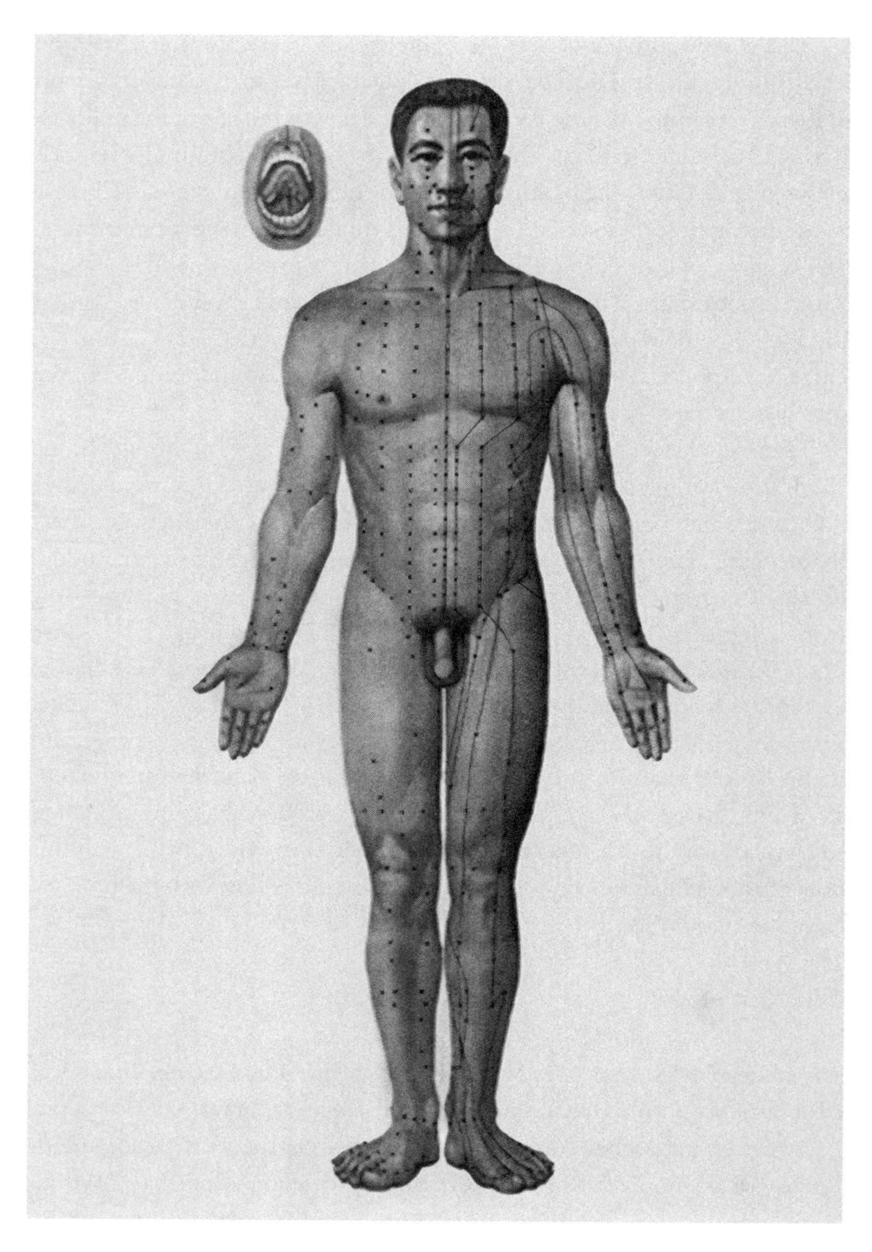

Figures 1.4–1.5. Modified traditional Chinese medicine charts, positive (*above*) and negative (*right*). Both modified by and courtesy of John Reardon.

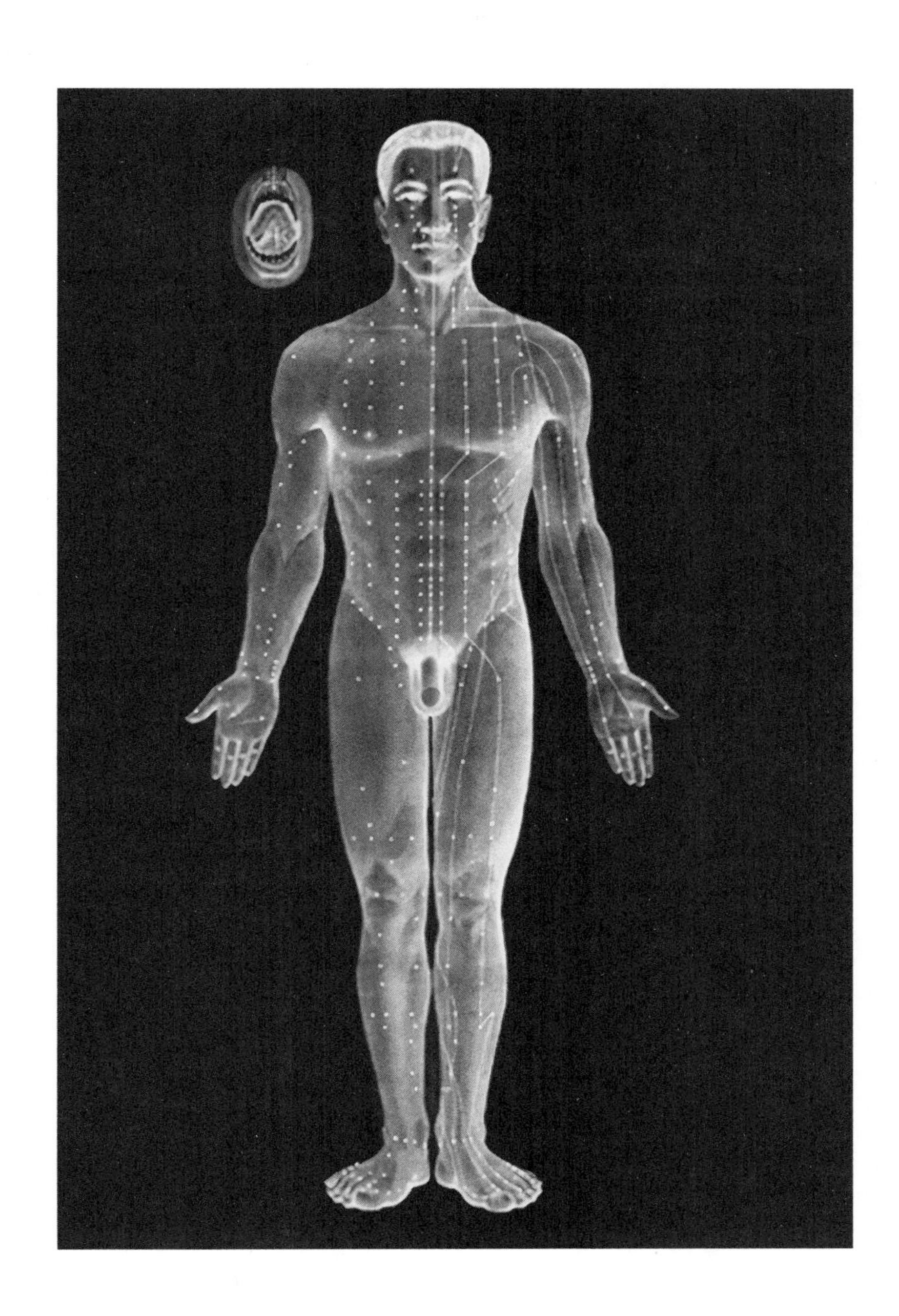

this encyclopedia, while a linear alphabetic listing of "characteristics" suggested a familiar form of categorization, it was immediately confounded by absurd taxonomic characteristics. Behind each order-establishing letter—a, b, and c—sat a wild-card description of a creature, with each description appearing as random, absurd, and whimsical as the next.[70] Animals, said this encyclopedia, were divided into (a) those that belong to the emperor, (b) embalmed, (c) tame, (d) suckling pigs, (e) sirens, (f) fabulous, and so on.[71] Serial categories that formed an order of things that appeared to offer no order at all would break up the certainty of Western knowledge and open what Foucault called the "unthinkable space" of "the non-place of language."[72] Here, then, is a shattering, revealing the non-place of language, in a language (Chinese) that Jacques Derrida argues partly falls outside the grip of "our" logocentric knowledge world.[73] Can one, then, from within this seemingly nonlogocentric language, imagine the unthinkable non-place of language and, through this, still faintly hear the possibility of another knowledge system incomprehensible to our own?

Instead of the imagination of Borges, let us turn to an "alteric" Chinese knowledge system that is historically grounded.[74] Think, for instance, of the

70 Note the role this alphabetic sequencing plays in ordering and connecting things. According to Deleuze and Guattari, "a is to b as c is to d is the defining frame of structural logic." For Deleuze and Guattari, this is a means to establish a series, but in Foucault's use of this work it is to question the certainty of knowledge claims. See Deleuze and Guattari, *A Thousand Plateaus*, 258.

71 Foucault, *The Order of Things*, xv.

72 Foucault, *The Order of Things*, xvii.

73 Jacques Derrida makes this contentious point in the opening section of *Of Grammatology*, arguing that because the Western tradition of metaphysics operates on a privileging of the phoné, it is both logocentric and ethnocentric. See Derrida, *Of Grammatology*, 25–26, 70. For Spivak's mild rebuke, see Spivak, translator's preface to *Of Grammatology*.

74 It might be prudent to note at this point that Borges's Chinese encyclopedia is widely believed to be a literary fiction. Whether it is real or imaginary, however, is of little consequence, as this encyclopedia is, for Foucault, merely a heuristic device to demonstrate a point about the nature of taxonomies framing our knowledge in particular ways. The fictive quality of Borges's Chinese encyclopedia, however, excited critical commentary within the field of Sinology and the Sinophone world. Zhang Longxi points to the dubious provenance of this use of

specialized language traditional Chinese medicine employs and the mapping of the body it undertakes. Strange names compound the esoteric quality of meridians and acupoints (Hundred Meetings, Yin Metropolis, Purple Palace, for example).[75] These conform to another world of understanding bodily functions. Now move from the legitimacy of that specialist knowledge form to a "dialect" or "slang" still operating within this same, seemingly nonlogocentric Chinese-language system,[76] but so "telluric," so earthy, and so "illegitimate" that it would remain as incomprehensible to the Chinese scholar-officials of Borges's imagination as it would to a traditional Chinese doctor. Imagine a telluric "dialect" and mapping of the body determined by context, timing, camouflage, and flow. This is not a dialect of absolute otherness but, rather, one of uncanny difference.[77] It is a dialect operating as a nodal point in the flow of daily conversations, yet it functions to establish an electrical current of recognition for the initiated. It would tie them together

the encyclopedia to develop his own critique of claims about the absolute "otherness" of the binary division in relation to philosophy more generally. See Zhang Longxi, "The Myth of the Other."

75 The Hundred Meetings, or *baihui* acupoint on the dorsal midpoint, is significant in terms of dizziness, headaches, numbness, apoplexy, rectal and anal prolapse, and uterine prolapse. The Yin Metropolis, or *yindu*, is an acupoint close to the navel that regulates *qi*, strengthens the spleen, promotes digestion, and is of value in treating gastric problems and upper abdominal pain, while the Purple Palace, or *zigong*, located on the upper chest, can be used to regulate *qi*, alleviate coughing, and treat asthma, bronchitis, tonsillitis, and pains in the gullet. Thanks to Rey Tiquia for these insights.

76 One needs to temper the claim of Chinese as a nonlogocentric language without losing the point that Derrida is making. It is, however, hard to make absolute distinctions of otherness in terms of Chinese language, as characters are not entirely pictographic and do have a phonetic component. In most cases, Chinese characters are picto-phonetic, which means they draw on a rebus rather than an alphabet system, which, in turn, leads back to the question of the phoné and Derrida's general point about the ethnocentricism of logocentric knowledge. On Chinese characters not being purely pictographic, see Kraus, *Brushes with Power*, 15–18. On Derrida's opening gambit, tying logocentricism and ethnocentricism, see Derrida, *Of Grammatology*, 3.

77 Uncanny, insofar as it "feels" *unheimlich* (unhomeliness) and, like the Freudian uncanny, raises a feeling of dread. On Freud's uncanny, see Freud, "The Uncanny."

in a shared imaginary world lying outside the mainstream.[78] This is the world in which *chundian* is spoken. It is this that opens a window to quite another type of system, culture, and identity buried within and weaving its way in and out of the Chinese mainstream.[79] This helps us attach a telluric element to the flow of the political and to chart the flow of the political within the body politic.

There are said to be over 40,000 or 50,000 Chinese characters in the lexicon of *chundian*.[80] Not wordplay, dialect, language, or even slang, *chundian* is earthy, pragmatic, humorous, disrespectful, and sometimes, quite misogynist and scandalous. *Chundian* is the gateway into a parallel Chinese universe and spirit. It is a spirit revealed in a language that, quite literally, turns the tables on authority. Growing organically out of words, phrases, and expressions uttered by traditional itinerant beggars, bandits, vagrants, artists, disgraced officials, magicians, as well as the socially despised lower-level merchant classes of old China, *chundian* reflected daily life with its focus on things at hand. This was a language revealing action, a language made up not of qualities, but of functions. Mixing words with deeds, merchants and lower-level professions practiced a quick-witted banter called *tiaokan'er* and, through banter

78 For this reason, *chundian* remains uncatalogued, save for an array of minor texts that pick up on certain illustrative words or phrases or on a few incomplete dictionaries. Lian Kuoru notes that it is so disparate and diffuse that it can never really be fully catalogued. See Lian Kuoru, *The Miscellany of Jianghu*, 4, for a fuller explanation. On the question of dictionaries, I know of only two, both compiled by Liu Yanwu. One, a classified text for the police titled *A Compendium of Slang and Hidden Language*, focuses on criminal slang. The other, *Tracing the Sources of the Secret Language of Chinese Jianghu*, is public and much more of a general compilation. More recently, Qu Yanwu has published *The Mysterious World of Gangster Jianghu Jargon*, but it deals mainly with China's classical times.

79 Wang Xuetai, *The Water Margin*, 32.

80 Lian Kuoru, *The Miscellany of Jianghu*, 4. Contemporary critic Wang Xuetai argues that the classic novel *The Water Margin* offers endless examples of this language being used that predates even the Song dynasty. Nevertheless, until the time of the last dynasty, the Qing dynasty, this "black language" was quite marginal. In that dynasty, different trades and triads employed it for specific purposes and, after that, the language developed thousands of characters. For details, see Wang Xuetai, *The Water Margin*.

laced with *chundian*, double-entendre, and wordplay, advanced their trade and commerce.[81]

Moneyed patrons became known as "fire spots" (*huodian*); poor men were identified as "water numbers" (*shuimazi*); and gamblers were "small tinkling bells" (*luanbadian*). There was a chance of sharp trade brought about through *chundian*, or banter camouflaging meaning. Yet there are also words that point beyond limited self-interest to a moral code. Good people become "loyal-looking spots," or *zhongyangdian*, while the lecherous were deemed "stinky spots," or *chouzidian*, and so forth. Not that *chundian* didn't have its fair share of lecherous and thieving bandits.[82] With them, *chundian* became another form of remapping the human body. More than just naming bodily parts, *chundian* turned the body into a veritable acupuncture chart of (male) sexual opportunity and/or financial profit.[83]

Either for monetary gain ("to eat from a heavenly window" [*chi tian chuang*], meaning to steal from the upper pocket of a shirt) or to describe sexual activity ("to lick from the plate" [*tian panzi*], meaning fellatio), the body was reimagined and then renamed. It was a largely masculinist, patriarchal world that *chundian* revealed, but it was also one with the complexities, contradictions, and paradoxes of a heterogeneous, wayward non-place of marginal (non)people expressing things through their non-language. Communities were tied linguistically through a lexicon that imitated their life in that it was always a life in flux. Never in place or of a place, this tactical language was always one of chance and opportunity. *Chundian*, like the people who spoke it, was always in flux and always used in a specific context. As if

81 Lian Kuoru, *The Miscellany of Jianghu*, 2.

82 Yu Yang says,

> In the hundred odd years of the Ming and Qing dynasties, not a few Chinese worshipped: "heroes in troubled times" [*luanshi xiaoxiong*] which is absurd in the extreme [*wuyi fujia*]. These worshipped idols [*ouxiang*] aren't real heroes . . . they are shifty characters, shifty warriors and hoodlum bandits of the *jianghu* who sit outside the system. The vast majority are outside ordinary society but a few look like they remain within, yet in reality, they are outside the system carrying out work that follows the customs of the *jianghu*. They are brave, courageous fighters [*haoyong doulang*] with tricks that are pungent and poisonous. (Yu Yang, *Chinese Jianghu*, 3)

83 For body maps that reframe the body being mapped by the *jianghu*, see Dutton, *Streetlife China*, 172–79.

in recognition of the mercurial nature of their fluid lives, those who spoke *chundian* were known as "rivers and lakes" or, more simply put, the *jianghu*.

Always hard to define, the *jianghu* are those who exist on the very edges of legality and visibility. *Jianghu*, as an imagined space, sits on the other side of a mystical river to the mainstream, yet it would shadow the mainstream and weave into it with words and deeds. Flowing in and out of the static, statist world of mainstream society, the *jianghu* proved as threatening as they were enticing and elusive. For the static world of mainstream Confucian society where the character *wen*—meaning stability—was a foundation, these were the people of *liu*, or flow.[84] Where the mainstream desired stability, *jianghu* relied on wily movement; where the mainstream relied on traditional, patriarchal, and place-based authority, *jianghu* relied on a patriarchal spirit of sworn brotherhood (*jiebai xiongdi*) and a telluric spirit of non-place; and where the mainstream advanced a spirit of harmony, *jianghu yiqi* (or the spirit of *jianghu*) lived life like a de Certeauian "tactic."[85] Novels would be written about them, stories and legends created around their adventures, but still they would be treated by mainstream society with the utmost suspicion and dread.[86] Untranslatable words, unthinkable categories, uncontrollable people: *jianghu* were not part of a vital energy flow that would replenish and bring harmony to the city, the body, or the household, for the *jianghu* were a flood.

Rivers that ran so fast that they could sweep away convention, lakes so deep they would drown the mainstream, *jianghu* composed a tidal bore surging in an intense and threatening fashion. This was life in Bataille's general economy for it was made up of the "worthless surplus" (*lingyu*) that would nevertheless live life as gift and as sacrifice.[87] Through sacri-

84 Even within contemporary Chinese one finds that the word *flow*, when treated anthropomorphically, still often carries negative connotations, such as *liumang* (meaning "hoodlum") or *mangli* (meaning "vagrant"). For details, see Dutton, *Streetlife China*, 62–65.

85 On tactics and strategy, see de Certeau, *Practices of Everyday Life*, 34–39.

86 On positive depictions within the Chinese literary tradition, see the "knight-errant" (*youxia*) literature in China. For an overview, see Liu, *The Chinese Knight-Errant*.

87 The idea that *jianghu* were made up of vagrants who were society's "worthless surplus" comes from Wang Xuetai, *The Water Margin*, 26.

fice, this worthless surplus became more than excess. It became the basis of the fraternal bonds of brotherhood that mimicked and replaced the static, "site-specific" patriarchal clan or lineage system that they had been forced to leave.[88] Together, these dispossessed souls became the shadowy side of the mainstream, yet, in their anthropomorphizing of the flow, the way in which they were fluid yet telluric, and the way in which they relied not on blood-based relations but on the shedding of blood to create a bond, they help us shed a somewhat different light on the concept of the political.

Turning their backs on mainstream notions of virtue that they regarded as having been corrupted, they carved out an imaginary, mobile guerrilla space of virtue that reproduced the code of chivalry in an imaginary, parallel universe to the mainstream. Righteousness that would countenance the spilling of blood for the honor of one's sworn brother constituted the cornerstone of their ethical world. From this form of floating ethics, freed from the land yet still telluric, freed from actual blood relations yet still deeply invested in consanguinity, freed from social constraints yet still obliging a patriarchal model through the spilling of blood, the bonds of *jianghu yiqi*, or the spirit of *jianghu*, were forged. Here was a reimagining of kinship without the fellowship of place, an ur-form that would directly flow into the construction of the Chinese political for it is just one step removed from the intensity of class struggle and, more generally, from the friend/enemy distinction so central to the Schmittian concept of the political.[89] The political comes into view with precisely this type of excess energy expenditure.

88 Wang Xuetai explains that economic and technical developments in the Song dynasty (960–1279) changed the nature of agricultural production, leading to peasants being driven from their land into cities where, as dispossessed itinerants, *jianghu* bonds were forged. See Wang Xuetai, *The Water Margin*, 26–27.

89 As noted earlier, the public nature of the enemy is central to Schmitt's rendition of the political (Schmitt, *The Concept of the Political*, 27). Here, the *jianghu* spirit of faux consanguinity forms a bridge between the public and the private by constructing a form of nonbiological consanguinity between brothers that lies somewhere between the genuine consanguinity of the clan member and the unrelatedness of the Party comrade. This will be dealt with in more detail in later chapters.

Substitutions

In the preface to Georges Bataille's magnum opus, *The Accursed Share*,[90] he recalls a moment when he was asked what he was currently working on and with a somewhat embarrassed shuffle he replied, "Economics." A strange response from the man Simone Weil claimed desired the "triumph of the irrational"[91] and whom André Breton had called the "excremental philosopher."[92] Strange, that is, until one realizes that this was no ordinary notion of economics he was talking about. Bataille was not so much working on economics as working on ways to explode its underlying myth.[93] He would do this by the simplest of means: substitution. "Scarcity" would be replaced by "excess" as the founding concept and . . . boom! . . . there goes the discipline! Enter "General Economics": the study of "excess energy translated into the effervescence of life."[94]

Expenditure and consumption replaced labor and production, excess rather than limit, and vomit, piss, and semen in place of a protestant ethic. The need to expend or *dépense*, Bataille would argue, was central to our world, but it would require a general economics to comprehend it.[95] Mainstream economics was too restrictive. It would confine the question of the flow to economic, commercial, and financial circuits. With this narrowing of focus, scarcity becomes the key concept, and market growth becomes central.

90 Bataille, *The Accursed Share*, 9–14.

91 "Revolution for him, the triumph of the irrational, for me of the rational, for him a catastrophe, for me a methodical action in which one should try and limit the damage; for him the liberation of instincts, in particular those considered pathological, for me a higher morality." Simone Weil, in a draft letter to the Democratic Communist Circle, of which Bataille was a leading figure, was differentiating her politics from his. For this quote and details of the quite complex relationship between Weil and Bataille, see Surya, *Georges Bataille*, 172.

92 For a critique of Bataille, see Breton, "Second Manifesto of Surrealism."

93 On the underlying myth and its spread into knowledge, see Foucault on how the economy became the crucial site of veridiction for truth statements in our modern world. See Foucault, *The Birth of Biopolitics*, 30–36.

94 Bataille, *The Accursed Share*, 10.

95 Hollier calls *dépense* the need for loss rather than the loss itself. See Hollier, *Against Architecture*, xiv.

Gone was the wanton, useless expenditure of the gift economies of old and along with them that feeling, within this process of exchange, where someone gave "part of oneself," part of one's "spiritual essence."[96] In other words, within mainstream (restrictive) economics, the capacity to understand and feel within oneself an economy of humanity and cruel sacrifice has been lost. Without this broader and more profoundly felt understanding of a general economics, there could be no appreciation of how "sacred horror" harmonizes with pleasure to form both the "base of erotics" and the intensity of the political Dasein.[97] Reread through the need for *dépense*, Bataille's employment of Marcel Mauss's theory of sacrifice becomes the basis of an altogether different ontology.[98] It is one that would highlight the mechanisms through which violence would demonstrate a struggle for recognition, offering a means by which "death lives a human life."[99] Sacrifice and potlatch[100] created spaces that today's market veridiction regimes tend to marginalize.

Modern markets alienated us from these excessive yet fundamentally affective human dimensions of the exchange relationship, thereby freeing us

96 Mauss, *The Gift*, 10.

97 Bataille, "Hegel, Death and Sacrifice," 18–19.

98 A different ontology, hinted at perhaps in Bataille's own work. See Bataille, "The Psychological Structure of Fascism."

99 Politics is, in part, a struggle bordering on the life-and-death question. Bataille, "Hegel, Death and Sacrifice," 18. Sacrifice, as a key technology of the struggle for recognition, was part of the master/slave relationship and, therefore, at the heart of both ontology and politics. Here one sees the influence of Kojève on Bataille. See Kojève, *Introduction to the Reading of Hegel*. Michel Surya, Bataille's biographer, suggests that by the time of his brief interlude with Marxism, Bataille no longer thought of revolutionary violence as simply useful but saw it as an end in itself. That end, one might suggest, was recognition. Surya, *Georges Bataille*, 172.

100 Potlatch was said to be practiced by northwestern American indigenous groups; while it is a key term for Bataille, his understanding rested on Marcel Mauss, who misread the practice. For Bataille, as Surya makes clear, potlatch is sacrifice (*Georges Bataille*, 384). Potlatch as sacrifice becomes part of the struggle for prestige and is therefore tied to sacrifice and recognition. As Christopher Bracken has shown, however, potlatch was an invention of nineteenth-century Canadian colonial law that was simultaneously trying to destroy it. See Bracken, *The Potlatch Papers*. As Surya explains, Mauss's understanding of potlatch as the squandering of wealth by giving or destroying gave Bataille's own work a new political element. For details on Bataille, see Surya, *Georges Bataille*, 174–75.

from the overweening obligations that were entailed in traditional societies.[101] Modern markets would liberate us, but only at the cost of ignoring or repressing the incalculable agonistic elements that had long been central to such exchanges and that continued unconsciously to be important in contemporary politics.[102] Indeed, were it not for the continuing importance of this element in contemporary political forms, this transition would be an entirely academic problem.[103] As a political problem, however, the incalculable opaque, agonistic elements of excess buried within the traditional gift economies of sacrifice would have an afterlife.

In cleaving apart the gift relation, modern market-based economics treated the gift as they would treat the political, focusing almost exclusively on the inanimate (and calculable) material "thing" while largely ignoring, ritualizing, or commodifying the affective, so-called spiritual dimension. Yet it is this incalculable, ethereal dimension that was central to the operation of a gift economy just as it is central to the production and reproduction of political intensity.[104] With orthodox economics geared narrowly to questions of market and financial flows and material supply/demand chains, affective expenditures outside these economic calculations (i.e., the extraneous excess elements) were repressed or drawn onto a material plane of explanation, production, desire, and/or sale.

Registered only in relation to this trading of material things, affective flows, if recognized at all, were translated into the only term that the supply and demand curve could readily harness, namely, desire. Thus, emotional connections that were forged with a material object and that had not been tapped into became a sign of the undervaluing of that object. If discovered, they became part of a new calculus that adjusted price to both recognize

101 Mauss notes the absolutely obligatory quality of traditional forms of exchange. In many instances, to refuse to give, like the refusal to receive, was equivalent to declaring war. See Mauss, *The Gift*, 11.

102 This much vaunted "break" with the past, according to Jean-Joseph Goux, begs the question of "What happens to the demand of the sacred in capitalist society?" See Goux, "General Economics and Postmodern Capitalism," 209.

103 Mauss pointed to this ontological transition when he notes, "For a very long time man was something different and he has not been a machine for very long, made complicated by a calculating machine." Mauss, *The Gift*, 76.

104 Bataille, "The Notion of Expenditure," 123.

and regulate any excess desire for the object. Price increases rectified what could only be read, on this grid, as a distorted "demand" signal; that is, the "x factor" made a material object more valuable than its pure utility. Not only did everything have a price but price itself helped re-world our lives through numbers.[105] Numbers were the "canon" of the enlightenment. As Adorno and Horkheimer tell us, "To the Enlightenment, that which does not reduce to numbers, and ultimately to the one, becomes illusion."[106] Numbers underpin a particular style of thought that, they note, underpinned the knowledge regime of a marketized order of veridiction.[107]

This veridiction regime would be founded on an analysis of utility tied to a series of highly restrictive understandings of (material) flow (the supply and demand curve, the availability of goods and services, etc.) that could be universally numerated around three key categories: demand, supply, and scarcity. Everything could be mapped onto this grid. The problem with this grid, however, is that it cannot calculate desire, only register its existence, and tap into its potential. The power of desire lies in its capacity to increase demand for a product and, in so doing, channel energy away from political intensities. Yet it was precisely the excessive aspects within these elements of the exchange relationship—factors crucial to an understanding of the political in the contemporary world—that were effectively written out or reduced to black-box variables in the modern-day economic understandings of the exchange relation. What was being left out, however, was precisely what was needed if we are to understand the ongoing production and reproduction of political intensity. While central to the growth of the modern market, these elements are, however, marginal to the calculations of the regime of market veridiction. The reduction of these elements to the status of mere "variables" thereby reduced their visibility and importance within the calculating machine. This machine, then, offered a promise, if not of perfect calculability then a close approximation to it. The seductive charm of a calculable future was the promised land of enlightenment rationality,

105 Groys, *The Communist Postscript*, xvi.

106 Adorno and Horkheimer, *Dialectic of Enlightenment*, 7.

107 For Adorno and Horkheimer, equations dominate "bourgeois justice" just as they do commodity exchange. See Adorno and Horkheimer, *Dialectic of Enlightenment*, 7–8.

and it would infect all specialisms and disciplines, even those not directly concerned with the market.[108]

All knowledge systems are increasingly falling under this calculative spell, producing specialized disciplines that could all be brought together under the sign of value. Mainstream American political science was both the beneficiary (in terms of the power it could wield) and also, ultimately, a major casualty (in terms of the knowledge limits it imposed on itself) of this tendency. Not only would it translate politics into numbers, but as a discipline, it would also hang out its shingle and offer its services as a science of autopsy and analysis, explaining limits and halting excess. Such arguments about limits quickly turned into action plans of utility yet did so while strengthening the rechanneling of energy flows into market values.[109] For the most part, the market could successfully accomplish its task of dissipating any potential political agglutinations by rechanneling desires toward an ever-increasing number of material aspirations that would simultaneously weigh the desiring consumer down with monetary burdens such as mortgages and loans. A new agglutinating desire would gain expression through a new commodity. Yet there was always spillage and sometimes it flowed into potential pools of political intensity. These pools became rivers and rivers became lakes, inducing currents and movements. Here is where Bataille's general economics helps explain the excesses of the political.

108 American political science is the one obvious beneficiary/victim of this sort of infection. With his call for a "science of politics," the Scottish economist Duncan Black played a crucial role in this process. Black's claim to "scientificity" rested largely on his view that political decision-making processes were analogous to the manner in which "prices are fixed by demand and supply." Black inspired the work of William Riker's within political science. Just as Kenneth Arrow took on Marxist economists like Maurice Dobb, so too, Riker would combat opponents within the discipline of politics largely defeating normative political science and rival quantitative approaches as well as the case-study approach to political science, which had been favored by modernization theorists and was central to the very idea of an area studies knowledge. For details on the relationship between rational choice theory and economics, see Amadae, *Rationalizing Capitalist Democracy*. On modernization theory and area studies, see Gilman, *Mandarins of the Future*.

109 Both modernization theory and rational choice theory within political science place the market at the center of their concerns and attest to this. On the history of rational choice theory, see Amadae, *Rationalizing Capitalist Democracy*. On the history of modernization theory, see Gilman, *Mandarins of the Future*.

2

Numismatics

The Magic of Money

There is magic in money, which is tied to the question of flow. Put simply, no movement, no markets, no money, no magic. The magic of money lies in its role not only as a technology to channel energy flows but also as a material artifact of the abstract process of circulation. The symbolic side of money's magic will be dealt with momentarily but, first, there is Karl Marx.

For Marx, the role of money in the commodity economy is magical insofar as it creates conditions under which things appear other than they are. This conjuring trick of capitalism ensures that money, while revealing flow, reveals only a restricted jurisdiction. Monetary flows limit things to the circuits of finance and trade and, in so doing, disguise the process (of production) by which value is transformed into surplus-value. It is this little trick of money—whereby fluidity is confined to these circuits, which enables it to disguise the site of value creation—that Marx reveals. Behind its appearance as an unchanging material token of exchange, there is fundamental change in its form, and it is the capitalist production and circulation process that produces this change. Money functions as the initiator of the process of commodity production and then, upon its return to the capitalist owner, it reappears as the "first transformed form of a value that originally enters into circulation in the commodity form."[1] In other words, it appears as one thing at the beginning of the process of production only to reappear, albeit with exactly the same surface appearance, as something else later in the process.

At these two moments of monetary flow within the production and commodity circulation process, Marx claims, the nature of value within capitalism becomes visible. Money, in other words, is both the "symptom" of the existence of value but also its "independent and palpable form."[2] Money, however, in making the notion of value visible, both disguised the way in which value is actually produced and masked changes in its own makeup as it returned to the capitalist not as value but as surplus-value.[3]

Money, in creating the appearance that circulation creates value and surplus-value, hides the social facts of value creation, Marx tells us.[4] He repeatedly insists that it is labor that creates all value through the expenditure of labor-power.[5] Workers are free only because they have the right, unlike the slave, to sell their (labor) power on the market, like any other commodity.[6] Labor is thus freed from slavery but also alienated by being

1 Marx, *Capital*, vol. 2, p. 127.

2 Marx, *Capital*, vol. 2, p. 137.

3 As expressed in Marx's M . . . M′. See Marx, *Capital*, vol. 2, p. 138.

4 Marx, *Capital*, vol. 1, p. 286.

5 Value, Marx insists, "does not have its description branded on its forehead; it rather transforms every product of labour into a social hieroglyphic." The meaning of this social hieroglyphic is revealed in "the belated scientific discovery that the products of labour, in so far as they are values, are merely the material expressions of the human labour expended to produce them," which, for Marx, "marks an epoch in the history of mankind's development." Marx, *Capital*, vol. 1, p. 167. Value, he insists, is only the congealed quantity of labor expended. Marx, *Capital*, vol. 1, p. 150. "As exchange-values, all commodities are merely definite quantities of *congealed labour-time*" (emphasis original). Marx, *Capital*, vol. 1, p. 130.

6 Marx, *Capital*, vol. 1, p. 270.

reduced to a commodity form. The social fact that labor is now free means that labor-power,[7] not the laborer, is bought and sold on the market. The sale of labor-power, decoupled from the human, leads to questions of labor alienation. Leaving the question of alienation aside, what is being bought and sold here is a discrete power or energy that is actually part of a much broader affective energy flow. Calculability, being essential for any regime of market veridiction, therefore requires the marginalization of certain unwanted and unused aspects of this energy. In this system, material production functions as one vast machine-assemblage that channels the flow of energy through the narrow vector of the money economy and siphons off and excludes that energy that it cannot calculate. Markets require calculation to ensure that the exchange value is greater than the value of inputs that go into the production of an item: hence profit, hence growth. Herein lies the key mechanism ensuring the health of the contemporary market system but also the source of its suicidal tendency. It is growing on the back of a nonrenewable resource—namely, the earth.

Marx inadvertently contributes to this view of the earth by treating it as nothing more than a larder or tool house,[8] enabling labor to create all (use) value. While Marx recognized that labor uses natural resources and is therefore "not the only source of material wealth," these elements are, like excess energy, excluded from the calculation of labor-power and therefore excluded from his analysis.[9] Labor-power in Marx's reading is registered only in what Georges Bataille would call the homogeneous realm.[10] At the same time, it

7 Marx defines labor-power in the following terms: "We mean by labour-power, or labour capacity, the aggregate of those mental and physical capabilities existing in the physical form, the living personality, of a human being, capabilities which he sets in motion whenever he produces use-value of any kind." Marx, *Capital*, vol. 1, p. 270.

8 Marx, *Capital*, vol. 1, p. 285.

9 For a contrary view suggesting Marx lays the basis for a historical environmental materialism, see Foster, "Marx's Theory of Metabolic Rift."

10 Louis Althusser noted this when he wrote, "Surplus value is calculable, defined by the difference (in value) between the value produced by labour power on the one hand, and the value of the commodities necessary for the reproduction of this same labour power (wages) on the other. And in this arithmetical presentation of surplus value, labour power figures purely and simply as a commodity." This leads Althusser to suggest that this fosters a neglect of other facts because it registers

is through Marx that we can see how the question of flow is broader than the abstracted and restricted set of concerns built around (market-based) exchange relations. To show this, however, Marx would build on the logic of the arguments he opposed, employing the same logic and leading to a highly restrictive notion of labor-power. In Marx, labor-power was restricted to the time of production when the laborer's energy was expended "usefully," producing what the market deemed a "use-value." Labor-power is, therefore, only that part of the overall affective energy flow that capitalism can make calculable. In the general economics of Georges Bataille, however, there is no such limitation.

As John Brenkman notes, Bataille's premise is quite straightforward: "The energies of the laborer are not completely exhausted (utilized) in the labor process itself. Surplus value represents the measurable portion of the worker's productive capacity which does not return to him or her as a wage. There is, however, another surplus, an unmeasurable excess, which does not return to the production process but is expended 'unproductively.' This unproductive expenditure Bataille calls heterogeneity."[11] That is excluded from Marx's concerns, for the only energy expenditure that concerns him is the one that can be slipped into the pocket of the capitalist as surplus-value at the end of each working day. Workers, when brought into and calculated within this machine, are registered only in the "disembodied" energy form of labor-power. Labor might well be said by Marx to create all value, but all the vital energy expended by labor isn't counted. Only that energy allocated "productively" gets counted. A similar narrowing of the flow is evident in other parts of Marx's analysis of capitalist markets.

"A cyclical movement complete in itself" is how Marx would describe this market-based exchange system, as from money to money or in the alpha

---

labor-power (which is itself, of course, an energy) only in its calculable form, he states: "You can in fact seriously question whether this misunderstanding concerning the arithmetical presentation of surplus value, taken for a complete theory of exploitation, has not finally constituted a theoretical and political obstacle in the history of the Marxist Labour Movement, . . . [leading to] . . . a classical division of tasks in the class struggle between the economic struggle and the political struggle, therefore to a restrictive conception of each form of struggle." Althusser, "Crisis of Marxism," 219.

11 Brenkman, "Introduction to Georges Bataille," 61.

and omega of the capitalist production process, M . . . M′.[12] Joining the dots between these M&Ms creates a circuitry that, while far from sweet, is nevertheless of value. Indeed, the entire measurement of "value" is reduced to this circuit of understanding bound by the binary form, profit and loss. This binary gradually extends its jurisdiction, moving beyond the economic question of value into the moral question of "worth" (the useful and the useless). In sum, this restrictive and reductive circuitry does not make everything visible as it claims, but instead makes everything commensurable. It is the means of commensurability that is actually rendered visible by this system.[13] This restricted cyclical movement leading to commensurability is what Bataille would call its "tendential homogeneity."[14] Such "tendential homogeneity" can, however, be disrupted.

When "money capital," as Marx called it, gathers into "a hoard" at the beginning of the production phase or if, in the final phase of the process, it accumulates as unsaleable stock, economic crises can turn political.[15] What begins as an economic bottleneck can inadvertently "jump track," inducing moments of class struggle that transform the notion of class from being an economic category into a political one. Commodity circulation attempts to avoid such intense and sometimes violent transformations through its flirtation with heterogeneous desire.

12 On this formula, see Marx, *Capital*, vol. 2, pp. 136, 138. Yet, as Marx elsewhere explains, M—M′ is merely another way of saying usury, which, for Marx, is "the most rightly hated" because it is not "based on nature." Speaking as though original use exhausts all use, Marx suggests that money, when used in usury, is not used as originally intended. It is "not used," he says, "for the purposes for which it was invented" and is, therefore, "contrary to Nature"! See Marx, *Capital*, vol. 1, p. 267.

13 On commensurability, Marx turns to Aristotle, saying that there can be no exchange without equality, and no equality without commensurability. For Marx, commensurability is tied to the question of direct exchangeability. It is here that the mystery of the equivalent form, which thereby enables this process, is revealed to be money. See Marx, *Capital*, vol. 1, p. 151, on Aristotle, and p. 149 on money.

14 Tendential homogeneity is the propensity to limit the world to a restricted field of calculation based on science, reason, and technic. It is a concept drawn from Bataille, "The Psychological Structure of Fascism," 137.

15 On these obstructions to the circulation of capital and their cost, see Marx, *Capital*, vol. 2, p. 133.

In becoming a "Crystal Palace," the commodity form inspires awe, wonder, and desire among the purchasing public and, in a notion from an increasingly bygone era, pride among workers who created the products. Here, the flow of emotions reinforces the desire to consume. This flow of emotions and intermixing of desire and "things" takes the commodity well beyond simple "use-value." In harnessing, channeling, and transforming desire, the commodity directs energy flows toward a material or immaterial attraction and away from potentially disruptive tidal bores that can turn into political intensities and actions. While market processes tend to draw us away from violent intensities, the contractual form of the legal code reinforces and naturalizes market-based thinking. Indeed, the contractual form that law takes means that it is little more than a legal summary and expression of the ideal market relation.[16] As a result, energy that surfaces as desire is redirected toward productive and calculable ends that are naturalized through the legal form and given value via the market-exchange mechanism. This channeling of energy toward "productive," calculable ends is central to the capitalist production process as it puts the "power" in the term "labor-power" and is critical to the production and reproduction of market desire. In other words, these "transcriptions" not only help neutralize political intensities, but also drive desire, which, in turn, powers economic growth.[17] The genius of the capitalist market system lies in its ability to transform almost all potential points of political intensity into profit flows and growth.

In the restricted realm of modern financial flows, such "transcriptions" take place through the money form. Appearing to offer nothing more than a universal token of exchange, the face value of currency offers a "facing" symbolism that can often take coins and notes beyond their denominated value. The face of a coin—that is, the clutch of symbols imprinted on its surface—demonstrates that money can be much more than a universal token of exchange and, in fact, can offer a telltale sign of a systematic "transcription."

16 There is a "givenness" to the contractual form that law takes that runs through the traditional scholarship of people like Sir Henry Sumner Maine right through to the radicalism of the commodity exchange school. For details, see Maine, *Ancient Law*, 168. On the commodity exchange school, see Stuchka, *Selected Writings in Soviet Law and Marxism*. See also Pashukanis, *Selected Writings on Marxism and Law*.

17 This notion of transcription used here comes from Boris Groys who claims that "the communist revolution is the transcription of society from the medium of money to the medium of language." Groys, *The Communist Postscript*, xv.

Figure 2.1. *Left to right:* Greek (Macedonian), Gaul (Limousin), and Gaul (Artois) coins. Image courtesy of Bibliothèque nationale de France.

Ill-Disciplined Numismatics

In his short essay titled "The Academic Horse," Georges Bataille sets the grotesque horselike figures on Limousin and Artois Gaulish coins alongside the symmetrically structured Greek coins of Macedonia (see figure 2.1). The monstrous and wildly extravagant equinelike creatures covering the face of the Gaulish coins stand in sharp contrast to the precise, geometric, and noble drawings of the horse appearing on the coinage of ancient Greece. At first glance, the coins of Gaul appear to materially and symbolically underline a history of dramatic civilizational decline. Greek perfection seems to be overrun and debased by Gaulish barbarism, captured in a rather clumsy and technically incompetent fashion by Gaulish artisan reproductions of Grecian equestrian imagery. This, then, reinforces the orthodox view of the Gauls as "people who calculated nothing and conceived of no progress."[18] For Bataille, however, the comparison reveals a debasement of an altogether different kind. Here, on the surface of the coin, he explains, is Gaulish excess lived as a deliberate and positive "extravagance."[19]

In ancient Greece, he notes, the horse had an exalted place because of the perceived perfection of its form. For the ancient Greeks, this creature was of such nobility and elegance that it came close to being an ideal. Indeed, it was just as much an ideal "as Platonic philosophy or the architecture of the acropolis." For Bataille, this equestrian privileging of the Greeks gave way to a

18 Bataille, "The Academic Horse," 237.

19 Bataille, "The Academic Horse," 238.

Gaulish "*ignoble equidae*" that produced creatures of "unspeakable morals" that were "ugly beyond compare" but that, in terms of the imagination, contained "grandiose apparitions" and "staggering wonders."[20]

An "aggressive ugliness," opening onto the monstrous other side of what Bataille calls the "academic horse" of the ancient Greeks, offered a grotesquely deformed picture of dark magic, "stirring itself with movements of anger" and opening onto a "succession of revolutions" that have continued to this day.[21]

20 Bataille, "The Academic Horse," 238.

21 Bataille, "The Academic Horse," 238.

Figure 2.2. The Gong coin, May 24, 2014, Jinggang Mountain, China. Photo by the author.

> In May 1928, the Soviet government of the Xiang-Gan border region established a financial department under Yu Benmin and, in the village of Shangjing, in the Jinggang Mountains region, that department established a mint. At this time, silver currency was in great demand. Old silver coins, jewelry and other ornaments confiscated from traitors were melted down, the silver extracted, and the raw material supplied to this Red Army mint which then produced coins using the mold of a Mexican silver dollar. To distinguish the Soviet base camp's Mexican coin from others used in "white" areas, the Red Army stamped on the surface of each of their coins one additional character. That character was *gong* [meaning worker-*trans*]. This was the first coinage ever issued by the revolutionary base camps. In 1929, however, this mint was destroyed by the enemy.[22]

This quotation is how the guidebook *Traveling in Jinggang Mountain* summarized the consensus, now established in Mainland China among specialist historians and numismatists, about the "Gong" coin ("*Gong*" *zibi*; see figure 2.2).[23] This would be the first coin of the first mint of the first rural Soviet base camp of the rapidly rusticating Chinese Communist Party.[24] This communist base camp was established at Jinggang Mountain—an impenetrable, inhospitable retreat that was bandit ridden, lying between two administra-

22 Xia Mengshu, *Traveling in Jinggang Mountain*, 52.

23 The name "Gong coin" (*Gong zibi*) would come later. Indeed, it came much later. "In 1975, the Finance Ministry and the People's Bank headquarters work unit groups carried out a check to determine the special name of the 'Gong' coins from the Jinggang Mountain mint. Their unified finding was that, despite the rustic manufacture and crude design patterning, the purity of the coin was high and the weight sufficient that they could stamp upon the foreign eagle coins the character *gong* or worker." Yu Shiquan, "My Views on the Silver Coins of Jinggang Mountain," 15n1.

24 A rather more scholarly account of the period, offering more detail than the tourist book but arguing along the same lines, is given by Yu Boliu and Chen Gang. They, too, refer to the Gong coin of Jinggang Mountain and offer a short history of the mint. See Yu Boliu and Chen Gang, *The Complete History*, 328–30. Meanwhile, Chinese numismatist scholarship also says much the same thing. For a short literature review of the earliest numismatically based research on this question, see Xin Guo, "Du Xiujing and the Jinggang Mountain 'Gong' Coin."

tive zones on the borderlands of Jiangxi and Hunan provinces. When the communist armies began to arrive in the area, two bandit gangs dominated the mountain. These two bandit gangs were closely aligned, with the gang leaders being "comrades" of an altogether different stripe. They were, in fact, more than comrades; they were blood brothers, living the telluric spirit of the rural *jianghu*.

Before the ragtag remnants of the defeated communist armies arrived at Jinggang Mountain, this telluric spirit of *jianghu* had dominated these mountains. It was a spirit that united two bandit gangs led by two sworn brothers, the so-called bandit kings of Jinggang Mountain. Their names were Yuan Wencai and Wang Zuo.[25] They, along with their gangs, would come to join the Communist Party and this would lead not only to the forging of the coin, but also to the infection of Marxism-Leninism with the *jianghu* spirit. This occurred despite the fact that those who had made possible this telluric transformation of the Party, namely the bandit kings Yuan Wencai and Wang Zuo, would end up being killed by their own Party comrades in February 1930.[26] Despite this, the Gong coin is evidence of the moment when,

25 For a detailed account of their lives, see the profiles offered in Averill, *Revolution in the Highlands*, 81–108.

26 While the details of their deaths are both complicated and murky and lie outside the scope of this study, two key factors precipitated their deaths and should be mentioned. The first and most important was the decision of the Party leadership (who were in Moscow) to use bandit gangs where necessary but separate the bandits from their leaders and then eliminate their leaders. The second was a flare-up in land and ethnic disputes between the Tu and the Ke peoples in which Yuan and Wang were involved. On Mao's role in their deaths, there are also many questions. Gregor Benton's detailed account of the period centering on the evacuation of the base camps for the Long March highlighted Mao's culpability in their killing, pointing to his acceptance if not support of the central Party leadership decision. Benton, *Mountain Fires*, 382–86. More recent Mainland scholarship, however, disputes Mao's culpability, pointing to his strong defense of Yuan and Wang at various times, including one key local meeting (the Bailu meeting) in January 1929 where he reminded the other base-camp leaders that Wang and Yuan weren't bandits but comrades. See chapter 4, section 4, "The Deaths of Yuan and Wang," in Yu Boliu and Chen Gang, *The Complete History*, 392–404. Edgar Snow's interview with Mao in the 1930s reports Mao's remembrance of events:

> Two former bandit leaders near Chingkanshan [Jinggang Mountain], named Wang Tso [Wang Zuo] and Yuan Wen-tsai [Yuan Wencai] joined the Red

paradoxically but significantly, the most brilliant figure of modernity, rationality, and science (the Communist Party) was joined to the continuing (re) emergence of rituals proper to the telluric spirit of the *jianghu*. The Party's cultural immersion within rural China did more than "rusticate" the Party. It produced a unique form of "telluric partisanship" that would power the revolution and, after that, produce a radical and unique rationality of government that still proves infectious.[27] The significance of this infection in terms of a concept of the political, however, is easily missed, for this event is now

---

> Army in the winter of 1927. This increased the strength to about three regiments, Wang and Yuan were each made regimental commanders and I was army commander. These two men, although former bandits, had thrown in their forces with the Nationalist Revolution, and were now ready to fight against the reaction. While I remained in *Chingkanshan* [Jinggang Mountain] they were faithful Communists, and carried out the orders of the Party. Later on when they were left alone at Chingkanshan, they returned to their bandit habits. Subsequently, they were killed by peasants, by then organized and Sovietized and able to defend themselves. (Snow, *Red Star over China*, 165–66)

Lastly, there are details that have emerged in more recent Chinese scholarship. As Zhang Xudong writes,

> On 22nd February 1930, because of the slander and deceit of Long Chaoqing, and without any investigation, the local Party leaders in Jinggang Mountain made up a list of the five crimes of Yuan Wencai, including leaving his post without permission, ignoring dispatches, and looking after his own people [*shanzilidui, buting diaoqian, baobu luokeshao*]. Yuan Wencai refuted these accusations, but the argument was heated and because the local Party leaders were frightened that Yuan's troops would rebel, the 5th Red Army Special Leadership Committee of the Xiang-Gan Border Region decided to surround Yuan's residence. Yuan Wencai was shot in his bed. Wang Zuo heard the commotion, leapt out a window, but unluckily fell into Dongguan pond and drowned. (Zhang Xudong, "The Two Heroes of Jinggang Mountain," 40)

27 It is infectious in two ways. First, echoes of this unique approach to governance can still be found in certain contemporary governmental techniques in China. This, at least, is the suggestion of Heilmann and Perry. See Heilmann and Perry, *Mao's Invisible Hand*, 7. At the same time, and within a broader global view, we can see how this question of the telluric transmission of intensity has energized other forms of politics and other political movements of the non-Western world.

little more than a minor and contested footnote in a larger tale of communist redemption of almost biblical proportions.[28]

Barely a year after the Communist Party had been wiped out in the cities of China, and soon after their own abysmal Autumn Harvest Rising had made their situation significantly worse, sections of the communist Red Army fled to this liminal zone of the *jianghu* that was beyond the reach of the state. It was at Jinggang Mountain where these remnants would regroup and rebuild. In the depths of rural China, the Party that claimed to represent the vanguard class of modernity, the proletariat, opened themselves to an ancient underground telluric connection. In opening themselves to that telluric connection, the communists were able to mint the Mexican silver eagle coin on which they stamped their character *gong*, meaning *worker*. Like the flipping of a coin, there are two sides to this tale. One would be to present these events as a "modernist" tale of communist pragmatism, while the other would highlight the subterranean flow of a telluric *jianghu* infection.

As a modernist tale, the forging of this coin is presented as pragmatic in nature and communist in intent. The story of the production of the coin becomes a modernist tale for it presents the Communist Party and their actions in this rural backwater as a harbinger of the new. By producing the coin and introducing currency into the area, the communists were said to have brought the idea of a modern money economy into a remote and backward part of China that knew only barter. Mao Zedong, the leader of the Jinggang Mountain Soviet base camp, authorized the production of this coin, and he appointed his new Party comrade, the former bandit king Wang Zuo, to set up the mint.

After Wang joined the Communist Party, he was appointed to a number of important positions both in the Red Army and on the camp's finance committee under Yu Bimin.[29] The reason why Wang was chosen to set up the

28 "We cannot deny that the Mexican silver dollar *gong* coin from the Shangjing mint in *Jinggang* Mountain existed," concluded Zhang Ying of the Shanghai mint after he investigated the veracity of the claim. He came to this conclusion, as Liang Jie wryly notes, without ever seeing a genuine verifiable original. See Liang Jie, "On Knowledge of the 'Gong' Coin." Skepticism has grown about the coin and has reached the point whereby the refurbished Chinese Numismatic Museum in Beijing no longer displays or even mentions it.

29 On Wang's position within the Party, he was a member of the Xiang (Hunan)-Gan (Jiangxi) Border Region special committee (defense) committee (*zhongyang xiang*

mint was because, as a local, he had the necessary contacts to undertake this work. To this end, Wang would approach two other Party comrades, the Xie brothers, Xie Guanlong and Xie Huolong, who had the vernacular indigenous skills, knowledge, and tools to forge the first communist coin. If the Xie brothers supplied the molds and the skill base, it was the Party that provided the premises and offered the cause.[30] Moreover, a Red Army official, Huang Huaju, sent from Wang Zuo's own regiment to inspect and check on coin production, would add the final touches to this story by marking the freshly minted silver coin with the character *gong*.[31]

It has been said, perhaps apocryphally, that Huang noticed a vertical scratch line on the surface of one of the Mexican silver dollar coins being produced by the mint. Huang seized the moment and scratched two horizontal lines on either end of the vertical line, thus completing the *gong* character. Simple and evocative, this mark of Huang was then said to have been stamped onto all future communist coinage from the Jinggang Mountain mint, turning the Mexican silver dollar into the Gong coin.[32] The Gong coin, in this account, then, was born of revolutionary invention and was a harbinger of the new.

Yet this revolutionary tale of the arrival of the communists at Jinggang Mountain could be retold very differently if stress were laid on slightly

---

ganbianjie tewei weiyuan) and deputy regimental commander of the 32nd Regiment of the 4th Army (*Hongsijun sanshi'ertuan futuanzhang*). See Li Zengwen, "Paying Homage at the Relics," 66. For his role in financial matters, see He Chonggong, quoted in Liang Jie, "On Knowledge of the 'Gong' Coin," 47.

30 On the equipment and the house, see Xin Guo, "Du Xiujing and the Jinggang Mountain 'Gong' Coin," 85. On the master workers Xie Huolong and Xie Guanlong (the Xie brothers), see Li Zengwen, "Paying Homage at the Relics," 67. Li explains how they used their clan's coin factory, casting machines together with equipment and materials supplied by the confiscations undertaken by the Red Army in the course of struggle. In Jinggang Mountain's Shangjing village, a traditional house confiscated from Zuo Jiagui became the Red Army mint. For details, see Li Zengwen, "Paying Homage at the Relics," 66.

31 Liang Jie, "On Knowledge of the 'Gong' Coin," 47.

32 Information on Huang Huaju comes from 1975 and from a then-aged Luo Dongxiang who was, at the time the mint was built, the Ciping village secretary and who spoke directly to the visiting research team from the Finance Ministry and the People's Bank. See Liang Jie, "On Knowledge of the 'Gong' Coin," 47.

different aspects of this story. This other account might begin by noting Wang Zuo's *chundian* name, Nan Dou or "Southern Compass," and might also draw attention, as many leaders within the Communist Party at the time had been doing, to his bandit connections and traits. It might also mention that his regimental leader, Yuan Wencai, known locally by his *chundian* name Xuan San, was also his sworn brother and the other bandit king of Jinggang Mountain. Wang Zuo had, in fact, followed Yuan into the Communist Party.[33]

Together, these two former bandit kings, along with their followers, would form a Red Army regiment that was led by Yuan with Wang as his deputy.[34] This regiment was involved in "financial" activities that became an important source of revenue for the base camp. In other words, these bandits joined the Party, but with revenue gathering as their main occupation, they never really left the *jianghu*. This continuing link to *jianghu* practices is hardly surprising. After all, at Jinggang Mountain, neither Wang Zuo nor the Communist Party could live without taking on at least some of the attributes of the *jianghu*. Indeed, Mao Zedong chose Wang Zuo for the role of mint maker precisely because he had never fully left the *jianghu*.

Wang Zuo and his sworn brother, Yuan Wencai, would bring their bandit gangs into the Party fold. They would bring in thieves, bandits, counterfeiters, and smugglers and now these vagabonds would work for the revolution. As bandit gangs bound as much by the spirit of *jianghu* as the spoils of banditry, they had lived as a brotherhood-in-arms and in this respect the transition into comradeship was an easy step for them to make. Wang Zuo had long relied on his *jianghu* brothers to survive in Jinggang Mountain,[35] and he would

33 According to Ouyang Hui, Yuan Wencai joined the Communist Party in November 1926. Stuart Schram dates it from early 1927. See Ouyang Hui, "The Two Wang Zuos's Period of Struggle," 42. See also Schram, introduction to *Mao's Road to Power*, xxv. For the nicknames and an investigation into their fate, see *Beijing Agriculture*, "Remembering the Two Heroes of Jinggang."

34 In terms of ethnicity, Yuan's regiment was made up of *Ke*, while the local Party committee was largely *Tu*. Tensions sometimes arose between the two groups and these were greatly exacerbated by divisions over land. While both groups were immigrants, they came from different places at different times. Benton's work highlights this division. For references to this in relation to the events surrounding Wang and Yuan's deaths, see Benton, *Mountain Fires*, 382.

35 There is a story of how Wang Zuo and Yuan Wencai became blood brothers. "In 1925, Wang Zuo's forces were torn apart by internal strife and Wang Zuo was forced

come to rely on them again when charged with the task of creating the mint that produced the coinage of revolution.

Xie Huolong was chosen by Wang to run the mint because he had been a local rural counterfeiter with a long history in the *jianghu*. He was, therefore, both knowledgeable and loyal. He had also, like the marker of the coin, Huang Huaju, been part of Wang Zuo's bandit gang. Having been chased from one province to the next, Xie had finally ended up at Jinggang Mountain in Wang's gang.[36] Faux consanguineous relations born of a brotherly bonding formed the basis of the masculine trope of *jianghu*. It was a trope that tied *jianghu* back to a memory of the patriarchal clan but could also move it forward toward an intensified, nonconsanguineous notion of comradeship.

---

to flee for refuge to Yuan Wencai. Yuan Wencai helped eradicate those estranged from Wang Zuo and restored him to power. From that time onwards, Yuan Wencai and Wang Zuo, who were both of the same age, became blood brothers. After this, Yuan Wencai went back down the mountain to Maoping while Wang Zuo went back up the mountain to the villages but now, in having '*lao geng*' relations and living under the same banner and standing side by side, these two gangs became two horns of the one beast with an illustrious name that echoed across the whole of the Xiang-Gan border region." Ouyang Hui, "The Two Wang Zuos's Period of Struggle," 42.

36 The Xie brothers were originally counterfeiters from Longchuan County in Guangdong Province, where they first set up their secret "Xie brothers mint." At the beginning of the 1920s, the Xie brothers moved to Jiangxi to flee the pillage and then lived in Dongkeng Village. As they were inept at farming in the rice fields, they started to forge coins again. They forged only small numbers of coins each time, just so they could make a living. But when Xie Rongzhen died, Xie Huolong (the younger brother) would not only continue the surreptitious business but also expand the venture. He collected bronze coins and mixed a little silver into the coins, making large numbers of fake coins. He then hired people to sell them in the remote areas of Guangdong, Hunan, and Jiangxi and made huge profits. When the government found out, Xie was put on a wanted list and fled. He moved his mint to Yongxin County and continued minting coins. When the government tracked him down there, Xie realized he had no choice other than to discontinue the business for a while. At that time, Wang Zuo at Jinggang Mountain heard about him and recruited him to forge coins for his *jianghu* gang. After Mao Zedong took the Red Army to Jinggang Mountain and met with Wang Zuo and Yuan Wencai, Wang Zuo decided to stop forging his own coins. When the mint reopened at Jinggang Mountain, it was the Red Army mint and became an important way for the Party to overcome the economic blockade the Nationalists had established. See Liu Qun, "The Silver Dollar 'Gong' Coin of Jinggangshan."

Leaving aside this question of whether the coin represents communist modernist commitments or the spirit of *jianghu*, the Sinologist in me still wants to know more about the veracity of either account of the Gong coin. After all, why mint a coin that could not be used outside a tiny area of communist control and minted on the back of a commitment to something that looked to have very little chance of survival? Was this coin really produced to promote commerce and trade with enemy-controlled areas?[37] How could it be said that the *gong* marking on the coin was a guarantee of purity when, in enemy areas, it was nothing short of being the Mark of Cain?[38] Perhaps, as a guarantee of purity, the coin flagged something else? Given the overwhelming odds against their survival, could this mark have flagged a desire for the purity of commitment? Then again, this might be nothing more than an elaborate hoax, built on myth, couched in reverential terms to disguise the fact that the Communist Party itself bears the bandit scar? Was it just another clever *jianghu* trick to hide the Party's *jianghu* infection? The Party, then, in this reading, becomes a *jianghu* trickster. Whether the mark on the coin is a hoax or not, one thing seems clear: this coin, marked or otherwise, announced the arrival of *jianghu* technologies into the Party and, with it, the *jianghu* mentality. It was this infection of *jianghu* intensity, as it was channeled toward class struggle, that formed the basis of the telluric partisanship of Mao Zedong. Maoism was the siren song heralding this transformation. And speaking of siren songs . . .

37 Liang Jie says that the "base camp needed their own finances, and the *Gong* coin alleviated the situation and enabled them to openly trade with white areas. Even though it had limited circulation, this 'indigenous coin' [*tuban huabiao*] was well received in the white areas and this enabled trade and helped resolve one of the more urgent problems, that was stabilising the economy." See Liang Jie, "On Knowledge of the 'Gong' Coin," 49. Li Jiakui, Ju Qizhi, and Li Zhenwu say, "In order to raise production, and enable commerce to recover, they decided that the resolution of their monetary problem could be addressed by the Xiang-Gan border Soviet Government establishing a mint to cast and modify coins." "The Jinggangshan Five-Point Star 'Gong' Silver Dollar," 6.

38 According to Wu Manping, the coins were pure silver whereas the original was 90 percent silver and 10 percent brass. Wu Manping, "Markings on the Jinggang Mountain Silver Dollar, Explored," 45.

3

Callings

Things That Sound Like Sirens from a Long Way Off

In Homer's *Odyssey*, Circe cautions Odysseus about his journey home. Beware the bewitching sounds of the Sirens that lure sailors to their deaths, she warns. Odysseus listens but does not heed her call. Instead, as currents lead his boat past the Sirens' lair, Odysseus avoids the fate of countless others by having his oarsmen plug their ears with wax while he, himself, is strapped to the ship's mast. Thus, while his oarsmen row on, oblivious to the Sirens' song, Odysseus is alive to its mesmeric yet tormenting call but, being tied, unable to act on it. Thrown into bliss but also tormented, he is unable to move. Odysseus avoids death by sacrificing free will.

Enter the cultural theorists Theodor Adorno and Max Horkheimer. Predicated on a Kantian-inspired understanding of the Enlightenment, Horkheimer proclaimed the *Odyssey* "the first document on the anthropology of man in the modern sense, that means, the sense of a rational enlightened being."[1] It is a parodic description of our contemporary dilemma. Oarsmen stand in for contemporary workers; the master, Odysseus, for the modern bourgeoisie. The modern worker, in being limited like the oarsmen, to the practical tasks at hand, is deaf to the Sirens' song. Theirs is a world dictated by the factory bench, the movie theater, or the collective enterprise.[2]

If that be the destiny of the modern worker, what twisted fate awaits the contemporary analogue of Odysseus, the bourgeoisie? For Adorno and Horkheimer, the modern bourgeoisie, like Odysseus, are strapped to the mast of a system of their own creation but no longer able to control or enjoy it. For worker and burgher alike, there is only a Taylorism of the mind in which instrumental reason comes to prevail over the call of the Enlightenment.

But can the Enlightenment be so readily identified in this fable of the Sirens' song? If reason is tied to a yearning, is it not, then, a paradox? After all, a yearning is far from rational. Can reason, then, be so readily aligned with the unreason of a yearning, of a Siren's temptation?

"The first document on the anthropology of man [*sic*] in the modern sense," therefore, seems to entail something other than "the rational enlightened being." Indeed, the allure of the Sirens' song seems to suggest the opposite of a rational enlightened being. It seems to suggest a being who cannot avoid the affective yearning to embrace the Sirens' song, and this will overrule all rationality. Perhaps what this fable does is merely repeat the tension between reason and revelation? Perhaps, what it suggests is that even when our actions follow the footsteps of reason into a plan to outwit revelation, a yearning pain still burns within? After all, the Sirens' song still burns in Odysseus's ears even though the ropes of reason stop him from acting. Despite the ropes, this yearning remains. The affective, intense, irrational, and violent desires that the Sirens' song brings to the fore are not satiated by reason but held back by it.

Less reason than temptation, less temptation than irresistible yearning, the Sirens' song takes us beyond calculation. At this point the Sirens' song takes us to the heart of religious and political intensities that, while not the enemy of Enlightenment reason, nevertheless operate in a parallel universe. Let us, then, reimagine this story of Ulysses and the Sirens' song not as enlightenment lost, but as political intensity outwitted. This yearning, this intensity, this sense of destiny, signals the way the political can entice but like Ulysses, the market has found a way to outmaneuver it, without ever being able to fully silence the ongoing threat.

1 Cited in Wiggershaus, *The Frankfurt School*, 329.

2 Adorno and Horkheimer, *Dialectic of Enlightenment*, 36–37.

Figure 3.1. Portrait of Mao Zedong and calligraphy of Lin Biao, from the frontispiece to the volume *A Compilation of Materials*. This book is identical in appearance to the Little Red Book. With a red plastic cover and diminutive size, this "Little Red Book of Chinese medicine" has an appearance that signifies its status. In the notes and bibliography, I refer to the book as *A Compilation of Materials*.

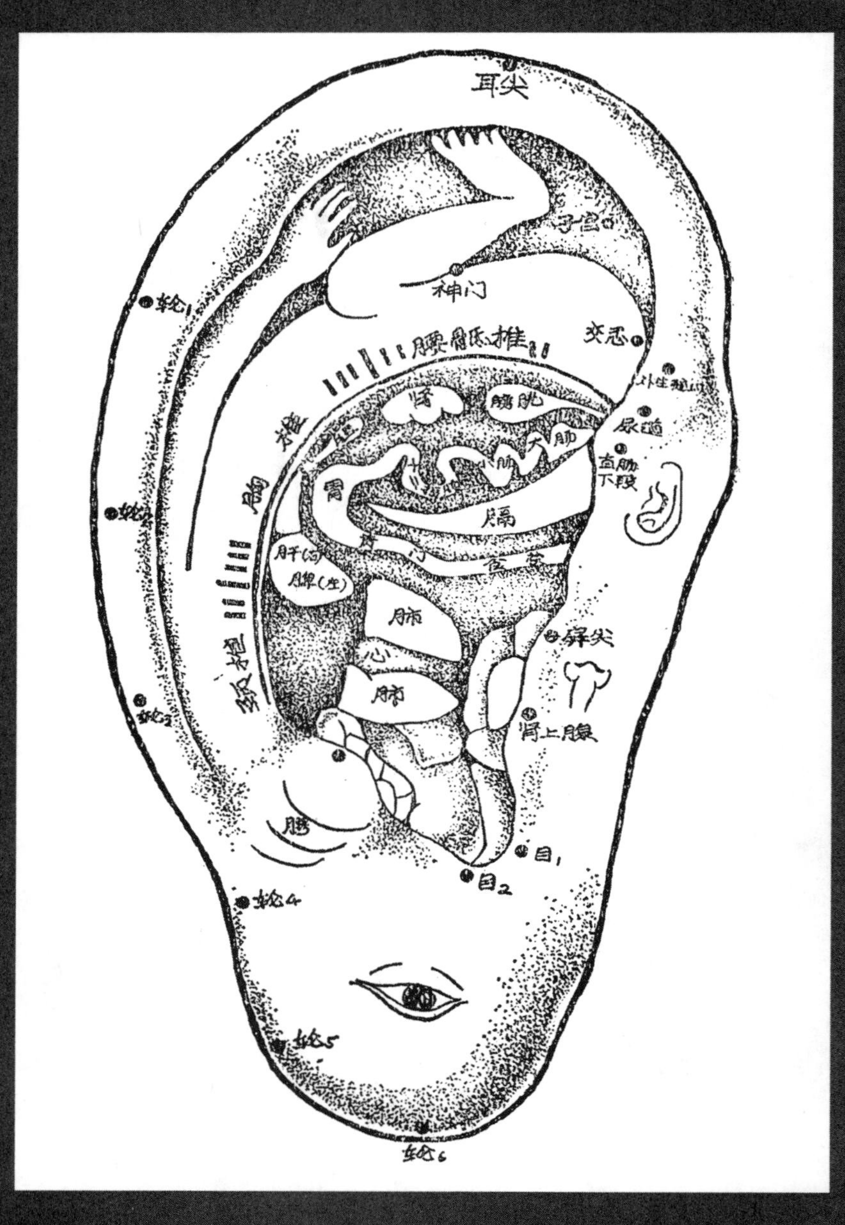

Figure 3.2. Left ear chart used in traditional Chinese medicine (TCM). From *A Compilation of Materials*, 189.

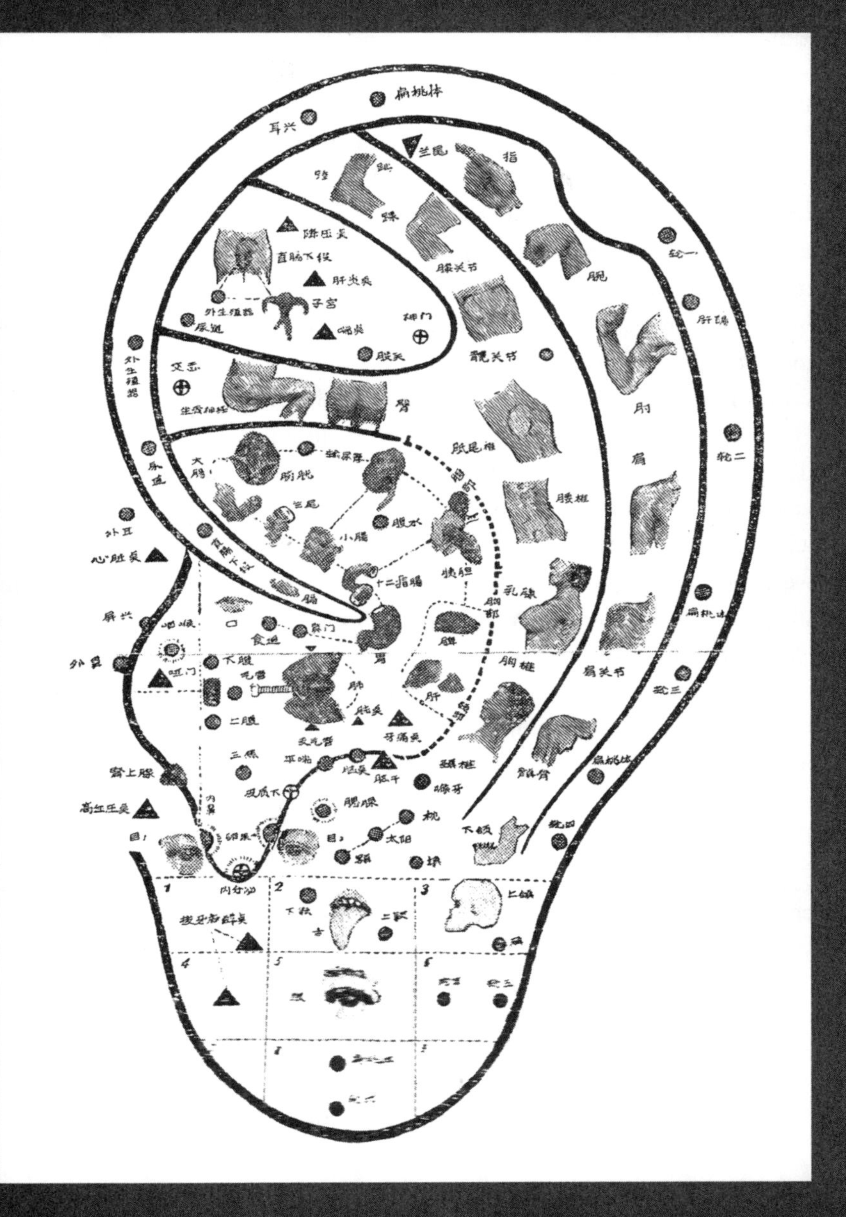

Figure 3.3. Right ear chart used in TCM. From *A Compilation of Materials*, 190.

Left behind the Ears

Figure 3.1 depicts the Great Helmsman with a dedication to him below that. Chairman Mao and the dedication to him are located right before the ears. The dedication is written in the hand of Lin Biao, who was, at the time he wrote it, Mao's closest comrade-in-arms and his chosen successor. It was written at the height of the Cultural Revolution on May Day, 1967.[3] The image of Mao and text by Lin form the frontispiece of a Little Red Book that came out in 1969 under the title *A Compilation of Materials on Following the Command of Mao Zedong Thought with New Medical Methods*. That is where the ears come in. They were part of the "new methods."

Two years after the publication of this Little Red Book, Lin Biao, who devised the red plastic-covered format back in 1963 and who wrote the sycophantic dedication to Mao, was dead. He had been trying to flee China after a failed coup attempt against the Great Helmsman. His charred remains were found, along with those of other family members and close allies, on the plains of Mongolia after a plane crash foiled his escape. Only his teeth were left to identify him.[4]

Stories of his teeth lead us away from the ears. They lead us back to his charred body and conjure up images of internal Party intrigues, disenchantment with the Maoist leadership, and high-level excesses fueled by Byzantine politics. By the time of economic reform, the story of Lin's teeth was but one element in an overarching critique of the whole sorry period.

"Ten years of chaos" is how the Cultural Revolution is depicted in reform-era China, and this depiction is also, rather surprisingly, the basis of most Western accounts of the period. Chastened by the "perspicacity" of some of

3 Lin's calligraphy reads as follows: "The greatest guide, the greatest teacher, the greatest leader, the greatest commander-in-chief, the greatest helmsman; Long live, long, long live Chairman Mao (Lin Biao, May Day 1967)." See the frontispiece to *A Compilation of Materials*.

4 Numerous books written on the Lin Biao affair have become increasingly revealing over the years about the plot that seemed as preposterous as the campaign against Lin Biao and Confucius that followed. It was only after the opening of archives in Russia, however, that details about the flight, crash, and death of Lin Biao over the skies of Mongolia were revealed. On this, see Hannam and Lawrence, "Solving a Chinese Puzzle."

their number,[5] the guilt and retractions of former fellow travelers;[6] the revelations in biographies, autobiographies, and recollections;[7] and the opening of newly available archives, Western scholars in search of horror would not be disappointed.

Local and county records were scoured, in-depth fieldwork and interviews undertaken, classified documents leaked. The result has been a series of micro-level studies of violence and terror, as well as studies of Byzantine intrigues in the court of Mao, as exemplified by those that documented the fall of Lin Biao and the discovery of his teeth.[8] These studies are far from uninteresting, unimportant, incorrect, or even consciously politically motivated. Rather, they are studies that operate along a line of veridiction that produces concrete data about the political movement, by occluding an understanding of the movement of the political. Thus, when it comes to the Siren song of Cultural Revolution, it is scholarship with wax in its ears.

Facts, not convictions, must rule scholarship, but when it comes to the Cultural Revolution, these are "facts as have scarcely ever become the basis of convictions," to steal a line from Walter Benjamin.[9] Facts, gathered out of earshot of the Sirens' song, are facts without conviction, teeth without ears. Yet it was precisely because "truth" was reconfigured around conviction that the Cultural Revolution moved beyond fact and reason and attempted to channel

5 Most obviously, Pierre Rykmans. His critique of Maoism, articulated during the Mao era when the French left were turning to China as an alternative to the totalitarianism of the USSR, was bitterly attacked at the time. Written under the pseudonym Simon Leys, Rykmans's account excoriates Western Maoists as naive and simplistic and his critiques of them and of the Cultural Revolution have now become widely accepted. See Leys, *The Chairman's New Clothes*, or Leys, *Chinese Shadow*.

6 Within American China studies, it led to much soul-searching, resulting in everything, from Mark Seldon revising his overly rosy picture of Yan'an, right through to the total repudiations of a leftist past by scholars like Edward Friedman.

7 Probably the most famous of these in the West is by Mao's doctor, Li Zhisui, whose memoir of his time with Mao became a best seller. See Li Zhisui, *The Private Life of Chairman Mao*.

8 Lin Biao's story was retold as scholarship by the daughter of Wu Faxian, commander of the air force under Lin Biao and one of the people implicated in the plot. See Qiu Jin, *The Culture of Power*.

9 Benjamin, *One-Way Street and Other Writings*, 45.

and transform affective energy into a form of intensity that had a political use-value. Culture became the vehicle through which this was attempted.

Culture, in this context, and only in this context, played a mechanical role. This was not the first time the idea of culture as machine had been rehearsed within the communist movement. That honor goes to Vladimir Tatlin's Machine Art. Nevertheless, this was the first time it had been mass-produced within earshot of the non-Western telluric. The ears help us hear of an indigenous telluric knowledge system that still listened to modernity's call.

"A healthy auricular [*er'ke*] is like an inverted fetus in a womb," says the Little Red Book of new medical methods (see figures 3.2 and 3.3).[10] It is the existence of this inverted fetal form within the ear that enables various ailments within the body to be located and treated, for the ear offers a "definite system regulating the distribution of acupoints."[11] This "systematizing ear," so privileged in the new Maoist methods, was not one of the acupoints located on the fourteen meridians identified in the classic ancient medical text *The Yellow Emperor's Book of Internal Medicine*, or *Huangdi Neijing*; nor was it part of any traditional Chinese remedy or cure. In fact, it wasn't even Chinese.

In 1957, a French neurologist, Paul F. M. Nogier, coined the term *auriculotherapy* and introduced the ear into alternative medicine.[12] It came along with a multitude of other additions, modifications, and importations into New Medicine. Maoism didn't save traditional Chinese medicine any more than it promoted Western medicine. Rather, it attempted to combine Western and Chinese medicine into a New Medicine.[13] Be it through the discovery of 361 new and "strange" acupuncture points or the addition of electricity to the needles during insertion, the use of measurements within the body or the

10 *A Compilation of Materials*, 188.

11 *A Compilation of Materials*, 188.

12 For a very brief introduction to auriculotherapy within alternative medicine, see Rider, "An Introduction to the Early History of Ear Acupuncture."

13 The goal was never to ensure the lasting presence of Chinese medicine in China, Taylor tells us, but rather to halt attempts to dismiss it as a body of medical knowledge. See Taylor, *Chinese Medicine in Early Communist China*, 120. For the Maoists, the question was not Chinese or Western medicine but new and old medicines. For other examples of foreign interventions, from nonspecific protein-otherapy to Soviet tissue therapy, see Taylor, *Chinese Medicine in Early Communist China*, 55–56.

recognition of the nervous system, the new Maoist methods attempted to develop techniques that were not only better but more economical. What was notable about this treatment was that it bore the birthmarks of a new cosmology built on the flows of the political. Public health increasingly became a mass campaign and, along with self-reliance and the simplification of techniques, enabled the development of the barefoot doctor system and the extension of medical care into rural areas.[14] It also forged the basis of the economic strategy that became known as the Great Leap Forward.

In the shadow of the unspeakable number of deaths that now scar the name of the Great Leap Forward, however, it is difficult to register anything positive. Kim Taylor, for example, begins her detailed assessment of medicinal developments in this period with the words "There is little that was good that came out of the Great Leap Forward" before listing a series of things that were good and that came out of the same telluric spirit that fueled the Great Leap's transition into the Cultural Revolution.[15] If the struggles within medicine that took place throughout the 1950s and 1960s, between red and expert, resulted in challenges to the centrality of Western medicine, then the answer was to redirect attention toward a more indigenous, telluric knowledge form, namely, Chinese traditional medicines.[16] These medicines, however, were far from being "pure," "traditional," or even singular. Even ideas of vital energy, or *qi*, *yin*/*yang*, and the *wuxing*, or five phases, were, as terms of reference, displaced by more Maoist concepts such as contradiction, self-reliance, and the mass-line. The balancing of *yin*/*yang* gave way to the idea of "different

14 See Taylor, *Chinese Medicine in Early Communist China*, 116–18.

15 An example of this is her praise of the idea of self-reliance, which, she notes, encouraged the use of home remedies as well as a simplification in procedure, which then led to the extension of medical care into the countryside and opened the experiment that led to the barefoot doctors' system. See Taylor, *Chinese Medicine in Early Communist China*, 116–18.

16 *Remedies* might be better than *medicines* but the use of the plural here is deliberate. Chinese traditional medical practices all worked from a similar Taoist-inspired understanding of the body and the cosmos, but the specific local techniques applied and passed on through an intimate master/apprentice relationship militated against a single medicine, as it meant that each of these practices would adopt a discrete set of remedies and cures. See Sivin, *Traditional Medicine in Contemporary China*, 6–7.

methods being employed to resolve different contradictions,"[17] while self-reliance, in practice, encouraged the use of homegrown localized remedies. Texts would adopt a more militant language and medicine would reflect this, becoming one of the many sites where the Maoist slogan of "greater, faster, better, [and] more economical production" was put into practice.[18]

Nevertheless, despite this, the fundamental question always remained a question of the flow, even if *qi* itself was occluded.[19] Here, then, was a form of medical treatment far from the shores of scientific socialism, yet equally adrift from the "reactionary" knowledge forms being smashed under the rubric of the "Four Olds."[20]

This understanding of "tradition" as a "treasure house" containing "thousands of years of our laboring people's rich experiences"[21] would be explained through the circumlocution of the revolution. Yet strangely, if *A Compilation of Materials on Following the Command of Mao Zedong Thought with New Medical Methods* is anything to go by, more revolutionary meant being

17 Under "Basic Principles": "The Great Helmsman Chairman Mao taught us to understand: Different contradictions can only ever be resolved using different methods." *A Compilation of Materials*, 169.

18 Note, for example, the words used in the Little Red Book of Chinese medicine: "This type of treatment whereby one inserts the needle less [*quxueshao*], doesn't leave the needle in too long [*buliu zhen*] and achieves good results, is easy to learn and understand, with simplified treatment methods that the masses can grasp and easily accept." *A Compilation of Materials*, 23.

19 Kim Taylor notes the way that, while the theory changed, fundamental practices did not: "Science might have replaced the theory of disease, altered the presentation of the body, changed hand techniques, and reformed the description of individual diagnosis. But in the 'new acupuncture' it did little in the role of diagnostics, and even less in the selection of acupuncture points." Taylor, *Chinese Medicine in Early Communist China*, 61.

20 A focus of attack in the Cultural Revolution, "the Four Olds" were old customs, old culture, old habits, and old ideas.

21 This claim of it being the work of the laboring people is made in *A Compilation of Materials*, 23, but is contradicted by Nathan Sivin, who has pointed out that the tradition that has been passed down is "almost exclusively from 'the elite literary tradition'" (*Traditional Medicine in Contemporary China*, 22). Later elaborating on the point, he added that "much of the hodge-podge we call popular curing has been officially classified as superstition for the past thirty years, and has been little studied as it continues to die out" (44).

more practical, technical, and selective. It meant dividing the body into parts and not treating it as a whole and it meant maintaining certain techniques of bodily cure, while breaking with the traditional universalizing cosmogony that underpinned it. Thus, the relationship between bodily and political flows was no longer tied by a shared cosmologically based concern with *qi*. Nevertheless, the Maoist political, more than most, was still haunted by concerns about the flow of energy. Here is where our analysis must begin, not with the complex rhythms that dictated past understandings of the flow in each and every area, but with the simple recognition that *qi* that is central to bodily flows opens onto a way of understanding political flows.

Pulsating, bunching up, creating pressures that need to be expended, expelled, or in some other way dissipated, the management of bodily flows opens a similar pathway to the management of the flow of the body-politic. Thus understood, it leads to a view that registers the Maoist machinery of state and government as exemplars of that politics of flow and recognizes the Cultural Revolution not as a moment of madness or chaos, but as an experiment in the channeling and harnessing of political intensity.

Something less than madness, but something not quite sane, this event and its project open a unique window onto the question of the political. It becomes one of the crucial examples and experiments in the channeling and intensification of revolutionary energies. It transformed parts of the state and Party into a war machine. As a war machine, it would speak not just as a state developmental model, but as a machine to channel and transform affective energy into an intensity that, through its Sirens' song, developed a political form. So how does one halt such contagions?

Figure 4.1. The Metropole Hotel, circa 2004. Photo by the author.

PART 2

Contagions

Figure 4.2. The hotel room number plate from the Metropole Hotel, from which, after SARS, room 911 simply disappeared. Mongkok, Hong Kong, circa 2004. Photo by the author.

4

911

On June 23, 2003, the following item appeared in the *South China Morning Post*: "The ninth floor of the Metropole Hotel in Mongkok—ground zero of Hong Kong's SARS epidemic—will be turned into a museum if the management can figure out the best way to 'package it.'" The Metropole Hotel, ground zero of Hong Kong's SARS epidemic, as the report put it, was where the Guangzhou medical professor Liu Jianlun had stayed during his brief sojourn in Hong Kong (see figure 4.1). From there, and in a writing style that was Trumpist before Trump, the article labeled the poor maligned professor "super-spreader Liu" and accused him of spreading the SARS virus from Mainland China to the rest of the world. Looking back on this type of description after Trump's relabeling of SARS-CoV-2 as the "China disease" casts it in an altogether different light. But what struck me at the time that I read it was not the use of language or even the spreading of the virus itself but the room number of the professor in the Metropole Hotel. It was room 911.

It made me wonder what tricks the gods were playing on us such that this minor footnote from the very first strain of the SARS virus to threaten humanity[1] redirects our mind's-eye, through numerical association, back to New York and to an act of inhumanity on September 11, 2001, that redefined the early part of this century.[2] Two historic events came together around this seemingly enchanted emergency number, 911.[3] Twenty years on, and this chance encounter in numerology looks more like a portent of things to come.

1 SARS is one of seven members of the coronavirus family that can spread to humans, with COVID-19 being the latest. On December 31, 2019, the first reported case in the COVID-19 outbreak was reported in Wuhan, China. By January 30, 2020, the World Health Organization had declared COVID-19 a Public Health Emergency of International Concern (PHEIC), giving rise to the expression "pandemic." For the details on SARS and how predictive models were being developed to track the spread of COVID-19, see Binti et al., "CoronaTracker."

2 Such a chance numerical encounter is reminiscent of Sigmund Freud's reading of *lapsus linguae*. Under the code of *lapsus linguae*, Freud studied the way a linguistic lapse created an association between two unlikely events. Indeed, for Freud, the importance of the link is evidenced by the merriment and derision caused by the linguistic error. This, he argues, speaks "conclusively against the generally accepted convention that such a speech blunder is a *lapses linguae* and psychologically of no importance." See Freud, "Psychopathology of Everyday Life," 84. Perhaps this linguistic complementarity is, like a joke, bringing out a "suppressed subsidiary thought." See Freud, *Jokes and Their Relation to the Unconscious*, 52. From the description given by the *South Morning China Post* reporter, who spoke of the Metropole Hotel as Hong Kong's "ground zero," this chance meeting of numbers is clearly not missed. I would like to thank Don Gasper for bringing this to my attention.

3 *Enchanted*, because the number 9 has special meaning in ancient Chinese (as well as other cosmologies flagging the completion or the end of things, while the number 11 is an event taking place on a physical plane). *Emergency*, because this sequence of numbers became the emergency telephone number throughout the United States from February 16, 1968, after a trial was conducted in Haleyville, Alabama. Until Bin Laden came along, the local switch manager, Bill Frey, was known as "the father of 911." The idea of three digits came from the Presidential Commission on Law Enforcement in 1967. The choice of the number 9 to begin the sequence might well have stemmed from its association with the British telephone emergency number 999 that came into existence in 1936. The following sequence of 11 was said to have been selected because of the ease of dialing on the old rotary dial-up phone systems. For further details and complications, see Holland, "Why 999 for an Emergency?"; K. Moore, "Dial 999"; and Dutton, "911."

If SARS was the beginning of a struggle against new and invisible deadly viral strains, the war on terror pitted the state against a no less shadowy (although far less deadly) manifestation of the telluric, namely, the (Islamic) terrorist. To combat these two shadowy infestations, governments felt compelled to marshal their resources, reach beyond themselves, declare their own laws and regulations void, and institute emergency measures that offered them the best opportunity to move past these viral infections and cut them off. These struggles against virulent flows occasioned within government a legislative fiat that Carl Schmitt famously labeled the state of the exception.[4] Thus, while SARS would speak of the revenge of nature, and New York's 9/11 of human terror, both events forced themselves on us, politically, as states of emergency. Until COVID-19, however, we in the West lived such threats as momentary or minor adjustments. Indeed, in terms of the war on terror, part of what made the contemporary Western state of the exception exceptional was that, for the nontargeted population, it was less a state of emergency than a state of adjustment. "Be alert, not alarmed" ran the antiterrorist slogan in Australia,[5] yet what were the beneficial "spinoffs" for both the market and the state? In the West, the war on terror saw a massive growth in surveillance technology[6] alongside a rush toward the commercialization of online data[7] as the internet of things (IoT) grew.[8]

4 The opening gambit of the book *Political Theology* offers the following line: "Sovereign is he who decides on the exception." For Schmitt, the exception is at the core of the question of sovereignty. See Schmitt, *Political Theology*, xxxvii.

5 One of the Australian contributions to the war on terror was to run an AU$15 million advertising campaign, advising people to be "alert but not alarmed" and telling the populace whom to contact in the advent of a terror attack. See Bossio, "Be Alert, Not Alarmed."

6 While pointing out that such technology has had mixed results, Ritchie King nevertheless notes a twentyfold improvement in the accuracy of facial-recognition technology taking place between the years 2000 and 2006. See R. King, "How 5 Security Technologies Fared after 9/11."

7 The global big-data and business analytics market, which was valued at US$168.8 billion in 2018, has grown exponentially since then. Taylor, "Big Data and Business Analytics Revenue Worldwide."

8 In 1999, Kevin Ashton came up with the term *internet of things*. It is a network that connects people via the internet to the objects around them. Connecting up all the objects around people requires the addition of sensors to things, enabling

The lockstep nature of advances in surveillance technology and online marketing was far from a chance encounter, as both relied on predictive algorithms for the extraction of (knowledge) value from "big data."[9] With an IoT business model relying on the online users paying for services with data rather than money, the services being provided were reengineered to maximize data-mining potential. As data sets grew, they were more accurately able to find anomalies, patterns, and correlations through which to predict outcomes. Predictive technology was, of course, of value to both commercial and security end users.[10] Hence, even though the war on terror led to diplomatic controversy, foreign interventions, invasions, and even long-term occupations; even though internally it increased racism, xenophobia, and intolerance as well as accelerating the development of new technologies of mass surveillance, superficially at least, it produced minimal disruption and came alongside an IoT industry designed to distract. Behind the distracting appearance of normality, however, things were rather different.

The so-called war on terror led to increased security at nodal points of population mobility, leading to certain types of people, particularly refugees, or certain places, such as airport transit lounges, becoming zones of legal exception.[11] It led to the harassment of Muslim communities and racial

---

these "things" to communicate real-time data without any human involvement. For further details, see Ranger, "What Is the IoT?"

9 "Big data" refers to those data sets that are too large or complex for traditional methods of data processing. See Liu Shanhong, "Big Data—Statistics and Facts."

10 See Levine, "Google's Earth."

11 It fueled, for example, a legal redefinition of refugee rights. From 2001, in Australia, for example, refugee claims from "boat people" were assessed "on-shore" while the refugee claimants themselves were shipped to camps "off-shore." Yet even in seemingly more "normal" places of transit, we saw changes taking place. Take the high-profile example of *Guardian* journalist David Miranda, who was held in Heathrow's transit lounge because he was carrying material from Edward Snowden, or even the case of Snowden himself, who was cut off for months in the transit lounge of Sheremetyevo International Airport in Moscow. Essentially, the airport transit lounge has become a new site of the exception where the laws of the land do not apply. See, for example, Maass, "How Laura Poitras Helped Snowden Spill His Secrets."

profiling in the targeting of suspects.[12] There was also an increased overlap between military, surveillance, and policing platforms with technological deployments in one arena quickly being picked up, modified, and redeployed in another.[13] Such technological overlap and integration has only increased since the COVID pandemic. Indeed, as one commentator put it, the COVID pandemic was "9/11 on steroids."[14]

Technological advances may have stoked this growth but the marketization of these advances made these technologies ones that we could no longer live without. From increases in online shopping[15] to the ubiquitous use of tracking and tracing, QR codes, and digital passports, everything pointed to a digital future based on industrial-scale data scraping, and the development of new, more accurate, and more pervasive predictive technologies.[16] Meanwhile, lockdowns, social distancing, and the wearing of masks inevitably reinforced a militarization of language. Hospitals were spoken of as war zones, hospital staff as front-line heroes, and patients as a battleground where this new deadly viral enemy would be fought.[17] Indeed the only place that seemed to avoid this militarization of language was the Orwellian double speak of the military itself. Putin's "special military operation" is but the latest example of this and draws on earlier practices adopted by Western governments.

12 See Bah, "Racial Profiling and the War on Terror."

13 On the militarization of the policing system, see Christie, *Crime Control as Industry*. On the "refit" of drones for internal police work, see Wolf, "The Coming Drone Attack on America."

14 The expression "9/11 on steroids" is said to come from one of the world's foremost experts on mobile phone surveillance as he assessed the use of new technology in response to the COVID-19 pandemic. See Roth et al., "Growth in Surveillance May Be Hard to Scale Back."

15 In the United Kingdom, the online retail index showed online sales surged in April 2020 to a ten-year high, up 23.8 percent year on year. See Radojev, "Coronavirus."

16 The differential consumption patterns of different generations during the COVID-19 lockdowns are revealing and examined diagrammatically by Katie Jones. See Jones, "How COVID-19 Has Impacted Media Consumption." From this, the future looks online.

17 Freshwater, "COVID 19."

As early as the 1990s, and with one eye on NATO's intervention in Kosovo and another on the first Gulf War, Michael Hardt and Tony Negri noticed the way modern warfare was being linguistically redefined as a policing action, but simultaneously, the description of the enemy was being "intensified." There is a linguistic trail through which we can plot this linguistic intensification. It stretches at least as far back as the criminalization of the enemy in the interwar years (1920–1930s)[18] but leads all the way forward to the absolute demonization of the enemy that is evident today.[19] In the West, at least, war is not a "struggle for recognition" but is instead rendered as a battle for survival waged against a viral strain that must be eliminated.[20] This increasing linguistic ferocity around the enemy suggests that the "war on terror" displayed a heightened sense of political intensity, yet paradoxically, on an affective level, the reverse was the case. While the rhetoric of "war" would offer security services "the rationale for claiming warlike freedoms of action," everyday life in the West would appear, at least superficially, to have returned to normal.[21] Appearances, however, can be deceptive.

The loosely framed emergency powers granted under the PATRIOT Act in the United States, for example, enable the appearance of business as usual while providing the legislative cover for a covert war to not only continue but be dramatically expanded. As a result of powers granted under this act, there has been a massive expansion of highly classified surveillance systems that are now being used as weapons on the front line. These sophis-

18 Carl Schmitt, back in the 1930s, wrote of the perverse effects of the creeping "pacifist vocabulary" surrounding war: "War is condemned but executions, sanctions, punitive expeditions, pacifications, protection of treaties, international police, and measures to assure peace remain. The adversary is thus no longer called an enemy but a disturber of peace and is thereby designated to be an outlaw of humanity." Schmitt, *Concept of the Political*, 79.

19 Hardt and Negri, *Empire*, 13. Comparing Schmitt's words to those of Hardt and Negri is revealing of this transition. Schmitt referred to the enemy as an "outlaw," while for Hardt and Negri, it is more virus-like.

20 Using the Hegelian master/slave dialectic, Alexandre Kojève argues that the struggle for recognition involves a chancing of one's own life. See Kojève, *Introduction to the Reading of Hegel*, 3–30.

21 Naughton, "Why NSA's War on Terror Is More Than Just a 'Neat' Hacking Game."

ticated technologies (PRISM, XKeyscore, Boundless Informant, and so on)[22] require covert government/private partnerships (the so-called upstream program with US telecoms, not to mention the forced partnerships with Facebook, Skype, Google, Yahoo, Microsoft, and Apple)[23] and the secret installation of equipment in service providers' systems to monitor internet traffic. These, along with other technologies (such as BULLRUN, which is used to break through encryption services, or DROPOUT JEEP for iPhone encryption), were alleged to have introduced backdoor vulnerabilities into all major encryption codes.[24] The US dominance of the virtual world and the internet industry generally enabled the US National Security Agency (NSA) to gain control over international encryption standards. These systems have

22 Greenwald and MacAskill, "Boundless Informant." Such technologies, of course, are extended beyond the United States by the "five eyes" data-sharing agreements between the United States, the United Kingdom, Australia, Canada, and New Zealand. For the United Kingdom's Government Communications Headquarters (GCHQ), this has proven invaluable as they have, through their Tempora project, directly tapped into the transatlantic fiber-optic cable of the major telecommunications corporations. See Ball, Borger, and Greenwald, "Revealed." On the role of XKeyscore, which allows analysts to search with no prior authorization through vast databases containing emails, online chats, and the browsing histories of millions of individuals, the whistleblower Edward Snowden told the Council of Europe that "this technology represents the most significant new threat to civil liberties in modern times," enabling the United States to mine and screen "trillions of private communications." See Harding, "Edward Snowden."

23 After such partnerships were put in place, the actual work of installing the technology to enable the harvesting of servers was then subcontracted to private companies, and said to account for 60 percent of the budget. James Bamford says of the National Security Agency that "one of the agency's biggest secrets is just how careless it is with that ocean of very private and very personal communications, much of it to and from America. Increasingly, obscure and questionable contractors—not government employees—install the taps, run the agency's eavesdropping infrastructure, and do the listening and analysis." Bamford, "Shady Companies with Ties to Israel." On the upstream program, see J. Ball, "NSA's Prism Surveillance Program." On the budget figure, see Wilson and Wilson, "The NSA's Metastasised Intelligence-Industrial Complex Is Ripe for Abuse."

24 On DROPOUT JEEP technology for iPhones, see Rushe, "Apple Insists It Did Not Work with NSA."

enabled the NSA to crack large numbers of foreign encryption codes.[25] All this has been hidden from the general public by a wall of secret subpoenas issued by specially convened Foreign Intelligence Surveillance Act (FISA) courts that are themselves operating *sub rosa*.[26] Despite the secretive and coercive nature of all of these arrangements, the state still attempts to make fig-leaf claims about due legal process. More importantly from a business perspective, the government is working within a user-pays logic because government agencies still pay for each view to access any confidential client data that it requires from private providers.[27] The "exceptional," then, in terms

25 With a yearly budget of US$254.9 million, which had, by 2013, increased to US$800 million, the NSA "actively engages US and foreign IT industries to covertly influence and/or overly leverage their commercial products' design," which meant inserting "vulnerabilities into commercial systems." In other words, private providers were paid to write weaknesses into their security program to enable backdoor access by US spy agencies. These weaknesses would be known only to the NSA. Working with these major internet service providers, the NSA not only controlled international encryption standards, but has, for the past decade, been researching ways to break into most encrypted data systems. In this particular code-cracking operation—which operates in partnership with the British GCHQ—it was reported that by 2010 the NSA had achieved considerable success with a technology breakthrough, enabling "vast amounts of encrypted internet data," previously discarded, to become exploitable. For details, see Ball et al., "Revealed."

26 This massively expanded covert system was designed to remain totally hidden, but the paradoxical effect of this massive expansion and dispersal of information is that the system became vulnerable to "leaks." The war against terror, therefore, quickly spread to become a war against whistleblowers and hacktivists. In 2012, James Clapper, the US director of national intelligence, declared cyber threats to be the greatest danger facing the United States, even greater than the threat of terrorist attacks. Quoted in Bamford, "Shady Companies with Ties to Israel."

27 There is an alignment of the internet businesses and government demands insofar as these business models are designed around the collecting and selling of people's demographic information. For details on US government payments to cover the cost of compliance arrangements for the PRISM corporate partnerships handled by the Special Source Operations, see MacAskill, "NSA Paid Millions." On the United Kingdom's GCHQ and their pay-per-view scheme, see Campbell et al., "Exclusive."

of legal or market veridiction regimes, enables government to push both law and the market into new frontiers.[28]

One sees this same sort of "spread" and "redeployment" of the legal exception and marketized solutions operating in the emergency financial measures undertaken during and after the 2008 financial crisis. Indeed, it was those discredited mechanisms of economic veridiction, the banks, that the state would first bail out, then turn to for help to solve the economic crisis, despite the fact that the banks had created the crisis. These institutions and their logic of recovery, far from being challenged by the "empirical proof" of their own catastrophic failure, became the medicine relied on to cure the ailing patient. Endless streams of money would be injected into the banking system to re-inflate it, inducing years of recession and austerity. Again, a similar case could be mounted in relation to the sole reliance on scientific and technological solutions to the looming environmental crisis. This crisis, after all, is simply the deleterious effects of the long-term application of the science and technology that created the environmental problem in the first place. The rationality underlying these various regimes of veridiction—be it directly tied to the market, the law, science, or the economy—is like the commodity itself: always new but always the same.[29] The "same" in this instance being the homogeneous, the ratio, and the market. Veridiction comes carrying claims about its scientific objectivity, the naturalness of its self-interest assumptions, or even the force of the better argument. It works because it avoids any signs of being "political." Until COVID-19 this, too, had been the leitmotif of the medico-logistic meta-narrative of the Western state of the exception.

For market-based liberal democracies, such a postpolitical stance is not just adopted during medical emergencies but has also begun to creep into the logic of the entire political system. It allows public policy to outflank and overrule a politics of intensity by reference to "due procedure." In first medicalizing before militarizing the language of the state of the exception, liberal democracies' "moment of emergency" is invariably made to appear to be purely technical. Borne of compassion it may well be, but when put into effect it is an attempt to develop pure utility. In a pandemic, millions

28 These thoughts were in part prompted (but in no means derived) from Horst Bredekamp's discussion of Schmitt's state of the exception in Bredekamp, "From Walter Benjamin to Carl Schmitt," 251.

29 Adorno, *The Culture Industry*, 44.

of lives will be saved by these measures, but they can only be implemented by momentarily reducing existence itself to what has elsewhere been called a "bare life."[30] In minor and quite modest ways, liberal democracy spread this logic into realms traditionally associated with politics. It was reflected, for example, in the minor shifts already noted in the language employed around war, not just in terms of relabeling what was once called war into policing action, but also in spreading the logic and name "war" to myriad other things.

There have now been wars on drugs, welfare, crime, and poverty, and, the biggest of all, the coronavirus.[31] These wars sit alongside the more conventional use of the term in relation to Afghanistan's Taliban, or Iraq's Saddam Hussein, even into the "war on terror" (which was code, first, for Al Qaeda and then, later, ISIS). Meanwhile, as noted earlier, armed struggles were redefined and relabeled as "policing actions."[32] These confusing and competing linguistic descriptions of war help highlight the changing nature of war itself. In the West, and because of modern technology, war increasingly operates without the need to generate, channel, and harness political intensities.[33] This is just as well, as modern Western states

30 The reference here is to Giorgio Agamben's concept of bare life. Briefly, bare life is life without the thrills or frills. Indeed, it is, in part, a state in which one can be killed but not sacrificed. Road carnage, the concentration camp, and the life-support machine are examples and we, more than most, have learned to live this state as natural. See Agamben, *Homo Sacer*.

31 Writing about the rhetoric of war surrounding COVID-19, Alex de Waal suggests that this metaphor of war—be it a war on terror or on COVID—locks us into a mindset that produces the problems in the first place. See de Waal, "War on Disease Is a Self-Fulfilling Prophecy."

32 Bush's war on terror was quietly dropped as an expression when Obama came into the White House. Even before that, Donald Rumsfeld had tried in vain to convince Bush to brand this "the global struggle against violent extremism or GSave" rather than have it labeled as a war on terror. See Burkeman, "Obama Administration Says Goodbye to 'War on Terror.'"

33 The decreased human input in wars is exemplified by the massive expansion of drone programs in the United States. The former secretary of defense, Robert Gates, suggested that the next generation of US fighter planes, the F-35, will be the last human-piloted fighter planes built. Oddly, however, the drones that will replace them come not out of aviation but out of advanced robotics. This, in turn,

are no longer "geared" to its production. Increasingly, neither the physical nor mental states needed for extended and sustained combat are available in the liberal-democratic state. Indeed, even in terms of fitness levels, the United States has now reached the point whereby the nation's fighting capacity is being seriously impaired by obesity, thereby triggering a "war on obesity."[34] Read symptomatically, this latter "war" is simply the manifest form of a far more significant, worrying, and latent mental change in the populace. That change was the loss of any sense of political meaning or purpose. Faced with the loss of political intensity, liberalism resorted to its own "unconventional" conventionality. The face of war was changing, and new technology and the logic of privatization were in the forefront of the neoliberal response.

During the Iraq War, outsourcing and subcontracting became so common that mercenaries came to constitute the third biggest allied military force on the ground. Indeed, it was even suggested that, at the war's height, there were more mercenaries who were ex-British Special Air Services than actual SAS soldiers on the ground.[35] As mercenary forces were often contracted to do the "dirty work," they significantly reduced the risk to ordinary soldiers and

meant that the Air Force was not the only wing of the armed forces that had a stake in this nonsentient weaponry. With new drones that are as small as flies and others that can walk, the field of warfare is about to be dramatically recalibrated, and the agencies involved in that process expanded. See Robertson, "How Robot Drones Revolutionized the Face of Warfare."

34 In 2010, writing in the *Washington Post*, two US army generals, John M. Shalikashvili and Hugh Shelton, pointed out that, as of 2005, at least nine million young American adults, or 27 percent of all Americans ages seventeen to twenty-four, were too overweight to serve in the military according to the Army's own analysis of national data. Obesity has now become the main medical factor leading to military rejection. Indeed, since 1995, the proportion of potential recruits who failed their physical exams because of weight issues has increased to nearly 70 percent, according to data reported by the Division of Preventive Medicine at the Walter Reed Army Institute of Research, leading to more than 130 retired generals, admirals, and senior military leaders calling on Congress to pass new child nutrition legislation. See Shalikashvili and Shelton, "The Latest National Security Threat: Obesity."

35 See *Economist*, "The Baghdad Boom."

thereby lowered the official military death toll.[36] In a post–Vietnam War era, this was seen as essential, as body bags still set the limits of the possible. For Western states, death needed to be transformed into a rarity. To further this end, Western armed forces also increasingly replaced ground troops with technological solutions.

In applying to the military, the administrative and technical solutions that were already becoming central to the world of commerce, the possibility of mass enemy casualties and limited "official" friendly ones was advanced. War no longer required political intensification for it no longer needed mass mobilization. Instead, it increasingly required cost/benefit analysis. Specialist technical and professional personnel would be trained to kill without personal hate by employing their video-game-style proficiencies to operate drones. Such abstraction removed any existential threat and with it much of the basis of the intensity. Meanwhile, for civilians back home, the horror of war was also kept at a distance, by media coverage that claimed "authenticity" by embedding journalists then practiced censorship to downplay the horrors committed by "our" troops. Paradoxically, then, the technology that enabled mass killing at a distance (through drone attacks, stealth bombers, and "precision" weaponry) also produced the conditions on the ground that enabled the question of death to be rarely felt or fully acknowledged. Existentially "back home," these wars troubled government far less than in the past. The format of new media technology often habitualized viewing patterns among the "home" audience, progressively draining away any existential dread associated with war. At least for those in the West and not in the military, war no longer excited existential dread, only concern; even then, it was concern expressed from a distance.

Whether the events into which we, in the West, are violently involved are called wars or merely referred to as "policing actions," the effects are much the same; unless we are on the front line, we, personally, remain largely uncommitted, somewhat distant, and reasonably detached. We are, in the main, freed from the necessity of having strong existentially felt com-

36 In Vietnam it is estimated that US forces suffered 58,220 deaths, while the number of US troops killed in Afghanistan and Iraq up to 2019 was just over 7,000. For Vietnam, see the National Archives, "Vietnam War U.S. Military Fatal Casualty Statistics," last reviewed August 23, 2022, https://www.archives.gov/research/military/vietnam-war/casualty-statistics. For Afghanistan and Iraq, see Crawford and Lutz, "Human Cost of Post-911 Wars."

mitments to the violent actions our governments involve our nations in. Instead of commitment and political intensity, there is the market, technology, and the expert. Personal political commitment and involvement evaporate on the gossamer-like wings of consumer distraction. Moreover, the distraction seems authorized by reference to experts who take care of any "serious business" in their reports, quality controls, and commissions, all of which go to "prove" that the course of action undertaken by government was, if not correct, at least "legal," reasonable, and, therefore, understandable. Opposition parties and movements, in challenging these perspectives, offer counternarratives that may or may not change outcomes but, collectively and over time, they, too, tend to reinforce not so much the narrowing of agendas but a narrowing of the way one can legitimately look at questions. This is because they, too, unconsciously accept the parameters of debate because they accept the underlying logic of this system of veridiction and this style of thought.

While the market and media draw us away from deep political commitments, and experts convince us to rule out other ways of seeing, any guilt or doubt that might be felt about killing is assuaged by a belief that, while not perfect, at least "our" political system is not only better, but also more democratic and more reasonable (and, of course, underpinning such views is the unconscious thought "more civilized and enlightened"). This politics of the "middle ground" (the ground of "reason") narrows the political spectrum available to us, leaving room only for a struggle in a market of experts. This, in turn, gives rise to the appearance of diversity, but it is always a restricted diversity, limited to forms that are judged "reasonable" and work within the homogeneous realm. In other words, it is argued within the limits set by the regime of veridiction itself. Thus, experts collectively control and are controlled by their field of knowledge; professional soldiers control and are controlled by the logic of the battlefield technologies; and our political masters control and are controlled by a particular rationality of government. In all cases, the language of the specialist, task-oriented, utilitarian figure prevails.

This professionalized, utilitarian language game of neoliberalism gained its own status as a "science" of politics, paving the way for the subdiscipline of public policy that systematizes this "style of thought" and works to drain the question of intensity from the field of politics proper. The effect is a growing sense of distance without guilt, for "we" (as opposed to the irrational "they") rely on specialized expertise that always knows best. Here is a discourse legitimized not by the strength of the political commitment it can demonstrate, but by claims of rationality, objectivity, and transparency that are backed up by specialized professional expertise. Here are the pillars on which the Western understanding of democracy is being reshaped into something less democratic but appearing more scientific because it takes the medico-logistic logic beyond the emergency and into daily-life practices. Even in arenas once unquestionably regarded as irredeemably political, we now see this form of apolitical medico-logistic logic being imposed.

Thus, when Western soldiers are dispatched either to save lives in times of disaster or to extinguish them in times of war, this same form of discursive logic always appears to undergird their movement. It claims to enhance good governance, to follow the science, and to be open and transparent. Here is a world that dreams of appearing like a shop window where everything seems to be "on display," despite the fact it isn't. Indeed, the political dream of this system, which is to transform all signs of politics into public administration, is always accompanied by a political daydream to camouflage all forms of control. If control cannot be hidden, then it must be shown to be utterly necessary given the circumstances and here is where the medico-logistic once again comes in. Alternatively, it can be rendered as desirable, given our needs and desires, and this is where the market comes in. This form of camouflaging of control has, if anything, intensified with developments in cyberspace. The a priori of knowing what we need and/or desire requires knowing us and, here, developments in cyberspace are apposite.

Appearing to offer total anonymity, the net ensures full disclosure. Social networking has become part of our way of life, occasioning its own revelations, celebrity crazes, social panics, and business models.[37] These models rely on mining private data for commercial potential in the same way that the government mines it for political meaning or surveillance systems mine

37 The rise of net porn offers examples of all these things. If the number of hits on porn sites is anything to go by, we all live secret lives. On the social panic this has occasioned, see Littlewood, "Cyberporn and Moral Panic." See also Salmon and Zdanowicz, "Net, Sex and Rock 'n' Roll!" The circulation of porn on the net has, according to one porn star, led to hundreds of young girls coming into the industry and driving down wages, while at the same time free net porn has driven down their individual profits. See Feeney, "Being a Porn Star Ain't What It Used to Be." On business models and a comprehensive overview of net porn and its history, see Jacobs, Janssen, and Pasquinelli, *C'Lick Me*.

it for potential subversion.[38] Whether it is business, government, or the security forces, all are tapping into this flow. Technology, as a result, renders the private/public divide obsolete just as it has problematized the division between the real and the virtual world.[39] Large cities such as London have been at the forefront of these changes.[40]

Even before the war on terror produced an argument for greater public surveillance—thereby snuffing out the last embers of Tony Blair's "Cool Britannia" image—London, the city at the heart of the revival of 1990s British "cool," was also at the forefront of a new panoptic private lifestyle.[41] It began with the all-pervasive CCTV security camera. First introduced en masse to London streets to reduce crime in certain "trouble spots," the CCTV cameras quickly enveloped the city as the new threat of terror emerged and turned every area into a potential crime scene/war zone. With claims of one CCTV security camera for every fourteen citizens, and one photograph taken of

38 One need only think here of the Cambridge Analytica scandal. For a brief rundown on the key points of this scandal, see *Wired*, "The Cambridge Analytica Story Explained."

39 At the June 10, 2013, Apple WorldWide Developers Conference, Boris Sofman, CEO of the startup company Anki, launched their intelligent system for gaming, in which multiple robots interacted and worked together through a computer operating system, effectively producing a physical version of what had previously been a screen-based video game. With this work in robotics, the virtual suddenly came off the screen and into a physical space, reversing a process of virtualization that had seen avatars taken on psychologically as embodied forms in one's alternative net life. On Anki and the launch of a physical form of the virtual game, see Sofman, "Anki DRIVE." The precarity of this new form of entrepreneurship, however, is captured in the rise and fall of Anki, which had, in banking on robotics and not software, chosen the wrong market trend. They announced the closure of Anki in April 2019, with Sofman and many other employees from Anki moving to Whymo, where their skills would be used to help develop autonomous vehicles. See Schleifer, "The Once-Hot Robotics Startup Anki."

40 See the largely US-oriented timeline created by James Spillane in "From Edison to Internet." It suggests London may well have pioneered the use of CCTV back in the 1960s.

41 No one knows how many CCTV cameras have been installed in Britain, but it runs into many millions, says Philip Hensher, who also notes that between 1996 and 1998 three-quarters of all crime-prevention budgets were spent on CCTV cameras. See Hensher, "Philip Hensher: The State Wants to Know What You're Up To."

every citizen every thirty seconds, London was transformed.[42] "Cool Britannia" attempted to transform this creeping securitization into a form of "happy panopticism."

"Strike a pose" was one "creative" response to CCTV surveillance, and it was in the advertising logic of Peugeot—that stylish French car manufacturer that sells "cool" as cars—that the power of style to transform the face of surveillance into something less menacing becomes apparent. A series of panoptic CCTV camera views that follow the car as it moves through the city turns the surveillance apparatus into an endless opportunity for "Madonna-like" moments. In other words, this 2006 advertisement for the Peugeot 207 hatchback turned panopticism into paparazzi. As the vehicle enters a parking lot, and the advertisement winds up, a computerized voice, read over an image of a faux security computer screen, quickly narrates the words "You are caught on camera over three hundred times every twenty-four hours." Then, with the car once again in the frame of a surveillance camera, the advertisement's "strike a pose" logic offers the following punchline solution: "Give them something to watch."[43] And while "they" watch us and we try to look

42 This figure of one in fourteen comes from the then former Conservative Party shadow Home Secretary, David Davis, but it was shown to be little more than a guess. See Channel 4 News, "FactCheck: How Many CCTV Cameras?" Despite doubts about the veracity of this claim, one thing is clear: London no longer holds the record. *Statista* reports that this dubious honor goes to Chongqing, China, which is said to have 168 CCTV cameras per 1,000 people, well ahead of London's 68.4 per 1,000 residents. See Buchholz, "The Most Surveilled Cities in the World."

43 While Peugeot's advertisement playfully employed this theme as a marketing strategy, more serious concerns have since emerged. In 2003, when Benetton—a company never far from controversy—used radio frequency identification chips (RFID) as part of its supply-chain management system, fears were raised that the company wanted to track their customers' purchasing habits after they left the store. While this concern proved ill-founded, it nevertheless offered a foretaste of technological uses to come. In 2005, a Silicon Valley area school installed RFID into its school badges to automate attendance. Such technology, while banned in many states in America, found its way to the streets of London in 2013, forcing the City of London Corporation to order the advertising company Renew to desist from using high-tech litter bins in the financial district that could trace people walking past by tracking their mobile-phone chips. Renew wanted to use cookies, which could track files across the internet into the physical world. "We will cookie the street," said chief executive Kaveh Memari. While governments scramble to legislate and limit such private intrusion, they have long ago adapted

"cool," a very different fate awaits those who are looked on coldly and with suspicion. For them, abduction would be called rendition; torture was "enhanced interrogation." That was, of course, until that strategy, which led to too much media attention and too many legal conundrums, was replaced by a simple kill list organized under the innocuous sounding title of the "dispositional matrix."[44] Here, then, is the dark side of a knowledge economy, producing a language game of depoliticization but this time in extremis.

---

and adopted this technology for their own use. An electronic passport system, first introduced by the Malaysian government in 2006, has been picked up and employed by the United States in relation to the twenty-seven countries with which it has a Visa Waiver Program (VWP). Meanwhile, in China, a new generation of resident identity card unveiled in 2006 embedded computer chips into all identity cards, making them instantly verifiable. On the Chinese government claims about the virtues of this second generation of card, see Xinhuanet, "Public Security Ministry Notice," concerning the issuance of second-generation identity cards. For Western press reports about the chips in Chinese identity cards, see Bradsher, "China Enacting a High-Tech Plan to Track People." On the electronic passport system and controversy in the United States surrounding it, see Nithyanand, "The Evolution of Cryptographic Protocols in Electronic Passports." On Benetton and the school's use of technology, see Kline and Martin, "ID Industry Fighting Big Brother Image." On Renew and the controversial rubbish bins, see Associated Press, "City of London Corporation Wants 'Spy Bins' Ditched." Peugeot was just one of many companies to play with the popular theme of surveillance. The Peugeot advertisement can be seen at "Peugeot 207 'CCTV' Ad," posted May 24, 2012, by djhyperuk on YouTube, 0:41 min., https://www.youtube.com/watch?v=jkWmxnZka8k. Givenchy provides a similar example: Givenchy Oblique, "Video Surveillance," September 2000, video by DDB Paris, 0:46 min., https://www.adforum.com/creative-work/ad/player/5687/video-surveillance/givenchy-oblique.

44 The dispositional matrix was organized by Michael Leiter, who had been head of the National Counterterrorism Center during the George W. Bush and then Obama administrations. Leiter used it to augment kill lists for suspects who were out of range of drones. Said to contain biographies, locations, known associates, and affiliated organizations of suspected terrorists, the matrix was, along with drone attacks, motivated by the political imperative to close secret CIA "black site" prisons and honor Obama's election pledge to close Guantánamo Bay. Rather than arrest or detain terrorist suspects, some have suggested that Obama simply authorized their killing by the use of drones. This, however, left a "dispositional" problem as to what one was to do about suspects who were out of range of the drones. Marshalling resources to track them down, the matrix includes sealed

Perhaps it is because of its ability to help spirit away the intensities of the political yet maintain an ability to kill and do so while maintaining the outward appearance of rationality, transparency, democracy, and justice, that this particular form of governmentality proves so enduring. Technology obviates the need for any political intensity in that there is no longer a need to draw on affective energy flows to produce mass political indignation. Indeed, in this system, there is a greater desire for political de-massification in the transcription of intensity into profit flows. Governments have tried to use policy to routinize, rationalize, bureaucratize, and "re-order" affective energy flows, directing them toward regimes of market veridiction. The result is that even the counterclaims of an opposition or "resistance" demanding political change end up speaking in the language of neoliberal rationality, for it is only in that language that things make sense. The language codes of postpolitical neoliberal, market-based utility, therefore, reflect a form of political monolingualism.

This desire for, and (obviously false) claim to have achieved, a post-political monolinguistic power freed by reason from the either/or emotions of the political was nailed to the philosophical cross of modern Western liberal democracy by Francis Fukuyama, who insisted that this shift away from intensities—which he labeled the spirit, or the *thymotic*—also constituted the end of history (in the Hegelian sense). For Fukuyama, history ends when *thymos*,[45] or spiritedness, and *ratio*, or reason, find themselves betrothed

indictments and clandestine operational materials that map out each agency's responsibility should these suspects surface. Moreover, agency responsibilities have changed over time. The NSA, which was once largely a signals intercept organ, is now the world's largest spy agency, while the CIA has moved from intelligence and espionage into overt military actions with the development and expansion of its lethal drone fleet. This includes drones that have a fully automated artificial intelligence capability, enabling them to pick out targets and then make life-and-death decisions based on the drones' capacity to correlate information from intersecting databases. It is said that drones have now killed more people than the 9/11 attacks. Essentially, as conventional wars wind down, the Obama administration was responsible for the institutionalization of this new form of warfare. For details of all of the above, see the following: Miller, "Plan for Hunting Terrorists"; Drum, "The Disposition Matrix"; Schneier, "What We Don't Know about Spying on Citizens"; and Mataconis, "The Never Ending War on Terror."

45 In Plato's *Republic*, we are told of the three parts that compose the human soul. One is desiring, another reasoning, and a third, called *thymos*, is a kind of spiritedness. This sense of spiritedness fuels the desire for self-esteem, and, that, for

in the vestibule of the liberal democratic state enabled by technology. With an economic heart pumping out technologically induced material plenty, *thymos* is not so much captured by reason, Fukuyama claimed, as seduced by the material plenty created by the industrial technology that enabled it. Spiritedness finds new expression in the desires generated by the commodities it produces. Yet, by its very nature, commodity seduction is only ever momentary. Indeed, the entire capitalist system and the whole raison d'être of contemporary market-based manufacture are built on this very point. While the system of capitalist (re)production is built on the temporariness of the products it manufactures, the side that is visible works in a somewhat different fashion. It relies not just on mass production, but on the mass production of small changes that will help "reenchant" the consumer with the new product. Sometimes the product is technically improved, and often it is improved in terms of style, but it is always, in whatever form it might manifest, "improved."

The Western political system has come to rely on these small changes and constant enactments of a new and improved version of the old as it attempts to re-create enchantment but redirect *thymotic* desires away from political violence. Are such shallow, short-term seductions that lead away from political violence enough to change human subjectivity and desire? Are these flows, which are little more than the circulations of the economy, enough to soften the tension between Athens and Jerusalem?

We have learned to live with, and cherish, short-term seductions: to remember back only as far as the last fad and to look forward to the next one with glee. Even in states of emergency, when life itself is threatened, we can still notice the effects of what might be called this logic of the short term on our contemporary Western mindset. The media that sells product through the seductive voice of advertising also provides the up-to-date news of the latest disaster. The binaries of politics never fully disappear; only now, like the "exclusive," they become part of the seductive market appeal of news channels. The information format never changes, for, just like the commodity

---

Fukuyama, with his Hegelian/Kojèveian reading of history, is the clarion call of humans for recognition. Following Hegel, Kojève registers this in the first moment of humanity as being that mythic struggle between master and slave. This struggle for recognition then becomes the struggle of politics that is only reconciled in Fukuyama with the space opened up by liberal democracy. See Fukuyama, *The End of History*, xvi–xvii.

itself, the content of the news is always new but (the form) always remains the same. Today's terror of nature quickly gives way to tomorrow's news flash. Whether it be a story of war, of SARS, of the coronavirus, or of a tsunami, the shock effect, while violent, will always remain short-lived. We live our world in "quick bites" and grow accustomed to the horrors these bites reveal. We are simultaneously outraged yet complacent. Indeed, when the outrage is at its peak, or in that moment when we are still trapped in the mild panic of a "that could be us" form of recognition (9/11, SARS, etc.), we have still learned to evoke only limited and specific expressions of concern when it is not directly about "us."

We will give money to relief agencies because we imagine it will go to the victims,[46] and we will protest the war, because we believe governments will listen.[47] Secretly, however, we know that it is more complicated than that. Irrespective of our personal concerns, it is invariably someone else who is acting on our behalf, someone else who represents us. We know that all our personal actions in these matters are mere tokens of concern. We know that the real story lies elsewhere, and it is this elsewhere-ness of the struggle or the problem, always threatening, but always some distance away, that dominates our world and our worlding. "Over there" becomes merely another way of saying "not us." Our happiness depends on ensuring it remains thus. Even at a site of disaster, such as the hotel in Hong Kong where SARS erupted, commodifying becomes a way of coping.

"We might turn the whole floor, or just room 911 where Professor Liu stayed, into a museum. It's a very creative suggestion. But it is also historic. We have to see how to package it," said the former Metropole resident

46 Of course, quite a bit of it does, but as the American Institute of Philanthropy suggests, administrative costs for servicing donations can take up as much as 40 percent of any donation received. See Charity Watch, "'Not So' Great Nonprofits." See also Craig, *The Great Charity Scandal*.

47 Indeed, the evidence of the authorities not listening is deafening. When the second war against Iraq was launched, an estimated ten to fifteen million people took to the streets in protest in more than six hundred cities worldwide. In Rome alone, crowds were estimated to be three million, while in London and Barcelona, over one million people were said to have participated. Who listened? For details, see Tharoor, "Why Was the Biggest Protest in World History Ignored?"

manager, Kaivin Ng.[48] We package our terror and thereby contain the dread. We limit its psychic effects by turning it into a form of distraction or remembrance. And when we cannot control a variable, when there is no way to halt this feeling of horror, we repress it. Once again, the actions of management at the Metropole Hotel illustrate the way this system operates. Having tried and failed to package the idea of a SARS museum in a way that could generate anything other than dread, the management eradicated the problem by employing another trick of numerology. Post-SARS refurbishments at the Metropole Hotel eliminated the problem by eliminating the room. Numbering skipped a beat and room 911 simply vanished from the room plates (see figure 4.2).[49] It is a shame they couldn't have so easily eliminated the virus!

We live in a world where neoliberal governments grapple with problems in the same way as the management of the Metropole Hotel. Society packages things to gain power over them. It does this by reducing them to their barest and most profitable components. That also means limiting their profundity in our lives by turning things, events, and people into packaged forms of distraction. Yet as we package our understanding of things, we also know that, at a more profound level, there is still a difference between the "real event" and the packaged simulacrum. Repackaging remembrance cannot "throw" us in the way that real events can. We do not "reel" from its effects, for an existential element is missing in this repackaging. We intuitively know that something has disappeared from *thymos* when it is seduced by this logic of the package.

When the reason of capital seduces the thymotic struggle for recognition, we do not reach the end of history but come face-to-face with that constant, nagging, and perpetual dissatisfaction we all feel toward the comfort and cocooned anxieties of the present. The point about the seduction of *thymos* is that it anesthetizes our response. Theodor Adorno knew this. That is why he said that consciousness is "disowned in the sphere of production which

48 Quoted in *Taipei Times*, "Hong Kong Hotel Is Eliminating Memories of SARS."

49 In 2005, after the shock of the SARS outbreak, the hotel refurbished the ninth floor, and room 911 disappeared. After refurbishment, however, the hotel also had a name change. The Metropole Hotel became the Metropark Hotel. See *Taipei Times*, "Hong Kong Hotel Is Eliminating Memories of SARS."

trains individuals to disperse themselves."[50] Commodification is but the most obvious sign and means of that dispersal.

In the world of the commodity, individuals and their desires are dispersed and temporarily satiated by packaged material purchases. In this world of material seductions, the power of ideas no longer seems able to intensify. Ideas are packaged when politics becomes policy and this, then, tends to drain the political of its thymotic affective element. In the end, we are caught between the calculated reason of postpolitical policy dissimulations and the depoliticizing dream desire of a material life promised on the hoardings of the advertising industry. Indeed, once politics no longer throws one toward the question of recognition, once our dreams of recognition are tied to the promises of the advertising hoarding, *thymos* can only ever be registered as "lack." This lack fuels our material desires and drives the consumer world. It produces an existence, Adorno suggests, that does not lack material desire but rather lacks a sense of purpose.[51]

When facing future threats (be they ecological, gender-based, class, ethnically based, or emerging for some other reason), we may desire this passionless form of rule because we believe that it will cocoon us from fear and anxiety. Yet, as each threat emerges, we become increasingly aware that this lack of passion equals nothing other than an expression of powerlessness. Pushed to extremes, our "homecoming" in reason leads not into the philosophy of Hegelian reconciliation[52] but back to fears that bring us to the edge of an existentially barer life.[53] That is what the 911 of SARS helps reveal but, in its revelation, what it cannot speak of is the world we have attempted, through the market, to break from. It is a world that still stalks our own. It is a world in which the political can still speak to us beyond the word or text to feelings of intense commitment.

50 Adorno, *The Jargon of Authenticity*, 71.

51 Adorno, *The Jargon of Authenticity*, 10.

52 Hegel would write of philosophy as a "homecoming," which was, as Trent Schroyer observes, the reconciliation of "objective discord and subjective consciousness." This totality was made meaningful precisely by the reflective mediations of critical reason. See Schroyer, foreword to *The Jargon of Authenticity*, by Theodor W. Adorno, xv.

53 And here, of course, we stand at the foot of Agamben's argument about *homo sacer*: the one who can die but cannot be sacrificed. See Agamben, *Homo Sacer*.

To glimpse this world, we need to move beyond SARS, beyond "policy," and beyond Enlightenment reason into a realm we more clearly associate with the terror of 9/11. Actions that precipitated this other, more familiar 9/11 are built on the very thing that arguments of utility and the seductions of the material world tend to make incomprehensible. This other, incomprehensible world is built on a fabrication of self that uses the political not just to press forth a particular political point of view but to "press out" from within us, a sense of ourselves that leads us beyond ourselves.

5

Heroics?

Build your cities on the slopes of Vesuvius! Send your ships out into uncharted seas! Live in conflict with your equals and with yourselves! Be robbers and ravagers as soon as you cannot be rulers and owners, you men of knowledge!
Friedrich Nietzsche[1]

There is more than excess that ties the 9/11 suicide bombers to China's Tian'anmen "tank man." From their extreme actions, one can discern a sense of "responsibility."[2] For good or ill, this responsibility overrides all other

1 To which Hannah Arendt replies, "The vehement yearning for violence, so characteristic of some of the best modern creative artists, thinkers, scholars, and craftsmen, is a natural reaction to those whom society has tried to cheat of their strength." Arendt, *The Human Condition*, 203–4. For the Nietzsche quote, see Nietzsche, *The Gay Science*, bk. 4, p. 283.

2 Derrida seems to regard this particular responsibility as part of a theological turn that takes him back to the work of Kierkegaard who, in turn, goes back to the

responsibilities. It is a form of responsibility that gives to actors the moral strength that enables them to undertake acts that put that which they most cherish at risk. Their actions require a higher calling. It does not require a god, but it does need to operate in that zone in which gods speak.[3] Heroic or villainous actions of this order mark out these figures as political Dasein. Why political Dasein? Dasein, because Being is an issue for them.[4] Political, because they existentially face the possibility of death, but do so willingly for a collective cause. Their orientations, therefore, are always political.[5] Indeed, in that moment of political intensity when antagonisms become extreme and action follows, the "I am" of their existence becomes an "I can be" of their own potentiality. Both figures come to us on the cusp of a friend/enemy divide that not only ties them to a collective cause but also sees in that cause something that is fundamentally tied to a "struggle for recognition."[6] Herein lies the political potential of this energy flow. While expressed in myriad ways, such energy flows are always shadowed by the specter of intensity.

biblical parable of Abraham and Isaac. See Derrida, *The Gift of Death*, 60–61.

3 As Derrida notes, "Every revolution, whether aesthetic or religious, bears witness to a return of the sacred in the form of an enthusiasm or fervor, otherwise known as the presence of the gods within us." Derrida, *The Gift of Death*, 21.

4 Martin Heidegger makes this quite clear: "Understanding Being is itself a definite characteristic of Dasein's Being. Dasein is ontically distinctive in that it is ontological." Heidegger, *Being and Time*, 32.

5 This collective sensibility of Dasein, which is a precondition of the political, is also the third priority of Dasein. Heidegger notes, "Dasein also possesses . . . an understanding of the Being of all entities of a character other than its own. Dasein has therefore a third priority as providing the ontico-ontological condition for the possibility of any ontologies." Heidegger, *Being and Time*, 34. On the collective nature of the political, Carl Schmitt's words are revealing: "A religious community, a church, can exhort a member to die for his belief and become a martyr, but only for the salvation of his own soul, not for the religious community in its quality as an earthly power; otherwise it assumes a political dimension." Schmitt, *The Concept of the Political*, 48.

6 Nicolai Hartmann makes the important point that while the dialectic of suffering is better known, the Marxist theory of class struggle actually comes out of Hegel's master/slave dialectic. In other words, Marxist class analysis comes out of the struggle for recognition. Quoted in Bataille, "A Critique of the Foundation," 114n4. The most famous Marxist-inspired reading of the Hegelian "struggle for recognition," however, comes from Kojève's *Introduction to the Reading of Hegel*.

And while Schmitt might have held his concept of the political in place by the binary thing-concept of friend/enemy, even he would gravitate toward an acknowledgment of intensity's importance.[7] Intensity is the ever-present looming precondition of a particular expression of the political and a clear sign that the political can never break free of affective energy flows.[8] It is in facing this real possibility of their own death as a matter of ego cogito that they have become intensely political.[9]

Those willing to commit acts that stretch the social instinct to its very limit and then push beyond those limits, those who move beyond social morality[10] and into the realm of a higher moral calling: these are the figures we will call political Dasein.[11] Society may sometimes deem them "robbers and ravagers," but in this land that lies beyond the law, they are also beyond such labels. In presenting themselves before the possibility of death, they show themselves to be impassioned by a commitment that lies beyond the everyday and calculable. To be willing to die for a cause or to kill without hate is nothing if not a sign of this. And this sign is, in turn, a mark of their own political commitment. Yes, they have built their lives on the slopes of

7 As noted earlier, Jan-Werner Müller has argued that, in his later years, Schmitt saw the political as "purely a matter of intensity, so that any antithesis, if it was strong enough, could become political." Müller concludes, "Thus, it was not the substance of enmity that mattered, but the intensity of an existential threat." Müller, *A Dangerous Mind*, 32–33.

8 "The political can derive its energy from the most varied human endeavours, from the religious, economic, moral, and other antitheses. It does not describe its own substance, but only the intensity of an association and disassociation of human beings whose motives can be religious, national (in the ethnic and cultural sense), economic, or of another kind and can effect at different times different coalitions and separations." Schmitt, *The Concept of the Political*, 38.

9 Heidegger notes that a stricter formulation of the Cartesian *ego cogito* as "I think" would be "I place something as something in front of myself." The something before one is the I of I-ness where the I emerges in moments of turmoil and where it is, perhaps, also about to slip away. See Heidegger, *The Principle of Reason*, 77. It is because of the importance of the "tumultuous" in parts of Heidegger's analysis of Being that I have retained the Heideggerian term *Dasein*.

10 Pashukanis, *Law and Marxism*, 155.

11 Derrida calls this a distinction between the social and the secret responsibility. See Derrida, *The Gift of Death*, 60.

Vesuvius, and, with their knowledge, they have come to an understanding of themselves and their world. From the suicide bomber to the Chinese tank man, from the irreverence of Pussy Riot to the publicists of WikiLeaks, Nietzsche's so-called men of knowledge do not share an agenda or even a gender, nor do they even feel the same degree of commitment or intensity. What they nevertheless all share is a high degree of political intensity.

The political, in this rendition, is painted with such blinding and intense binary colors that any other shade can appear difficult to discern. Politically, both suicide bomber and tank man exist in a world of elemental binary distinctions. Good and evil is the way we commonly describe this distinction, but good and evil is merely the moral inflection of that primordial binary, "us and them." Individually, it could be thought of as the binary that "worlds" their world. Yet "us and them" proves to be a wholly inadequate way of describing the circumstance in which, as a collective force, they are propelled by ideas that lead them to face the ineffable nature of their own existence. "Us and them" lacks the political intensity of the collective but nevertheless captures something of the existentially and individually felt nature of the commitment as a sensation. Goosebumps on the surface of the skin, lumps in the back of the throat, tears welling in the eyes of the believer: these can all be signs and bodily symptoms of a political intensity that is intensely and personally felt. Such intensity, therefore, is intensely affective.[12] Through the friend/enemy divide and the technologies deployed to channel its eruption, goosebumps, tears, and lumps in the throat are all symptoms of affect harnessed and channeled into action. Life-and-death struggles are still stalked by fear but not by animal fear. If it can be said that animals use violence to ensure self-preservation, the actions of the suicide bomber are a far cry from this world. What their actions speak of is something that takes them beyond the survival instinct, for it is a willingness to lose, not preserve, life that is the quintessential feature of such figures. What propels their actions is not animal fear but what Heidegger might have called human anxiety.[13] Such anxiety

12 How these are "measured" and, through that process, become unfelt in our world of calculability is described in Massumi, "The Autonomy of Affect."

13 Heidegger's employment of a distinction between anxiety and fear is useful to understand at this point. Fear is directed at something, while anxiety is that which "makes manifest in Dasein its *Being towards* its own most potentiality-for-Being—that is, its *Being-free for* the freedom of choosing itself and taking hold of itself. Anxiety brings Dasein face to face with its *Being-free for* (*propensio in . . .*) the

seems to propel such figures into actions driven by a struggle for recognition.[14] Rendered thus, the struggles are, then, the antithesis of animality. Indeed, these are the traits not just of the human, but of History.[15] It is this quality, be it for good or ill, that enables us, as humans, to carry out actions based on conviction. The power that such convictions have over us perhaps gains the greatest illumination in the language of theology, for behind every intense "friend and enemy" distinction, there always lurks—at a subterranean, unconscious, individual level—the anxiety created by the binary of I and Thou.[16]

Facing the possibility of death leads one to face one's own mortality. In the language of Martin Buber, the question of mortality is simply another way of saying "Thou."[17] Even if we do not follow Buber all the way down this path of theological enlightenment, we can, at the very least, assume that this question he calls "Thou" brings to the surface another way of facing the possibility of Being. Being before Thou yet simultaneously denying the godhead. As politics becomes submerged in government, this side of the "political" is increasingly repressed as politics is transcribed into policy formulations and intensities into commodity desire. In sum, affective energy that could potentially become an intensity is dispersed, enervated, and redefined in and through the system of market veridiction.

---

authenticity of its Being, and for this authenticity as a possibility which it always is." See Heidegger, *Being and Time*, 232.

14 "One being only recognized, the other only recognizing" is how Hegel came to describe the struggle for recognition that constitutes the mythic moment of an originary binary of humanity he describes as master and slave. See Hegel, *Phenomenology of Spirit*, 113.

15 Hegelian history, that is. More importantly, however, it directly relates to the history of recognition and to Kojève's approach to Hegel's struggle for it. See Kojève, *Introduction to the Reading of Hegel*, 7–9.

16 Here, it is important to note that one can think of I and Thou as anxiety creating, based on the Kierkegaardian paradox, and it is this that Heidegger draws on in developing his notion of anxiety. For an elaboration on I and Thou, see Buber, *I and Thou*.

17 Buber's thought, dominated by the I-Thou and I-It, roughly matches the binary combination of Strauss with Athens and Jerusalem, but where Strauss would harness "tension," Buber is in search of an experiential knowledge space, which, like the Taoists, was a search for harmony not propelled by tension. See Buber, *I and Thou*.

The resulting style of thought that emerges from this system of market veridiction all too often blinds us to those human traits that give meaning to our sense of Being. Yet blindness does not mean that these traits no longer exist: only that we no longer recognize or value them. Indeed, just when political intensity seems far removed from our rational everyday world, when a sullen postpolitical peace comes to reign over our land, we are forced to once again confront the consequences of this other ethereal presence, this other potentiality, this other way of Being that still lurks within . . . and when we finally face this and recognize it as part of our reality, we do so, with a thud. More often, however, the blow is softened for it is revealed only at a distance, through images on television and internet screens or in a past remembered by monuments or plaques on a wall. Speaking of which . . .

Figure 6.1. Plaque to the deserter, Göttingen, Germany, June 2001. Photo by the author.

6

Monumental Hiccup in Göttingen

FROM LIVING DANGEROUSLY TO A BARER LIFE[1]

The secret of realizing the greatest fruitfulness and the greatest enjoyment of existence is to live dangerously!
Friedrich Nietzsche[2]

1 "Hiccup" or "hiccough" is often tied to the idea of a "hitch" or "cock-up." Yet, in this case, it also subliminally carries something of the meaning of the Old English word *ælfsogoða*, as elfin spirits were thought to cause hiccups. "Hiccup" (n.), 1570s, "hickop," earlier "hicket," "hyckock," "a word meant to imitate the sound produced by the convulsion of the diaphragm." Palmer, *Folk-Etymology*, 170. The modern spelling was first recorded in 1788. "Hiccough" came into being in the 1620s and was a variant of "hiccup" (q.v.) because of a mistaken association with the cough. *Etymonline* (etymology dictionary), s.v. "hiccup," last modified September 28, 2017, https://www.etymonline.com/word/hiccup.

2 Nietzsche, *The Gay Science*, bk. 4, p. 283.

"Live Dangerously," that victorious hiccough in vacuo, as the national anthem of the true ego exiled in habit.
Samuel Beckett[3]

On September 1, 1990, after much heated debate, the Göttingen city Social Democratic Party (SDP) mayor, Arthur Levi, decided to "live dangerously," unveiling the town's controversial response to its blighted militaristic past.[4] Beside a rose garden next to the town square, on the front wall of the old barracks of the 82nd infantry regiment, the city council bolted a large stone plaque commemorating the valor of the deserter (figure 6.1).[5] The location was important. The 82nd had been one of the key regiments in the September 1, 1939, invasion of Poland that led to the declaration of war in Europe.[6]

The 82nd's regimental motto *Bis zum Tode Getreu* (loyalty until death) was covered over, and in its place was a large rough-hewn stone plaque with the words "Not for fear of death but in order to live!" (*Nicht aus Furcht vor dem Tode, sondern aus dem Willen zu leben!*) The words were a verse from a poem by Alfred Andersch who was himself an army deserter. As if to accentuate the contrast between the two sentiments expressed by Andersch's words and those of the old Nazi-era military slogan, Andersch's poetic words

3 Beckett, *Proust and Three Dialogues*, 20.

4 There is some debate about whom the plaque was intended to honor. While the Social Democratic Party (SDP) wanted to confine its meaning to those who had deserted the German army during the Second World War, the Green alternative list councilors wanted it to include all deserters and conscientious objectors anywhere. The Christian Democratic Union (CDU) and elements in the army were against the whole idea as a matter of principle, believing it might encourage deserters in the contemporary armed forces. The CDU called the whole episode a "*schauspiel*" of drama, while simultaneously complaining about the costs associated with it. "Sour cherries of freedom" (*Säure Kirschen der Freiheit*) was how the *Göttinger Tageblatt* would describe this plaque at the time of its unveiling. Their claim was merely the last hurrah of a "sour grapes" CDU opposition that had failed to halt the combined SDP/Green council's support for the creation and placement of the plaque. See L. Stein, "Sour Cherries of Freedom." I wish to thank Suhail Nazir for helping with the research and translation of German texts used in this section on Göttingen.

5 The 82nd had used it as their barracks from 1835 until 1945.

6 For more details, see Stedeler, "Der Stein des Anstoßes," 134–40.

were haphazardly scrawled across the surface of a roughly hewn stone plaque. The idea of killing by compulsion (*Zwangsverpflichtung zum Töten*) was being overwritten by the idea of civil courage (*Zivilcourage*),[7] just as the idea of desertion as an act of cowardice was being reinvented as a sign of individual valor.

What leads me to recount this tale of a plaque to the deserter is the way that the ideal of civil courage finds form in the figure of that most despised of political universals, the deserter. A poem by a deserter, about the nobility of desertion, placed on the side of a former military barracks, lays down what appears to be a radical moral challenge to society. Yet in this land of a crime so evil (the Holocaust) that it cannot be politicized (Žižek), there now appears a reaction so extreme (the plaque to a deserter) that it cannot be anything other than an abstraction. Through this form of abstraction—where affectivity, far from being the ur-form of a political intensification, is rendered as the warm inner glow of self-satisfaction—a universally negative signifier (the deserter) could be given a positive meaning and thereby embraced. This weak embrace of abstracted heroics, with all its attendant "feel-good" factors, defines the entire political project of liberal democracy. Think of the abstracted embrace of the heroic whistleblower, only to be undone when the "real thing" makes an appearance, or more philosophically, think of the abstracted embrace of equality when all around us there is only inequality.[8]

7 Stedeler, "Der Stein des Anstoßes," 138. The term *Zivilcourage* first appears with Bismarck in 1864 when he talked of the existence of heroism on the battlefield and how it was less common off the battlefield. It has been defined as being "to dare to act because of one's convictions, even at the risk of paying a high price for this conviction," which is a definition that could easily include the suicide bomber. It has, however, in more recent times been used to speak of the whistleblower Edward Snowden. In a television debate between Angela Merkel, of the Christian Democrats, and the leader of the Social Democrats, Peer Steinbrück, before the September 22, 2013, election, Steinbrück spoke of his civil courage (*Zivilcourage*). See Connolly, "Merkel Wins Narrow Victory." For a definition and an examination of this term in relation to a case study, see Swedberg, "Civil Courage."

8 The Chinese have an expression conveying this kind of hypocrisy—*yegong haolong*. It is a phrase literally meaning "Mr. Ye loves dragons" and comes to us from ancient China where, it is said, a man who spent his entire life painting, researching, and composing verse about dragons finally gets to meet one, at which point, he flees.

Jacques Rancière tells us that equality is the founding norm of modernity, but not as an ontological principle or condition, but rather as something that exists only when put into action.[9] The question of "action" is important here. What action is being undertaken to reinforce equality here? Equality can draw us like a telos toward action, but it can also draw us toward the limited action that still carries within it a "feel-good" factor. That is to say, we have come to live a life wherein equality and democracy as principles stand in place of actions designed to achieve them. Does an intermittent and abstract vote to elect national leaders ensure democracy when, at the level of the workplace, there is no such democracy? Like the plaque, the notions of equality and democracy are kept at bay by their aloofness and abstraction from daily life while nevertheless acting as though these principles are being lived in daily life affairs.

Here, then, with this plaque and the abstraction it produces, we find a monument to the necessarily weak symbolic power of the political in our modern Western liberal democratic world. The *thymotic* element, that spirited fore-thrown-ness that would once have driven the committed deserter to action, far from being revealed by the plaque was, in some respects, entombed by it. The momentary but monumental political rancor that accompanied the unveiling of this plaque simply underlined the limits of what was at stake. Moreover, once the plaque was in place, even that momentary outrage it brought with it evaporated as memorialization and historicization gave way to gradual habitualization. As a minor adornment on a wall in the city square, the plaque has long since distanced itself from any ability to move people or move political discourse.

The acceptance of a plaque to the deserter is a sign of our own gradual acceptance of the normalization functions of our political system that carries the promise of liberation, but only ever as an abstraction, in much the same way a commercial brand works in relation to a product. It is in this land that the radical possibilities offered via the political are abstracted by the very processes that make them concrete. The concrete materialization of them actually reduces the action-event to the more limited, liminal, and "realist" possibilities offered by policy-oriented actions. We can admire the deserter but only at a distance and as an abstraction on something like a plaque. There, it can be separated from the "real thing," and debates can abound around its "real" meaning—was it just about the Nazis, or did it mean all deserters?

9 Rancière, *The Politics of Aesthetics*, 52.

Here is a politics transformed by the fact that even questions of significant political difference become staging posts for expert opinion or for detailed think-tank reports and government commissions.

This regime of the expert produces, if nothing else, a historic inversion. Politics no longer flies its flag over policy but is subsumed and muted by it. Notions like equality or even demos find only a weak echo in the habits of this everyday acceptance and, once habituated into these weaker forms, draws us away from both the allure and the sting of the Sirens' song of the political. What is left on the ground of politics are the cobblestones of policy indicating reason and the law are now in charge. The Situationist might once have graffitied *Sous les pavés, la plage!* ("Beneath the pavement, the beach!") but on these pavestones of neoliberalism only a hollowed-out notion of the political lives on, always as a habitualized abstraction much like Andersch's plaque.

"Habit is the ballast that chains the dog to his vomit," Beckett once wrote, and the vomit that spews forth, like the chains that bind the dog, seems inescapable in a politics largely emptied of the intensities necessary to generate real *Zivilcourage*.[10] Here, however, we must tread carefully, for habit also contains a paradox. We need habit and routine for a world that is daily, hourly, and by the minute speeding up. With growth as the new anxiety-creating mantra, habit calms us and makes at least some parts of our lives seem more predictable, manageable, and worthwhile. Yet to overindulge in habit is to turn it into a poison that slowly kills the humanity it sets out to calm. It robs us of the very feelings that make us human. It is like Andersch's monumental plaque in that it can only memorialize but cannot feel the events it attempts to recall, still less bring those feelings back to life. Like all such monuments of abstraction, this habituated life can no longer affectively concretize and congeal into meaningful intensities and/or events. These monuments are no longer remembrances of the events they claim to be about but have instead become monuments to the political limbo that our lives have fallen into under the spell of neoliberal democracy. Why political limbo? Saint Thomas explains.

The fate of the unbaptized child who dies with no fault other than that of original sin cannot be given "afflictive punishment, like that of hell," for they have done nothing wrong. Instead, they suffer only what Saint Thomas calls "the punishment of privation." That, says Giorgio Agamben, consists

10 Beckett, *Proust and Three Dialogues*, 19.

of the "perpetual lack of the vision of God." Such a lack is far from painful. On the contrary, it is a joy, but as Agamben then points out, it is "a joy with no outlet."[11] Joy with no outlet may not quite describe our modern liberal-democratic state of being, but it comes close. We populate a land of liminal commitments and sublimated and dispersed minor intensities. As policy envelops the notion of politics, our lifeworld suffers the punishment of privation. It can tolerate anything just as long as that which is to be tolerated has been abstracted to weaken or dismiss its affective dimensions. It becomes a land in which commitment rarely extends beyond the contractual agreement signed when taking out a mortgage; when any intense emotional outburst is privatized or limited to love, sport, fashion, or an individuated connection to one's god(s); where dreams lead no further than the faux and momentary satisfaction provided by that parallel universe of products that the market offers to cater to our multiple "weakened" desires. Here is joy with just one outlet, the market.

Limbo and neoliberalism produce similar constraints. Knowing neither the sublime truth of God nor the horrors of the damned, the not-quite-damned-not-quite-saved of limbo are, like their modern neoliberal counterparts, confined to this neither-world in which, like limbo, everything equates with comfort and anxiety. But with liberalism it is largely expressed through the money form. "We have set our chairs down in the middle," writes Nietzsche, "as far away from dying warriors as from contented swine."[12] With chairs perched in the middle and eyes downcast, we still seek comfort, but do so within an all-enveloping, narrow, habitualized acceptance of the anxieties the monetized market system creates. As is all too obvious by the alienated state of this comfortable, habitualized existence, however, such contentment does not equate to care.[13] Liberalism shares with limbo the comforts derived from this state of alienated nothingness. It offers a form of sociability that draws us back from the possibility of a state of Being that can throw us. Instead, it leads us into a world of material things that turn our heads while simultaneously

11 Agamben, *The Coming Community*, 5.

12 Nietzsche, *Thus Spoke Zarathustra*, 190.

13 Here I refer to the Heideggerian notion of "care" as rehearsed in *Being and Time*. This suggests that the Being of Dasein is made visible as "care." Care, in this sense, is ontologically focused and means that Dasein always is a way of Being-in-the world. Heidegger, *Being and Time*, 83–84.

reinforcing the anxieties the system creates. At the same time, we draw comfort from the distance we have created between our own sense of self and the violence of the political.

We, in the West, live this limbo liberalism as though it were the promise, indeed the only workable promise, of life itself. In the main and for the most part, we know, firsthand, neither the enchantment of political fore-thrownness nor the existential horrors or joys of anything other than individuated, self-serving sacrifice. Political excess as a lived existential state is, in the main and for the most part, only a memory or an abstract construct. It is always a state that is somewhere else. In place of the burden of commitment we are given financial burdens; in place of faith, there is the distraction of the phantasmagorical, the feeling of superiority that comes from being moderate, and endless, remorseless, work-based assessments that lead us to the view that we are productive and useful. But to be ethical do we have any other choice? J. M. Magaziner thinks not.

In our repertoire of conduct, he seems to suggest, we humans face a stark choice: be ethical or be heroic, for it is impossible to be both! The ethical, argues Magaziner, is built on "moderation and precision," while the heroic always drives us to actions that go "beyond duty" and that are, in turn, often (mis)understood as ethical.[14] We have this choice, but, collectively, rarely do we recognize, much less exercise it. Like dozy commuters on a rush-hour train, we carry our ethics like backpacks as we follow the crowd. Pushed out of the carriage and onto a newly renovated station platform named "democracy," we discover that this newly refurbished and fully appointed place was once known by another name: "averageness."[15] Here, in this average state of ethical Being, we are lionized as democratic by being disburdened of any individual ethical responsibility to make a stand.[16] This is because all decisions are taken by the anonymous "they" of the collective crowd and this,

14 Pashukanis, *Law and Marxism*, 155n4.

15 On averageness, see Heidegger, *Being and Time*, 164–65.

16 For Heidegger, the "they" disburden and accommodate Dasein and reveal the "levelling down" tendency in Dasein. They do this through Dasein tendencies to take things easily and make things easy. And because the "they" "constantly accommodate the particular Dasein by disburdening, the 'they' retains and enhances its stubborn dominion." See Heidegger, *Being and Time*, 165.

for Heidegger at least, would be a "levelling down" of possibilities.[17] That, for Adorno, at least, is simply the law of value reasserting itself.[18] Criticizing the authoritarian elitism of the Heideggerian position, Adorno notes that the elites have the prerogative over this and, these days, it is run by regimes of "benchmarking" in an audit culture in which elections, Gallup polls, surveys, and statistics constitute the basis of the system's claim to value, transparency, and superiority. The a priori assumptions underpinning such mechanisms of transparency, however, remain opaque. Yet it is precisely because the preconditions are occluded that we can adopt a style of thought that enables us to believe we are moral and democratic and our system is, if not equal, at least merit based and transparent.[19] Habit is indeed the ballast that chains this dog to its vomit, but as Beckett then goes on to add, "Breathing is habit. Life is habit!"[20] How easy it proves to be, however, to breath and to live in such a habit.

It is easy to live with because it is hard to imagine another way. This socially accepted mode, based on our existing regime of market veridiction, constantly leads to the view that there is no better way forward. After all, this regime of veridiction always works on the market decision, which is ultimately framed as the democratic decision, for it is a crucial and profitable subset of the most commonly held view. Under these conditions, our life focus shifts. Desirous of staying within the norm but unsure of the direction of the crowd, we tread carefully—no point slipping on vomit!

17 For Heidegger, it is from the world discovered that Dasein draws its possibilities but led by the "they" restricts itself. See Heidegger, *Being and Time*, 165.

18 Adorno's use of the law of value arises in his critique of Heideggerian notions such as the "They" and "averageness." It rests essentially on the charge that elite notions of "levelling" tip the balance of forces toward an unequal exchange. Where Heidegger seems to only look down disdainfully, Adorno looks and sees exploitation. See Adorno, *The Jargon of Authenticity*, 104.

19 Elisabeth Noelle-Nuemann argues that what we perceive to be the majority viewpoint is something we, as a group, not only gravitate toward but that we come to wear it like a social skin that protects us from social estrangement. See Noelle-Neumann, "The Spiral of Silence."

20 Beckett quickly adds that "life is a succession of habits," in which habit is defined as "the generic term for the countless treaties concluded between the countless subjects that constitute the individual and their countless correlative objects." Beckett, *Proust and Three Dialogues*, 19.

We gain relief from the burden of life-threatening decisions by a system that makes these decisions for us but presents them as a summarization of "our" collective will. We bury ourselves in the crowd and gain ethical reassurance because these decisions are based on the collective will and if elections aren't held to verify this viewpoint, then increasingly, expert opinion and surveys by think tanks take their place. These then guide government actions just as they help mentally frame ours. The problem here is aptly summed up by Pierre Bourdieu when he famously remarked that the problem with public opinion polling is that it assumes the public have an opinion.[21] Precisely because of this assumption that the public have "spoken," we come to regard any decisions that flow from such polling as being inherently moral because it is self-evidently democratic. Thus, the pragmatic, rational, and utilitarian is also translated into the ethical for it is a decision-making process arrived at through a method that can claim to be both scientific and democratic. We therefore follow procedure and measure our steps. To live measured lives is to be ethical and reasonable and, in that vacuum of a world in which the possibilities offered by any sense of fore-thrown-ment has diminished if not been altogether eliminated, reason and objectivity are the closest we come to presenting ourselves before any sort of enlightenment pathway.

Our political commitments to causes, our moral commitments to social justice, even our institutional or religious commitments to "Thou": all come to know the limits of this normative world, and these limits always result in moderation and measure. The mass-line becomes a mass-retreat into a form of self-restraining "democratic" reasoning. We no longer encounter those "beyond calculation" moments as anything other than "private" concerns, for we come to fully accept and embrace the fact that "nothing is without reason" (*nihil est sine ratione*). Unlike Leibniz, however, for whom God would gain definition as reason itself, for we moderns, the logic is reversed.[22] In the humanism that followed this reversal, something slowly slips away from us. Stripped of an ability to understand flow, much less the possibilities of affective energies flowing in other directions, our new secular god of reason is

21 Pierre Bourdieu's words were that "every opinion poll supposes that everyone can have an opinion or, stated otherwise, that the production of an opinion is within everyone's range of possibility. At the risk of offending a naively democratic sentiment, I contest this." Bourdieu, "Public Opinion Does Not Exist," 124.

22 Here, I am merely following Heidegger who points to the way that, in Leibniz, "God is called reason." See, Heidegger, *The Principle of Reason*, 27.

largely incapable of throwing us into any state other than self-congratulatory conceit, sure in the knowledge that our worlding is the true worlding for this world, and the material wealth that has accompanied its growth confirms this.

As creatures of this god of measure, we have learned all too well of the need to tread carefully, yet what has been all but forgotten, in the West at least, is that this moderation could have been part of a fall from grace. This, at least, is a viewpoint Max Weber leads us toward in what could also be thought of as a stinging indictment of modern capitalism. From Weber, the paradoxical twist comes from the fact that it was a deeply held and spiritual asceticism that has led us into our modern materialist world of growth and straight into the arms of *homo economus*. Yet, as Weber also explained, this fall from grace into a world of *homo economus* and moderation came not as an effect of our alienation from God, but as an exalted moment of inspiration that "intensified" our belief in that spirit.

Paradoxically, then, it was not with disenchantment that the moderation, secularization, and reason of *homo economus* begin a long journey to dominance but with a particular form of reenchantment known as Calvinism. In rechanneling all our "this-world" material concerns into a re-intensified religious devotion to Thou, Weber says, the path from the fore-thrown-ment of devotion into our contemporary deracinated world of things begins. It is in his seminal text, *The Protestant Ethic and the Spirit of Capitalism*, that these crucial points were made, and these points guide us toward a clearer understanding of our current predicament. It is, after all, through Weber's work that we realize that our own contemporary sense of "joy with no outlet" is little more than the heir to a tradition that began with Luther and the idea that life is to be endured, not enjoyed, which, in the Calvinist spirit, was translated into action as "accumulation without expenditure."

Through Weber's Calvin, we are offered a very different rendition of the counter-reformation. Crucial to his argument is the reinterpretation of God's work as the spirit of acquisitiveness and the self-restraining quality Calvin's notion of predestination produces within the heart of any true believer. This figure of religious excess was wed to a Spartan disregard for the fruits of material wealth. Expenditure was therefore severely limited, for it excluded even the hint of anything that might be interpreted as promoting self-aggrandizement or satiating worldly desires. Hence, only expenditure that was truly and demonstrably doing God's work was acceptable. These religious strictures produced a lifestyle of self-restraint, modesty, and acquisitiveness that resulted in a state of accumulation that limited in the extreme the possibilities of expenditure. Money could not be expended for pleasure or prestige but like the humble, human servant of God, it had to be put to work . . . but only in God's name and doing God's work. Reinvested, these monies grew and produced the material foundation on which an entrepreneurial ethos based on acquisitiveness, thrift, and hard work would be born. While borne of a gift-like devotion to God, it led increasingly to the fractious world of markets and mammon.

While borne of devotion, it would not live by it and, over time, the ethic that fueled this endeavor was its own gravedigger. Over time, the restrictions placed on expenditure would be forgotten, as would the Calvinist origins of this process. It is indeed ironic that the very mechanisms designed to ensure a pious life produced what could be thought of as its very opposite. It is into this world that we, in the West, were eventually born. It is this world we have come to inhabit and know intimately. Because we have been worlded in this way, we have come to regard it as "natural" and to put down our deposit and agree to pay the monthly installments on our very own version of the "iron cage."[23]

Through habituation, we come to feel safe, and while the habitual can sometimes offer a space to escape into our own thoughts, it often only makes us comfortable and complacent in our own iron cages. Moreover, the habits of the market open us more fully to the possibilities offered by a recognition of ourselves not as political Dasein but as "individual rational utility maximizers."[24] The habits formed that are based on market rationali-

23 On Max Weber's iron cage, see the famous quote in Weber, *The Protestant Ethic and the Spirit of Capitalism*, 181. Also, note Weber's own prescient assessment of the effects of the cage in Weber, *Economy and Society*, vol. 2. Regarding the Prussian bureaucracy, Weber claims that "all advances of the Prussian administrative organization have been and will in the future be advances of the bureaucratic and especially of the monocratic, principle. Today, it is primarily the capitalist market economy which demands that the official business of public administration be discharged precisely, unambiguously, continuously, and with as much efficiency as possible." Weber, *Economy and Society*, vol. 2, p. 974. Later, Weber extends the claim to the state itself. "In a modern state the actual ruler is necessarily and unavoidably the bureaucracy, since power is exercised neither through parliamentary speeches nor monarchical enunciations but through the routines of administration." Weber, *Economy and Society*, vol. 2, p. 1393.

24 This, of course, is all based on the description of the individual offered by rational choice theorists. See Brogan, "A Mirror of Enlightenment."

ties help channel the flow of our aspirations into the realm of marketplace distractions and aspirational acquisitiveness. For everything else, as the advertisement tells us, there is Mastercard . . . or, more precisely, a world of calculation and debt.[25]

Joy is therefore not unalloyed but tinged with calculation, risk, aspiration, financial fear, and anxiety. Debt in this context is not the debt of the gift economy. This is not a debt repaid out of the moral obligation to reciprocate but, rather, a calculation that comes in the form of the ratio of labor time expended and compensated for, set against the fear of financial ruin caused by repayments for things that once temporarily satiated our needs or, increasingly, our desires. It is into this world that we have carved out a moment of joy in the materiality of this world, and in that materialistic form, we gain a sense of our own worth as social beings. Yet anxiety, too, is found in this type of materiality. Anguish comes from the fact that while we live lives in which we must constantly calculate and balance, we tend not to add up all that we have but instead focus on all that we have to lose. This fear of the possibility of loss undergirds our trepidation, and this trepidation increasingly makes us obey an ever-weaker and yet ever-more-complex notion of the binding rules of law.

For government, too, calculations are underpinned by rational choice assumptions, for government is the machine-assemblage of this flow bounded by the same laws, rules, regulations, logics, and roots.[26] As it surveys its "market" (the constituents) in this version of rational choice, the people emerge as categories from polls and surveys that then steer policies toward various "stakeholder" ends. The logic used is a deracinated parody of the logic of Maoism. "Take the ideas of the masses scattered and unsystematic . . . , [and then] concentrate them" until they are embraced once more by the

25 This expression is a play on a slogan first used in October 1997, in the Mastercard "Priceless" advertising campaign. This campaign led Mastercard to jump from ninety-ninth place in 2008 to twenty-fourth place in 2012 in the BrandZ one hundred most valuable brands rankings. Shown in 112 countries and translated into 53 languages, this campaign has led to "spinoff" campaigns such as the "Priceless Cities" campaign. All this flowing from a single sentence: "There is always something money cannot buy, but for everything else, there is Mastercard." See Zmuda, "Mastercard's Priceless Evolution."

26 Weber, *Economy and Society*, vol. 2, p. 1394.

masses "as their own."[27] This now finds echo in the liberal democratic notions of policy and polling. "Take the ideas of the masses . . . and turn them into numbers, then, out of these numbers make policy," our liberal democratic leaders and think tanks seem to say. Yet, in doing this, what these leaders do not tell us is that the reason of policy is itself a form of "push-polling" or predictive marketing that replaces the very possibilities opened by the political. What an electorate will "buy" increasingly becomes the "measure" of what politics will sell and, outside of that, there are only the extremes.

To pull away from such extremes, the political is both limited in scope and tamed by the distracting pleasures of the "phantasmagoric." It leads to a world of the everyday wherein idle talk, curiosity, and ambiguity distract us and bring forth *Verfallen*, or a falling.[28] For Adorno, such idle talk would already be in decline if the "expenditure of advertisements disappeared."[29] Far from disappearing, however, advertisements increasingly form the basis of an aspirational way of looking at life. Increasingly, this world of advertising seduces us and materialism cushions the fall. The technically modern economy offers the possibility of purchasable pleasures and, as we fall, we are comforted by the possibilities offered to us by these ongoing, momentary distractions algorithmically determined for our individual pleasure. Added to this are the deracinating effects of institutional politics and the ever-increasing demands of a rationalized work regime undertaken to survive. All this adds up to a dulling of our political senses as policy is decoupled from the political and works against it to limit its impact and redirect its flow. The wellspring of this expression of the political is no longer directed toward intensification. While the friend/enemy distinction still shadows the world, it now gives way to technology designed to slow the flow, dissipate the energy burdening us with debts, mortgages, and work while simultaneously stimulating our material desires.

Working alongside the "phantasmagoric," which offers endless temporary enjoyment in the minor moments of commodified distraction and circulation, are the language games of professionalism. This is because it is policy

27 Mao Tse-tung (Zedong), "Some Questions concerning Methods of Leadership," 119.

28 This, at least, is how Magda King reads the central claim of Heidegger with his notion of the everyday. See M. King, *A Guide to Heidegger's Being and Time*, 88.

29 Adorno, *The Jargon of Authenticity*, 101.

implementation and not the political intensification that drives this system. This further distances us from the political by instituting various versions of the force of the better argument. The possibility of disruption still exists and comes from many sources: the poor migrant, the other nation, the other belief system, the other culture, the other sexuality. This fear can even lead to momentary eruptions of political intensity but in the West, at least, liberal democracy has, until very recently, always held such eruptions in check, citing a belief in the higher ideas of a civilization founded on notions of enlightenment reason. And reason emboldens us. Only we would be bold enough to valorize that which we don't actually believe in or practice. What government, what people, what nation ever supports the deserter? What system could possibly embrace this figure as its own? Only in abstraction can it do so, yet in abstraction it counts for little and threatens even less. This is the only way, it seems, for the deserter, the refugee, or the outsider to be embraced.

Blinded and yet emboldened by such dissimilitude and habituated by daily concerns, the possibilities of the political are narrowed to the point whereby only the regime of veridiction becomes important. In place of collective action, one looks toward the more individualizing confirmations of subjectivity offered from within our rational market-based world. Corporealized, individualized, and existentially felt, the fore-thrown-ment, which was once the province of the collective, the sacred, and the political, is now, in our modern, Western, and increasingly bare-life existence, largely restricted to the individual passions associated with love, pleasure, or religion. In the main and for the most part, it is in the passions of love that we can rediscover in our Western world that one remaining possibility of everyday disruptions to our otherwise distracted yet increasingly measured state of being.

It may well have been Victor Hugo who said it, but it was Freud who reported it to us: "Only when we are in love have we blind faith in humanity; everything is perfect. . . . It puts us on a level with the gods and incites us to all sorts of artistic activities. We become real poets; we not only memorize and quote poetry, but we often become Apollos ourselves."[30] In love, we are, in fact, beyond good and evil, for "the lover loves beyond reward and punishment."[31] The intensities of the soul have, in this mode, been confined to

30 This is from Freud quoting affirmatively a source he describes as a very brilliant woman who, in turn, quotes Hugo. See Freud, "Psychopathology of Everyday Life," 47.

31 Nietzsche, *Thus Spoke Zarathustra*, 273.

matters of the heart. Passionate love becomes one of the few outlets through which any "intensity" felt by the majority can be channeled and displayed. And it is one of the few points at which the power of commitment politics can be challenged. "The world of lovers is no less true than that of politics. It even absorbs the totality of existence, which politics cannot do," says Georges Bataille.[32] It is, therefore, an all-enveloping embrace.

As a point of obsessive rechanneling of feelings that are potentially bound for the political, passionate love becomes a channeling of emotions endowed with "strange and sometimes terrifying powers,"[33] but now deployed in a new and quite private form of secularized monotheism. Love, therefore, quite literally, has no measure, yet at the very moment one recognizes this measureless passion, we are also forced to recognize how it is a rechanneling of affective flows into regimes of market veridiction. In other words, that which is without limit finds its limit through values attributed to it in the market.

While Rousseau would attempt to limit love by reference to pity,[34] the sly subversions of market forces channeled it far more effectively. The market did not offer a "measured" way out, but rather produced a series of phantasmagoric material objects that, as signifiers of intense love, were an aid to help us find a way in. Thus, while we cannot measure love for it is incalculable, we can still measure its market potential. Indeed, its incalculability becomes one of the key selling points in that its calculable market appeal and appetite for that "little something" always helps raise the price of the commodity being sold.

From the dominance of the love song in popular music through to the burgeoning bridal-gown industry, our commodified society has managed to find a way to make individualized expressions of even total enchantment fold back into our "this world" commodified existence. Herein lies the power of that which Adorno once labeled the culture industry. This industry helps "world" our bare-life mentalities and ensures that all forms of fore-thrownness lead back into commodity circuits in search of the best deal.

If the political is a unidirectional flow reaching toward a cathartic point of eruption, the commodity circuits rechannel potential affective intensities in

32 Bataille, *Oeuvres completes*, vol. 10, *L'Erotisme*, quoted in Surya, *Georges Bataille*, 255.

33 Deleuze and Guattari, *A Thousand Plateaus*, 307.

34 For an analysis of Rousseau, passion, love, and pity, see the extensive discussion in Derrida, *Of Grammatology*, 171–77.

other directions. They become constant loops of minor sparks, excitements, and distractions.[35] The dominant economic form leaks into the political, transforming it into similarly endless circuits of desire-loops selling policies to an ever-expanding and variegated series of "stakeholders." Politics mimics the form of commodity sale and, in the process, enters the culture industry as an albeit privileged part of a series of calculated distractions. This is not a world in which enlightenment reason is brought to a standstill, but rather, it is one caught in the paradox of knowledge circuits transforming the monotheist—be they political or religious flows—into looped and looping circuits of disaggregation and rechanneling.

This "polytheist" looping process is central to the circuitry of the commodity flow but it is a narrowing of that flow around the economy, rather than a narrowing and intensifying of the flow to create a tidal bore. What, then, of those technologies of the tidal bore? To examine these, we need to move from contemporary Germany to the China of Mao Zedong where we will find machines dedicated to the production of political intensity.

35 In that sense, the modern Western political is "in advance" of its own advertising industry, which is gradually moving from funnel to loop. See Baar, "The Funnel Is Dead."

PART 3

Reconstructions

Figure 7.1. Anren reconstructed.

7

Channeling Intensity

A DESIGN PROCESS

At the last Venice Biennale of the twentieth century, the Chinese conceptual artist Cai Guo-Qiang was awarded the Golden Lion for a performative installation that had once been the frontispiece of revolution. Cai's *Venice's Rent Collection Courtyard* was based on a partial reconstruction of an episodic, 118-meter-long socialist artwork, *Rent Collection Courtyard* (see figures 7.2, 7.3, and 7.4).[1] The original monumental installation featured

1 To be accurate, Cai's work was modeled on the Beijing re-creation of the work. The work, first exhibited in Anren, became a national sensation and soon there was a demand for it to appear in Beijing. As the Anren exhibition was made up of statues that were not kiln dried, it meant that they would need to be remade in Beijing. Therefore, sculptors who had made the original work were dispatched to Beijing in 1966. Information on Cai modeling his installation on the Beijing exhibition comes from an interview that I conducted with Cai Guo-Qiang in his New York studio on March 24, 2010. Information on the remaking of the statues in Beijing comes from an interview that I conducted with arguably the most

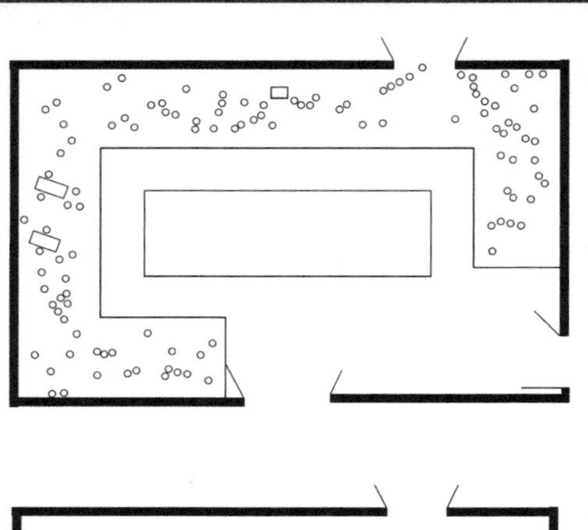

Figure 7.2. *Rent Collection Courtyard* (RCC): *The flow.*

The three diagrams are from the RCC exhibition, drawn from the work of the original sculptures in Anren in 1965. All from Hebei Art Press, *The Public Sculptures of Rent Collection Courtyard*, 8–9.

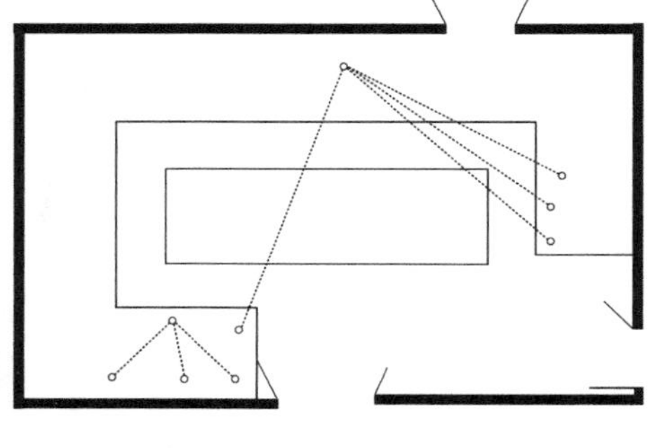

Figure 7.3. RCC: *The gaze*

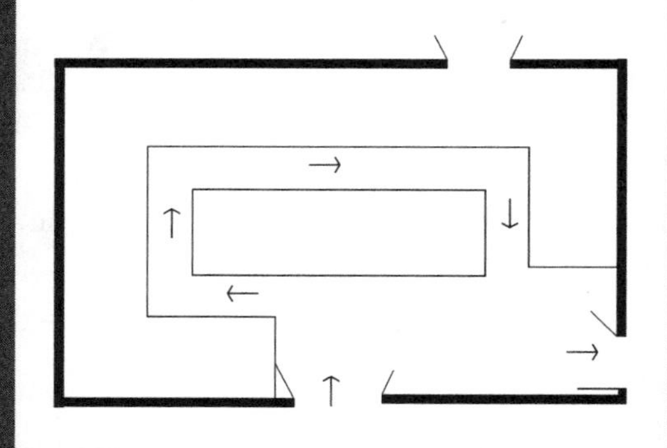

Figure 7.4. RCC: *The emotion*

114 life-sized mud statues and was created on the cusp of the Chinese Cultural Revolution in the manor house of a former landlord, Liu Wencai. In a series of four episodic parts, the statues depicted Liu's cruel and exploitative practices of measuring, weighing, and collecting grain from tenants. Liu was a widely known landlord in Sichuan but after this revolutionary work was completed in October 1965, he became (in)famous nationwide as the epitome of evil landlordism.[2]

Cai's *Venice's Rent Collection Courtyard* was not a replica of the original work but, rather, a partial fabricating of this work to raise questions about process. Cai's partially completed and slowly deteriorating mud statues led to reflection on questions about the cycle of life—birth, death, and authenticity.[3] In terms of concrete practices, it led to Cai paying close attention to the fabrication methods of the original Maoist sculptors who wrapped their socialist artwork in traditional Chinese customary methods and practices of statue-making.[4]

If the original socialist project led to an installation comprising mud statues and associated objects ordered in a fashion that told a story that would tug at the heartstrings, thereby channeling emotions into political intensities, Cai's work was radically different. Cai's redoing of this work comprised statues in various states of assembly and decay but largely set adrift from the episodically constructed storyline of peasant exploitation that had been the central theme of the original work. Cai's work was designed to induce contemplation, not anger. By removing the political storyline, Cai

important classically trained sculptor on the project, Zhao Shutong, Chengdu, Sichuan Province, August 17, 2011.

2 See Erickson, "The *Rent Collection Courtyard*, Past and Present," 123.

3 As Anne Wedell-Wedellsborg says, it involved "questions of authenticity/originality/copying in art works as well as formal copyright, of socialist realism versus postmodernism, of the process of creation and destruction, individual and collective, of timeliness, context and site specificity, of local and global, of the concept of aura, and of course again of different expectations, China versus the West." Wedell-Wedellsborg, "Contextualizing Cai Guo-Qiang."

4 On his focus on process, Cai says, "The key is to focus on the process of fabrication of these artworks, to pay attention to the process of the artists making these sculptures, rather than where these sculptures will end up and how they will look in the end." Pearlman, "Cai Guo-Qiang with Ellen Pearlman."

effectively takes this work to Venice. That is to say, Cai takes the work "out of [its political] context and just focus[es] on the goal of fabrication and artistic production."[5]

The shadowy aura of the political intensification process, buried within the original work, however, still lurks. It is registered in the cold glass eyes and facial expressions of some of Cai's "remade" mud statues, even though, in his work, such emotional expression appears only in relic form. In Cai's rendition, there is no cathartic ending, no character identification, no process of intensification, only estrangement and aestheticization. In decentering the original artwork's (political) content and moving the work out of Maoist aesthetics, Cai Guo-Qiang's process-driven work could, therefore, be said to be an aestheticization of the political, yet (paradoxically) it is precisely in this process of aestheticization and estrangement that the techniques of the art of the political come to the fore. This is because Cai's *Venice's Rent Collection Courtyard* pays close attention to the techniques and process-based methods of the original that extend well beyond the material objects themselves. In other words, the objects have a "surplus."[6]

Site specificity, the use of found objects, and the employment of readymades might all be at home in contemporary Western art practices, but they are also central to this Maoist "model" art form.[7] The root of these innovations, however, does not lie in experimentation from within the tradition of Rodin any more than they are drawn from Soviet-era art forms. Instead, these innovations, Cai explains, come from the telluric tradition of the artisan-artists of the eighteen Buddhist arhats. Cai's work shares this connection to Chinese tradition, but where the Maoist tradition draws on

5 Pearlman, "Cai Guo-Qiang with Ellen Pearlman."

6 Harman, *Immaterialism*, 20.

7 In February 1966, alongside the model operas and ballet, which she created, Jiang Qing, Mao Zedong's wife, identified the *Rent Collection Courtyard* as a model for other artists to emulate in a speech titled "Summary of the Forum on Literature and Art in the Armed Forces with Which Comrade Lin Piao Entrusted Chiang Ch'ing." This speech is translated in Chung Hua-Min and Miller, *Madame Mao*, 208. For further commentary on this work as a model, see Zhang Youyun, "The Roots of the Changing Appreciation of the *Rent Collection Courtyard* in Popular Perceptions," 46.

a quotidian telluric base to produce character identification and political intensity, Cai's interests propel him toward an engagement with more ethereal forms that turn on the flow of *qi*, or vital energy.[8] It is here, in this meeting of the telluric and contemporary forms of art practice, where the Taoist flow of *qi* has the potential to be transformed into the tidal bore of Maoist political intensity and where estrangement from the art objects themselves helps us see the techniques used to channel affective flows, that this process of aestheticization opens onto the methodological basis of an art of the political.

An art of the political is neither a political science nor the rationality of government (governmentality).[9] Rather, it is a broader style of thought that turns on understanding a set of culturally and site-specific process-driven practices and techniques that intuitively work within the fluidity of power to produce political outcomes. Directional rather than intentional, an art of the political focuses on those socially embedded technologies and processes that attempt to channel, harness, and make concrete the fluidity of the affective

8 Like his pyrotechnical work, the ephemerality of Cai's decaying mud statues underlines the transience of all things in much of his work and brings to mind traditional Taoist concerns. Indeed, as Cai himself says of his gunpowder work, "I feel good with the volatile nature of gunpowder; I am looking for the unchanging through the always changing. Nature always changes but the fact of change—or evolution—never does. I also associate it with the discipline and spontaneity of calligraphy, that most honored Chinese art form. In calligraphy the artist is a 'perpetual amateur.' This is the model I identify with as an artist." Crane, "Cai Guo-Qiang: Taoist?"

9 This is not to reject the notion of governmentality but merely to highlight the limits of thinking of this flow as being restricted to matters governmental. Rather than being about rationalities, this form of thinking in some ways works from irrationalities and resembles the broader frame that Edward Said has called a "style of thought." This, Said notes, informs all writing, thinking, and acting on "the Orient." Thus rationalities are only part of the question. Having said this, it should also be acknowledged that the rendition of the political given here draws heavily on the Foucauldian insistence that power is fluid, mobile, and relational rather than "a thing." On governmentality, see Foucault, "Governmentality." On the Said notion of a style of thought, see his description of Orientalism in Said, introduction to *Orientalism*, 1–28. On Foucault's rendition of power as fluid, see Foucault, *The History of Sexuality*, vol. 1, pp. 94–95.

realm.[10] An art of the political in the contemporary moment focuses on the channeling and transcriptive technologies that enable the heterological, intangible, and affective flows to be either turned into political intensities or transformed into dissipated (material) desires. An art of the political is concerned with those technologies and processes that work either to intensify or to de-intensify the power of affective energy flows. If commodity markets are the central means by which the flow is deintensified and dissipated in "our" world, the *Rent Collection Courtyard* and all the other "model" artistic works of the Cultural Revolution open onto the technologies and machinery of class struggle designed to produce and expand the production of political intensity in theirs.

Collectively, these "model" technologies of the Cultural Revolution worked to turn the rational cognitive processes that produced a strong intellectual belief in revolution into goosebumps on the surface of the skin, lumps in the back of the throat, tears in the eyes of the believer, and anger in the heart of the revolutionary.[11] This, then, was the basis of the claim, at the beginning of the Cultural Revolution, that they would "touch people to their very souls."[12]

The novelty and invention of this Maoist political apparatus lies precisely in its experimentation with technologies of fusion that brought together, and intensified, idea and affect. Maoism undertook a series of experiments in synesthetic homologization to bring "idea" and "affect" into correspondence and, through that process, to "weaponize" their union.[13] If Maoist "machines" brought affective energy flows to the surface as a clustering of

10 It could, in the language of Deleuze and Guattari perhaps, be called a (political) "becoming." For details of how this might be the case, see Massumi, *A User's Guide to Capitalism and Schizophrenia*, 94–95.

11 How these are "measured" and thereby become unfelt in our world is described in Massumi, "The Autonomy of Affect."

12 *People's Daily*, "A Great Revolution," 1.

13 Spinoza distinguishes between idea and affect in Axiom 3, Section 2, of *Ethics* where he notes that while modes of thinking about, say, love cannot exist without an idea of the thing loved, the idea of love can itself exist separately from the state of being loved. See Spinoza, *The Ethics*. Drawing on this, Gilles Deleuze notes that ideas are representational whereas affects are not. See Deleuze, "Gilles Deleuze, Lecture Transcripts." The Maoist "trick" was to devise techniques to weave affect and idea into one form.

intensely felt political feelings, emotions, and ideas, it did so by channeling them through the ever-narrowing vector of the friend/enemy dyadic structure of the political.[14] This enabled the velocity and intensity of the affective flow to be constantly and rapidly increased. This machinelike quality was, however, many miles from the type of Machine Art that had once been heralded as revolutionary within the socialist tradition.

"Art is dead—long live Tatlin's Machine Art," the Berlin Dadaists would proclaim in May 1920.[15] Thought of as part of a scientific push within Soviet socialism, Vladimir Tatlin's *Machinenkunst* was, in fact, regarded as the death knell of old art forms. For Tatlin and the entire Constructivist movement, life became more precise, more mathematical, and more scientific. Their studios became "laboratories," just as the square, the line, the point, and the grid became their point of reference.[16] Where Tatlin's Machine Art was produced in the age of steel and made iron "stand on its hind legs" in search of an artistic formula,[17] the Maoists drew on a telluric partisan tradition that led them to mud, not steel, and toward a political rather than artistic formula. Where Constructivism, after its transition to a productivist approach, would lead to the production of everyday objects that fitted into society, Maoism sought model art forms that would stand out. These models would condense and intensify past peasant experiences of exploitation and turn them into an artistic expression. Where Maoism

14 The friend/enemy distinction is, of course, what Carl Schmitt calls the unique criterion "to which all action with a specifically political meaning can be traced." On this, see Schmitt, *The Concept of the Political*, 26. As I have shown elsewhere, this duality can be traced all the way to China where it would sit at the heart of the Maoist political. On the centrality of this to the Maoist political, see Dutton, *Policing Chinese Politics*.

15 This "slogan" came from the Berlin Dadaist Fair of May 1920 when leading Dadaists George Grosz and John Heartfield held up a large work taken down from the gallery wall with this quote about Tatlin written on it. Posing with it, they had their photograph taken and from there, it captured the imagination of the artworld. See Lynton, *Tatlin's Tower*, 30–67. See also Tafuri, *The Sphere and the Labyrinth*, 131.

16 Rodchenko, *Experiments for the Future*, 145.

17 These are the words of Viktor Shklovsky, in Shklovsky, *Knights Move*, 69–70. See also Tafuri who points to differences within the Dadaists precisely around questions of the political. Tafuri, *The Sphere and the Labyrinth*, 130–33.

sought identification with these model forms, Tatlin and the Constructivist movement sought estrangement from this type of everyday. Molding mud into message and peasant into revolutionary required that this process-driven artwork revolutionize all thoughts and techniques, including those of the sculptors themselves.

"The process of creation is also a process of thought reform for the artists concerned," said Li Shaoyan, as he explained how a plotline designed to touch the peasant audiences required the sculptors themselves be touched.[18] To be touched, the sculptors would have to bury themselves in the peasant life they were trying to depict. To this end, they would go and live with the peasants, collect their stories of exploitation, and join in their daily work routines. Gaining an understanding of peasant life and then intensifying that feeling of bitterness, their project work was thought to have ontological effects not just on those who saw the finished product but also on the sculptors who created it. In other words, the making of this work involved the remaking of self.

From the peasants, the sculptors learned both the indigenous techniques of mud-statue making and a pedagogy of frugality and self-reliance. These techniques would then be used to alter the practices of these Western, classically trained, sculptors. Moreover, the demand that this be a collective rather than individual enterprise forced them to reflect both on their craft and on their own egoistic motives for engaging in art.

As a machine created specifically to channel the flow of the political, *Rent Collection Courtyard* was, therefore, to have cognitive effects on those who worked on the design and production of these statues. The work required intense thought being given to the emotional effects these material objects would have on those who viewed them—"wax statues in the exhibition offer gloomy, frightful figures that evoke real fear," one sculptor would say. "Ah

18 Li Shaoyan, who was head of the Sichuan Arts Council at the time, made these remarks in relation to the weight being placed on the collective nature of the enterprise, which he claimed helped combat the individualism of the artist. See Li Shaoyan, "Learning from the Sculptural Workers." He was not the only one to hold such views. Ma Li, who was the Wenjiang area committee propaganda ministry chief at the time, addressed the sculptors, saying that "in going through the process of creating this work, you also go through your own type of ideological reform, and toward your world view, and view of humanity, you undergo your own huge revolution." Quoted in Wang Zhi'an, *The Heavens Thundered*, 191.

yes, but the reality of the old society was about a hundred times gloomier and more frightful," came the reply . . . and so the debate on appearance and its ability to carry a message continued.[19] It required experimenting with various indigenous materials and knowledge forms to "place" the work, not just in a site-specific location but within a specific style of thought that was readily intelligible to ordinary Chinese peasants.

Using everyday materials and motifs that local people were familiar with meant learning from the masses. "From April 1965 onwards, I understood our role as being to offer support, which meant 'learn at work and work in learning' [*gongzuozhong xuexi, xuexizhong gongzuo*]," the classically trained lead sculptor on the project, Zhao Shudong, would say.[20] It meant living and working with peasants, developing a sense of self-reliance, and adopting a collectivist and self-critical attitude toward oneself and one's work. Lastly, this attitudinal change also meant that they came to regard challenges and hardships encountered as honors bestowed rather than burdens carried. "In those days it was really hard . . . things were really hard but no one had any demands because, from our perspective, we really felt honored," a junior sculptor on the project, Long Taicheng, would later say.[21] The process was profoundly experiential and utterly Maoist. Indeed, it was an exemplification of the Maoist idea of "greater, faster, better, [and] more economical" production (*duo kuai hao sheng*) being applied not to the economy, but to an economy of art.

The sheer scale of this project made it "greater" (*duo*). The honor felt by young sculptors like Long Taicheng was harnessed in a Stakhanovite-like work-drive that led them to produce this massive work in just four and a

19 Wang Zhi'an, *The Heavens Thundered*, 140.

20 The indigenous element played the primary role, according to Zhao Shudong, lead sculptor of the Sichuan Academy of the Arts team. According to Zhao, the role of the academy in the construction of *Rent Collection Courtyard* has been overstated. This is a very different view to that held by Wang Guangyi, another leading sculptor who worked on the project. Wang's views tend to accord more with the prevailing position, which is, according to Paul Clark, that the statues were made by teachers and students of the Sichuan Academy of the Arts. See Clark, *The Chinese Cultural Revolution*, 206.

21 Interview with Long Taicheng, August 21, 2011. All further quotations from Long come from this interview, unless otherwise noted.

half months (faster, *kuai*). The use of simple, cheap, and indigenous-based artisan technologies brought a new economy to the work, reducing the cost of each statue to just three Chinese dollars per statue (economical, *sheng*).[22] Moreover, through the fusion of modern political energy and demotic indigenous telluric technology, the art of sculpture was transformed (better, *hao*). Here was a process in which sculpture, sculptor, and spectator were transformed. "It is a revolution in sculpting," crowed the official Party organ, the *People's Daily*.[23] Declared a "model work" in 1966, it was hailed as the harbinger and prototype of a new type of revolutionary practice in the plastic arts. What it shared with all the other "model" or *yangban* artworks was that, like them, it was built around the typification of characters and designed to channel and heighten political intensity by stretching the boundaries of the art form through a fusion of modern and indigenous telluric technologies and knowledges.[24]

Such hybrid practices—that brought the telluric into the modern—stretched well beyond the arts to include just about all those things that were being labeled newborn socialist things (*xinsheng shiwu*).[25] The new medical methods, for example, demonstrated a similar hybridic form, realigning and fusing modern Western medical techniques and aspects of traditional Chinese healing practices to produce a new model science.[26] Model art, model science, model theater: this concept of the model, as Børge Bakken dem-

22 Three Chinese dollars is the figure given in the *People's Daily* on June 11, 1965. At today's exchange rates, that is less than US 50 cents per statue. See *People's Daily*, "*Rent Collection Courtyard*," 6.

23 *People's Daily*, "*Rent Collection Courtyard*," 6.

24 Paul Clark claims that the model operas made just these sorts of claims and it was on this basis that they were deemed "models." While not untrue, the key thing that makes models exemplary for this study was their function as the machine component of what one might call, to steal a line from the Dadaist about Tatlin, a Machine Art form. Maoist art forms were the technologies used for the channeling and intensification of the flow into a single political and cathartic end. For a more prosaic account of the characteristics that led to them being technologies of the flow, see Clark, *The Chinese Cultural Revolution*, 57–58, 73–75.

25 See Laurence Coderre's work, which offers more details about some of the newborn socialist things, albeit ones that focus largely on their relationship with the commodity form. See Coderre, *Newborn Socialist Things*.

26 See *A Compilation of Materials*.

onstrates, is deeply embedded in traditional Chinese cultural practices and spreads to educational and even social control discourses.[27] What turned model-making from a traditional into a revolutionary practice, however, was not just the ability to set a norm but rather the ability to turn that norm into a device to incite political intensity. Liu Wencai, the landlord featured in *Rent Collection Courtyard*, would be used to do just that. Tales of his excesses would be used to tap into affective emotions, channeling, transforming, and harnessing them such that they all turned into a single political torrent. And it was Cai Guo-Qiang who would reveal this aspect of the work when recalling his own schoolboy experiences:

> When I was a schoolboy and first saw the *Rent Collection Courtyard*, I was moved by the adult next to me who looked at it and cried because he had really suffered at the hands of his landlord. I felt his pain. The exhibition guides who explained the story of the *Rent Collection Courtyard* to [our class] also cried as they spoke . . . and then when they cried the whole class began to cry. They gave us some inedible food that tasted like straw, and they explained that this was a peasant staple in the old society. We forced the food down, looked at the statues while having the severe hardships of the old society explained to us. Now that I look back on this from an artistic point of view, this whole thing is really very interesting. It was a work not just about statues, but about the tears of the guide who explained things, and the horror of the disgusting food we were being forced to eat. . . . These things were all part of the same big concept.[28]

The statues, the tears, the food, the horror were existentially felt effects tied together by one big concept. "When the laboring masses viewed this work, they cried so much pain that they lost their voice [*tongku shisheng*]

27 Bakken traces this penchant for typification, the exemplary, and the model back to traditional times, noting that Chinese pedagogy contains a "fundamental assumption . . . that people are capable of learning from models." See Bakken, *The Exemplary Society*, 8. Ouyang Zongshu illustrates Bakken's point with reference to the exemplary ancestors being used as models for future generations in the late dynastic lineage records. See Ouyang Zongshu, *Chinese Genealogies*. For further details on how this late dynastic tradition might have fed into a Maoist pedagogy, see Dutton, "Mango Mao."

28 All quotations from Cai Guo-Qiang are from the interview conducted on March 24, 2010, in New York, unless otherwise noted.

but simultaneously developed a heightened sense of class hatred," the *People's Daily* reported.[29] The "one big concept" produced this effect by channeling affective flows into a single intense point of politicization. One of the lead sculptors on the original project would later recall how, even before completion, this work unsettled emotions: "Because we left the courtyard gate open when we were working, a lot of the peasants got a sneak preview and when they were invited in they were intensely aroused [*qunqing jifen*] and couldn't hold back their tears [*qibu chengsheng*]. Some even fainted [*hundai zaidi*]."[30] Here then, one begins to see the crucial affective element that was being channeled by a series of staged, "technical" manipulations. The machinelike quality of the artwork, which enabled it to function as a technology unifying and then transforming affective flows into emotional flows, was, for Maoism, the artwork's raison d'être.

Sipping his tea and talking to the sculptors while they were creating the work, the local Party chief and patron of the work, Ma Li, said, "Concerning the creation of the *Rent Collection Courtyard*, I want to raise a small request. The spirit [*qifen*] of the overall statues needs to be grasped and grasped accurately, for the aim of this work is to lay stress on the overwhelmingly positive aspects and if this healthy trend does not prevail, then a perverse or evil energy flow [*xieqi*] will."[31] To employ this positive spirit, or *qifen*, and ward off the evil or bad energy flow [*xieqi*] was something, however, that would only work within an overarching and specifically directed political culture and technology.

The art-ful-ness of the original *Rent Collection Courtyard* project, then, lay not in the aesthetic itself but in its "use-value" in harnessing, channeling, and directing affective energy within an overarching political culture. Its artfulness in this particular cultural setting was to act as a key pressure point, transforming affect into emotions such that they would intertwine and be channeled into a single and powerful political intensity. It would function in this way not just by appealing to a cognitive knowledge of past oppression but in reproducing in facsimile the taste, tears, and pain of past suffering via a mud-based "condensation" centering on an anthropomorphized enemy.

29 *People's Daily*, "*Rent Collection Courtyard*," 6.

30 Wang Guanyi, "Looking Back on the *Rent Collection Courtyard*," 38.

31 Quoted in Wang Zhi'an, *The Heavens Thundered*, 191.

Designed to reignite revolutionary enthusiasm, it re-created the taste, tears, and hatred of what the communists had overthrown.[32]

Peasants fainting as they saw their own pasts captured in mud, visible pain developing into class hatred, teardrops welling in a schoolboy's eye as food is ingested but proves as hard to swallow as the evils of Liu Wencai: these were all physical manifestations of a visceral connection being made between cognitive and affective states of being. Here, then, were affective transformations produced through technologies of channeling and the harnessing of memory. The original statues were therefore designed to collect, heighten, and then channel affective energy flows by tapping into three emotional states: crying, enmity, and spiritedness.

> [If] we want the masses, when viewing the *Rent Collection Courtyard*, to think about old China . . . then, in emotional terms, we need to induce three emotional changes within them: crying, enmity, and spiritedness.
>
> Crying—This will deeply arouse the masses, allowing for the production of a mass consciousness by moving them with feelings of tragedy.
>
> Enmity—Here we want the audience to hate the landlord class, hate reactionaries, and hate the old society.
>
> Spiritedness—After undergoing "speak bitterness" sessions the people would be inspired to a higher class consciousness, transforming their class hatred into a form of powerful resistance.[33]

That channeling process being described involves syncopating emotional responses with the calibrated plot line of the *Rent Collection Courtyard* narrative. It is a narrative that leads toward a collective cry for revolutionary organization, and it was in the penultimate section of the original Anren

32 The *People's Daily* said, "We have many young people in this country who have never seen the reality of man's exploitation of man, and man's oppression of man. And even though many people have obviously seen this, it was quite a while ago and the influence of this upon them has grown ever fainter. Therefore, the role of these mass clay statues, in reflecting the leadership of Mao Zedong thought, is to awaken people from their light sleep and to get them to rise up, getting them to recognize and reflect upon what the old society actually did to people, and from this vantage point, strengthen their love of the current new society of socialism." "*Rent Collection Courtyard*," 6.

33 Wang Zhi'an, *The Heavens Thundered*, 202.

Rent Collection Courtyard work, a section entitled "resistance" (*fankang*), that crying, enmity, and spiritedness would be transformed into this desire to organize. Wang Zhi'an explains how these energy flows were channeled through these emotional states into one single unidirectional torrent:

> The final section of the work was themed "resistance" and the focal point here was enmity [*chouhen*]—the enmity of the peasants toward the landlord. Here, there was a self-generating notion of struggle tied to a growing consciousness of that struggle. Hence, [resistance and enmity] were two halves of the same coin: one expressed an abstract "hatred" [*hen*], and the other expressed the peasants' growing self-awareness of where that hatred would lead. Here, the idea of hate is expressed as a form of spontaneity [*zifaxing*], while the growing peasant self-awareness pointed toward organization.[34]

To understand concretely how to better channel this spontaneity and self-awareness into revolutionary organization required the artists to understand how the revolution itself had done this. The artists, therefore, packed their bags and went to live in a former partisan base camp, known locally as "little Yan'an."[35] There, they would live the spartan peasant life, eat peasant food, and work alongside peasant laborers and hear their stories of struggle. "This was all part of the creative process," Li Qisheng, who was "in charge of the creative side," would insist.[36]

This experience of living, working, and struggling with the peasants was all part of a Maoist pedagogy and, when combined with the use of mud and indigenous technology and knowledge, produced the telluric ingredients for a political transformation that was constantly being contextualized in terms of an idealized view of the revolutionary potential of peasant life. The use of "found objects" in the *Rent Collection Courtyard* project (things such as desks, an abacus, and a grain thrasher), the site-specific framing of

34 Wang Zhi'an, *The Heavens Thundered*, 210.

35 The official name of the place they went to was Three-Fork Commune (*Sancha Gongshe*), and it was, originally, in the war years, the underground base camp of the west Sichuan Communist Party branch. See Wang Zhi'an, *The Heavens Thundered*, 163, for further details.

36 Wang Zhi'an, *The Heavens Thundered*, 162–63, 167.

the work (using the courtyard of the landlord's manor house as a stage for and a staging of the work), and leaning mud statues on doorways or against pillars were all novel innovations that came not from contemporary Western art theory, but out of a profoundly Maoist idea of "making do." Making *Rent Collection Courtyard*, then, was far more complex and process-based than might have been imagined. Yet this process-based work was all part of the "one big concept" of Maoism, which could only be imagined in terms of affective productivity within the larger, sociopolitical context of that time, that place, and that revolution.[37] Site specificity here is understood in two ways.

First, in terms of the broader society, this form of art incitement could only work when the veridiction regime was not market based or founded on the flow of money. In other words, it was "site specific" in terms of a telluric, revolutionary veridiction regime that required the production, reproduction, and harnessing of poetic, political intensities. Wedded to both cognitive and affective flows within that society, the artwork was charged with the task of channeling and transforming these flows into a political torrent.

Second, in terms of the local context, the original mud statues of Anren must be thought of in the broader context of their role in Liu Wencai's Manor House Museum. It was here, in its original form and original locale, that the *Rent Collection Courtyard* exhibition was but one (albeit penultimate) technology within a larger machine-assemblage known as the Landlord Manor House Museum. Once again, site specificity takes on a particularly political hue, for it was art technologies like the *Rent Collection Courtyard* project that helped transform Liu Wencai's manor house. How this *Machinenkunst*

37 In a discussion on faces, Long Taicheng, who worked on both the Anren and the later Beijing statues, explained how Mao's one big concept was translated from an abstraction into a concrete set of concerns. In moving the work from Anren to Beijing, recontextualization was required. Speaking of his own practice, Long said, "When I went to Beijing to reproduce the statues, I had to observe numerous faces. Every day as we took the bus from Hepingli to the Art Museum, we observed many northern children's faces. In my work, I tried to mix the faces of northern children with faces from the south. I also studied their expressions of anger and resistance. They looked very different from the anger and resistance being displayed on the faces of adults."

(the *Rent Collection Courtyard*) did this within the larger context of this particular machine-assemblage (the manor house) requires a step out of the courtyard back into the manor house proper, for the statues were but the most important lesson in a residence that had become what the Maoists at the time would call a classroom of class struggle.[38]

38 Wang Zhi'an describes the manor house as a classroom of class education in his book. See Wang Zhi'an, *The Heavens Thundered*, 19.

8

Anren

FRIEND AND ENEMY IN PEACE AND BENEVOLENCE?[1]

"Who are our enemies, who are our friends?" Mao Zedong once asked at the beginning of his revolutionary career.[2] By the end of it, the entire radical revolutionary movement of China would be posing the same question. This question came to be the opening line of Mao's *Selected Works* just as

1 Anren is the name of a small town in Sichuan that is the home of Liu Wencai's Manor House Museum and, more recently, the Jianchuan Museum Cluster. The characters that form a compound that make up the town's name are *an*, meaning peace, and *ren*, meaning benevolence.

2 *The Selected Works of Mao Tse-tung*, vol. 1, dates this remark back to a text from March 1926. See Mao Tse-tung (Zedong), "Analysis of the Classes in Chinese Society," 13. Schram and Hodes, however, have traced it back to December 1, 1925. See Schram and Hodes, *Mao's Road to Power*, 249.

it came to frame the opening gambit of his revolutionary politics.[3] It was a gamble that paid off. The revolution would turn China on its head just as the nature of that revolution would turn the political on its head. It would invert that famous dictum of Carl von Clausewitz that war was the continuation of politics by other means. Politics infused with intensity became the most extreme form of war by other means.[4] Here was a war machine, in the process of formation. As Clausewitz did cartwheels, the Chinese revolution showed that miracles could be made.

The communists survived the massacres of 1927, lived through the "extermination campaigns" of the 1930s, turned themselves into legends through the Long March, and set out a new mode of governance in Yan'an. Finally, they proved victorious with the defeat of Japanese imperialism and their own internal ally turned enemy, the Guomindang or Nationalist Party. Through struggle, the revolutionaries become masters of their own destiny. Rewritten by Maoist hagiographers as an anthropomorphized struggle between two "lines," this was destiny lived on a knife's edge.

The peace that the communists brought to China in the wake of their victory was, paradoxically, built on this ever-extending metaphor of war. War became a metaphor of life as the binary of class struggle was sutured into the "peace" the Communist Party spread into all domains of life. Moreover, it was extended with such detail that even the smallest cogs in this system gained existential meaning through the pulsating rhythms of the life-and-death struggles that the political realm produced and promoted.[5]

For those who are part of the movement, the political in moments of "high tides" (*gaochao*) is always a surge, a tidal bore, and felt personally as a cognitive "leap." In Maoism, such "leaps" were often produced by a series of machinelike operations designed to produce an intensification of the class struggle and to eclipse any other rendition of the political.

Clothed in the garb of struggle, the political becomes the all-defining, thus all-redefining question of the everyday revolutionary body. Collec-

3 I have made this argument before, as the opening gambit of Dutton, *Policing Chinese Politics*.

4 "Politics is war without bloodshed, while war is politics with bloodshed," says Mao in "On Protracted War" (May 1938). See Mao Tse-tung (Zedong), "On Protracted War," 153.

5 This is an effect of Mao's idea that, under socialism, class struggle actually intensifies.

tively, the people would learn to chant the words "class struggle" like a mantra and, in this way, the slogan "never forget class struggle" (*qianwan buyao wangji jieji douzheng*)[6] would be etched in the mind such that it became a habitual reflex when facing any problem. Moreover, it would also touch the subject individually and profoundly. "Struggle against self, criticize revisionism" (*dousi pixiu*)[7] became the catch-cry of this new Maoist revolutionary breed. In this way, the revolutionary government of China attempted to become one bio-disciplinary regime, tying cognitive knowledge and noncognitive affective knowledge to a collective ethos of struggle that also individualized by individualizing the means of self-rectification.

Machines of correction, then, were not just the preserve of the penal sector nor were they simply coercive. Rather, they become multiple in form and productive in their outcomes. They were the everyday "appliances" for channeling the energy of the political into a revolutionary positivity. Through the machinery deployed in the political and biopolitical spheres, the revolution would "world" the Maoist world such that the collective class enemy became the individual's own question as a figure.[8]

It is, of course, a truism to say that not all Chinese were seduced by this revolutionary process. Many within China did not support the revolution, much less feel the fervor that an intense political leap would produce. But herein lies the "tension" driving this particular flow of energy. The enemy would become a key component in the machinery of intensification. The enemy would be the key device to ignite and drive an energy flow that would then reconstitute the political. A large part of the power and intensity the revolution had at its disposal derived from any resistances it encountered that would be recoded as being "signs" of an "enemy." This technique of intensification stands in sharp contrast to the technologies by which energy was guided in traditional Chinese society. Where once harmony had been sought through balance, with the Maoist political, energy channeled through class struggle into a friend/enemy grouping was energy intensified.

6 *Qianwan buyao wangji jieji douzheng* comes from a slogan out of a speech by Mao Zedong given on September 24, 1962, at the tenth plenum of the 8th Central Committee. See *People's Daily Online*, "Nineteen Sixty-Two."

7 This term was coined by Mao on a tour of the regions in mid-1967.

8 Here I am merely reiterating a point Carl Schmitt makes when he says the "enemy is our own question as a figure." See Meier, *The Lesson of Carl Schmitt*, 44.

For the Chinese Communist Party, then, the friend/enemy dyad became central to the forward movement of the revolution, and it was this that framed their entire revolutionary history from 1926 up until 1976.[9] The state that emerged after 1949 was built on this fault line. It is a fault line along which coursed an energy flow that the state attempted to harness through a process of ongoing rechanneling. It was a form of experimentation designed to suture into the structure and operation of government an endless series of technologies of direction and incitement. The bold, simple, and crude dyadic formulation of friend and enemy, in being specified in this fashion, might splinter into a series of more complicated and complicating formulations, theories, and actions, but in all its diverse fields, it was always held together through a "principal contradiction" that guided the way for concrete, pragmatic, and detailed action. In this way, the machinery of state intervened to guide the flow toward an end point: productive revolutionary ends.[10]

The socialist state held a monopoly on these machine-assemblages of dyadic navigation and channeling. Government effectively became one long series of campaigns, institutions, and programs to establish a rhythm and channeling mechanism directing this binary of class struggle. Class struggle produced practices that were designed to propel a "continuous revolution" (*jixu geming*), and the machinery of state offered the Party the machinery through which it would attempt to direct the tidal bore productively toward revolutionary ends.[11] Read in this way, everything from Mao's "On Contradiction"[12] to the campaign to study an "All-Round Dictatorship of the

9 For the historical detailing of this particular argument, see Dutton, *Policing Chinese Politics.*

10 *Productive* and *positive* as used here are not morally loaded categories but terms employed to describe the usefulness to the ends "things" are being put.

11 This, at least, is what I have argued and hopefully shown in sufficient empirical detail in my earlier book *Policing Chinese Politics.*

12 "On Contradiction" was one of Mao Zedong's most important texts. Written prior to his full ascendency to leadership, it argued for the importance of the contingent moment over any notion of a transcendental binary. In presenting the possibility of primary, secondary, and tertiary contradictions it was, according to Louis Althusser at least, deeply anti-Hegelian. In allowing politics, not reason, to determine the rank order of contradictions it is perhaps more accurate to say that Mao's Hegel was more in tune with Kojève's reading of the master/slave relation than the original Hegelian dialectic. That, however, is an argument for another

Proletariat" could be rendered as different developments within, inflections of, and experiments about ways to channel the life-affirming / life-threatening dyadic force that enabled the political to pose its existential questions and threat. Read thus, the decision to open to the public the manor house estate of one of China's most notorious enemies, the despotic landlord Liu Wencai, falls into perspective.

Liu Wencai's Manor House Museum was one of the concrete sites where the theoretical explorations of channeling took on a material form. The Sichuan Provincial Cultural Bureau's 1959 promise to restore the manor house of Liu Wencai to its former glory was no simple act of conservation but an attempt to turn this Manor House Museum into a machine-assemblage for the channeling of political flows. The restoration of Liu Wencai's manor house as a *chenlieguan*, or "display site," was a moment when political theory would take on a concrete design form. The restoration and reform of the manor house was, therefore, part of a series of experiments into how best to channel the multiplicity of possibilities offered by affective energy flows into an intense political expression and experience.

The restoration work began with a call to local peasants from the Party's Cultural Bureau to return all property taken from the manor house.[13] With much of the property returned, some twenty or so "educators" were then brought in to curate and reorganize the household goods so that they could be used to serve the revolution. With class struggle as their "organizing principle,"[14] these curator-educators aimed to contrast the hard lives of the peasants outside the manor house with the hidden decadence and luxury that

---

time. For the official English translation of "On Contradiction," see Mao Tse-tung (Zedong), "On Contradiction." For an annotated translation of the original prewar manuscript, see Knight, "Mao Zedong's 'On Contradiction.'" For Louis Althusser's argument, "Contradiction and Overdetermination," see Althusser, *For Marx*, 89–128. Finally, for an elucidation of Kojèvian-Hegelianism, see Kojève, *Introduction to the Reading of Hegel*.

13 On August 30, 1959, the government call for all looted goods to be returned as preparations for opening the house as a museum gathered pace. See Wang Zhi'an, *The Heavens Thundered*, 134.

14 According to Wang Zhi'an, the key role of the museum at the beginning was restoration albeit reorganized to (1) highlight and expose crimes, (2) highlight the contrast between past and present China, (3) get former employees of the household to speak out, and (4) open ten exhibitions within the house and then invite the

lay within. This attempt to produce a shock effect by revealing a hidden history through the redeployment of found objects that originally existed within the manor house shares something of a family resemblance to the methods that would later be employed by Fred Wilson in his celebrated 1992 exhibition *Mining the Museum*.[15] Wilson's goal was to reveal institutional racism, not produce what one China scholar has called "class racism."[16] Nevertheless, he shared a general approach with the Manor House Museum's curators, which saw him reach back into the museum's archives to bring out objects that could be recurated to reveal a hidden, darker history behind the museum's display of past opulence. Where they differed was that Wilson used radical, sometimes horrifying, juxtapositions to highlight absences from the historical record,[17] whereas the Chinese curators, initially at least, believed the objects, if correctly displayed, could speak for themselves. "The exhibition only needs to let the genuine objects, the original material objects, speak the truth and they will expose the tyrannical feudal landlord class," one educator-curator was claimed to have said.[18] Display, it was thought, would reveal, enlighten, and educate. If that was what they hoped for, then the educator-curators were in for a shock.

"It all began with a bed," said the lead sculptor, Zhao Shudong, as he recalled the process that led him to Anren and to the creation of the *Rent Collection Courtyard* project. "It was a beautiful old bed . . . and when peasants came in and saw that rather opulent bed, instead of wanting to overthrow the old system, they looked upon it with awe."[19]

---

leaders to comment (which led to six more exhibitions being added). For details, see Wang Zhi'an, *The Heavens Thundered*, 135.

15 The exhibition was held at Baltimore's Maryland Historical Society in April 1992.

16 Leading scholar Lee Haiyan claimed the manor house produced "class racism." See Lee Haiyan, *The Stranger and the Chinese Moral Imagination*, 202. For an argument that suggests that although such discriminatory practices were horrific, they were not racist, and that, therefore, the Cultural Revolution was not like the Jewish Holocaust (as author and critic Ba Jin claimed), see Schwarcz, *Bridge across Broken Time*, 110–32.

17 See Stein, "Sins of Omission."

18 Wang Zhi'an quotes anonymous curators suggesting this. See Wang Zhi'an, *The Heavens Thundered*, 140.

19 Interview with Zhao Shudong in Chengdu, Sichuan Province, August 17, 2011.

"Too much of an emphasis on things and not enough on the landlord's crimes"[20] would be the complaint after the early openings of the manor house to the public produced little more than envy and jokes. Youths were overheard muttering things like "Wow, the landlords had such comfortable lives"[21] or "Liu Wencai's bed looks so comfortable! I'd be willing to die just for a chance to lie in it for a spell."[22]

Where Wilson had radically juxtaposed objects—silver goblets, urns and decanters, sitting next to a pair of rusty slave shackles; an old, gnarled whipping post in the center of a semicircle of ornate Victorian chairs labeled "Cabinet Making 1820–1910"; and busts of three white non-Marylanders next to three empty plinths of three famous Black Marylanders (to mark the absence of a history of enslaved Black people from the museum)—the Manor House Museum curators relied only on signage to carry their message. From the Party's perspective, these educator-curators had fallen into a form of "naturalism." "Culture and art are twins; they are one family. Getting closer to the reality isn't enough, that's a type of naturalism, and given the passing of time, the effects of such things will weaken. We need to be able to aid the exhibition, develop an ambiance so that model statues can be used to expose the tyranny of the landlords and enliven the people's hatred of the old society."[23]

Rather than Wilson's juxtaposition of found objects, however, the Party critique of "naturalism" led to fabrication, which was sometimes overt but often hidden. As an "advance command post [*qianyan zhendi*] in class education . . . every brick, tile, blade of grass and stick of wood [*yizhuan yiwa, yicao yimu*] should be used for one and only one purpose, . . . to circle around the facts of class struggle."[24] To circle around the facts of class struggle meant increasing the degree of political intensification, which, in turn, led to a "typification" of Liu as the embodiment of the crimes of the entire landlord class. Instead of merely exhibiting objects of wealth and decadence and hoping for indignation to result, the manor house exhibition now set about adding displays that would be aimed at producing it. Exaggerated descriptions of

20 Wang Zhi'an, *The Heavens Thundered*, 138.

21 Wang Zhi'an, *The Heavens Thundered*, 138.

22 Interview with Zhao Shudong.

23 Wang Zhi'an, *The Heavens Thundered*, 140.

24 Wang Zhi'an, Wang Fei, and Wang Shao, *The Secrets of the Manor*, 98, 144.

Liu's decadent, cruel, and evil lifestyle had been written on signage, but with low peasant literacy rates, the curator-educators focused on "visualization."

By 1960, seventeen small statues of "real events" were added to the Manor House Museum.[25] In 1961, a further eighty-seven sculpted exhibits were put on display. Created in the lamp case, or *dengxiang* style and made of wax, these statuettes further detailed Liu's alleged class crimes.[26] As a result of the success of these experiments, more figurines were added to the museum and more "crimes" attributed to Liu. Every statue carried a criminal accusation, until finally, in 1963, a series of small statuettes in gypsum called "The Display of 100 Crimes," or *Baizuitu*, led to Liu basically becoming a model of evil.

This diorama was said to have been very popular despite the fact that its statues were small and not well made. By this stage, however, for Liu at least, it didn't matter as he was being portrayed not just as a typical landlord, but as a stand-in for landlordism in general. His desire for wet nurses to supply him with human milk, not to mention his opium smoking, and his cruel treatment and cheating of the peasants were all being highlighted as the manor house gradually moved into its new role as a "classroom for class education" (*jieji jiaoyude ketang*) and a "battlefield against imperialism and revisionism" (*fandi, fanxue de zhanchang*).

With Mao's 1962 call to never forget class struggle ringing in their ears, the authorities set up a Reform the Exhibition Hall Committee which, by early 1964, had devised an elaborate plan for Liu and his manor house. Costing somewhere in the vicinity of 100,000 *yuan* (Chinese dollars), the reform of the manor house would see the exhibition divided into five sections, each of which would introduce Liu's many crimes, pointing to his cruel exploitation and oppression of the peasants and, finally, to the peasants' own spontaneous revolutionary resistance against him. Hanging over this entire exhibition would be the slogan "never forget class struggle."[27]

As if the statues detailing Liu Wencai's numerous crimes were not enough, another far more graphic exhibition, the *shuilao* (water dungeon), was being created in the dank, dark bowels of the manor house. Restored largely on the basis of testimony from the water dungeon's only alleged surviving victim,

25 Eight of these crimes were later said not to have even involved Liu. See Xin Jiyuan, "The New Era."

26 Wang Zhi'an, *The Heavens Thundered*, 137.

27 Wang Zhi'an, *The Heavens Thundered*, 144.

Leng Yueying, it was claimed that it was the site of Liu Wencai's most disgusting and heinous crime.[28]

Leng's tale of despair transformed her from a local cadre to a national model hero. From her lips came a harrowing tale of gothic proportions.[29] With her help came an exhibition displaying a floor covered with dank, dirty, and icy water, with a splattering of thin, watery blood stains covering the room and the hand marks of the wretched etched into the walls. The centerpiece, added in 1964, was an iron cage with triangular spikes at its base which was just big enough to contain one tortured human body.[30] Having created an "earth dungeon" of torture implements in one room above ground, and a water dungeon below, the stage was now set for a revolutionary extravaganza. With these additions, the museum was finally proving to be a huge success.[31]

"Oh, the water dungeon had so many people visiting it, you wouldn't believe it," said the sculptor Long Taicheng, who was on duty doing "reception work" at the museum in October 1965 when the dungeon was a major draw.

28 It was said at the time that Leng Yueying was "the other side of the coin to Liu Wencai." She gained something of a name for herself in the 1950s, as had Liu Wencai, but both were only local figures at that stage. Leng became nationally renowned only after her tales of horror from the water dungeon captured the nation's imagination. As the only survivor of it, she surfed the tidal bore of political intensity, becoming known as "Mama Leng" and eliciting teary responses from adults and children as she toured the country telling of her victimhood, before later, in the period of economic reform, being denounced as a fraud. See Xiao Shu, *The Big Landlord, Liu Wencai*, 24–25.

29 For a detailed account of the legend of the water dungeon and Leng's role in setting it up, see Xiao Shu, *The Big Landlord, Liu Wencai*, 23–41.

30 See Ming Hong, "The Manor House of the Liu Family," and Lee Haiyan, "The Enemy Within." Information on the timing of the addition of the cage and further details about the water dungeon came from an interview with Mr. Wu, the former head of the Manor House Museum exhibition, in the Jianchuan Museum Cluster, Anren, on August 18, 2011.

31 Although later denounced as a fraud, Leng would be interviewed by the sculptors of the *Rent Collection Courtyard* so that they could get a "feel" for that moment they were sculpting. For a convincing account of the role of the water dungeon, putrefied bodily parts, excrement, blood, and tissue all tied to the abnegation of the "enemy," see Lee Haiyan, "The Enemy Within." As far as I am aware, Leng now claims she was confused and taken to the house of a cousin of Liu Wencai, and in the cousin's house, not Liu's manor house, she was put in a water dungeon.

"It was just incredible. It was so crowded . . . the tours of it were nonstop."[32] Like a ghost-train ride into hell, the manor house was taking the peasant visitors on a wild ride that began with displays of decadence and ended with a gothic horror version of their own past. With gothic horror framing both the manor house and the biography of Liu, the man and the site captured the national imagination. By 1964, Liu's estate was attracting thousands of visitors daily.[33] By 1965, in an effort to "further the needs of the class struggle" and increase interest in the Manor House Museum, another major "theme" was developed. This one would simply be called the *Rent Collection Courtyard* exhibition.

Dramatically illustrating the tyrannical nature of the landlord system by the personification of the struggle, this display laid out, along the walls of the inner courtyard, life-sized, lifelike statues that depicted the tearful scene of rent being collected in kind. It immediately gained revolutionary acclaim in terms of its "class educational" value. Even during the Cultural Revolution, when Red Guards stormed this museum to "smash the Four Olds,"[34] the theme-park attractions of the *Rent Collection Courtyard* and the "water dungeon" remained open and on display. By this stage, the Landlord Estate Exhibition Hall had been renamed the "Class Education Exhibition of Sichuan Province, Dayi County."[35] The manor house was now a form of episodic theater with the opening scene being the display of opulence designed to produce indignation, the second scene being the "water dungeon" created to fill the audience with fear and dread, and the third act was the *Rent Collection Courtyard*, designed to instill anger and hatred against the landlord class. Each affective moment was designed to link to and build to the next, each scene designed to spark a specific set of emotional eruptions, each point of

32 Interview with Long Taicheng, 2011. Long was a first-year student in sculpture at the Sichuan Academy of the Arts when he was sent with his class to Anren to work on the *Rent Collection Courtyard*.

33 Wang Zhi'an et al., *The Secrets of the Manor*, 99.

34 "Smash the Four Olds," or *posijiu*, being old customs, old culture, old habits, and old ideas.

35 The first name change came in early 1959 in a document numbered 58, note 79, which changed the manor house to the Landlord Estate Exhibition Hall. See Wang Zhi'an, *The Heavens Thundered*, 131. In the autumn of 1966, the name was changed again, this time to the "Class Education Exhibition of Sichuan Province, Dayi County." See Wang Zhi'an et al., *The Secrets of the Manor*, 101.

the tour adding a further pressure point of intensification until a meridian line of revolution was created. Where a peasant had entered, a revolutionary would leave.

That was almost sixty years ago. The museum still stands today, but its name and role are no more. What was once named the Landlord Estate Museum, or a Class Education Exhibition, is now called the Liu Family Estate Exhibition. Class education long ago ceased to be its raison d'être, for it no longer functions as a machine-assemblage promoting and producing political intensity. Instead, the Manor House Museum now channels affective flows in a very different direction because, essentially, it now caters to an entirely different audience.

No longer part of a state-sponsored pedagogical technology of incitement, the manor house has been transformed into a state-sponsored heritage site. "Only the rich peasants and landlords can afford to visit the manor house now!" said one local peasant rather ruefully.[36] As the channeling of political intensity gives way to nostalgia, the manor house displays have been aestheticized and historicized. Gone are the descriptions that were designed to incite revolutionary fervor; gone, too, were the water dungeon and torture chamber after historic research revealed them to be fraudulent.[37] Now the focus was on historical accuracy and re-creation.

"A typical reflection of the nature and architectural form of landlord class estates in Sichuan in the modern era," says one contemporary tourist guidebook before going on to add that the manor house "epitomizes the rise and

36 As one local peasant rather wryly commented, no peasant could afford to go there anymore. Interview with one peasant who wished to remain anonymous (interviews undertaken in Anren, October 2004). His claim was slightly hyperbolic and only partly true. The museum is free to all local residents but outsiders must pay. From being free in the 1960s to only 20 Chinese cents in the 1970s, the museum-estate has gradually seen its ticket price rise as economic reform required the museum to pay for itself. In the 1980s, the price rose to $20 (Chinese), and by the 1990s it went up to $45 (Chinese).

37 The most significant changes in this regard came on April 5, 1988, when in an effort to return the manor house to its historically "accurate" form, curators dismantled two exhibitions completely. The water dungeon (*shuilao*) and the torture chamber (*xingxunshi*) were dismantled and "returned" to what was claimed to be their original use when Liu lived there. The water dungeon was said to be an opium storage space, and the torture chamber was said to have been a stable. See Wang Zhi'an et al., *The Secrets of the Manor*, 104. Interview with Mr. Wu.

fall of feudal class production in the modern era of China."[38] Indeed, the only telltale signs of its former role are the faded Maoist slogans on the exterior wall of the manor house and the continued occupation of the central courtyard by the mud figures of the *Rent Collection Courtyard* collection. Yet even this continued occupation by the statues was no longer quite the same as it once had been. Now encased in glass, the statues appeared more like prisoners to the past than revolutionary occupiers of the site.

In the service of the tourist industry, *Rent Collection Courtyard* is now described as an artistic masterpiece and viewed for the artisan skill that went into the making of the mud statues rather than the affective responses these statues were able to conjure up and tap into. A museum, which once operated as part of a vast "machine-assemblage" designed to produce and intensify a sense of fore-thrown-ment by intensifying class hatred, has been quietly and successfully transformed. The statues, the manor house, and indeed the town itself became part of a new assemblage that turned the township of Anren into a cultural hub. Rebuilt as a simulacrum of its own past, each and every museum, shop, and street has been rebuilt to produce touristic-historical nostalgia. In some respects, the long march of the Manor House Museum of Liu Wencai from revolutionary machine to tourist attraction plots the same trajectory as contemporary Chinese politics.

With the death of Mao and the demise of a state built on political intensity, the days of experimentation designed to transform state technologies into component parts of a war machine were over. Across the land, there has been a very public and comprehensive repudiation of the Cultural Revolution and class struggle, followed by a reassessment of Maoism. With Mao gone and class struggle no longer employed to mobilize the masses into ongoing political campaigns, the development of the productive forces became the Party's new mantra. Despite resting on claims of Marxist orthodoxy, early economic reforms proved to be a body blow to the older Maoist-Marxist body-politic based on developing the productive forces of political intensity. With the growing dominance of contract-based employment, with calls to obey the newly esteemed rule of law, and with the ongoing development of socialist market economics that gradually moved from the introduction of material incentives to a fully blown commodity economy, the question of friend and enemy became, like Liu Wencai's Manor House Museum, a matter of historical curiosity and (Red) tourist interest.

38 Wang Zhi'an et al., *The Secrets of the Manor*, 103–4.

"We came to Anren and the manor house because, when we were kids, we learned about Liu Wencai and therefore thought that it would be worth taking a look for ourselves," said the peasant tourists from Shaanxi as we chatted and sat sipping tea opposite the manor house in July 2010. Soon the Shaanxi peasants I was talking to were being called to join the rest of their tour group as they went off to visit another Red nostalgia site. They didn't have to travel far. Just down the road from the Manor House Museum and dwarfed by it is the huge privately owned Jianchuan Museum Cluster. One of Sichuan's leading property developers, Fan Jianchuan, had come to town and built a massive new museum complex that was designed, for the most part, to recall China's revolutionary past and induce a moment of Red nostalgia around that most troubling of postliberation political moments, the Cultural Revolution. As the tragedy of revolution gives way to the farce of phantasmagoric commodity production, the friend/enemy divide returns to Anren not as political incitement but as tourist nostalgia. It is on the flow of tourists, rather than the tidal bore of intensity, that this town begins to pin its hopes of revival.

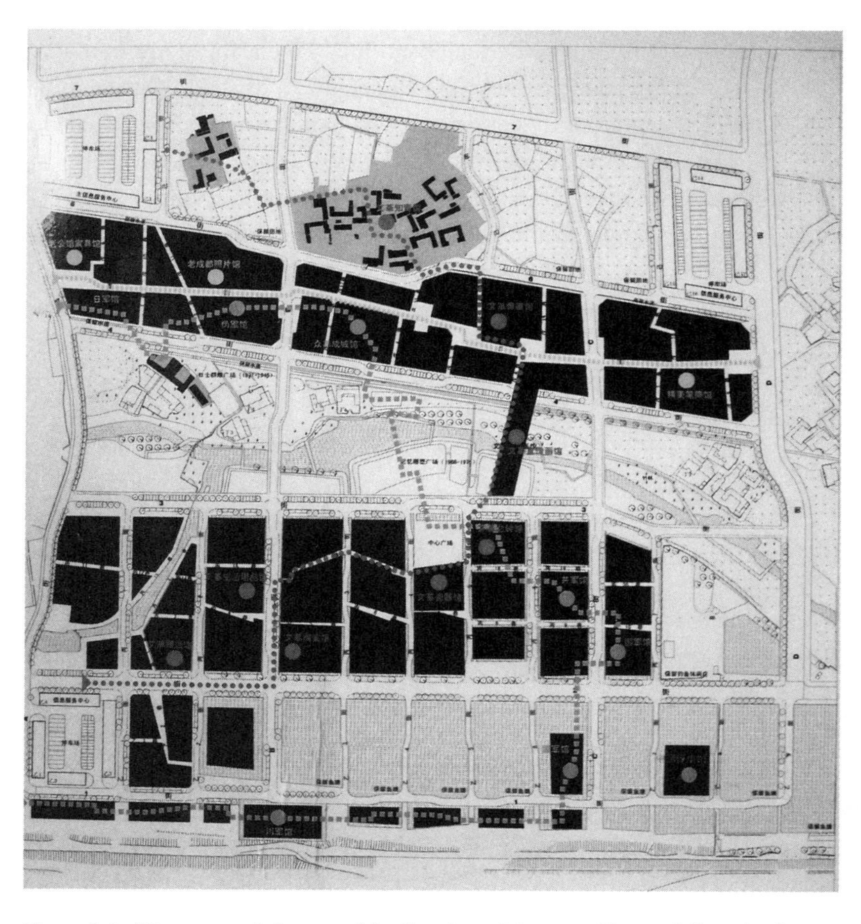

Figure 9.1. Diagrammatic layout of the Jianchuan Museum Cluster: follow the dots to Cultural Revolution. Anren, China, circa 2004. Photo by the author.

9

From Hiccup to Habit

FROM CULTURAL REVOLUTION TO CULTURE INDUSTRY

In 2004, plans were afoot in Anren for a new museum.[1] It would not replace Liu Wencai's historic Manor House Museum, but complement it. On 33.3 hectares of requisitioned land, China's first museum to the Cultural Revolution was about to be built.[2] It was designed to be the centerpiece of a plan to

1 For more details and different approaches toward this new museum, see Denton, "Can Private Museums Offer Space for Alternative History?" For an alternative way of tying the Manor House Musuem of Liu Wencai to this museum cluster, see Ho and Li, "From Landlord Manor to Red Memorabilia."

2 Following this publicity surrounding the announcement of the Anren museum project, a much smaller-scale museum was built in Shantou's Chenghai district in Guangdong Province. Founded by Peng Qi'an, a former deputy mayor of the city, the small pagoda-shaped museum to the Cultural Revolution was built with money raised from private donations, including, it is claimed, one from the Hong Kong billionaire Li Ka-Shing. See French, "Scenes from a Nightmare." For a very different approach to politics, see the contrasting approaches being taken to Fan

transform the small township of Anren into a cultural and tourist hub, and it was the brainchild of one of Sichuan Province's most successful sons, a developer and collector of Cultural Revolution and wartime memorabilia, Fan Jianchuan. With the Cultural Revolution at its heart, Fan wasn't just constructing a museum, he was reconstructing the political.

Ba Jin, the famed novelist, onetime anarchist, and prominent victim of the Cultural Revolution, first mooted the idea of recasting history through building a Cultural Revolution museum back in the mid-1980s. For Ba Jin, it would be dedicated to the victims and designed to ensure that it would never happen again. Nevertheless, while its goal was anti–Cultural Revolution, in terms of curatorial practices, it shared something of a family resemblance with curatorial practices adopted in the early days of the Manor House Museum. Both were overtly didactic, and both claimed to involve no more than laying out "real objects" to reveal new truths. Where the Manor House Museum had intended to show Mao-era peasants why class struggle was absolutely necessary, Ba Jin's classroom-museum to the Cultural Revolution, in contrast, would show them why it was absolutely necessary to avoid it. Of his own idea of a museum, Ba Jin would insist it must be a place where "masks would fall, each will search his or her own conscience, the true face of each one will be revealed, and large and small debts from the past will be repaid."[3]

To achieve this, however, Ba Jin did not turn to the early Manor House Museum practices when framing the idea of an anti–Cultural Revolution Museum; instead, he looked at the memorialization of the Jewish Holocaust.[4] It would be a museum designed to make those involved "take responsibility for the very act of . . . voluntarily forfeiting his [or her] individual responsibility," as the cultural critic Hu Ping put it.[5] Whether the Holocaust memorialization

---

Jianchuan's museum cluster and the only other Cultural Revolution museum, in Shantou, by Quartz, "Two Museums in China about the Cultural Revolution."

3 Ba Jin, *Random Thoughts, Volume* 5, 137.

4 Taking a strongly anti–Cultural Revolution stance, Vera Schwarcz nevertheless disagrees with Ba Jin and rejects the analogy he draws between the Cultural Revolution and the Holocaust. For Schwarcz, Mao's Cultural Revolution was a war of Chinese against Chinese in which, as she puts it, "every Chinese was, in principle, capable of total obedience to the Red Sun." That is to say, rehabilitation was possible in a way it was not with Hitler, who, as she notes, simply wanted Jews exterminated. Schwarcz, *Bridge across Broken Time*, 111.

5 Hu Ping, *The Thought Remolding Campaign*, 150.

could produce these desired effects is highly questionable,[6] but the strident Party opposition to Ba Jin's idea came not from the impossibility of producing the desired effect but from the way this effect, if it were produced, would implicate the Communist Party. For the Party, the Cultural Revolution was an event they wanted to brush over, if not airbrush out of their own history. The Party had, at the very beginning of the reform era, called for a total repudiation (*chedi fouding*) of the Cultural Revolution, and the last thing they wanted was a museum to remind the Chinese people of such a divisive issue for which they were responsible. Silence reigned while the Party struggled with the fear that any revival of the memory of Cultural Revolution spelled immediate political trouble for them. Ba Jin's proposal fell on deaf ears, but where he failed, the market succeeded. The appeal of the taboo alone made this idea a marketable commodity.

Enter the real estate developer Fan Jianchuan. Here was an entrepreneur with a bold, alternative vision not just for his private museum complex, but for the entire township of Anren. Jianchuan, whose name literally means "construct Sichuan," was about to reconstruct the small Sichuan township of Anren by turning it into a major cultural and tourist hub. In so doing, he would reveal the mechanisms by which a new set of technologies designed

6 The problem with this form of memorialization is that, as the French Jewish artist Christian Boltanski once said when asked if he would ever make a Holocaust memorial, "If one were to make such a memorial, one would have to remake it every day." Forty, "Introduction to the Art of Forgetting," 185. Boltanski is not the only critic. *Bus Stop* took eleventh place in an international competition held to select a design for the Holocaust memorial in Berlin. The designers published a 128-page booklet in the form of a timetable, listing Holocaust-related sites and telling how they could be reached by public transportation. Their entry was based on a critique of the static nature of traditional museum designs. They say, "We want to make clear that there is no need for monumental construction in order to commemorate the victims. The entire country and many parts of Europe are full of places and histories that must not be forgotten. A visit to a former concentration camp creates uneasiness; the earth trembles, and the knowledge of atrocious events as well as glimpses of devastating documents are seared into memory. It is a very strange idea that says that the incomprehensible can be experienced through tall concrete walls and narrow passages, or that a sense for the Holocaust can be simulated by a space attempting to generate a mixture of angst and meditation in the middle of the new capital." See Schnock and Stih, *Bus Stop*. I would like to thank John Reardon for this information.

to dissipate the effects of political intensity through the use of market veridiction was to be set in place.

With local government support, Fan acquired enough land (166.6 hectares) to enable him to build a housing project around his huge museum-cluster development plan. Travel time between the township of Anren and Sichuan's provincial capital, Chengdu, would be cut from two hours to just twenty minutes due to an eight-lane highway between them. With these developments, Anren would become not just a cultural and tourist hub, but also a gentrified satellite suburb of Chengdu.[7] The irony of the anticapitalist Cultural Revolution being the centerpiece of a museum that is itself the centerpiece of a capitalist, culturally driven urban-development plan is hard to miss. Yet such an irony also demonstrates how markets can turn anything into a "value" just as long as they can harness the "phantasy" element of the commodity form. Playing on what Svetlana Boym once called "restorative nostalgia,"[8] Fan's museum would, however, be as distant from the spirit of the Cultural Revolution as it was from the type of museum Ba Jin had envisaged.[9]

Ba Jin's dream was not so much being fulfilled by Fan Jianchuan's project as being channeled elsewhere. Fan's plans offered no hint of a social reckoning. Instead, his museum would redirect the flow of affective energy toward

7 In an interview with the main architect of the Jianchuan Museum Cluster project, Mr. Liu Jiakun, I was told that the land acquired by Fan Jianchuan was 166.6 hectares, with the museum occupying 33.3 hectares of it. The museum was to be the centerpiece of a new housing development that would be connected to the city of Chengdu by an eight-lane freeway. Interview with Liu Jiakun, Chengdu, December 2008.

8 Svetlana Boym uses the term *restorative nostalgia* to distinguish it from a more introspective form she names *reflective nostalgia*. Nostalgia, she notes, was institutionalized in the West in the mid-nineteenth century through the development of the museum. In this process, she argues, "The past became heritage." See Boym, *The Future of Nostalgia*, 15, 49–50.

9 Denise Ho and Jie Li make a different argument. They suggest that Fan Jianchuan has skillfully played the system, testing the limits of things by displaying within the museum cluster "guerrilla exhibits." Far from disagreeing, I would point out how, within the culture industry, appearing edgy pays. Take the Chinese cynical realist art movement (*wanshi xianshizhuyi*), which, at its peak, offered powerful financial rewards to any marketable rebel voice or trend. In other words, the significant coda enabling such a strategy was always the market. See Ho and Jie Li, "From Landlord Manor to Red Memorabilia," 28–29.

a pathway marked by the words "Red nostalgia." Where Ba Jin's dream museum wanted to channel affective energy toward an intense revelation, Fan's museum would dissipate that energy by producing a museum focused on nostalgia. Translating his own vast personal collection of Cultural Revolution memorabilia into a business proposition, Fan would sell the idea of a museum to Ba Jin's family as being Ba Jin's dream fulfilled and, to the local council and the Communist Party, as a business proposition with urban-development potential that reinforced the Party line: Anren as cultural hub, Anren as a local center of the Red tourist industry, Anren as part of the city's wealthy commuter belt. Granted, this was no easy "sell" to a Party that continued to harbor fears that Ba Jin's "large and small debts" may one day reappear on the debit side of socialism's ledger,[10] but with so many development opportunities flowing directly from this project, Fan's idea proved too tempting.

With the commissioning of this museum cluster, Anren could now boast two museums to the Cultural Revolution—one to a former enemy who was partly being rehabilitated (Liu Wencai), and the other to an erstwhile revolutionary friend (the Cultural Revolution) that could now only ever be comprehensively denounced. Behind such claims, however, lies something far more important than symmetry. Together, these two museums tell us something about the nature of China's transition from a regime built to harness political intensity into a regime of market veridiction that dissipates and transforms such energy flows. Together, these two museum complexes signal the end of an era of experimentation that was designed to use the dyadic intensity produced by the friend/enemy binary to propel the revolution onward. "Struggle" would now be remembered but only once it was quarantined behind glass cases and exhibited as something at a distance and as something of an abstraction.[11] While the Party would finally give permission for Fan's museum to go ahead, conditions were attached. One minor amendment to the museum's name was necessary before approval would finally be granted. "Just one thing," Fan's assistant said to me in Anren in 2004 before the museum was built, "please don't refer to this as a Cultural Revolution museum. If you

10 Zhu Shengguo, "What Is Being Managed at the Cultural Revolution Museum?"

11 According to Julie Makinen, the Cultural Revolution is just one of the "touchy" subjects that the Jianchuan Museum Cluster tackles. See Makinen, "China Museum Builder Lets History Speak."

have to call it something, call it a Cultural Revolution arts museum."[12] In the end, they settled on a far more prosaic title, the "Jianchuan Museum Cluster," for it was now to be much more than a Cultural Revolution museum.[13]

Where the Cultural Revolution had turned everything, including art, into the political, Fan was now turning everything, including the Cultural Revolution, into a Red tourist attraction, leading toward a nostalgic, proud nationalism. With a pavilion largely devoted to the display of Mao-era ration coupons, another to the porcelain statues and propaganda posters of that time, and, of course, one entirely devoted to the display of the once-ubiquitous Chairman Mao badge,[14] these artifacts of the political lost their intensity and induced only nostalgia. No tears, no enmity, and no spiritedness would be produced through this type of museum-machine. Instead, there was the simple act of distanciation, which enabled the display value of the artifacts to be appreciated.

Being neither a restoration of the Cultural Revolution–era spirit nor a display of artifacts to induce a shock effect, this museum produced an almost total separation of artifact and event while employing the mesmeric effects of those moments to recontexualize this historical event. The reclassification of objects produced a "total aestheticization of the use value of these artefacts."[15] The energy that had once powered a movement was now dispersed through a process of reclassification and artifact rearrangement. It was as though the

12 The assistant's words and request for it to be called a Cultural Revolution arts museum are echoed in an early article on this project in *Beijing Youth Daily*: "Beautiful Writings Give Birth to Evil Flowers."

13 While still centered on the Cultural Revolution, the museum cluster reflects the acquisition habits of the collector and owner of the cluster, Mr. Fan Jianchuan. Pavilions now cover his entire collection, including artifacts from the War of Resistance, embroidered shoes for traditional bound feet, and classical porcelain.

14 In the diagrammatic plan of the museum site (see figure. 9.1), one finds dotted pathways to all pavilion halls devoted to the Cultural Revolution. For further details of the pathways created within the Jianchuan Museum Cluster, even in its planning stage, see Wang Hua and Wang Li, *The Jianchuan Museum Cluster*, 179.

15 Susan Stewart argues, in fact, that not only do collections aestheticize artifacts but their aim is also never restorative. She goes on to argue that "in the collection, time is not something to be restored to an origin; rather, all time is made simultaneous or synchronous within the collector's world." Stewart, *On Longing*, 151–52.

magic of the Maoist "one big concept" had shattered and given way to another "big concept" centering on nostalgia, but undergirded by market veridiction. Yet, in the different curatorial practices adopted, the Manor House Museum and the Jianchuan Museum Cluster would become something of a microcosm of two modes of being political. Yet they were two modes that could only work within the larger social constellation that gave them both protean life.

In the era of a socialist market economy, Ba Jin's commitment to a moral crusade that would pick at the scars of the Cultural Revolution could never compete against political forces that wanted the stories suppressed and market forces that judged them only on their ability to garner profit—either by visitor numbers or by the sale of apartments. The politically dissipating effects of the commercial world that Fan's museum represented sidestepped Ba Jin's moralism by working on an altogether different enunciative plane. Far from producing a cognitive realization of personal responsibility, Fan's museum produced excitement, amusement, nostalgia, and, with nostalgia, a sense of distance. In Fan's museum, consumers and tourists alike could relax and amuse themselves, safe in the knowledge that there was distance between themselves and these "crazy" events. Nostalgia could reign as they encountered the sights and sounds of a Cultural Revolution tamed, taxonomized, and made into a sign of the curious rather than the threatening. In gathering communist paraphernalia in the hope of attracting tourists, Fan's project shares more in common with other postsocialist theme parks such as Lithuania's Stalin World than it does with either the original Manor House Museum exhibition or Ba Jin's Holocaust memorial.[16]

In such parks, the visitor is safe in the knowledge that they are sitting at the crossroads, not of revolution and reaction, but of knowledge and entertainment. Knowledge, in the form of the brief introductions and explana-

16 Lithuania's Stalin World was the creation of Viliumas Malinauskas, the so-called Mushroom King. Having made a fortune growing and selling mushrooms, Malinauskas used his money to create a theme park, Stalin World (officially known as Grūtas Park), featuring full-size state-produced Lenin statues, as well as statues of other communist leaders, badges, flags, hangings, and other paraphernalia of the Soviet era. These artifacts were transported from various parts of the eastern bloc to his tourist park, which had been specially designed as a concentration camp for visitors' amusement. See Anusaite, "Welcome to Stalin World!" For his efforts, Malinauskas was awarded the 2001 Ig Noble Peace Prize. See "The 2001 Ig Noble Prize Winners," 8.

tions that carry through a political rejection of the event; entertainment, in that each "display" then lifts the visitor out of the everyday as they recollect to their children their own life in hard times past. At the same time, all such parks and museums tend to draw on this sense of personal nostalgia and it is with this sense of nostalgia as its phantasmagoric "trump card" that Fan's museum turned the intensity of the past into a fantasy for the "real" world present.[17] This form of distanciation and abstraction enables the contemporary visitor to recall the event, but see it now only at a safe distance. Once again, the intolerable is made tolerable by a form of abstraction. And it is precisely in abstracting the Cultural Revolution from its political conditions of existence that the museum is reproduced as entertainment.

In this respect, Fan's museum would be quite different from Ba Jin's original concept. For Ba Jin, the museum would attempt to correct the record and remember "truth." That response, however, opens the way for disputation. Truth claims, after all, can always be countered and contradicted and, as they fall into dispute, they raise the prospect of renewed intensity. Truth always asserts a righteousness that is alien to the commodity world. The dynamics of the commodity world are not fueled by attempts to prove truth but are driven by the commodity's need to prove itself desirable and profitable. Attempting to prove a truth is to enter into a quest for justice. This quest is alien to the commodity world, for only truth quests can drink that heady elixir we call justice. The commodity offers another truth, registered on an altogether different plane. In the everydayness of a fully commodified world, veridiction comes in the form of growth through sales. Being challengingly seductive rather than challenging, the commodity world offers the capacity to compress the space in which a counterpoint can emerge. A truth claim can always be challenged but how does one challenge a theme park? In transforming the objects of the Cultural Revolution into a taxonomized form of exhibit, the Jianchuan Museum Cluster is, therefore, less like Ba Jin's museum of historical correction and more akin to Sigmund Freud's explanation of a joke. Why? Because jokes, like the commodity form and like the museum cluster, produce no stable counterpoint.

Jokes, by inducing laughter, create a means of countering truth claims by undercutting rather than challenging substantive argument. Where arguments are based on reason that builds into a case that will draw the listeners

17 For, as Schmitt observes, "history can be turned into a romantic use as well." Schmitt, *Political Romanticism*, 69.

over to its side, the joke endeavors simply to push the criticism out the window and laugh at it as it falls. Jokes fight a war of maneuver with truth claims and, in that war, says Freud, "There is no doubt that the joke has chosen the method which is psychologically the more effective."[18] This is because truth can only ever act in a solemn fashion. Truth can only ever act from a position that asserts righteousness and this, in turn, is always open to the charge that it is humorless. The joke, therefore, offers a form of enjoyment that is forbidden to reason, for it is a form of discourse taking us beyond reason.[19]

In this respect, jokes offer a means of subverting humorless political truth claims. Like theme parks, jokes potentially change our perspective on things without the need for the clamorous dichotomization that works in the language of either/or. Jokes are disarmingly seductive and position an opponent in a way that withdraws from them the possibility of declaring a winning hand. In changing our position by challenging our perception, they nevertheless produce techniques that can lead back into the world of politics. "He who wants to kill most thoroughly," says Nietzsche, "laughs."[20]

The two museums of Anren form the perfect, if petrified, metaphor of the political-past as viewed from the present. Indeed, with the Cultural Revolution pavilions within the Jianchuan Museum Cluster on one side of town and the mothballed technologies of political intensification within Liu Wencai's Manor House Museum on the other, this small town becomes a spatial depiction of the mummified friend/enemy divide. These two museums, therefore, constitute two models for a museum of the political. Seventy years after Mao first gave birth to his revolutionary question "Who are our enemies, who are our friends?" Anren's museums of the political attempt to put this question to bed, by putting all exhibits behind glass, in temperature-controlled and sanitized environments. If, in Göttingen, politics rendered in stone failed to generate political intensity so, too, in Anren, the glass cases block any excitations of political passion. In other words, if Göttingen failed to generate intensity, neither does Anren. Intensities, it seems, require more than machines; they require contexts. In a climate of limited opposition, pessimistic fatalism, and a hefty dose of capitalist idealism, the social landscape of Anren, like China more generally, is being transformed, with the two museums of

18 Freud, *Jokes and Their Relation to the Unconscious*, 6:184.

19 Freud, *Jokes and Their Relation to the Unconscious*, 6:177.

20 Nietzsche, *Thus Spoke Zarathustra*, 324.

Anren flagging processes of modernization and development that highlight this process of rechanneling. Such rechanneling is designed to aestheticize the dangerous elements within the political. Unlike Göttingen's plaque to the deserter, however, the Cultural Revolution pavilions within the Jianchuan Museum Cluster are attempts to aestheticize the political such that former technologies of intensification (be they badges, books, sayings, or posters) become, in a diverse range of ways, "collectables" and things of one's youth, not quite art but tugging on the heartstrings. The association of the Cultural Revolution pavilions within the Jianchuan Museum Cluster with the Manor House Museum of Liu Wencai brought to mind Adorno's phrase about a Taylorization of the mind but it also led me to recall Walter Benjamin's claim that museums were the "secret blueprints" of the industrial exhibitions.[21] Benjamin would make this claim while examining the legacy of the Crystal Palace.[22] It is, perhaps, time for us to do the same.

21 Benjamin, *The Arcades Project*, 176, G/G2a, 6.

22 Benjamin, *The Arcades Project*, 182–84, G/G5.2–G6a.2.

PART 4

Becoming Modern

Figure 10.1. *Prospectus Turris Babylonicae* (view of the Tower of Babel). From Cruyl, *Prospectus Turris Babylonicae*, 40.

10

From the Crystal Palace to the Eiffel Tower

The age of reason under the influence of the market led to a "world dominated by its phantasmagorias," says Walter Benjamin, and it is this, he adds, that we have come to call "modernity."[1] How the phantasmagoric became central to modernity and the route modernity would take lead us back to Jerusalem and revelation.

In the beginning, there was the word, and it was the quest to recover that word that would mark early European thought by shaping early modern intellectual inquiry. The quest would begin biblically on the plains of Shinar, where Noah's three sons, Shem, Ham, and Japhet, attempted to build a tower so tall that it would touch the gates of heaven (figure 10.1). Guilty of the sin of pride, God's response was as swift as it was devastating. He would turn their search into a curse that would haunt Christendom until the nineteenth century.

1 See Benjamin, *The Arcades Project*, 26.

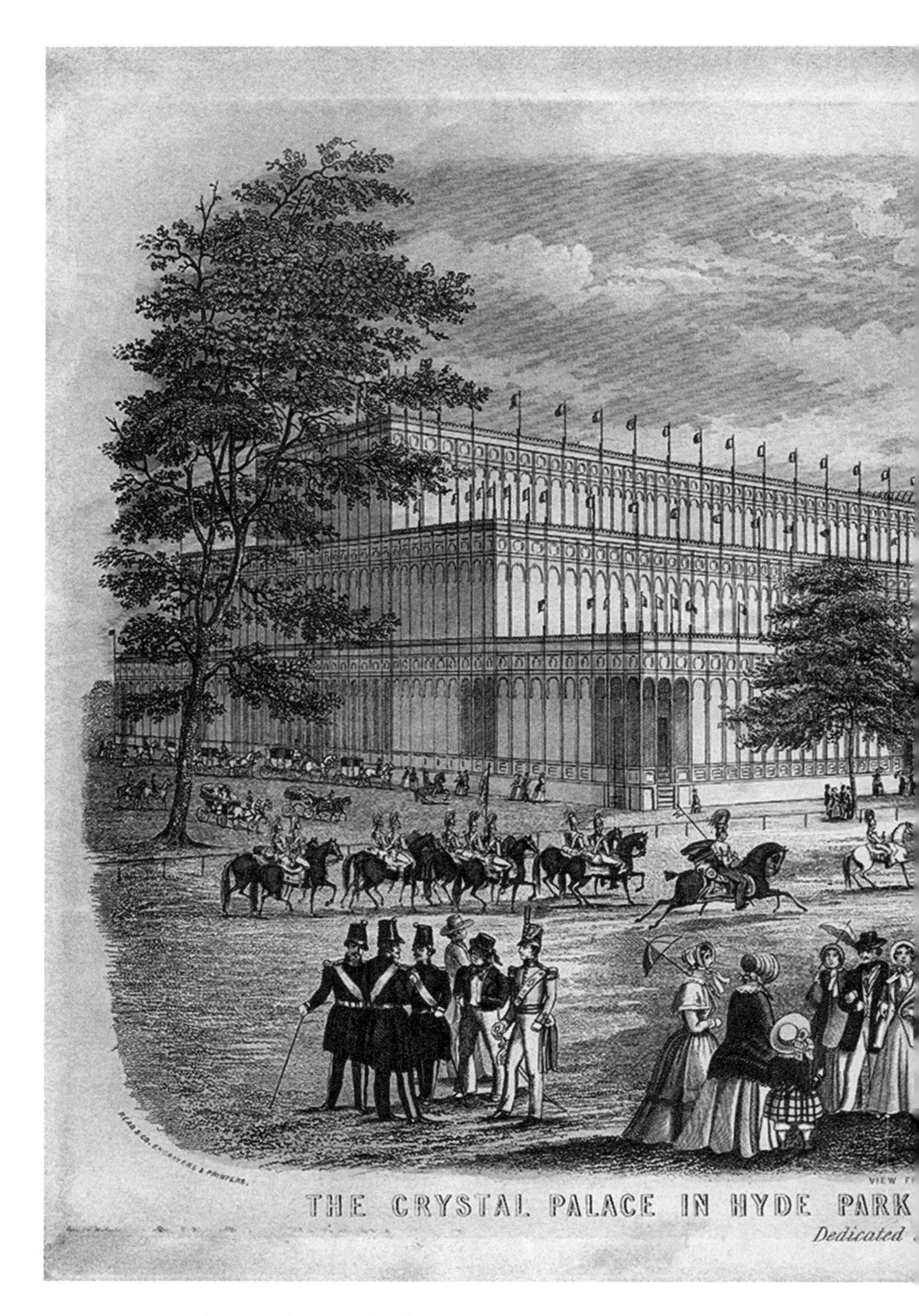

Figure 10.2. Read & Co, *The Crystal Palace in Hyde Park for Grand International Exhibition of 1851*, Harvard Art Museums / Fogg Museum, transfer from Photograph Collection. Photo © President and Fellows of Harvard College, M22958.

10, JOHNSON'S CT, FLEET ST, LONDON.
D OF
D INTERNATIONAL EXHIBITION OF 1851.
mifsioners.

Where once "word" and "thing" had been one and people united, after Babel, there was a scattering of "peoples" and a confounding of tongues. Words, which were once thought to be important in humanity's attempt to unravel the mysteries of God and the cosmos,[2] gave way to a very gradual acceptance that what humans faced was what John Locke would come to call the "trick of words."[3] Nevertheless, whether starting from the book of the original scribe, Enoch,[4] or following a pathway leading back to Babel, all roads led through language toward what Jacques Derrida once described as the theological prejudice.[5] That is to say, from the sixteenth century onward, "in becoming Bible-conscious, Europe became Babel-conscious."[6]

2 Note, for instance, Luther's remark on Adam: "What an ocean of knowledge and wisdom there was in this one man!" It was a wisdom because there was no distinction between word and thing. For Locke, of course, the idea of no distinction is simply a "trick," as this distinction between the word and thing is inevitable. Locke saw words as signs of ideas and language itself as a human invention. Words had no essence that would tie them back to objects any more than languages were divinely inspired. The whole idea of a search for an original universal language was, therefore, for Locke, a complete misunderstanding of the nature of words and language. For more details, see Aarsleff, *From Locke to Saussure*, 42–83.

3 For a much more detailed examination of the effects of the discipline of philology in the spawning of this quest, see Dutton, "Lead Us Not into Translation."

4 While some have regarded Enoch as "the scribe" and therefore become interested in the language in which he wrote, Augustine believed that Enoch, the seventh generation from Adam, was simply too ancient to be a reliable witness, and that his book, therefore, could not be included in the ecclesiastical canon, for false things may have been inserted in it. I wish to thank Allen Kerkeslager (Department of Theology, St. Joseph's University, Philadelphia) for his help in positioning Enoch in this debate.

5 See Derrida, *Of Grammatology*, 323n3. Hans Aarsleff also puts stress on this theological prejudice, calling it Adamicism, explaining contra Foucault that it went well beyond the question of "resemblance," for it was too infected by religious concerns to be reduced to a seemingly semiotic or linguistic role. For the Jesuit Louis Marin, too, Foucault's reading in *The Order of Things* suffers because of its lack of attention to the theological, thereby making the linguistic history appear too simplistic and secular. For details, see Aarsleff, *From Locke to Saussure*, 2; Marin, *Food for Thought*, 4.

6 Bodmer, *The Loom of Language*, 444.

The search for the original language would take many forms but it would always involve sacred scripts and arcane and defunct languages.[7] Whether it began as a search for sacred root words through comparative studies of verbs and nouns,[8] through Kabbalist techniques revealing hidden textual meanings,[9] or with the valorization of nonphonetic languages that, because they were pictographic, were thought to reduce the gap between word and thing,[10] the desire for the original language of Adam produced new techniques of scholarly language inquiry. Techniques designed to enable a pathway back to the original language of Adam gradually gave way to a scholarly interest in the structure and syntax of language itself. As "the word" gave way to the sentence, the search for an original perfect language gave way

7 With Babel viewed as history and the Bible as fact, early Christian scholars of the Western world not only set out to rediscover the original language, but also used the Bible as their guide. Naturally, this led all the early fathers of the church—from Origen to Augustine—back to Hebrew, but it also generated a range of counterclaims. Apart from the influential coupling, that Derrida would refer to as the "Chinese" and "Egyptian" prejudice, there were a vast array of other pretenders. Luther, for example, believed German to be the closest language to the language of God, while Becanus posited a "Flemish thesis." One of the most bizarre claims comes from Andre Kempe, who demonstrated that an anti-Gallic tradition was alive and well even in the seventeenth century. Kempe argued that while God spoke to Adam in Swedish and he responded in Danish, Eve was being seduced by a French-speaking snake! By this stage, as Umberto Eco notes, such claims were coming close to parody, yet it is important to note that all such claims tell us a little about the way in which national identity was being forged through the formulation of claims about the privileged status of the language of their peoples. One can see, in these very early and crude attempts to render one's own national language as sacred, the beginnings of claims that would later lead to a wedding of language, race, and privilege. With this homology, an "Aryan thesis" becomes possible and imaginable. See Eco, *The Search for the Perfect Language*, 49. More generally, see Olender, *The Languages of Paradise*, for details on this period.

8 On the importance of the verb, see Foucault, *The Order of Things*, 92–96.

9 Eco makes a distinction between the Kabbalist techniques of Raymond Lull's *Ars Magna*—"About logic we will be brief, for it is to talk about God," he would thunder—and the theological movement relating to the Torah, yet both would still share a faith in a return to the word. See Eco, *The Search for the Perfect Language*, 69.

10 Nor was this purely religiously inspired. With algebra at this time starting to become part of the new language of science, interest in the use of characters grew alongside interest in the use of symbols. See Dutton, "Lead Us Not into Translation," 511.

to a desire for a language key. This, in turn, led not only to the "unlocking" of old languages but to the invention of new "rational and scientific" ones. Techniques of decipherment, the art of military decoding, not to mention the more recent artificial languages that underpin the contemporary virtual world, were all products of this shift in knowledge toward "a universal matrix for all languages."[11] This desire led straight into logarithmic and algebraic principles[12] and, from there, straight into the arms of what Peter Sloterdijk has labeled a "faith in the geometric."[13]

Herein lies what appears to be a return to the tension that Leo Strauss believed exists between Jerusalem and Athens, but for Sloterdijk the route to this question of faith was not via the city, but by sea. For Sloterdijk, the risks attached to the life-defining and life-threatening journeys of early European adventurers, conquerors, and seafarers demanded faith. Faith, he suggests, was confirmed in their acts of adventure.[14] For Sloterdijk, world history begins with the miracle of their safe return. Moreover, it was a miracle that also yielded a bountiful material harvest. God had given these voyagers a vocation, rewarded them with wealth from another world, and, most importantly of all, revealed to them that their world was, in fact, spherical.

With this revelation, the world became whole and, over time, this faith in a spherical world became a more generalized faith in the laws of science and their technical application to concrete this-world problems. Across all fields, knowledge would gradually be reorganized into this systematic and scientific form, then translated into a series of techniques that would lessen the risks associated with travel.[15] This, insists Sloterdijk, was modernity's insurance

11 Eco, *The Search for the Perfect Language*, 49.

12 Bodmer, *The Loom of Language*, 443–44.

13 Sloterdijk, *In the World Interior of Capital*, 161.

14 Sloterdijk is obviously drawing on a Nietzschean tradition: "The free man is a warrior," Nietzsche would tell us. What characterizes this freedom? Not the warrior's individuality but his or her (individual) willingness to chance life, to be willing to die for a cause. In contrast, to plot a path of life is but "a short step away from tyranny, right on the threshold of the danger of servitude," Nietzsche tells us. See Nietzsche, *Twilight of the Idols*, 65.

15 While Sloterdijk wrote of this discovery as initiating a move from cross to orb, for Michel de Certeau, it was a shift from the exegetical to the "scientific" and signaled a movement from symbol (where hidden textual meanings were interpreted

policy. As its terms and conditions were laid out, faith in God would lead into a belief in the power of technology. Technology diminished risk, enabling safer passage of people and things, and opened the way, eventually, for global trade. Modern logistics were a founding technology of global trade and, as Stefano Harney and Fred Moten remind us, established the basis for the "first great movement of commodities, the ones that could speak."[16] Global trade as slave trade, imperialism as battering ram, and colonial occupation as a consequence, all covered by the cloak of theology; these do not feature in Sloterdijk's "enframing" of the world, which for him, was made up of markets syncopated with the diminution of risk.[17] With (white) risk diminished, discovery gave way to the regularization of trade routes and the regularization of a generic calculable commodity form. With this, the ships of the adventurers gave way to what Sloterdijk would call "real floating capital."[18]

"With every ship that is launched," says Sloterdijk, "capital begins the movement that characterizes the spatial 'revolution' of the Modern Age: the circulating of the earth made possible by financial investment and its successful return to its starting account. Return of investment—this is the movement of movements that all acts of risk-taking obey."[19] From then on, journeys would be built around a written bill of lading, rather than as an adventurer's tale. Journeys that were gradually brought into a system of capitalist risk calculation therefore flowed along a channel circumscribed not just by cartographic charts but also by Marx's expression M—C—M′.

This dual journey caused the tectonic plates of knowledge, economy, and understanding to shift away from the concerns of Babel. Faith in the one true God of Christendom would remain but, gradually, the ways of approaching the question of the Almighty started to change. A new vocabulary

---

by authorized commentary) to the "cipher" (where analytical techniques offered a "totalizing taxonomy" and "universal instruments" to ensure "comprehensiveness"). On cross to orb, see Sloterdijk, *In the World Interior of Capital*, 161. On symbol to cypher, see de Certeau, *Practices of Everyday Life*, 74.

16 Harney and Moten, *The Undercommons*, 92.

17 For the way the world would be enframed as a world of trade through the world exhibitions, see T. Mitchell, *Colonising Egypt*, 34–62.

18 Sloterdijk, *In the World Interior of Capital*, 83.

19 Sloterdijk, *In the World Interior of Capital*, 84.

of understanding humanity's relationship with the world and with God was coming into being.

From the late eighteenth century onward, the quest for "the word" gave way to new meanings and a proliferation of new words. Old words, like *economy*, began to be used much more precisely to demarcate a very specific domain that drew it away from any vestige of the old Greek word *oeconomy*.[20] By the middle of the nineteenth century, words like *objectivity* came into being and they were soon joined by other words, like *scientist* (1833), *physicist* (1840), and *prehistoric* (1851).[21] This avalanche of words, however, marked the shift from concerns built around Babel to a new world of concerns captured concretely in the creation of what some have called Babel's ante-type, the Crystal Palace (figure 10.2).[22]

Where Babel sought the recovery of knowledge, the Crystal Palace sought its production. Where the beginning for Babel was "the word," the Crystal Palace generated a multitude of new technical terms[23] as an epiphenomenon of the new world it was helping to create. Neither a founding moment of that

20 "The word 'economy' which in the sixteenth century signified a form of government, comes in the eighteenth century to designate a level of reality, a field of intervention through a series of complex processes." Foucault, "Governmentality," 93.

21 On the dates for the word *objective*, see T. Mitchell, *Colonising Egypt*, 19. The word *scientist* was coined by William Whewell: "In response to a challenge by the poet S. T. Coleridge in 1833, Whewell invented the English word 'scientist'; before this time the only terms in use were 'natural philosopher' and 'man of science.'" Snyder, "William Whewell." *Prehistoric man* was "a term that the Victorian archaeologist and anthropologist Daniel Wilson coined in the year of the Great Exhibition" (1851), in his book *The Archaeology and Prehistoric Annals of Scotland*. The term was defined as those "specimens of humanity almost completely 'unaffected by those modifying influences which accompany the development of nations.'" See Young, "Mission Impossible," 12–13 (quoting Wilson, Prehistoric Man, vii). See also Wilson's 1851 book, *The Archaeology and Prehistoric Annals of Scotland*.

22 On the claim that the Crystal Palace was the ante-Babel, see John Tallis who quotes "one wiseacre," who, at the time of the exhibition, said that "the Great Industrial Exhibition was only the revival of its ante-type, the Tower of Babel." For further details on this, see Tallis, *Tallis's History and Description of the Crystal Palace*, 335.

23 Melvyn Bragg notes that it was at the Crystal Palace that the terms *self-acting mill*, *power loom*, *steam-press*, and *cylindrical steam-press* first appeared. See Bragg, *The Adventure of English*, 239.

new era nor its full embodiment, the Crystal Palace nevertheless constitutes a point at which the movement from the word to the thing becomes concrete in the West. The Crystal Palace gave things new meaning as they were routed through imperialism and the circuits of capital. It would constitute a gradual reworlding that would organize life around the logic of markets, machines, money, and science, drawing them into new, ever-extending domains and, in so doing, create a new ecosystem.[24] The Crystal Palace became the showcase of this process of growing market veridiction.

Built as a temporary structure in London's Hyde Park in 1851 to house the world's first Expo[25]—the Great Exhibition of the Works of Industry of All Nations—the Crystal Palace was a massive glass structure, designed around a central nave that proved to be as inspiring as any cathedral.[26] Where before

24 For some in the religious community, the Crystal Palace was Belshazzar's feast revisited. The Crystal Palace was, after all, uniting humanity through trade in the way Babel had attempted to through language when God had made his judgment. As one text noted, "The reversing of the judgement at Babel is left for the kingdom of God at Jerusalem. He that scattered must gather." See V., *Belshazzar's Feast in Its Application to the Great Exhibition*, 11.

25 There were many national exhibitions that predated the Great Exhibition, although what is not in dispute is the unprecedented scope of the Great Exhibition of 1851—namely, that it was the first that had aspirations to be international. D. Eldon Hall alleges that "the Marquis D'Aveze collected an 'Exhibition of Native Art Manufactures' in 1798. . . . [This] was followed up and enlarged by . . . Napoleon, whose instinctive sagacity quickly appreciated the stimulus which rivalry and pride would lend to the industrial resources of the country." "Belgium and Holland have . . . held 'National Exhibitions,' modelled upon the French system. . . . Germany, Spain and Portugal also had, to a greater or less extent, these National Fairs. But it remained for the Anglo-Saxon race ('that nation of shop-keepers,' as Napoleon called it), to develop, in its widest form, the fraternity of commerce, and the possibility of universal peace." Hall, *A Condensed History*, 6–10. After Henry Cole visited the 1849 Paris Exhibition, with plans afoot for a British Exhibition, Prince Albert said to Cole, "It must embrace foreign productions . . . it must be international." Quoted in Beaver, *The Crystal Palace*, 13.

26 Church architecture was commonly used to describe the Crystal Palace: its main body, running east to west, was called the nave. Leapman, *The World for a Shilling*, 10. Patrick Beaver also comments on this: "One cannot help being struck by the ecclesiastic terminology and religious sentiments that pervade much of the contemporary comment on the Great Exhibition. Queen Victoria was 'filled with devotion,' while *The Times* felt a 'sense of mystery' and referred to the Throne of

Babel there had been a desire for the unity of "word" and "thing," after the Crystal Palace, the focus was firmly focused on the desire for the "thing," and this "thing," as a commodity form, began to contour life itself. "Crystal Palace was an event distinguished by its capacity to engender universal consensus by material means," claimed Paul Young, and with the commodity form as its material means it promised a new tomorrow.[27]

It was Prince Albert who pointed to the lingering shadow of theology that still hung over this new tomorrow in his speech opening the Crystal Palace exhibition. In a speech which, quite graphically and remarkably, captured the shifting tectonic plates of thought at this time, Albert argued that the laws of science were none other than "the laws by which the Almighty governs His creation." Because science could make these laws into a "standard of action," he said, it had enabled humanity "to conquer nature to his use."[28] Science, in discovering "the laws of power, motion and transformation," thereby enabled industry (i.e., the "standard of action") to dominate nature. Being modeled on a greenhouse, the architecture of the Crystal Palace building reinforced this sense of dominance over nature. The greenhouse was, after all, one of the earliest technologies enabling humans to overcome nature by controlling the atmosphere. It enabled plant life to grow and flourish anywhere at any time under any conditions, just as long as it was protected by the greenhouse structure. The Crystal Palace was a massive industrial-sized greenhouse within which plant life from across the globe—even Hyde Park's own famous giant elms[29]—joined the industrial fruits of labor and flourished to-

---

God. The building itself was described in terms of church architecture—the nave, the aisle, and the transept—while the opening ceremony with its organs, choirs, prayers and Hallelujahs resembled a cathedral service." See Beaver, *The Crystal Palace*, 42.

27 See Young, "Mission Impossible," 39.

28 Prince Albert's speech at Mansion House, London, March 21, 1850, to launch the Public Campaign for the Exhibition of 1851 was the same speech he gave at the opening of the exhibition. See T. Martin, *The Life of His Royal Highness the Prince Consort*, 247–48. It is also reproduced in Prince Consort Albert, "Speech at the Banquet Given at the Mansion House," 110–13.

29 When public concern was raised about Hyde Park's famous elm trees, Paxton's answer was simple: he designed the transept with a semicylindrical vault elevated 112 feet above ground, which could accommodate a whole row of elms. Benjamin, *The Arcades Project*, G6, G6a, 1, 183.

gether. This greenhouse-based fantasy of a new world coming to life would therefore be built on the power of humanity and industry to actually transform nature. Indeed, the process of building the Crystal Palace was itself a demonstration of that power.

It took only ten months to construct what was, at the time, the largest prefabricated building in the world.[30] Prefabrication enabled rapid assembly and disassembly. Both were essential. Rapid assembly was necessary because of the limited time for construction work before the exhibition was due to open, and rapid disassembly was necessary because of the contractual obligation to ensure a rapid reestablishment of Hyde Park to its original condition after the exhibition ended.[31] Prefabricated components produced in factories around the country were transported to the Hyde Park site by a new national railway system.[32] Once on site, workers then assembled the 1,060 iron columns

30 The new mass-production factory and site processes enabled them to build what was, according to Thomas Markus, a huge shed made of iron, glass and timber. See Markus, *Buildings and Power*, 225. Benjamin quotes Albert de Lapparent, *Le Siecle du fur* (1890), who noted that the cast-iron girders were hollow and thus easy to transport, hence "their chief merit was that they were economical. . . . Moreover, the execution of the plan was remarkably rapid, since all the parts were of a sort that the factories could undertake to deliver quickly," Benjamin, *The Arcades Project*, 167, F7, 6.

31 Details of the contract were as follows: "Mr Paxton . . . encouraged by the gracious approbation he met with from Prince Albert . . . went forthwith to Messrs. Fox and Henderson, to ask them if they would make a tender for the building on his plan, which they accordingly did. . . . The contract was finally taken by these gentlemen for the sum of £79,800, and the materials after the close of the Exhibition; or for £150,000 if the building should be permanently retained. This was subsequently proved to be the lowest practicable tender that was submitted to the Building Committee; and not the least admirable thing connected with it, was the wonderful quickness and exactitude with which the necessary estimates were formed. . . . By the aid of the electric telegraph and railway parcels, the great iron masters and glass manufacturers of the north were summoned to come up to town on the Monday, to contribute their several estimates to the tender for the whole. . . . Within one week from this meeting, the cost of every pound of iron, every inch of glass and every pound of wood required for the building was calculated, and every detailed working drawing prepared." Tallis, *Tallis's History and Description of the Crystal Palace*, 10–11.

32 "It was on the 30th of July, 1850, that possession of the ground was obtained; on the 26th of the following September the first pillar was fixed. . . . Thursday, the

holding in place 300,000 panes of glass and secured by 200 miles of sash bars. Prefabrication, lighter building materials, and the scientific division of labor combined to enable the construction of this building with industrial speed. The prince marveled at the building and at the "great principle of the division of labour" that had produced it at record speed. The division of labor, he went on to say, "may be called the moving power of civilization."[33] For Prince Albert, the division of labor was, therefore, almost a divine mission. Even those of a more secular persuasion knew its power.

Adam Smith, of course, regarded the division of labor as being the single most important factor in the wealth of nations,[34] while Marx regarded it as constitutive of the growth and development of advanced capitalism. For Marx, it was through this division that labor-power was interpolated into the operations of the advanced capitalist production system. This full integration of labor-power Marx came to call real subsumption. He would contrast this with formal subsumption, which only incorporated production processes through the money economy and left the structural, social, and historic forms of production "intact."[35] The Crystal Palace was an admixture of goods drawn from both realms of production but privileged only the most advanced. As if to underline the dominance of real subsumption, it established a competition designed to stretch across the world of industry, but which would, in actuality, privilege only those items produced under the most advanced conditions

1st of May, the auspicious day, at length arrived—the day originally fixed upon . . . when England's queen, attended by the nobles and proudest of the land, should in her own person open to the admiring world a palace more glorious than the sumptuous abodes of royalty." Tallis, *Tallis's History and Description of the Crystal Palace*, 11–21.

33 With this suggestion Karl Marx would agree because the idea that labor creates all value is but a secularization of the general principle Prince Albert makes in his speech opening the Exhibition of 1851. For details of that speech, see Albert, "Speech at the Banquet Given at the Mansion House."

34 "The greatest improvements in the productive powers of labour, and the greater part of the skill, dexterity, and judgement with which it is anywhere directed, or applied, seem to have been the effects of the division of labour." Smith, *An Inquiry into the Nature and Causes of the Wealth of Nations*, 13.

35 For a more detailed analysis of the relationship of formal and real subsumption in relation to questions of temporality, history, and culture, see Harootunian, *Marx after Marx*.

of production. While formal subsumption functioned as "the battering ram of colonial capitalism," to use Harry Harootunian's phrase,[36] it was real subsumption that was winning all the prizes.[37]

The internal arrangement of displays within the Crystal Palace reinforced this dominance. The colonial mentality was not only a color code based on race but race tied to a veritable hierarchy of the world according to each nation's level of industrial advancement. With the vast majority of products from the non-West being supplied by European colonialists, their lands, like their commodities, seemed to be from a world that the West had left behind.

36 Harootunian notes that while there is a tendency to read formal subsumption as always in transition to real subsumption, it is, in the language of Althusserism, a transition that comes only in a last instance but in which the last instance never comes. See Harootunian, *Marx after Marx*. If Paul Young is to be believed, the "always in transition" thesis was even evident in the exhibition catalogue that enacted a pronounced drive to strip non-European communities of cultural and historical significance in order that they might more easily and profitably be assimilated into a global economy. In this way, the Crystal Palace served at once to coordinate, naturalize, and celebrate a process of industrial capitalist expansion that would see "barbarian and semi-barbarian nations become the countryside to Britain's town." Young, "Mission Impossible," 16. For more on the Crystal Palace and the techniques of the market, see Young, *Globalization and the Great Exhibition*, 3–26.

37 Evidence of this claim can be found in the two types of prizes awarded at the Great Exhibition. The Prize Medal was given for the standard of excellence in production or workmanship while the larger Council Medal was awarded for the novelty of invention or application and beauty of design. It was claimed the two prizes marked the merit of different kinds and character. The Prize Medal, it stated, "should be conferred wherever a certain standard of excellence in production or workmanship had been attained—utility, beauty, cheapness, adaptation to particular markets, and other elements of merit being taken into consideration according to the nature of the object. . . . In regard to the other and larger Medal (the Council Medal) . . . the conditions of its award should be some important novelty of invention or application, either in material, or processes of manufacture, or originality combined with great beauty of design; but that it should not be conferred for excellence of production or workmanship alone. . . . It follows, therefore, that the award of a Council Medal does not necessarily stamp the recipient as a better manufacturer or producer than others who have received the Prize Medal. It is rather a mark of such invention, ingenuity, or originality as may be expected to exercise an influence upon industry more extended, and more important, than could be produced by mere excellence of manufacture." See Great Exhibition (1851, London), *Reports by the Juries*, i–ii.

Costumes, trinkets, carpets, and hookahs appeared to be the standard array of goods from the non-West, and these were exhibited, somewhat uncomfortably, alongside the latest technologies of the West.[38]

More than just a transparent showcase display that privileged advanced industry, the Crystal Palace was an early sign of the will to power of markets and their veridiction regimes as they become technologized, systematized, and universalized. It was also the first sign of the power of the phantasmagorical. In the same way as real subsumption constituted the full integration of labor-power into the advanced capitalist production process, so, too, the Crystal Palace would now discipline and domesticate the Western workers politically. It transformed Western working-class sentiment, which had, up until this point, felt exploited, disenchanted, alienated, and on the brink of revolution, into something far more docile and compliant. In the 1850s, such a transformation was desperately needed.[39]

The mid-nineteenth century was a time of revolt against the existing order in Europe. The year 1848 was famously dubbed the year of revolution, yet even if one left aside conflict on the continent and focused only on the labor problems of the English, the picture was little different. There were riots in Bradford in 1837, Chartist riots in 1840 and 1842, not to mention the plug drawing riots of 1844. In the year that Marx published the *Communist Manifesto*, these "disturbances" set the ruling class on edge.[40] Strangely, however,

38 Fay, *Palace of Industry*, 8.

39 As Young notes, "The Exhibition, it appeared, would thus rid the age of their confusion and anxiety. Where the world went past them in the streets of London, fragmented by a fleeting and commodified aesthetic, at the Palace, it would be pinned down, systematized and rendered whole again. The display was therefore a comforting rationalization of the complex processes and interactions that made life in the Victorian metropolis what it was." Young, *Globalization and the Great Exhibition*, 3.

40 In the early months of 1848, turmoil broke out all over Europe and, at around that time, the Chartists announced a mass rally on Kennington Common in south London, followed by a march on Westminster to present a petition signed by five million people. Such was the fear at the time that the Bank of England was protected by sandbags at ground level and guns on the roof. Queen Victoria left the capital on the advice of her ministers. See Leapman, *The World for a Shilling*, 46–47. The dissipating effect the 1851 Exhibition would have on the threat to social order was observed by Fay: "Colonel Sibthorp . . . feared the irruption of foreigners, pickpockets and Socialists. Three years after the revolution of 1848 such fears might be quite legitimately felt. As we shall see, the fact that the Queen

by 1851 a miracle had happened in London. The revolutionary atmosphere had dissipated and been replaced, it seems, by a sense of wonder.

While labor-power turned the wheels of industry and transformed nature's raw materials into mobile and malleable use-values, the Crystal Palace would stimulate the senses such that the mobile and malleable use-value would surface not just as utility but also as a material manifestation of the flow of desire. By stimulating the crowd in ways that are almost the opposite of the *Rent Collection Courtyard*, the Crystal Palace quieted the masses. Within a framework of Victorian didacticism, it demonstrated its capacity to mesmerize with consumer goods, spectacle, education, and fun. More than that, its architecture embodied key characteristics of the commodity form itself. In particular, the Crystal Palace, as spectacle, functioned as a phantasmagorical form through which the phantasmagorical aspects of the commodity world were put on display.[41]

The Crystal Palace was not just an exhibition; it was the harbinger of the mass entertainment industry.[42] Wrapped in the garb of religious and scientific Victorian didacticism, it became the harbinger of the modern museum[43] yet,

---

could move freely among great crowds in the Exhibition was regarded as a major triumph for the British political system." Fay, *Palace of Industry*, 8. The "Press" is quoted as having written an "obituary with near reverence": "The tale of Hyde Park in 1851 will fall on the page of history. Fallen thrones will lie around it: here the Saturnalia of power—there the wild excess of popular freedom . . . everywhere anarchy, repression, conspiracy, darkness, dismay and death. In the midst of all these struggling spirits rises up the great figure of the Crystal Palace, to redeem the age." See Beaver, *The Crystal Palace*, 67.

41 Benjamin quotes Julius Lessing, who noted how the building appeared as a "wonderland" bringing the old fairy tale back to life. Here, however, the new phantasmagorical qualities of the commodity form, captured in the phantasmagorical qualities of the building that houses them, made all this possible. Lessing quoted in Benjamin, *The Arcades Project*, G6, G6a, 1, 184.

42 The entertainment value of this exhibition was not lost on the Americans. The New York exhibition of 1853 that directly followed the Hyde Park exhibition was not only architecturally modeled on the original Crystal Palace building but had, within a year of its opening, appointed none other than Phineas Barnum, of Barnum and Bailey Circus fame, to run it. See Benjamin, *The Arcades Project*, 186, G6, G6a, 1.

43 "Industrial exhibitions as secret blueprint for museums. Art: industrial products projected into the past," writes Walter Benjamin. Benjamin, *The Arcades Project*, G2a, 6, 176.

in organizing its displays behind turnstiles that rotated in the direction of profit, it would also lead into a world of organized commercial fun. It would be the precursor to the theme park,[44] the progenitor of organized tourism,[45] not to mention the inventor of the public bathroom.[46] The turnstiles at its entrance regulated and counted its customers and its profits,[47] and refresh-

44 According to Deborah Phillips, "The Great Exhibition of the Industry of All Nations established an international paradigm for the 'Grand Exposition' and the 'World's Fairs' that were to become a major influence for Walt Disney. . . . The Great Exhibition was laid out around a series of national 'courts,' a structure that was replicated in later Grand Expositions and World's Fairs and which continues in the pavilions of Disney World's Epcot World. The spirit of the 'Industry of All Nations' remains strong in the displays of national commodities and architectures at Epcot World Showcase." Philips, *Fairground Attractions*, 19.

45 Timothy Mitchell argues that Thomas Cook "launched the modern tourist industry" on the back of his early excursion train tours to the Crystal Palace in conjunction with the Midland Railway Company. See *Colonising Egypt*, 21. Mitchell is correct to point to the crucial role of the Crystal Palace in proving the success of this business model, although it was far from being the first such package tour. As Kate Colquhoun notes, prior to the Crystal Palace, Thomas Cook had already operated many tours, with its first packaged tour beginning as early as 1841. That tour was for the Temperance League and was a train ride from Leicester to Loughborough (*The Busiest Man in England*, 152). What made the Crystal Palace unique (and for Thomas Cook so profitable) was that it constituted the "greatest mass movement of people in Britain's history." For details, see Colquhoun, *The Busiest Man in England*, 190.

46 "The greatest innovation at the exhibition was the provision of public toilets, these included 54 urinals at no charge, 22 water-closets for gentlemen and 47 water-closets for the ladies. In the central refreshment area, however, charges were levied. It was 2d [pence] and 1d [pence] in the eastern and western refreshment areas," Ken Kiss tells us. These were the first instances of both public and "user pays" toilets and, according to Leapman, the Crystal Palace exhibition would prove a catalyst for the more general provision of public lavatories. "Legend has it that it was also the source of the euphemism 'to spend a penny' as the charge of 1d listed above suggests. Over 827,000 people were said to have 'spent a penny' and the design of these lavatories was soon copied not just in the streets of London but in other cities across the world." Leapman, *The World for a Shilling*, 91–95. See also Kiss, *The Crystal Palace Museum*, 10–11.

47 The entrance price was hotly debated, and the prime minister, Lord John Russell, wanted free admission. This was rejected, and the pricing scheme can be seen in Kiss, *The Crystal Palace Museum*, 11.

ment rooms inside fed its hungry clients. Its printed catalogues guided the public around the displays of industrial inventiveness and educational delights. It even had its own board game.[48]

Bradford workers, who had but a few years earlier been rioting about working conditions, became proud recipients of twenty-one medals for their cloths and yarns, having earlier demonstrated their newfound pride in industry by being, per ratio, the biggest subscribers to the Crystal Palace building fund.[49] Even before the Crystal Palace was built, workers from around the country had been forming special social clubs and paying weekly installments for train and exhibition tickets.[50] No one, it seems, wanted to miss out on visiting what was billed as the greatest show on earth.[51] Whether it was the pride of the worker in receipt of prize medals,[52] a sense of national pride in

48 Released in 1851 to coincide with the opening of the exhibition, "the Crystal Palace Game" promised players a "Voyage round the world, an entertaining excursion in search of knowledge, whereby geography is made easy." Young, *Globalization and the Great Exhibition*, 58.

49 It was a public subscription but by royal charter. Leapman, *The World for a Shilling*, 43.

50 On Priestly's travel club, see Leapman, *The World for a Shilling*, 43. For Thomas Cook, see Leapman, *The World for a Shilling*, 225–29.

51 In the 140 days that it was open, the Hyde Park Crystal Palace exhibition attracted six million visitors, with the *Times* reporting that nothing like it had ever been witnessed before. Colquhoun, *The Busiest Man in England*, 186.

52 There were fifteen thousand exhibits, half of which were from Britain and the remainder came from overseas. Colquhoun, *The Busiest Man in England*, 180. The introduction of the medals succeeded despite some financial problems. In the planning stage of the exhibition, the commissioners "had enough money pledged to be able to set aside £100,000 for whatever structure they chose, although to achieve that they had been forced to scrap the original plan to offer cash prizes. People would have to be persuaded to compete just for medals, for global honour and acclaim, rather than financial reward." Leapman, *The World for a Shilling*, 40. However, the number of articles viewed and prizes awarded demonstrated the importance of this honor and acclaim. "The number of Prize Medals awarded is 2,918. The number of Council Medals is 170. . . . The number of exhibitors was about 17,000. . . . The task of the Juries involved the consideration and judgement of at least a million articles; the difficulties attending it being not a little increased by the want of a uniform system of classification of the subjects in some of the foreign divisions." See Great Exhibition (1851, London), *Reports by the Juries*, ii.

a labor force that had created this wonderland of industry, or just the sheer pleasures of the theme-park-like entertainment available there, the Crystal Palace proved to be a major success.[53] Even the Queen was impressed.

The opening ceremony, she recounted, was a "sensation I shall never forget . . . magic and impressive"; it was "a day to live forever."[54] When cheaper tickets finally became available some two weeks after the opening,[55] the working class arrived and they, too, were awestruck. As one newspaper reported, they "seemed to stand in awe of the building: its greatness paralysed them."[56] The regularity of the glass paneling and the use of natural light created an almost religious atmosphere.[57] While its prefabricated industrial design was shocking to some at the time, the Crystal Palace was, in fact, a foretaste of things to come. "Buildings without the noodles" was how Adolph Loos would later come to call

53 After awarding Paxton £5,000 and settling all outstanding accounts, the commissioners were left with £180,000. In addition, nearly £100,000 worth of exhibits were presented to them. It was decided to purchase Gore House and twenty-two acres of land near Brompton Road and to erect there a permanent exhibition building to house the gifts, together with other objects that, in the opinion of the commissioners, exemplified good taste and design. This was the beginning of the center of art and learning that still flourishes in South Kensington. It now includes the Victoria and Albert Museum, the Science Museum and Library, the Natural History Museum, the Geological Museum, the Imperial Institute, the Royal College of Science, the Royal School of Mines, the City and Guilds College, the Royal College of Art, the Royal College of Music, the Royal College of Organists, and the College of Needlework. This, according to Beaver, is England's legacy from the Great Exhibition. Beaver, *The Crystal Palace*, 65.

54 The Queen's Exhibition Journal, quoted in Fay, *Palace of Industry*, 47.

55 As Beaver noted, "25,000 season tickets had been sold at three guineas for gentlemen and two guineas for ladies. The holders of these tickets had the privilege of attending on the day when the Great Exhibition was opened by the Queen. For the two days following the opening the price of admission was to be one pound and thereafter five shillings until 24th May. Then it was to be reduced to one shilling from Mondays to Thursdays, half a crown on Fridays and five shillings on Saturdays. There would be no Sunday opening. Smoking, alcohol and dogs were prohibited." Beaver, *The Crystal Palace*, 35.

56 Leapman, *The World for a Shilling*, 12.

57 The satirical magazine *Punch* joked that the unusual structure was a Crystal Palace and the name stuck. See Fay, *Palace of Industry*, 15.

the unadorned style that the Crystal Palace pioneered. It was a style that would later come to characterize modernism in architecture.[58]

The prescience of the Crystal Palace goes well beyond architecture. For Peter Sloterdijk, the Crystal Palace produced a momentary flash of Victorian light to illuminate a posthistorical world into which the bored Dasein was born. The basic disposition of this bored Dasein, Sloterdijk tells us, comes from life being devoid of any life-affirming or life-threatening challenges.[59] The Crystal Palace, paradoxically, paved the way for this bored Dasein by acting as the hothouse of faux ("safe") adventure: colonialism would be turned into an Aladdin's cave of exhibited goods from around the world while labor exploitation would be transcribed into the nobility of labor through exhibition prizes and displays. In reordering the world, not as it was, but as it should be—a world of trade—the Crystal Palace would attempt to reorder humanity in the way horticulture had reordered nature. Little wonder, then, that in thinking about who should construct this building, the authorities would come to call on the services of a master gardener, Joseph Paxton. In fact, the Exhibition Building Committee had little choice.

The committee appointed to oversee the exhibition project, having failed to find a suitable building design by early 1851, found themselves running out of time.[60] They needed a design that would fall within budget and also be easy to assemble and dismantle. With Paxton's greenhouse design, they achieved these ends and much more.[61] Paxton's innovations in greenhouse design came from his experience as chief gardener on the Derbyshire estate of the Duke of Devonshire. The duke's immense wealth enabled Paxton

58 For an example of just how negatively Adolf Loos viewed ornamentation, see his essay "Ornament and Crime."

59 Sloterdijk, *In the World Interior of Capital*, 172.

60 Indeed, by the time Paxton was given the brief, he had only twenty-two weeks to complete a building structure that, on this scale, was largely untested before interior decoration was undertaken and then the exhibits arranged. See Colquhoun, *The Busiest Man in England*, 172.

61 "The origin of all present-day architecture in iron and glass is the greenhouse," writes A. G. Meyer, and Paxton brought the greenhouse into the world of architecture. A. G. Meyer quoted in Benjamin, *The Arcades Project*, 158.

to fund his scientific experiments in design with ever larger and more radical greenhouse designs.[62]

On the duke's Derbyshire estate Paxton created Lily House, the world's largest greenhouse housing the largest lily ever grown in an artificial climate.[63] It is said that Paxton devised the unique load-bearing greenhouse design of Lily House by mimicking the structure of the lily pads themselves.[64] In this respect, the greenhouse was one of the earliest machines to tame and transform not just nature but also the telluric. Through science, even the wild beauty of the natural world, it seems, could be brought under human control.[65] If greenhouses could be said to have created "the dream of a happy

62 "A century earlier the Duke might have built a temple or mausoleum as a permanent memorial to his passion, but this was the age of scientific discovery and scientific obsession." Colquhoun, *The Busiest Man in England*, 65.

63 Temperatures in the Lily House were kept at between 80 and 90 degrees Fahrenheit. Colquhoun, *The Busiest Man in England*, 158.

64 The design of the Crystal Palace was said to be inspired by observations of the structure, unusual size, and great strength of the leaves of a water lily called Victoria Amazonica. P. Ramachandra Rao notes that Paxton, a gardener by profession, was fascinated by the intricate ribs and cross ribs on the back of a lily leaf and built a greenhouse, the roof of which incorporated a similar scaffolding structure. See Rao, "Biomimetics." Unfortunately, this is also said to be one of the "myths" about the relationship between exhibitions and nature that Julian Vincent says are almost unavoidable: "Unfortunately, simple copying can also become urban myth, such as the idea that the Eiffel Tower has design progenitors in the medullary structure of the head of the human thigh bone, or that the design of the roof of the Crystal Palace was inspired by the leaf of the Victoria Amazonica lily." Kate Colquhoun disagrees: "The lily house's structural system had come from the lily leaf itself and its extraordinary load-bearing capacity, which he [Paxton] called a 'Natural feat of engineering.'" See Colquhoun, *The Busiest Man in England*, 158. Despite this statement by Paxton, Julian Vincent sees no evidence, written or observational, for this popular interpretation. Indeed, the ridged roof structure of the Crystal Palace, he claims, was based on a design that had "simply allowed more sunlight into the greenhouse at Chatsworth Park." See Vincent, "Biomimetic Patterns in Architectural Design," 76.

65 According to one of the nineteenth century's greatest innovators in greenhouse design, John Claudius Loudon, the greenhouse was part of the "liberal and improving age." The glass house, he remarked, could "exhibit spring and summer in the midst of winter . . . to give man so proud a command over nature." Quoted in Hix, *The Green House*, 19.

unity between nature and man in the first part of the industrial age," could this same technology not now be redeployed to tame and discipline the savage beast within?[66] The Crystal Palace would offer the experimental artificial environment to tame, discipline, and channel not just nature, but also the telluric within human nature.

The artificial atmosphere that it created helped channel affective energy flows away from the wild, violent, and capricious. It led to workers looking in wonder at the products of their own creation, consumers awakening to a new set of desires that took them beyond use-value, and tourists being attracted by the sheer phantasmagoric allure of the theme-park events. Just as the greenhouse had domesticated plant life, so, too, would the Crystal Palace take the sometimes-violent telluric tendencies and domesticate them through the signs of wonder it had created. Whether it was displays of their own industrial brilliance, their ability to display the splendor of the East in the heart of the West, or merely the sheer spectacle of the building itself, the Crystal Palace constituted an incubator of modernity and, as modernity's greenhouse, it would incubate seedlings that would later blossom, not just into the largest lily, but into the world's largest tower, namely, the Eiffel Tower (see figures 10.3 and 10.4).

Stretching 324 meters (1,063 feet) into the Parisian sky, the Eiffel Tower was, at the time of its construction, the largest structure ever built.[67] With a form said to resemble nature,[68] Eiffel's tower was, according to Andre Antoine, "the first realization of the aesthetics of iron."[69] Using load-bearing iron girders connected in a manner reminiscent of common plant life, Eiffel created a tower that was anything but "common."

Purpose-built for the 1889 Exposition Universelle, the tower was the ultimate sign of Western (and bourgeois) dominance over nature and the world. It was as if the world of trade that had been incubated in the Crystal Palace

66 See Kohlmaier and von Sartory, *Houses of Glass*, 14.

67 At that time, it was said to be the largest structure ever built, according to Dorrian, "Cityscape with Ferris Wheel, Chicago, 1893," 21.

68 Some said that the Eiffel Tower was structured like *Ceratium algae*; others that it was modeled on the head of the femur in the thigh. Rao, "Biomimetics," 661; P. Ball, "Life's Lessons in Design," 413. Still others have suggested that the base of the structure was modeled on a tree trunk: see Forbes, "Building on Nature."

69 Andre Antoine was director of the controversial Theatre Libre in 1889. For more detail, see Lynton, *Tatlin's Tower*, 86.

was now strong enough to grow outside of greenhouse conditions. At the foot of the Eiffel Tower, a French-built Egyptian exhibit reproduced perfectly a winding back-street scene from Cairo, thereby confirming Western global mastery, because of the technical ability it demonstrated to replicate, in the heart of Paris, what appeared to be the heartbeat of Cairo.

Here was a streetscape complete with traditional Egyptian house veneers and the facade of a mosque modeled on one in Qaitbay. Here was a streetscape populated by imported Egyptian donkeys, complete with handlers offering rides, Egyptian dancing girls entertaining the passersby, and French traders dressed as Arabs selling trinkets from their bazaar stalls. Old Cairo was literally brought to Paris in summary form. As Timothy Mitchell summed up this Arabesque sideshow, even the dirt on the painted buildings was replicated.[70] Old Cairo was transported and in the process transformed. Yet this process of transformation—from lived social form to sideshow commodity—only confirmed the power of the West to extract, replicate, and make anything, anywhere, portable and intelligible to the Western mind's-eye. As a topiary of iron and glass growing out of the greenhouse of modernity's ever-extending claims, the Eiffel Tower would look down on this streetscape, cast that mind's-eye upward in wonder, outward in ambition, and also, perhaps, forward in time to a period when this aesthetic wonder could be wed even more firmly to a use-value.

That day of utility would come on July 1, 1913. Newly refitted, and bristling with electronic instruments, aerials, and other technical equipment, the Eiffel Tower would be the site of the first global radio transmission of a time signal and with this, says Stephen Kern, "The independence of local time began to collapse."[71] As the world awoke to the buzzers and bells of globalizing capitalist trade in the machine age, the division of labor spawned a political division. This would be monumentalized by two works that both took the Eiffel Tower as their point of reference. One, in the United States, would take capitalist modernity for a ride, while the other, in the Soviet Union, would offer a view of modernity designed to unseat that. One was the Ferris wheel; the other, Tatlin's Tower.

70 T. Mitchell, *Colonising Egypt*, 1.

71 Kern, *The Culture of Time and Space*, 14.

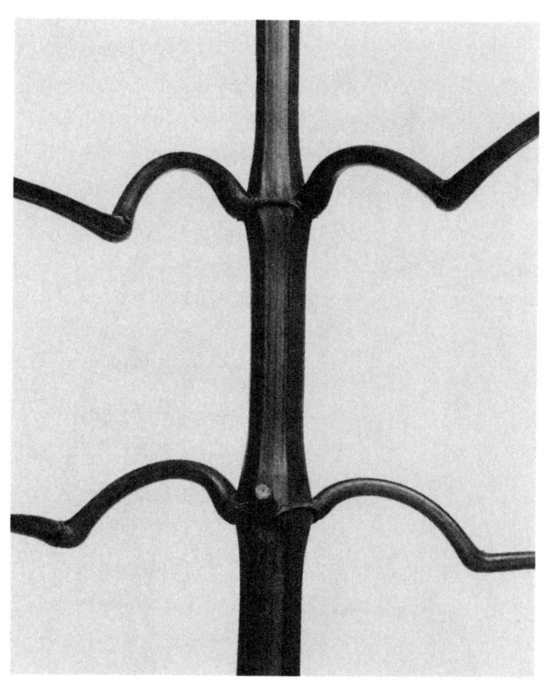

Figures 10.3–10.4. *Above*, Karl Blossfeldt, *Plantstudie: Urformen der Kunst*, 1928. Photograph, paper, and ink. Rijksmuseum, Amsterdam. *Below*, the Eiffel Tower, photo by the author.

Figure 11.1. The original Ferris wheel, World's Columbian Exposition, Chicago, 1893. Wikimedia Commons, last modified July 1, 2022, https://commons.wikimedia.org/w/index.php?title=File:Ferris-wheel.jpg.

11

Eiffel Tower–Ante

THE FERRIS WHEEL

It had always been George Ferris's goal, when designing the Ferris wheel (figure 11.1) for the 1893 World's Columbian Exposition in Chicago, to outdo Gustave Eiffel. In some respects, he did.[1] In tying the motion of the wheel to the production of market-based profit, he captured not only the general movement of capital but also, more specifically, the movement of things along an assembly line. The precursor to assembly-line production had, in fact, originated in Chicago just a few decades before the Exposition. In 1867, the Chicago abattoirs had installed a disassembly line that would prove to be the inspiration behind what later became known as Fordism.

1 At the time, the Ferris wheel was said to outdo the Eiffel Tower in sheer engineering brilliance, says John Kouwenhoven. He argues that in the two structures, one finds the sensibility of two nations on display. The Ferris wheel, he suggests, flagged mobility and change, which became the leitmotif of a newly emerging United States. Kouwenhoven, *Half a Truth Is Better Than None*, 109–24.

"I believe that this was the first moving line ever installed," Henry Ford would write of the Chicago meatpacking industry that pioneered a prototype of assembly-line production. As a young boy, Ford tells us, he had toured the plant and it left a deep impression. "The idea [of the assembly line] came in a general way from the overhead trolley that the Chicago packers use in dressing beef," he would later write.[2] This process hoisted the animal carcass onto hooks and chains and then slowly moved them along the disassembly line from station to station until they finally came out as cuts of meat. Here was a new means of killing without hate, but this time provided by industry. Slaughter was being sanitized by being mechanized. "For the first time machines were used to speed along the process of mass slaughter," writes Jeremy Rifkin, "leaving men as mere accomplices, forced to conform to the pace and requirements set by the assembly line itself."[3]

The break with nature that modernity initiated was, therefore, no break from slaughter, only its routinization and distanciation from everyday life. Routinization, distanciation, and, most importantly, calculability and profitability were hallmarks of this new world. Fordism, like the Ferris wheel, could thereby set a clock on the expenditure of human energy. If Fordism did this in order to discipline labor and extract from it maximum labor-power, the Ferris wheel drew its profit from the days when the laborer had time off. Indeed, the Ferris wheel could be said to have pioneered the assembly line of fun that was always calculated to end in profit. In the Chicago World's Columbian Exposition, such endpoint calculations proved correct.

The financial success of the Ferris wheel saved the Chicago exhibition from financial ruin[4] and, metaphorically, displayed the cogs of American industry moving forward and beyond material use-value assumptions. The

2 The slaughterhouse that Ford visited was most likely located in the Union Stock Yards, although he did not specify which slaughterhouse it was. See Ford, with Crowther, *My Life and Work*, 81.

3 Rifkin, *Beyond Beef*, 120.

4 Maranzani, "7 Things You May Not Know." Patrick Meehan says that by November 6, 1893, which was five days after the exhibition had closed, the profits were calculated, and it was found that 1,453,611 people had paid for admission while possibly a thousand or more free trips had been given to various important people. The gross earnings were $726,805, of which $513,403 was retained by the company, giving them a profit of $395,000. Meehan, "Ferris Wheel in the 1893 Chicago World's Fair."

Ferris wheel would, quite literally, be selling an experience, thereby "dematerializing" the commodity form, even though, at the time, it was thought of as the materialization of American engineering know-how.

Encapsulating the idea of the anti-ornament, Ferris would strip the wheel's design back to pure functionality: rotation. The rotation of the wheel was like the circulation of the commodity on the market: always moving, but never going anywhere; always new, but always the same.[5] More structure than building, more concerned with functionality than style, the wheel was a monument to an age of engineering brilliance, yet it also flagged a significant social and economic transformation. Here was a world moving out of the production of pure use-value and into a dreamlike state of fun, fantasy, and the phantasmagorical that would become the leitmotif of the modern consumer age. As America became the harbinger of the new, modernity moved continents and changed form. A new and more dynamic rendition of modernity was about to emerge, not from Europe, but from the shores of the United States.

> Have the elder races halted?
> Do they droop and end their lesson,
> wearied, over there beyond the seas?
> We take up the task eternal, and the burden, and the lesson,
> Pioneers! O pioneers!
>
> All the past we leave behind:
> We debouch upon a newer, mightier world, varied world.
> Fresh and strong the world we seize, world of labor and the match,
> Pioneers! O pioneers!
> (Walt Whitman, "Pioneers! O Pioneers!")

Plumbers were pioneers Adolf Loos would tell us: pioneers of cleanliness. They were "the first artisan of the state . . . the billeting officer for civilization, for the civilization of today,"[6] and "today," for Loos, was America. This "apostle of the 'American way of life'"[7] would take cleanliness beyond hygiene and into the realm of architecture and style. Cleanliness would be-

5 Adorno, *The Culture Industry*, 44.

6 Loos, "Ornament and Crime," 86.

7 Damisch, "L'Autre 'Ich,' L'Autriche-Austria, or the Desire for the Void," 35.

come clean lines for Loos, thereby inspiring the work of Le Corbusier.[8] Clean lines would become streamlined and begin to speak beyond aerodynamics and functionality, to everything, from fashion to footwear.[9] As streamlining spread beyond the realms of aerodynamics, life itself began to speed up. "In New York you always have the feeling there must have been an accident somewhere," Loos would ruefully comment.[10] Speeding up, streamlining, and making functional—this was the nineteenth century moving into the twentieth; yet only in America was there a new aesthetic emerging that offered an unencumbered embrace of this form of modernist immaterialism. How appropriate, then, that the monument that celebrates this movement within modernity from one continent to another was created by an American bridge builder.[11]

Inspired by horticulture, Paxton's Crystal Palace might have begun to tame the telluric, but it was only with the engineer George Ferris that this transition was taken for a ride.

George Washington Gale Ferris Jr. would put his name to a wheel that would monumentalize this shift away from pure industrial utility and into ways of capturing and calculating fun. If we can say that industrial power had been nurtured and displayed in the greenhouse of the Crystal Palace, and grew strong with the Eiffel Tower, then, with the Ferris wheel, it became phantasmagoric. The Ferris wheel was a machine that could tap into a human desire that had been exhibited in embryonic form, from the time of the very first Great Exhibition.

As the first world trade exhibition with a dedicated amusement park, the Chicago World's Columbian Exposition created a new channel of profit.[12] The fairground was the progenitor of the amusement park in much the same

8 von Moos and Sobiesky, "Le Corbusier and Loos."

9 Loos, "Ornament and Crime," 94–99.

10 Loos, "Ornament and Crime," 95.

11 To be fair, George Ferris was not the first bridge builder to erect a major structure at a world exposition. Gustave Eiffel was also a bridge-building engineer. See Schivelbusch, *Disenchanted Night*, 3.

12 "The week-by-week sales report reveals that 1,453,611 tickets were sold between July 1 and November 6, earning $726,805.50, with the largest number of tickets sold (151,201) the week of October 16." See Chicago History Museum, "Ferris Wheel, Standard of Business by the Week."

way as the amusement park became the (real) subsumption of the fairground into industry. Organized on an industrial basis, the amusement park channeled affective energy flows, not toward material desires but toward immaterial ones. Here was the moment when the phantasmagorical moved beyond any direct attachment to material objects, hinting, in fact, that the pre-given dominance of use-value as central to this economic system was insufficient. Instead, the system of market veridiction was now being extended into the calculation, calibration, and profit of emotions, thrills, and heightened sensations. The Ferris wheel would be a monument to this channeling process.

Gradually, intensities—be they religious, erotic, or political—would be diffused, rechanneled transformed, or, if all else failed, repressed. The power that could fuel an intensity would be directed into the market and there it would become the euphoric element in the phantasmagoric—the roar of the crowd, the elation at a performance, the thrill of the ride. Alternatively, energy would be dispersed into smaller rivulets that would flow, in varying degrees of intensity, into material forms—the now-familiar "desire element" within use-value. In other words, energies that could potentially produce political intensity would instead be channeled into the promiscuous world of diverse consumer desire. The market functioned as a nodal point in this recalibration of energy flows by continuously bringing about new alignments, creating new intersections, and launching new trajectories. Slowly, unevenly, and sometimes with setbacks, these swirling flows around the market welled into a new mode of worlding our world. In this world we begin to encounter Sloterdijk's bored Dasein, as well as the momentary, partial antidote to this form of boredom and despondency. It is here, on the cusp of the twentieth century and at the foot of a mechanical wheel, that industry meets the culture industry and channels energy toward an era overlaid with phantasmagoric experiences. These are the first tentative steps toward that nonmaterial form of materialism that could still turn a profit. Yet it so very nearly didn't happen.

It is a fair guess that in 1891 Daniel Burnham was a troubled man. Already one year behind schedule, the man in charge of building and creating in Chicago the world's biggest trade fair was simply unable to find a monumental structure to rival the already iconic Eiffel Tower.[13] The buildings for the exhibition were being designed in classical and conservative Beaux Arts style

13 In the end, the exhibition had to be delayed for a year, but when it was finally opened, it was a huge success, with an estimated twenty-seven million people visiting it. See Rose, "Welcome to the Fair."

which Burnham favored as the governing principle of his plans to rejuvenate the city of Chicago. This style, however, did not capture the imagination in the way Eiffel's tower had done in Paris.[14] Burnham, twice, had the chance to commission Eiffel to repeat his efforts with an even taller tower for Chicago. Twice, Burnham and his committee members said "no."[15] National pride, it seems, determined the rejection.

Chicago had to be an exhibition of American know-how, they insisted. If the trade fair in Paris had created Eiffel's tower as the centerpiece of French celebrations of the one hundredth anniversary of the Revolution, then surely American know-how should be able to create an even bigger and more spectacular symbol of the New World of engineering and industry to celebrate the four hundredth anniversary of Columbus's landing?[16] The problem was that plans submitted by American architects proved less than satisfactory.[17] Towers proposed by Americans—such as W. L. Judson's 1889 Tower that would allow car and tram entry, or David Proctor and the Columbian Tower Company's proposal that would offer a much larger viewing platform than Eiffel's and thus a greater return on investment—seemed uneconomical or unviable.[18] At this point, in 1891, with little time left, Burnham was forced to turn from architects to engineers. In a speech at a dinner of engineers, Burnham challenged anyone present to rise to the occasion. Legend

14 To see how successful Eiffel had been at capturing the public's imagination, see Jay, "Taller Than Eiffel's Tower," 146. To see the influence of Burnham's Beaux Arts style on the city of Chicago, see Böger, "Envisioning Progress at Chicago's White City," 270.

15 Jay, "Taller Than Eiffel's Tower," 149, 153.

16 Jay, "Taller Than Eiffel's Tower," 145–56. One should not assume from the above that everyone welcomed Eiffel's tower. Indeed, there is probably little need to remind the reader of the petition of artists and others against it or of Roland Barthes's story of Guy de Maupassant, who, he claimed, regularly ate at the restaurant in the tower despite not caring for the food. Why? It was the only place in Paris, he used to say, where one did not have to see it. See Barthes, *The Eiffel Tower and Other Mythologies*, 1.

17 See Jay, "Taller Than Eiffel's Tower," 149, 153, for a discussion of the costs and benefits of each scheme.

18 Apart from over-budget proposals, the length of time needed to build the proposed structures and the difficulty of assembly and disassembly all played a part in their decisions. For details, see Jay, "Taller Than Eiffel's Tower," 149–50.

has it that this is exactly what George Ferris did. Scribbled on a napkin that was passed to Burnham during the course of the evening meal was the first draft of the Ferris wheel design, complete with pricing details, passenger loads, and revolutions per reload.[19]

There was, initially, some hesitancy to take this proposal seriously. Put simply, many of Burnham's fellow committee members thought Ferris was a "man with wheels in his head."[20] Strong objections presumably resulted in Ferris not being given a concession in Jackson Park where the trade fair was taking place but in the less prestigious fairground attached to the trade fair.[21] Built on Central Avenue in Midway Plaisance, the Ferris wheel was to be the centerpiece of this purpose-built fairground. Where the Eiffel Tower had proudly stood at the center of the entire Exposition Universelle, Ferris's wheel would be consigned to the fairground and demoted to the rank of fairground attraction. Ferris's wheel would, therefore, never achieve the iconic status or aesthetic acclaim of the Eiffel Tower. Nevertheless, after the Chicago

19 It has been said that a napkin with the design of the wheel on it was presented to Burnham at a dinner with friends, but Mary Bellis (among others) suggests that it was actually given to him at a banquet of engineers that Burnham addressed. See Explore PA History, "Ferris Wheel Inventor Historical Marker"; Bellis, "Circus and Theme Park Innovations." Norman D. Anderson cites an interview with Ferris in which Ferris outlined a dinner at a "chop house." It was there that Ferris remembered remarking to people that he would build a huge wheel. "A monster," he called it. Ferris then continued, "I got some paper and began to sketch it out. I fixed the size, determined the construction, the number of cars we would run, the number of people it would hold, what we would charge, the plan of stopping six times in the first revolution and loading, and then making a complete turn—in short, before the dinner was over I had sketched out almost the entire detail, and my plan has never varied an item from that day. The wheel stands in the Plaisance at this moment as it stood before me then." Anderson, *Ferris Wheels*, 43.

20 Bolotin and Laing, *The World's Columbian Exposition*, 23.

21 For example, Patrick Meehan of the Hyde Park Historical Society, in noting the concession was not in Jackson Place, said this: "The engineers and architects of the Saturday Afternoon Club believed he was making a fool of himself as they loudly proclaimed that his wheel could not be built or, if it could, it could not be operated. But Ferris persisted and after much effort, the Committee granted him a concession to build the Wheel, not in Jackson Park, the main grounds, but in Central Avenue on the Midway." Meehan, "Ferris Wheel in the 1893 Chicago World's Fair."

Exhibition, what fairground in the world would ever open its gates without a Ferris wheel?[22]

With its focus on leisure, the Ferris wheel helped move questions of capital accumulation beyond industry and use-value. If Columbus was said by Sloterdijk to have launched "world history" with his journey to America—because risk would now give way to trade—could we not say that it was on the four hundredth anniversary celebration of his landing that history's page was turned again, when affective energy flows were channeled toward satiating momentary fantasy desires of both a material and immaterial kind? It was as entertainment that the Ferris wheel helped channel affective energy flows away from political intensities—not by tying desire to ownership of a material thing with a "use-value," but by creating a nonmaterially based series of attractions/distractions that produced a profit. By splitting the cell-like structure of the commodity form, extracting the phantasmagorical element, then redeploying it to channel affective energy flows toward fun, leisure, and entertainment, we enter into a world that continuously, daily, hourly, spontaneously, and on a mass scale makes calculable profits by momentarily capturing the desires of Sloterdijk's bored Dasein.[23] Under these conditions, free time entered the free market.

The "vacation is the successor of the festival," Roger Caillois tells us[24] as he traces the flow of energy from the ancient collective frenzy of the festival through to the vacation. The festival, writes Caillois, was an event of "intense emotions" that transformed subjectivity by transforming the way subjects accessed the sacred. Caillois came to call this Great Time and Great Space.[25] It was when Great Time and Great Space gave way to the Great Exhibition, however, that they were transformed into what Walter Benjamin would call the Great Myth, which was, in fact, just another way of describing the era of the commodity form.[26]

22 To offer but one of the many sources that make this point, see Meehan, "Ferris Wheel in the 1893 Chicago World's Fair."

23 This rhetorical flourish is, of course, a rewriting of Lenin's famous dictum about small-scale capitalist production. See Lenin, "'Left-Wing' Communism," 24.

24 Caillois, "Festival," 302.

25 Caillois, "Festival," 288.

26 Benjamin's Great Myth, according to Richard Wolin, was little more than another way of saying "the reproduction of the always-the-same under the semblance

In this brave new world, commodity forms began to contour energy flows away from spiritually intense, uplifting moments in which subjects would be "thrown" into frenzy, reverence, or sacrifice. Instead of this, the subject was to be "tossed" into atomistic sites of collective leisure. Temporary, dispersed, and occasional, sometimes material, sometimes not, the trajectory of this market-based commodity culture would spread into virtually all aspects of life, including sport. Indeed, for Norbert Elias and Eric Dunning, the channeling of this energy into organized sport had helped create the conditions enabling liberal governance to come about.

Formalized in England in the nineteenth century at public schools and spreading to the cities as the Industrial Revolution developed, organized sport began as a key pedagogical technology for inducing a sense of civic knowledge, duty, discipline, and morality in public school children. The playground lay at the center of these endeavors and pedagogy was at its heart.[27] David Stow's conception of classroom practice that marshalled and ordered schoolchildren into disciplined rows under the "authoritative and superintending eye" of the teacher would be joined to his idea of the playground as an "uncovered schoolroom" where children showed their "true character and disposition."[28] By joining the rules and discipline of the classroom to the "freedom" of playground games, organized sport became part of what Elias

of the production of the perpetually new." Wolin, *Walter Benjamin*, 174. This always-the-same quality under the rubric of the new was, of course, the very definition of the commodity. Thus, while Caillois's description of the time of the festival gave rise to Cesaire's scathing postcolonial critique, this transformation that takes us from what Caillois called Great Time and Great Space into Benjamin's Great Myth is worth recalling. Caillois, "Festival," 282.

27 David Stow devised the influential "Glasgow System" of education that tried to overcome the mechanical qualities of the "Lancaster method" by focusing on the pupil. Stow's rendering of the playground as an "uncovered classroom" was an attempt to make this linkage. For further details on how this became an influential part of English pedagogy, see Hunter, *Culture and Government*, 58–61.

28 The words "authoritative and superintending eye" come from Mathew Arnold and relates to play more generally. Ian Hunter has noted the way that this Arnoldian model of education has little to do with the idea of culture as art and relied as much on the playground as on the classroom. Indeed, Hunter even argues that the "moral and physical well being of the whole population of public schools would be secured through the moral supervision wherein organized sport could be thought of as an extension of governmentality." Hunter, *Culture and Government*, 18–20.

and Dunning have called the "civilizing process."[29] Nor did the development of organized sport simply herald a space of pedagogy for the player to learn and be disciplined by the rules of the game. Over time, it came to offer a place of mass excitement and entertainment as stadium productions created the space for the mass spectator-consumer-sports spectacle.

Nevertheless, even in this earlier phase, Elias and Dunning insist, the discipline imposed by organized sport was not unconnected to a "spurt" in the process of "parliamentarization" and a concomitant decline in political "cycles of violence."[30] It was this "affinity" between parliamentary contests and sporting contests that Elias and Dunning would contend was crucial to this process.[31] In place of the telluric violence of the past, sport would impose discipline, first on young players and then later on the crowd. As mass spectator sports developed, a corralled and controlled form of often violent excitement showed how the rules of the game spread into the conduct of life.

As a form of pedagogical amusement that increasingly falls under the sway of the commodity form, the mass sporting event, much like the vacation, the Great Exposition, and the amusement park, helped disperse political intensities not as part of a unified political project but in search of greater profit flows. With thirty-six cars carrying sixty passengers, each paying fifty cents a ride, the Ferris wheel played its part in supporting this rechanneling of intensities by turning affective flows into profit streams.[32] The amusement park became the liminal space from which would spread across the globe this more limited and dispersed version of intensity, driven by market veridiction and the flow of profits. In this space, and with this rechanneling of intensity, the Ferris wheel would literally grind out a profit with each rotation.[33]

29 Elias and Dunning, *The Quest for Excitement*, 26.

30 Elias, "The Quest for Excitement in Leisure," 97.

31 Elias and Dunning, *The Quest for Excitement*, 37.

32 "By the terms of this concession, which was granted December 16, 1892, the Ferris Wheel Company was to retain $300,000 received from the sale of tickets, after which one-half of the gross receipts were to be paid to the World's Columbian Exposition." Rice, "The Ferris Wheel," 476.

33 At a cost of fifty cents a ride, it was twice the price of a ticket to the fair and with a load of 2,160 people per ride, the wheel earned more than US$1,000 per rotation. Largely because of the Ferris wheel, it has been said that the Midway enabled stockholders to realize more than a 100 percent profit on their investment. On the

More sideshow attraction than monumental art form, the Ferris wheel was stripped of any aesthetic or pedagogical pretense, operating purely as a technology of fun, directing the flow of affective energy toward enjoyment and, through that, financial return. People would pay to ride on the Ferris wheel precisely because it was exhilarating, romantic, entertaining, and spectacular. Here, then, affective energies were being spirited away from political intensities by the intensities produced by this fairground attraction. Yet what made the Ferris wheel attractive to the trade fair of 1893 was not this. Rather, it was attractive to the American organizing committee because it captured the late nineteenth-century zeitgeist built around industry, utility, and profit. As an example of American engineering prowess that could be turned into profit, the Ferris wheel was, therefore, state-of-the-art technology.

Towering 264 feet into the air, the wheel was the tallest attraction at the Exhibition. Like a bicycle wheel, its spokes maintained its structural integrity. Like a vertical merry-go-round, it was suspended on a forty-five-foot axle, which was itself the largest piece of single-span steel ever constructed. This axle supported 140 feet of steel framing, on which were hung its thirty-six wooden boxcars that collectively carried sixty passengers per rotation.[34] To drive the wheel, two 1,000-horsepower reversible engines were added, as were air brakes. To erect this structure required knowledge of struts, beams, supports, and metal tensions. Ferris had been one of the first engineers to focus on metal tension in his earlier career as a bridge builder, but the stresses on this gigantic wheel were such that even he had to begin his design from first principles.[35] The result was an engineering feat that was said to display the American spirit of industry and enterprise,[36] and with three thousand of Edison's newly invented incandescent light bulbs mounted on all struts, that spirit would light up the night sky in the way neon signs would later come to light up the city.[37]

Ferris wheel costs, see Maranzani, "7 Things You May Not Know." On Midway investor profits, see Meehan, "Ferris Wheel in the 1893 Chicago World's Fair."

34 For a more detailed description of the technical elements, see Meehan, "Ferris Wheel in the 1893 Chicago World's Fair."

35 Meehan, "Ferris Wheel in the 1893 Chicago World's Fair."

36 Bellis, "The History of Theme Park Inventions."

37 Meehan, "Ferris Wheel in the 1893 Chicago World's Fair." On the history of the light bulb and an argument suggesting the close relationship between enlighten-

While the Ferris wheel turned leisure into industry and industry into leisure, inside the Exhibition itself the public were shown how the wheels of the railways and later automobiles would drive the country's industrial production.[38] Ferris helped turn the cogs of industry by showing the way rotational calculations could be turned into profit, presaging time and motion studies on the factory floor yet also, as a pleasure machine, foreshadowing the arrival of the new consumer world. According to Rem Koolhaas, it even gets enlisted into the journey of urban design.

In Koolhaas's account, Ferris's wheel was shipped from Chicago to Coney Island, where, alongside other sideshow attractions, it became part of a series of fairground technologies that presaged the emergence of the futuristic city of Manhattan.[39] While the amusement parks of Coney Island were, in some respects, explicitly modeled on the Chicago Exposition's Midway Plaisance, their design, Koolhaas contends, implicitly pointed forward in time to the skyscrapers and speed of Manhattan.[40] Coney Island showed the way in which

ment (reason) and illumination (by technical means), see Schivelbusch, *Disenchanted Night.*

38 Even the newly invented dynamo, which "created a new phase of history," was spinning away on display at this Exposition. Kern, *The Culture of Time and Space*, 93.

39 Koolhaas's account, however, while poetic, is contestable. A wheel was built in Coney Island but it might not have been the original Chicago wheel. Patrick Meehan's alternative account of the original wheel is more abject than poetic. After the Exhibition, there were numerous attempts to keep the wheel operating in Chicago but all failed. Eventually, the wheel was dismantled and sold to the organizers of the 1904 St. Louis Exhibition (the Louisiana Purchase Exposition). Failure to repeat the financial success it had achieved in Chicago led to criticisms that it was an eyesore, leading to its demolition. Its metal parts were sold as scrap for just $1,800 and its boilers and engines were shipped to Pennsylvania for industrial use. What little remained of the structure on the ground was dynamited in a controlled blast. For further details on the fate of the Chicago wheel, see Meehan, "Ferris Wheel in the 1893 Chicago World's Fair." For Koolhaas's reference to the purchase of a Ferris wheel from the Chicago World Fair of 1893, see Koolhaas, *Delirious New York*, 37.

40 Koolhaas, *Delirious New York*, 24–27. It is, in fact, remarkable just how many of the new industrial technologies first emerge in the circus. Wolfgang Shivelbusch notes, for example, that inventions such as the thermoclamp (a precursor to the street gaslight) and the steam engine both began their lives in circus acts. See Schivelbusch, *Disenchanted Night*, 23–24.

technology, in turning to fantasy and entertainment, could be used to mollify the masses and reduce political intensity, not by drawing people back toward pastoralism, but by harnessing the speed and intensity of the city and then transforming that into a series of profitable rides and distractions that actually intensified the urban experience. As he concludes, this turned the whole of Coney Island into a parody of "real" world intensifications and, as it did this, it became the fetal form of Manhattan.[41] Koolhaas reminds us of what this fetal form would grow into when he quotes Count Alexis de Sakhnoffsky. Looking upward from his office at the clean lines of Manhattan's skyscrapers, then downward to the ground and the commuters below, de Sakhnoffsky commented, "Now let's streamline men and women!"[42]

In America, *streamlining* became the buzzword for progress. Here was a word that would capture the imagination of architect, engineer, and stylist alike. Here was a word that would connote rapid frictionless, forward movement; a new addendum to a positivist creed propelling the modernist fantasy of the early part of the twentieth century. Here was a word that would accelerate this movement away from telluric intensities by mimicking the aerodynamic modifications that made vehicles move faster. A technical term that had once been restricted to physics was now being granted a much broader license on the back of a range of perceptual changes taking place in the West. It was a vision that moved streamlining from physics into aesthetics and, finally, in America, with the work of Raymond Fernand Loewy, into style.

Arriving in New York in 1919, shortly after being demobbed from the French army, Loewy, who had been trained as an engineer, was both awestruck by the industrial might of the United States yet also dumbstruck by its foul-smelling machinery. That, coupled with the dullness of its color, and the haphazard and disorderly appearance of its industrial products, led him to believe they had been put together by engineers who only ever seemed to ask the engineering question, namely, "Would it work?" Aesthetic questions, he noted, had been left to "well meaning 'artistic' men," who, having "admired

41 Koolhaas, *Delirious New York*, 30.

42 Quoted in Koolhaas, *Delirious New York*, 230. It was de Sakhnoffsky's 1930s illustrations, in *Esquire*, of car designs that were said to introduce "streamlining" to the broader American public. See Theobald, "Count Alexis de Sakhnoffsky."

the angels of Tintoretto, the garlands of Roas Bonheur, or the stone lacework of medieval Chartres . . . applied 'Art' to the machine."[43]

"Misguided decalcomaniacs" was how Loewy would describe these artists; "ungainly" was how he described their designs.[44] "Locomotives festooned with garlands of roses, steam rollers with pink angels, and coal stoves peppered with quails, butterflies, and nosegays of forget-me nots" were just some of his disparaging depictions. Fresh from the war, Loewy now took aim at what he called this "age of decalcomania."[45]

Loewy was not interested in decorating the machine. Instead, like Michelangelo's sculpting of stone, Loewy claimed to be interested in bringing out the machine's own intrinsic nature. "What you are calling sheathing," he would tell one interviewer, "is really the self-expression of the machine; when design and engineering work together toward a concern for shape (whether because of a physical principle or beauty or even a safety consideration), there is as much working backward *from* an optimal form *to* mechanics as there is from the machinery to what you have called sheathing."[46]

Rather than adding ornamentation, Loewy wanted to streamline the mechanical form. What had begun as an aerodynamic concept concerned with reducing drag suddenly took on new meaning. "It satisfies one's craving for tidiness and simplification," Loewy would say, "and if streamlining accomplishes nothing else, it is justified."[47] From his very first commission for Gestetner in 1929, he would use clay rather than the more conventional steel frames to design his models and, while this choice may well have stemmed from his lack of money, machinery, and time, it nevertheless resulted in a smoothing out of the harsh lines of the machine.[48] Despite Loewy's focus on

43 Loewy, *Never Leave Well Enough Alone*, 11.

44 Loewy, *Never Leave Well Enough Alone*, 11.

45 Loewy, *Never Leave Well Enough Alone*, 12.

46 Loewy, *Industrial Design*, 13 (emphasis in original).

47 Kobler, "The Great Packager."

48 In 1929, when Sigmund Gestetner, a British mimeograph manufacturer, gave Loewy the commission to redesign his Gestetner machines, Loewy turned his apartment into a studio and, without much time, money, or machinery, began his first design using clay. The result was a simplified form redesigned to prevent oil, ink, and paper from clogging, so it not only looked better, but also proved a step forward in terms of functionality. Loewy, *Industrial Design*, 10.

reshaping rather than decoration, he was no avant-garde formalist. Indeed, he was fond of saying that the most beautiful curve of all was a rising sales graph.[49]

"Design exists within the marketplace and helps define it," he would say. "Design acceptance," he argued, was the gold standard sought; and the acronym he coined, MAYA (more advanced yet acceptable) was the design ethos through which he would achieve success.[50] His breakthrough design, the 1934 Coldspot refrigerator for Sears Roebuck and Company, was exemplary. Not only did it combine sleek, clean lines with technical innovation, but also, most importantly, it was the first device to feature both technical and aesthetic detail in the advertising campaign built around it. For the first time in history, a product was being sold as much for its beauty as its utility.[51] The result was electric. Sales quadrupled, jumping from 60,000 units to 275,000 in just two years.[52] Coldspot, quite literally, put Loewy's industrial designs on the map.

What was remarkable about the Coldspot refrigerator (figures 1.1, 1.2, and 11.2) was the fact that it was released at the height of the Great Depression. At a time when the pragmatic, utilitarian, and "rationally" self-interested subject should have been dominant, what Loewy showed was that fantasy, not pragmatism, ruled. "Between two products equal in quality, price and function," Loewy would say, "the one that is esthetically correct is the one that sells."[53] In the middle of the Great Depression, Loewy had shown that something as seemingly inconsequential as style had the power to do something that even the great recovery schemes of government found almost impossible to accomplish. In modest and manageable ways, he had sold fantasy alongside utility. What was important, then, was not so much the way this aided the discipline of industrial design but the recognition of profit from within the dream side of this new commodity epoch. Little wonder, then,

49 Gibney and Luscombe, "The Redesigning of America."

50 Loewy, *Never Leave Well Enough Alone*, 278.

51 This change of direction in advertising was not Loewy's but came from "the Sears people," Loewy insists. Loewy, *Industrial Design*, 13.

52 "Quadrupled" was the word Loewy used. Loewy, *Industrial Design*, 13. The actual figures appear in Raymond Loewy, "About Raymond Loewy."

53 Kobler, "The Great Packager," 111.

Figure 11.2. The Coldspot refrigerator, 1934 advertisement. Image courtesy of Sears.

that Marx would refer to the world of spirits to help him explain the American republic![54]

The streamlining of the machine eventually led from design to the "streamlining" of brand logos,[55] and that, in turn, would lead to the streamlining of employees with the emergence of what sociologists called "aesthetic labor." "Brand embodiment" would become a catch-cry in retail[56] while terms like *branding*, *customer journey*, and *advertainment* would become business buzzwords. What had begun as a search for "the word" finally reached the moment of the buzzword. As work rates and life sped up, even parliamentary politics were "streamlined" by advertising agencies that became branding consultants and spin doctors before they became data analysts and behavioral scientists. On the back of brand-creation techniques, political campaigns were streamlined to iron out contentious points and reduce the space for error. Electoralism turned constituents into clients while the branding of political parties helped reduce the scope of the political spectrum by transforming the form and nature of argument. Jean Baudrillard pointed to this narrowing scope when he noted that it was "not by chance that advertising after having, for a long time, carried an implicit ultimatum of an economic kind, fundamentally saying and repeating incessantly, 'I buy, I consume, I take pleasure,' today repeats it in other forms; 'I vote, I participate, I am present, I am concerned.'" This process, explains Baudrillard, is "a mirror of a paradoxical mockery, mirror of the indifference of all public signification."[57]

What is the aspirational voter if not a political translation of the market's "aspirational lifestyle branding" process? Isn't the idea of "brand embodi-

54 And it was Walter Benjamin who would point this out. He noted how Marx, in the *Eighteenth Brumaire of Louis Bonaparte*, had suggested that "the feverish and youthful movement of material production . . . has left neither time nor opportunity for abolishing the old spirit world." Then he commented, "It is remarkable that Marx invokes the world of spirits to help explain the American republic." See Marx, "The Eighteenth Brumaire of Louis Bonaparte," 155. For Benjamin's comment, see Benjamin, *The Arcades Project*, 358.

55 Hauffe, *Design*, 110–11.

56 Wolkowitz, "The Working Body as a Sign," 85.

57 Baudrillard, *Simulacra and Simulation*, 91.

ment" simply a new mode of replacing the notion of commitment?[58] Can one not recognize in the term *aesthetic labor* a marketized version of the "cultural turn" taking place within social and public policy? In summary, the new engineers of politics and advertising are increasingly using the same skill sets and same scientific methods to test the popularity and durability of their policies and products. In a perverse way, the system of market veridiction has increasingly provided technologies to enable Mao Zedong's ideal form of leadership.[59] That is to say, through sampling, polling, and drawing on data analytics, algorithms, and machine learning technologies, "predictive marketing" offers a means to target products for advertisers and politicians alike that could be "from the masses to the masses." As contemporary algorithmic-based advertising and the scandal around Cambridge Analytica show, however, these strategies are designed to "know the masses" so that they can draw on their emotions to push them into buying something.[60] This has all been possible, however, only because market-based capitalism has seen off the other main secular political challenge to its market-based perception of modernity.

This alternative modernity that could have developed offered a similar set of commitments to science, reason, utility, and growth, but promised an end to the capricious, illogical, and immoral operations of the capitalist market. It promised liberation from the Taylorization of the mind that market veridiction was increasingly imposing on the social subject while simultaneously demanding its own Taylorization of the factory floor to increase production.[61] It promised a more rational pathway to modernity yet, paradoxically, attempted to intensify this rationality through a politics of revelation. In place of a capricious market, scientific socialism would offer the revelation of rationality through an ordered and centralized economic

58 On brand embodiment, see Wolkowitz, "The Working Body as a Sign." On "aspirational lifestyle branding," see Pettinger, "Brand Culture and Branded Workers."

59 Mao Tse-tung (Zedong), "Some Questions concerning Methods of Leadership," 119.

60 For details of how Cambridge Analytica achieved its "marketing feat" through machine learning, see Hern, "Cambridge Analytica."

61 As Carmen Claudin-Urondo notes, "It does not occur to Lenin for one moment that the 'refined brutality' of the Taylor system is not in essence due to its use by the bourgeoisie but, much more fundamentally, to its intrinsic characteristics." Claudin-Urondo, *Lenin and the Cultural Revolution*, 92.

planning model. In this system, market veridiction, which had once streamlined the flow of affective energy into profit, gave way to an attempt to wed political intensity with science through the scientific strictures of historical materialism. Once again, like Ferris's wheel, this new message would be broadcast from a monumental structure that was responding to the symbolic challenge of Eiffel's tower.[62] This other tower offering another version of modernity was Vladimir Tatlin's unrealized plan to build a Monument to the Third International of the Communist Movement. It was this unrealized project that Svetlana Boym called the anti–Eiffel Tower.[63]

62 "Tatlin's tower, however, was less a source of national pride than a class response to the 'bourgeois' Eiffel Tower." See Boym, *Architecture of the Off-Modern*, 10.

63 See Boym, *Architecture of the Off-Modern*, 10.

Figure 12.1. Tatlin's Tower ("Vladimir Tatlin and a model of his Monument to the Third International, Moscow, 1920"). Wikimedia Commons, last modified November 18, 2020, https://commons.wikimedia.org/w/index.php?title=File:Tatlin%27s_Tower_maket_1919_year.jpg.

12

Eiffel Tower–Anti

TATLIN'S TOWER

"Be Creators"

As a creator-rebel, I am telling you who are still capable of demolishing, to destroy everything old, everything outmoded, everything that's in the way, everything dying, everything superfluous, everything enslaving, everything oppressing us.

To you who are in power, to you, the victors, I say: Do not stop on the path of revolution, move ahead, and if the framework of your parties and treaties hinders you in life creation, destroy them, be creators, don't be afraid of losing anything, for the destructive spirit is the creative spirit, and your revolutionary procession will give you the power in the creative spirit, and your revolutionary path will give you the power of creative invention and bright will be your path of revolutionary-creation.

To you who come into power, you, the victors, brothers in spirit, creators of the brush, the pen, and the chisel, to you, who only yesterday starved in attics and today are commissars of art, I say: Do not barricade yourselves behind desks of your collegiums and bureaucratic offices, remember that time is passing, and you have not yet done anything for your brothers, and they are still hungry, as they were yesterday. . . . Remember the creative work of the rebels.

To you, who have come to life, to all living humankind, I say: May you all be gods and sovereigns, do not wrap yourselves in old blankets of our grandmothers' art, do not sleep on the feather beds of our great-grandfathers' love, do not chew the cud of science's old words. Do not fear a life of rebellion, build your life without guardians and prejudices, be heroes for yourselves! Move ahead, invent, search . . . be rid of and destroy everything superfluous, unneeded. Be free eternally youthful seekers. . . . In short, be creators, and not a herd, O you, living people!

Aleksandr Rodchenko (May 17, 1918)

Aleksandr Rodchenko wrote these words in the pages of the journal *Anarkchina* (*Anarchy*) using the pseudonym "Anti."[1] If the pen name captured his nihilism, the statement itself revealed his Nietzschean streak. In the thrall of revolution, he revealed a Nietzschean "secret"—a secret to the "greatest fruitfulness and greatest enjoyment of existence"—which in Nietzsche's words, added up to a wager for the modern world: "live dangerously."[2] To live dangerously in revolutionary times can lead to many things, but whatever it leads to, in such times, it is always an encounter with "the political."[3] Manifesting in this mode, the political is always registered as a tightening of life around "friend and enemy groupings"—as an "intensification of internal antagonisms"—and, ultimately, as "the real possibility of physical killing."[4] In other words, revolutionary movements always reside within this broadly Schmittian framing of the political because, at the very moment when the possibility of revolutionary violence is on the horizon, it is touched by an intense sense of commitment and thereby gains a sense of enchantment. It

1 Reprinted in Rodchenko, *Experiments for the Future*, 82.

2 Nietzsche, *The Gay Science*, 283.

3 "'The Political' can be anywhere along the spectrum of intensity," and revolution is nothing if not a form of directed intensity. Arditi, "On the Political," 8.

4 Schmitt, *The Concept of the Political*, 49, 32.

transforms the intensity of the Schmittian "either/or" of violence into a source of inspiration and sacrifice.

"Unyielding antagonism and stinging rebuke," claimed Martin Heidegger, can lead to a "thrownness without mastering it."[5] Heidegger's theological reach and existential leanings bring forth terms like *thrownness* that lead Adorno to dismiss this work as jargon.[6] The "thrownness" of this Heideggerian political example shares, however, a strange kinship with passionate love, religious commitment, music, the poetic, the gift, and all other forms that tap into affective currents, none of which are ever "mastered." These domains, therefore, share, to varying degrees and in different circumstances, a capacity to fundamentally throw the subject such that their own sense of self can be called into question. Haunted by this inspired and enchanted sense of being thrown, one is inevitably drawn to the question of Being. The political, if reduced to a simple binary of friends and enemies, captures neither the channeling process that leads away from the binary into a world of market veridiction nor the importance of the thrownness of Being that is so central to the intensities of revolutionary politics. Rightly or wrongly, for good or ill, this sense of thrownness, in revolutionary politics, is lived as an intensity, yet, when the phantasmagorical commodity form begins to world our world, it is this intensity that is "disaggregated," washed away, siphoned off, or otherwise diverted. In revolutionary politics, that intensity is lived as a single political form and it is this world that opened up in the Soviet Union in 1918 with the violent lyricism of Anti's manifesto.[7]

As Rodchenko's pen name "Anti" of 1918 gave way to the nom de plume Constructor Rodchenko in 1920, his newly established Constructivist school promised much more than a new art form. In the words of Manfredo Tafuri, it constituted nothing less than a homology of the revolution itself.[8]

5 See Heidegger, "What Is Metaphysics?," 105.

6 Directly drawing a parallel between political disenchantment and the authentic in Heidegger, Adorno compares the effects of disenchantment to Siegfried Kraucauer's celluloid-collar proletariat who thought of themselves as "special" while they were simultaneously losing their jobs. See Adorno, *The Jargon of Authenticity*, 20.

7 Boris Groys argues that communism was "the project of subordinating the economy to politics in order to allow politics to act freely and sovereignly." See Groys, *The Communist Postscript*, xv.

8 Tafuri, *The Sphere and the Labyrinth*, 120.

Art would forethrow in the same way revolutions would because this was an art form linked to the science of historical materialism. Art was not the only field that underwent this revolution in understanding.

Evgeny Pashukanis would riffle through the pages of Marx's *Capital* to uncover a buried critique of bourgeois legal forms such that law itself was shaken to its foundations. Through his work, and the work of others in the commodity-exchange school, there was the specter of a withering away of law under socialism, just as Marx had spoken of the withering away of the state.[9] Valentin Nikolaevic Volosinov made no mention of Marx's *Capital* in his dialogical engagements, but his linguistic methodology would, nonetheless, carry the "philosophical spirit of Marxism" into a study of the sign by challenging the "I" of speech signification with a more fundamental "we" of the collective.[10] And then there was Alexsandr Bogdanov, the father of Proletkult and one-time rival of Lenin. He would develop his revolutionary theory of tektology by pushing Marxism toward a new science of organization, centering on a new organization of culture.[11]

Tektology, coming from the Greek word *tektron*, meaning "builder," would chime in unison with Rodchenko's own notion of Constructivism but would pull away from orthodox Marxism in that it would privilege systems theory and organizational forms over property relations. Politically, however, Marxism and Bogdanovism would pull together in their shared claim that the scientifically highest form of humanity came from the technically highest mode of production. The machine age would, therefore, herald a new sense of Being in the world, and in the age of the machine, this subject-class was one that had the highest level of education in the advanced organizational forms that technological advances had enabled. They would be the masters of the machine. These people were, in both Marx's and Bogdanov's works, the proletariat.[12]

9 Pashukanis, *Law and Marxism*.

10 Matejka and Titunik, translator's note, 1.

11 Bogdanov, *Essays in Tektology*. On Bogdanov's challenge to Lenin, see Sochor, *Revolution and Culture*, 127.

12 See Bogdanov, *Essays in Tektology*, 32–33. According to Sochor, for Bogdanov, workers as a category were like "the chosen people," acting as a source of inspiration and the principal participants in the creation of a new proletarian culture. See Sochor, *Revolution and Culture*, 131.

In this continued romance with the machine, albeit one that would lead to the (abstract) lionization of its operator (the proletariat), one begins to tap into an alternative stream of modernist thought and an alternative form of art. This alternative modernism took root in the Soviet Union and took on a concrete and monumental form in the plans of Vladimir Tatlin. The tower that he planned was to be the headquarters of the Third International, had it ever been realized. Going beyond "the first realization of the aesthetics of iron" (the Eiffel Tower), Tatlin's Tower was, as Vladimir Mayakovsky described it, "the first monument without a beard" (figure 12.1).[13] This was to be the age of Tatlin's Machine Art.[14]

While Tatlin and the Soviet Constructivists' work had drawn on the rich, telluric traditions of Russian folk art, in a time of revolution, life needed to become much more precise and scientific.[15] "Constructivism was a metaphor for the technical organization of the real," Tafuri suggests. "Geometry" versus "the organic" was how El Lissitzky described their struggle.[16] It was at the point where struggle becomes real in the realm of the aesthetic, that the geometrical and the political mind became fused.[17] They fused because, as Boym makes clear with regard to Tatlin's Tower, Constructivism managed to wed machine and myth.[18] And it is here, under the shadow of Eiffel's tower, turning away from Ferris's wheel and carrying the spirit of the political to

13 Quoted in Lynton, *Tatlin's Tower*, 90.

14 As previously mentioned, the association of Tatlin and Machine Art comes from the Dadaists. It was at the Berlin Dadaist Fair of May 1920 that George Grosz and John Heartfield held up a large placard taken down from the gallery wall with the slogan "Art Is Dead—Long Live Tatlin's Machine Art" written across it. They were then photographed. For them, *Machinenkunst* flagged the death of art. See Lynton, *Tatlin's Tower*, 30–67, for details. See also Tafuri, who points to differences within the Dadaists precisely around questions of the political. See Tafuri, *The Sphere and the Labyrinth*, 130–33.

15 "Constructivism was a metaphor for the technical organization of the real," according to Tafuri, *The Sphere and the Labyrinth*, 137. On the Russian Futurists' connection to peasant and modern art, and how this combined in a figure like Tatlin, who offered a radical alternative to Cubism, see Lynton, *Tatlin's Tower*, 3–8.

16 Lissitzky, *Russia*, 62.

17 Todorov, *Red Square, Black Square*, 17.

18 Boym, *Architecture of the Off-Modern*, 12–13.

new heights, that Tatlin would develop his ideas and build his tower, albeit only in his head.

Designed to spiral four hundred meters into the St. Petersburg sky, its angled, iron, spirelike superstructure[19] would have been an engineering masterpiece, yet what captured the imagination was its ability to wed form and function and carry the message of revolution to the world. With a spiraling exoskeleton wrapping itself around a core until it reaches the point where it pierced heaven, the reference to Athanasius Kircher's painting of the Tower of Babel is obvious (see figure 10.1). For Lynton, this resemblance to Babel is the return of myth, but myth tied to a monumental calling.[20] If Babel was the first attempt to break free of God's will by (paradoxically) (re)uniting humanity through His language and His knowledge, Tatlin's Tower seemed to suggest that a new world where Being is unified and humanity united could be achieved through the homology of science and revolution.[21] Despite the secularity of science, the death of God, and the victory of the revolution, in Tatlin's Tower one still finds a sense of a Babel-like calling, still gains a sense of the idea of fore-thrown-ment, and still appears to have a driving desire to retrieve a sense of Being's wholeness. Its spiraling tower was designed to produce this sense of awe and anticipation. Quite simply, it was inspirational.

Inside this Babel-like skeletal form, attached to a central column, Tatlin wanted to construct three revolving vaults, each a different shape but each big enough to house a workforce. This internal structure of the tower, masked by the skeletal spire, reveals the power and political structure of an organization charged with the concrete task of fomenting world revolution, namely, the Comintern. Here was a monument to international communism and a workspace that would make it happen. Here, then, was a monument to the future, not the past. Spinning at different speeds, each of the

19 According to Boym, the tower "sabotaged" the perfect verticality of the Eiffel Tower by its off-centered spiral. Boym, *Architecture of the Off-Modern*, 10.

20 According to Lynton (Lynton, *Tatlin's Tower*, 76), Athanasius Kircher's famous seventeenth-century representation of the Tower of Babel was evident in the design. Catherine Merridale says of this point that "the incorporation of Orthodox, mystical and folk traditions in Tatlin's work is uncontroversial." Merridale, "All Wood and Dreams."

21 Heidegger points back to Gottfried Wilhelm Leibniz and the first employment of the notion of reason in the seventeenth century when he proposes that "as the first existing cause of all beings, God is reason." See Heidegger, *The Principle of Reason*, 27.

three internal "compartments"—a semispherical structure, a pyramid, and a cylinder—would house different branches of the Comintern.

The semispherical structure situated at the top of the tower would rotate once a year and would be used for lectures and legislative purposes by the Soviet of the People's Commissars of the World (*Sovnarkom*). A pyramid-shaped vault located directly below this would rotate monthly and house administrative offices and committees of the Third International. At the bottom was a cylindrical vault that would rotate daily. That vault contained the propaganda department that would be in charge of "disseminating information to the world proletariat."[22] If the annual rotation of the semispherical structure at the top suggested the careful, yet decisive, decision-making of a leadership, the vault below, housing the administration, suggests a faster pace of implementation (hence its monthly rotation). The need for rapid grassroots responses was registered in the daily revolutions of the propaganda department offices in the cylindrical vault at the base. As a functionalist mapping of communist power, the building reflected the utopian dynamics of the Soviet revolution. Where Ferris's wheel would spin for pleasure, profit, and entertainment, Tatlin's Tower used each revolution of the vaults to capture something of the revolutionary temporality of Soviet political power. Where the Eiffel Tower was, in the words of Barthes, a pure signifier of seeing and being seen,[23] Tatlin's Tower was a working space that revealed a utopian version of the internal dynamics of communist power.

Yet this internal structure only relates to organizational structures, not revolutionary appeal. To bring forth revolution, to connect to the affective flow, required more than instrumental-functional knowledge and movement. It needed the type of sacred intensity that the Babel-like form of its exoskeleton seemed to suggest. It required the world to listen and understand the language of revolution.[24] In presenting this, however, it functions like Walter Benjamin's allegorical tale of the chessboard, the puppet, and the hunchback in his first thesis on history. As in that thesis, Tatlin's Tower revealed a sacred

22 For details and disputes about this internal structure, see Lynton, *Tatlin's Tower*, 100. See also Boym, *Architecture of the Off-Modern*, 9.

23 Barthes, *The Eiffel Tower and Other Mythologies*, 5.

24 As Boris Groys notes, "Capitalism appears in the medium of money not in the medium of language, and most particularly not in the medium of rational language." Groys, *The Communist Postscript*, 22.

sense of thrownness that only the weak Messianic power within the science of historical materialism could supply.[25]

This thrownness of Tatlin was based on a form of politics that moved beyond questions of engineering and into the realm Bataille once called the heterogeneous.[26] Here, pushed by a sense of political intensity rather than religious faith, Tatlin moved Machine Art from the homogeneous realm of geometric precision into an entanglement with the heterogeneous realm. Tatlin's Tower was a monumental form that merged a "faith in the geometrical" based on the rationality of the industrial age into a structure that would drive the affective flow, not toward Loewy and a materialism of endless consumer distraction, but toward revolutionary fore-thrown-ment.

Tatlin's Tower, like Constructivism more generally, however, inspired a cerebral rather than emotional sense of thrownness. This is because the Constructivist movement was based on producing a form of cognitive or mental "estrangement"[27] through its focus on materials: on squares (Malevich, 1915);[28] on lines, grids, and points (Rodchenko, 1919);[29] and on collage and photomontage. Yet, despite their desire for scientific precision, the Constructivists would produce what Svetlana Boym would call "enchanted technology." "Founded on charisma as much as calculus, linked to premodern myths as well as to modern science," enchanted technology is quite different from the "technology of fantasy" that Koolhaas claims built Manhattan.[30] It differed in that the estrangement the Constructivists tried to induce flagged the need for revolutionary change outside regimes of market veridiction.

25 Benjamin's first and second thesis on history makes this materialist encounter with the theological clear. See Benjamin, "Theses on the Philosophy of History," 245.

26 As previously noted, Georges Bataille makes the distinction between the homogeneous world of science, reason, and technic on one hand and the heterogeneous realm of excess, exuberance, and the sacred on the other. See Bataille, "The Psychological Structure of Fascism."

27 Boym, *Architecture of the Off-Modern*, 7, 19–22.

28 Petrova, *Malevich*.

29 Rodchenko, *Experiments for the Future*.

30 On "enchanted technology," see Boym, *Architecture of the Off-Modern*, 19–22; Boym, "Tatlin, or, Ruinophilia." On "technology of fantasy," see Koolhaas, *Delirious New York*, 29.

"The monument is made of iron, glass, and revolution," Viktor Shklovsky would write, claiming it was analogous to literary language. The "air of revolution," he added, was its "glue" and the masses, its glue makers.[31] For Constructivism more generally, it was time to turn art into glue. "It is time for art to merge with life," Rodchenko would thunder. "Down with art as a bright patch on a mediocre life of a propertied man. . . . Down with art as a means of escaping a life that isn't worth living. Work for life and not PALACES, TEMPLES, CEMETERIES and MUSEUMS. Work in the midst of everyone, and with everyone."[32] Rodchenko's battle cry tied the Constructivist movement to the flow of the everyday and, by the 1920s, that led them back to the factory floor. Here, the Constructivists designed dishes, teapots, work clothes, textiles, interiors, and furniture.[33] Like Loewy in America, they, too, were streamlining the everyday, but unlike Loewy, their work was not based on the beauty of an upward sales curve, but on helping to reinforce and produce a rising revolutionary consciousness.

The Constructivists would call their approach Production Art and its purpose was to redesign the nature of revolutionary life, not just sell products.[34] Production Art was not industrial design, for the radical aesthetic that the Constructivists were creating worked against the kind of "acceptability" Loewy's MAYA (more advanced yet acceptable) demanded. Instead, the Production Art of the Soviet Constructivists had another agenda: to inspire a form of revolutionary estrangement that would simultaneously enchant. As Vladimir Mayakovsky's work on propaganda poster design made clear, their task wasn't simply to advertise or decorate the revolution, it was to inspire revolution by drawing out the potential in each of us: "It meant Red Army soldiers looking at posters before a battle and going to fight not with a prayer but a slogan on their lips."[35] Production Art developed a lyrical joyousness because, as Mayakovsky said, "The streets became their brushes and the squares their palettes."[36]

31 Boym, *Architecture of the Off-Modern*, 15.

32 Rodchenko, *Experiments for the Future*, 142–43 (capital letters in the original).

33 Rodchenko, *Experiments for the Future*, 141.

34 Rodchenko, *Experiments for the Future*, 141.

35 Lynton, *Tatlin's Tower*, 112.

36 "The streets our brushes, the squares our palettes" is drawn from the Mayakovsky poem "An Order to the Army of the Arts." See Berger, "Art and Revolution."

Here was an aesthetic practice designed to break through the barriers separating art from practice and, in the main, produce "real things" in the service of everyday life.[37] With Constructivism, this homology was designed to induce a radical estrangement based on a "faith in the geometrical" that, in turn, required a radical political faith in the virtues of the revolution.[38] Yet this revolution would build on the same language game that had once led to Prince Albert suggesting the laws of science were the standard of action. Taking it in a radically different direction did not lead to a questioning of the underlying positivism underpinning this language game, but it did bring to the surface a radically different way of living within the positivist frame undergirding modernity.

Both the market-based capitalist and Soviet-based political veridiction systems offered a break with past forms based on their shared commitment to modernity, growth, and overcoming the telluric. While the former would grow on the back of the infusion of the phantasmagoric into the material object, the latter wanted estrangement from the commodity form that would strip away its mythic quality to reveal another higher truth. At the heart of both of these two projects, however, was the figure of modernity. Both displayed a desire not simply to contour and discipline the telluric, but to build over it and overcome it. Be it socialist or capitalist, both worked within the broad parameters of enlightenment reason, and both would attempt to steer the affective energy flow toward a notion of profit, be that economic in the West or political in the Soviet Union. Indeed, both worked to overcome, not embrace, the telluric. This shared desire to overcome the telluric stands in contrast to certain strands of Maoism that attempted to both draw from the indigenous-grounded knowledges of the peasant, as well as from science. This opened onto another way of engaging with the telluric. Just how central this was to become to Maoism is clear from the very first moments of communist rustication, and it is to this that we will now turn.

37 R. French, *Plans, Pragmatism, and People*, 39.

38 See Boris Groys, who argues that this is where the avant-garde and Stalinism connected, evidenced by Stalin's appropriation of the idea that "writers are the engineers of human souls." See Groys, *The Total Art of Stalinism*, 37.

PART 5

Becoming Political

Figure 13.1.

13

Becoming Maoist

An Introduction

The political is at its clearest when it's at its most intense, Carl Schmitt tells us,[1] and it is at its most intense, he later adds, in the "telluric partisanship" of Mao Zedong. It was Mao Zedong's telluric partisanship that gets us closer—"closer than Lenin," Schmitt tells us—to "the core of the matter."[2] The core of the matter for Schmitt was, of course, the concept of the political.

1. "The political is the most intense and extreme antagonism, and every concrete antagonism becomes that much more political the closer it approaches the most extreme point, that of the friend-enemy grouping." Schmitt, *Concept of the Political*, 29.

2. "With Mao there is still a concrete factor with reference to the partisan, whereby he came closer than Lenin to the core of the matter which made it possible for him to think the partisan through to the end. In short: Mao's revolution was more telluric." Schmitt, *The Theory of the Partisan*, 57.

"The war will come, the wolves will become Bolsheviks," but then Freud would come and the wolf man, cured.[3] Not Mao Zedong. Instead of being cured, he chose to go up the mountain (*shangshan*).[4] There, in his mountain hideout, the absolute antagonism of Mao's telluric partisanship produced an intensity that was rendered in action, in political action, in a form of "wolfing." The intensity of the pack—interlacing telluric and filial elements into the modern political by turning affective energy flows into powerful emotional intensities—yielded a political outcome. The merging and accretion of interlacing affective flows under the rubric of revolution bring us, theoretically, to the question of intensity but geographically to the birthplace of the Maoist revolutionary telluricism: Jinggang Mountain. It was at Jinggang Mountain that Mao's telluric partisanship first came into being in a process that began almost by chance soon after the ragtag remnants of the Red Army arrived there.[5]

In 1927, a band of defeated Red Army soldiers found their way to Jinggang Mountain, a remote mountainous region that offered them respite after the massacre of communists in Shanghai and the failure of their Autumn Harvest Rising. There, in this former bandit lair, they would build a munitions factory (*junxiechang*), a print shop (*yinshuachang*), a Red marketplace (*Hongse*

3. This is a quote from Deleuze and Guattari. The reference to wolves is a reference to the "pack," and that pack mentality enters into the revolutionary spirit of the Bolsheviks. The cynical reference to a cure for the wolf man takes Deleuze and Guattari away from that connection and back to the Freudian critique they offered in *Anti-Oedipus*, that is, the ongoing questioning of the Freudian "cure." Pulling away from psychoanalysis and moving into the realm of the political, the "curing" of the Bolshevik wolf might well be thought of as the stultifying effects of the bureaucratic structures imposed on the Soviet Union after the revolution. Deleuze and Guattari, *A Thousand Plateaus*, 43.

4. We first encountered Mao Zedong using this expression as early as July 1927 when he urged the Provincial Peasant Association to "go up the mountain." According to Yu Boliu and Chen Gang, this idea becomes very important for understanding the move to the countryside. On Mao's idea of "going up the mountain," see Yu Boliu and Chen Gang, *The Complete History*, 40–46. Examples of Mao's urgings to go up the mountain can be seen in a range of early texts, such as "The Hunan Problem" (July 4, 1927) and "The Overall Tactics of the Peasant Movement at the Present" (Central Committee Circular, Peasant Series no. 9, July 20, 1927), in Schram and Hodes, *Mao's Road to Power*, vol. 3, pp. 11, 19.

5. Communist forces are said to have begun entering this part of the country from September 25, 1927. Yu Boliu and Chen Gang, *The Complete History*, 3.

xuchang), a Red Army hospital (*Hongjun yiyuan*), and a Red Army mint (*zaobichang*).[6] These enterprises would only survive for a matter of months, destroyed when Jinggang Mountain fell to the enemy in January 1929.[7] Nevertheless, the construction of these things showed communist intent. Building a munitions factory, print shop, and hospital showed the centrality of the military struggle at this particular moment[8] while the market and mint were said to be signs of the importance being placed on developing the economy of this impoverished region.[9] What the Red Army hospital and Red Army mint also show, however, is that something other than socialist modernity or military concerns was at work. The hospital and mint help reveal two early transformational engagements that Chinese socialist modernity had with

6. Liang Jie, "On Knowledge of the 'Gong' Coin," 45.

7. The Jinggang Mountain base-camp mint existed between May 1928 and January 1929. In five huge military campaigns, the Nationalist army tried to dislodge the Red Army from this entire region. They succeeded only on their fifth attempt in 1934, thus occasioning the legendary Long March. The actual Jinggang Mountain base camp fell during the third of these enemy encirclement campaigns. For one of the most contemporary and detailed works on this particular base camp, see Yu Boliu and Chen Gang, *The Complete History*, 328.

8. After the failure of the Autumn Harvest Rising, Mao Zedong criticized the bookish subjectivism of some Party members and said that "from now on we need to focus attention on military matters." Mao Zedong, "Speech at the Emergency Central Committee Meeting," 2. Again in August 1927, Mao Zedong pointed to the need to focus on military matters saying, "Our Party's past mistake has been to ignore military matters, now, we must put 60% of our effort into military affairs and realize that if we want to construct political power, we need to seize political power through the barrel of a gun." Mao Zedong, "The Hunan Autumn Harvest Rising," 7. According to Stuart Schram, Mao's writings were, unsurprisingly given his situation, dominated by military affairs. See Schram, introduction to *Mao's Road to Power*, vol. 3, p. xxi.

9. He Xiaowen notes the role played by coins produced at Jinggang Mountain in the development of trade and the local market. He Xiaowen, "Jinggangshan's Silver 'Gong' Coin." Mao Zedong actually mentions military and economic powers as two of the five conditions enabling the establishment of an armed worker peasant liberated zone. The other three were the suitability of the military terrain and having the support of the masses as well as a good Party to lead them. See Mao Zedong, "The Struggle on Jinggang Mountain," 21.

indigenous telluric knowledge forms. In both cases, necessity proved to be the mother of Maoist invention.

It has been said that the first communist hospital was established soon after Mao Zedong arrived in Maoping, Ninggang County, in October 1927.[10] The arrival of the Red Army resulted in Maoping's Panlong Bookshop (*Panlong shudian*) being turned into a makeshift hospital with around forty staff members.[11] In such makeshift facilities, facing a constant shortage of Western medicines,[12] instruments, and trained staff,[13] the Party had little choice other than to rely on local indigenous treatments and cures. To deal with shortages, Party health workers would go up the mountain in search of medicinal plants and herbs.[14] With precious few other options, the Party had little choice other than to go up the mountain.

10 The 4th Red Army hospital was said to have been built in October 1927 when the Red Army entered Ninggang. In the summer of 1928, however, the hospital was moved to the village of Xiaojing. Stuart Schram says that Mao went up the mountain at the end of October 1927 and, while he found no substantial texts available from September 1927 to May 1928 to verify this, we do know from Mao's writings on October 5, 1928, the importance placed on the hospital. A good hospital, along with strong fortifications, and an ample amount of stored food are the three key ways to ensure base-camp consolidation, Mao says. For Stuart Schram's comments, see Schram, introduction to *Mao's Road to Power*, vol. 3, pp. xxiv–xxv. On the three key points to consolidate a base camp, see Mao Zedong, "China's Red Political Power," 18.

11 The unit was headed by Cao Rong with Zhao Fazhong as Party chief, according to Yu Boliu and Chen Gang, *The Complete History*, 70.

12 Yu Boliu and Chen Gang chronicle the requests and the various means the communists at Jinggang Mountain used to get more Western medicine and help. One informant from the period recalled to Yu Boliu and Chen Gang the dire straits the communists were in in October 1927, when this hospital began with only one Western-trained doctor and two Chinese doctors with only three more Chinese doctors arriving in November 1927. The base hospital lacked Western medicine, but with local help, they were able to dig up over seventy medicinal forms of plants that could then be used for cures. For details, see Yu Boliu and Chen Gang, *The Complete History*, 71–72.

13 Yu Boliu and Chen Gang point out that nurses were even having to improvise by "using bamboo to make tweezers [*niezi*] and knives to apply ointments, and containers to put the ointments in." Yu Boliu and Chen Gang, *The Complete History*, 72.

14 Yu Boliu and Chen Gang record one informant telling them this. See Yu Boliu and Chen Gang, *The Complete History*, 72.

For a Party that had a leadership made up of iconoclastic, modernist urban intellectuals and tied to a nineteenth-century positivist ideology, this transition into the countryside must have been particularly difficult. After all, in those days, it was just this sort of modernist influence in China's urban areas that had led to the dismissal of all traditional Chinese thought, including its medicinal cures as unscientific and irrational.[15] On Jinggang Mountain, however, the modernist communists had little else to rely on. Thrown back on such resources, the communists would learn to "make do" and, in so doing, they would gradually come to recognize the value of traditional indigenous treatments and cures. Thus, despite variations and changes in emphasis over time, the idea of bringing Western and Chinese traditions together into one field became the basis of Maoist medical practice. While this would later grow to become the basis of traditional Chinese medicine (TCM), the general approach and style of thought that would lead to that new field being developed were born on the Red Army hospital beds of Jinggang Mountain.[16]

Traditional cures and treatments would become part of the new Maoist medicine, but there would be a price for such an inclusion. Where traditional cures were tied to a Chinese cosmogony that recognized that the flow of vital energy, or *qi*, was, like the Tao itself, everywhere and in everything, with the new Maoist medicine, this universalizing cosmogony gave way to a narrower understanding centering on a knowledge not of the cosmos, but of

15 Indeed, a case in point was the declining fortunes of traditional Chinese medicine. Ken Rose argues that had it not been for the Chinese Communist Party "the subject may have continued to decline and recede into China's hinterland." See Ken Rose, new foreword to *The Yellow Emperor's Classic of Internal Medicine*, v. For details on this decline, see also Lei, "How Did Chinese Medicine Become Experiential?" The case of Chinese medicine's decline is, however, somewhat more complicated than either of these two texts suggest. If Rose is right, how does one explain the existence of Chinese medicine in Chinese communities outside the Mainland? Indeed, even trying to unify the various strands of traditional Chinese treatments, remedies, and cures into something we might recognize as a discipline or "field" (i.e., traditional Chinese medicine) is problematic. As Kim Taylor makes clear, this "field" was never unified and was consistently changing emphasis from the very earliest of times. Taylor, *Chinese Medicine in Early Communist China*, 4. Thanks to Judith Farquhar for alerting me to this.

16 See Taylor, *Chinese Medicine in Early Communist China*, for a detailed history of the later process that led to the field of TCM being named.

the human body.[17] In much the same way as capitalist economies tended to focus on finance, trade, and economic flows, the new Maoist medicine confined concerns about the flow of vital energy largely to matters of the body.[18]

Nevertheless, vital energy flows would continue to underpin this form of health work. If the Red Army hospital at Jinggang Mountain shows the early effects of this indigenous knowledge encounter with modern Western medical sensibilities that would eventually lead to the hybrid knowledge form (i.e., TCM), the construction of a Red Army mint would reveal another effect of indigenous knowledge on communist practices and thought. This time, it would be an encounter leading directly into the realm of the political. Work around the mint would lead Maoism "up the mountain" not to collect herbal remedies, but, instead, to collect an altogether different form of telluric remedy.

17 This is not to suggest that the idea of vital energy was not important in other fields (such as architecture or design, calligraphy, or martial arts), only that the disciplinary concerns of Western medicine that centered on the body established the boundaries of the concerns of traditional treatments expressed under the nomenclature of TCM.

18 This engagement with Western medicine, with its focus on science and the body, led, over time, to changes and additions to Chinese medical discourse. Even key traditional concepts such as *qi*, *yin/yang*, and the five phases (*wuxing*) would find themselves being redescribed (*qi*), replaced (*yin/yang*), or ignored altogether (*wuxing*). Taylor notes how Zhu Lian's important text *The New Acupuncture* (1954)—which became an early and key document of the Maoist New Medicine—abandoned the concepts of *qi*, *yin/yang*, and the *wuxing* because they were thought to be unscientific and outmoded. See Taylor, *Chinese Medicine in Early Communist China*, 26. By the 1960s, these key terms were being worked around through references to Mao's work. In February 1969, the medical version of the Little Red Book (*A Compilation of Materials on Following the Command of Mao Zedong Thought with New Medical Methods*) was published, and it does not mention the *wuxing*, demotes *qi*, and replaces the idea of balancing forces through *yin/yang* with the more Maoist idea of resolving contradictions. In place of traditional concepts, references are made to Mao Zedong and the key idea of focusing on practice. Hence, the practical nature of this Little Red Book, which was small enough to carry around and use as a practical reference. The manual was designed for medical workers to aid them in carrying out diagnosis, treatment, and cure. As a practical manual for medical workers rather than a theoretical tome, why certain old concepts had been dropped, replaced, or decentered was left unaddressed.

Like the hospital, the mint was born of a hybrid knowledge encounter but, unlike TCM, the infections that came through mint work would relate to the body-politic, not just the human body. Moreover, unlike traditional cures and treatments that became codified as part of a particular technical knowledge regime (TCM), the mint reveals a communist encounter with a set of techniques, not just for forging and counterfeiting coins, but for intensifying affective bonding through a shared sense of righteousness. This, in turn, intensified the notion of comradeship within Maoism by adding to it the shadow of an ethical bond born of the "brother."[19]

For this reason, the infections of the mint were quite unlike those of the Jinggang Mountain hospital. Unlike traditional healing practices, the techniques of the mint workers did not contribute to any consciously extending knowledge bank that would, like Chinese remedies and techniques, one day become a field (i.e., TCM). Instead, the influence of the mint lay in its unconscious effect on communist practices and thought.

The mint draws us not toward circuits of capital as we might expect, but toward the fluid and the telluric elements within the Maoist political. It helps us trace the affective flow as it is transformed into political intensity. This heterogeneous current would flow into communist partisan practices through an encounter with the *jianghu*,[20] and it is this current through which the politics of intensity can be traced. This, however, is only possible through a closer examination of the Red Army replica mint museum of Jinggang Mountain.[21]

19 It is interesting to note here that in the early Communist Party parlance, familial terminology (for example, the use of the epithet "elder brother" rather than "comrade") was often used in correspondence between Party members. So extensive was this use of familial terminology that it became almost a trope. Stuart Schram points out that Mao's early writings to various Party officials, and their responses, were full of familial terms. See, for example, Schram, *Mao's Road to Power*, vol. 3, p. 49n1. See also the Provincial Committee's use of the term in Schram, introduction to *Mao's Road to Power*, vol. 3, p. xxix. Thanks, here, to Professor Xu Zhangrun for first pointing out to me this early trait of the Chinese Communist Party.

20 "To hide in forests and mountains, to roam the *jianghu* [rivers and lakes]" (*Yinju shanlin, dunji jianghu*) is how the slogan of old would refer to this ideal. See Liu Yanwu, *Tracing the Sources*, 1.

21 It is important to note that the Nationalist Party also had a *jianghu* infection, albeit of an altogether different nature. Criminal elements had helped the Nationalists massacre the communists in Shanghai, thereby forcing them out of the cities and into the rural "badlands." The Nationalist leader, Jiang Jieshi, had very close

"If you want to understand the revolutionary history of China," writes Li Zengwen, "Jinggang Mountain is both the birthplace and cradle of the revolution."[22] It is a "must-see" for any Chinese "Red tourist," and Li Zengwen, who works at the Bank of China, was one such tourist. Being interested in both politics and finance, Li had traveled all the way from Shijiazhuang to the village of Shangjing in the Jinggang Mountains, principally to visit the newly rebuilt mint museum that honored the first communist coin makers. Opened in 1998 by the local Jinggang Mountain government tourist authorities, the Red Army Mint Museum is said to be a full-sized replica built on the foundations of the original mint that was established seventy years earlier by the nascent and beleaguered Red Army of Mao Zedong.

Li Zengwen said he was moved to write about his visit to this mint museum because he was inspired by the bravery and resourcefulness of the original mint makers.[23] Part Red tourist, part numismatic pilgrim, part amateur historian, this "Red from the bank" would momentarily forgo the spectacular sights of the Jinggang Mountain region for the somewhat more prosaic site of the replica mint museum. "There were no walls surrounding it, nothing fancy, just a traditional 'three entrance' Hakka (Kejia) style house," Li Zengwen wrote of the architecture of the mint museum. The architectural indistinctiveness of the museum building is hardly surprising. The original building, after all, had been the house of the landlord Zuo Jiagui until it was

personal ties and alliances with city-based criminal gang leaders, which were of a very different nature to the ties being grafted into place in the rural Jinggang Mountain region. Mao explicitly refers to gang members, not only leaders, and differentiates by region. In the south, Mao says, many bandits already acted under the slogan "robbing the rich to help the poor." On this, see Mao Zedong, "The Overall Tactics of the Peasant Movement at Present" (Central Committee Circular, Peasant Series no. 9, July 20, 1927), in Schram and Hodes, *Mao's Road to Power*, vol. 3, p. 18. On the relationship between the Green Gang and the Nationalists, see B. Martin, *The Shanghai Green Gang*. On the communist critique of this form of personal bonding and on drawing a clear line between that and revolutionary comradeship, see Teng Yong, "A Viewpoint on Friendship."

22 All references to the visit of Li Zengwen to the mint are drawn from Li Zengwen, "Paying Homage at the Relics," 66–77.

23 "I wanted to quickly go there to pay homage to the mint that was there and carefully listen to the story of the first mint and its place in the history of Red Army coin-making." Li Zengwen, "Paying Homage at the Relics," 66–67.

confiscated by the Red Army and turned into a mint. The building, then, was indistinguishable from other larger households in the area. In using a typical Hakka household as their mint, however, the Red Army were not only "making do," but also "making local." "Making local" became a "taken-for-granted" form of camouflage. An indigenous Hakka household architectural form would disguise the fact that this was no ordinary indigenous Hakka household; it was the mint of the revolution.

Inside the museum, Li's account chronicles the display of rudimentary tools of the rural coin makers: furnace anvils, hammers, a cooling vat (*rongyin'ou*), a press or vise (*chongyajia*), and a series of handmade stone devices designed to pound metal into shape.[24] The display cases of the museum reveal the rustic, ad hoc nature of the original coin-making enterprise. They show how the Maoist ideal of self-reliance and "making do" were very much tied up with the simple question of survival.

"The financial and economic basis of Jinggang Mountain rested upon self-reliance," the communist veteran He Changgong once wrote. He should know: he was there at the time. "This base was created early on," he said. "People were few in number and time was short. We simply didn't have time."[25] The mint, he writes, had to use materials that were "at hand" and only on that basis could it operate. As He Changgong wrote, "Because we didn't have a bank, we didn't make paper notes. Besides, we didn't even have a lithographic machine."[26] Self-reliance meant reliance on indigenous technologies and knowledge. For the Maoists, self-reliance was a survival tactic that would go on to become an ethical way of being. And that was not the only silver lining.

Living on the land, the communists would harvest, as bandits before them had done, from the fields of the rich. Jewelry, ornaments, and coins confiscated from the gentry, the landlords, traitors, and pawnshops were said

24 No one quite knows what actual tools might have been used. Yu Shiquan takes issue with the view that they used a stone mold and traditional methods of molding to make the models. He says they could not have used a stone mold as that would have been too crude for the design on the coin. See Yu Shiquan, "My Views on the Silver Coins of Jinggang Mountain," 15.

25 Quoted from "A Record of Interview with Comrade He Changgong," in Liang Jie, "On Knowledge of the 'Gong' Coin," 48.

26 Quoted from "A Record of Interview with Comrade He Changgong," in Liang Jie, "On Knowledge of the 'Gong' Coin," 48.

to have been melted down and the silver supplied to the mint.[27] From the top of Jinggang Mountain came former *jianghu* bandits with the indigenous knowledge, skill, technology, and molds to turn this silver into communist "Gong" coins (figure 13.1).[28] Class struggle met the *jianghu* at this moment of minting. The replica-mint museum, in displaying the coin makers' tools, inadvertently revealed a *jianghu* bag of tricks.

Each tool used to chisel, stamp, and mold the coin was part of an indigenous-local technology that was tied back to the fluid world of the *jianghu*. That is to say, the telluric techniques, devices, and know-how being used by the mint makers presupposed a very particular way of being in the world. It was a way of being that was summarized and romanticized in the tales of 108 bandit rebels who populate the pages of the classical Chinese *jianghu* novel, *The Water Margin* (*Shuihuzhuan*).

Written sometime in the Ming dynasty (1368–1644) but set in the Song (960–1279), it is the story of the heroic adventures of 108 bandits, each of whom had previously fought corrupt officials or dynastic injustices in the name of righteousness, and who had been forced to flee to the remote hideaway of Liang Mountain. These 108, however, were no ordinary bandits but tied to demon spirits marking the night sky as stars. Of these 108 stars, thirty-six were heavenly spirits and seventy-two lesser earthly spirits, but all of them made up the legendary band of brigands of Liang Mountain. It was from their mountain lair, led by their illustrious leader Song Jiang, that these bandits would become legends.

The similarity between the *jianghu* bandits of *The Water Margin* and the Maoist rebels of Jinggang Mountain is striking. Both were inspired by charismatic leaders, both fought under the banner of justice and righteousness, and both were forced to flee to remote mountain hideouts. One would be "forced to go to Liang Mountain" (*bishang Liangshan*), while the other would be forced to go to Jinggang Mountain, but both offered a version of what Mao called "going up the mountain" (*shangshan sixiang*).[29] In "going up the mountain," Mao's forces didn't just appear to make a similar journey to the *jianghu* rebels of Liang Mountain, but, at Jinggang Mountain, they brought

27 The claim that the silver was melted down is made in Xia Mengshu, *Traveling in Jinggang Mountain*, 52.

28 See Liang Jie, "On Knowledge of the 'Gong' Coin"; Xia Mengshu, *Travelling in Jinggang Mountain*, 52.

29 Yu Boliu and Chen Gang, *The Complete History*, 40; for details on Mao's use of the term, see 236n4.

the bandit pack into the Party. Jinggang Mountain was where Chinese communism met the rustic *jianghu*. Back in Shanghai, the underground central Party leadership were far from pleased with these Mao-inspired developments. Regarding rural bandits as nothing more than useful tools who could later be disposed of, they rebuked Mao for having far too accommodating an attitude toward them.[30] For Mao, at Jinggang Mountain, they were potential recruits.[31] In recruiting the rustic *jianghu* to the Party, however, parts of the *jianghu* ethos and mentality began to be unconsciously woven into the fabric of the communist partisan's lifeworld. In the Jinggang Mountain region, rustication involved more than going up the mountain to collect herbs and medicines; it meant an encounter with this *jianghu* spirit. And what better place could there be for such an encounter than in a remote hiding place (*yinju changsuo*) like Jinggang Mountain? This place would become the Party's Liang Mountain, not just because it was a remote, mountainous hideout but, rather, because it constituted a specific indigenous knowledge encounter that would leave its mark on the nascent Chinese Communist Party. This was the moment when the bonds of the "*jianghu* spirit" (*jianghu yiqi*) would begin to be transformed into sentiments of revolutionary comradeship (*geming qingyi*).[32] It was this, then, that constituted the first, quite concrete, yet tentative and unconscious step toward "becoming Maoist."

"Under conditions of severe armed struggle," Li Zengwen tells us, the Party "chose a local man familiar with the situation to establish the mint."

30 Stuart Schram notes that, while on Jinggang Mountain, Mao received "repeated criticisms" for his intimacy with bandits and lumpen proletarians. See Schram, introduction to *Mao's Road to Power*, vol. 3, pp. xxiv–xxv.

31 In some ways, they shared the same goals. Mainland sources underline the point being made by Mao about the bandit gangs of Jinggang Mountain. On the lower reaches of the mountain, the gang, led by Yuan Wencai, were said to have derived the bulk of their income from "fishing" (or *diaoyang*) from local tyrants, while on the upper reaches, Wang Zuo's band was said to have fought under a banner which read "Stealing from the rich, aiding the poor, eradicating violence and giving peace to the people" (*jiefu jipin, chubao anmin*). On Yuan Wencai's fishing trips, see Kuang Sheng and Liu Xiaonong, *The Heroic Pair of Jinggang*, 47. For Wang Zuo's slogan, see Ouyang Hui, "The Two Wang Zuos's Period of Struggle," 42.

32 The term "*jianghu* spirit" and the sentiment of "revolutionary comradeship" are drawn from the work of Teng Yong, but where he sees them as being oppositional concepts, I see them as the beginning and ending points of a fluid journey. See Teng Yong, "A Viewpoint on Friendship."

Li is being circumspect here.[33] When they chose Wang Zuo to run the mint, they chose the *jianghu* connection.[34] Before joining the Communist Party, Wang had been king of the mountaintop (*shan dawang*) and, along with the gang of his sworn brother, Yuan Wencai, from the lower reaches of Jinggang Mountain, they lived the *jianghu* spirit (*jianghu yiqi*) of righteous rebellion. That, at least, seems to have been Mao's assessment.[35]

"They are a green wood army and we are grass topped kings so it will be easy for us to form a family. If we get a chance, we will pay our respects to the

33 Li Zengwen, "Paying Homage at the Relics," 66–67.

34 Wang Zuo was one of two bandit kings at Jinggang Mountain at the time of Mao's arrival. The other was Wang Zuo's sworn brother, Yuan Wencai. Wang and Yuan had become blood brothers after Yuan had saved Wang Zuo from a bandit rebellion by restoring him to power on the top of the mountain. According to Stuart Schram, Yuan had joined the Communist Party as early as 1926 (Schram, introduction to *Mao's Road to Power, Volume III*, p. xxv). Wang would later follow his blood brother into the Communist Party, bringing his bandit gang with him. The strength of the feelings of *yiqi*, or spirit, among bandits of this area, and of Wang Zuo and his sworn brother, Yuan Wencai, are discussed in Cui Youfu, "How Mao Zedong Incorporated the Mountain Kings Yuan Wencai and Wang Zuo," 53–54. Ouyang Hui makes the same point while discussing the basis of their relationship:

> In 1925, Wang Zuo's forces were torn apart by internal strife and Wang Zuo was forced to flee to Yuan Wencai for refuge. Wang Zuo helped eradicate those estranged from Wang Zuo and restore him to power. From that time onwards, Yuan Wencai and Wang Zuo, who were also both the same age, became blood brothers. After this, Yuan Wencai went back down the mountain to Maoping, while Wang Zuo went back up the mountain to the villages. Being the same age and very close friends, living under the same banner and standing side by side, they were said to have "*laogeng*"relations that made them two horns [*jijiao*] of the one beast with an illustrious name that echoed across the whole of the Xiang-Gan border region. (Ouyang Hui, "The Two Wang Zuos's Period of Struggle," 42)

35 This is the argument of Cui Youfu, "How Mao Zedong Incorporated the Mountain Kings Yuan Wencai and Wang Zuo." Two texts, Ouyang Hui, "The Two Wang Zuos's Period of Struggle," and Zhang Xudong, "The Two Heroes of Jinggang Mountain," show how important this principle of *yiqi*, or what could be called "righteous energy" or "righteous spirit," was to the bandits at Jinggang Mountain. These texts also emphasize how Mao Zedong, steeped in this culture, traded in this language to bring Wang over to the communist cause.

mountain."[36] Mao would pay his respects to the mountain soon after arriving at Jinggang Mountain. Both Yuan's and Wang's bandit gangs would receive alms/arms.[37] One hundred and eight rebel spirits inhabited the pages of the legendary *jianghu* novel *The Water Margin*, while in one report, 108 rifles were said to have been given to the bandit gang of Yuan Wencai.[38] Neither bartered nor sold, the rifles were given as gifts to cement relations and to produce an affective connection. As if to confirm the idea that there is no such thing as a free gift,[39] Mao's gifts induced a debt of kindness (*bao'en*) and, for Wang Zuo, a sense, perhaps, of destinies tied.[40] As Mao inched up the mountain, Yuan would introduce Mao to the king of the mountaintop, Wang Zuo.

36 Mao Zedong quoted in Zhang Xudong, "The Two Heroes of Jinggang Mountain," 39.

37 Mao Zedong claimed that, in October 1927, Yuan Wencai and Wang Zuo's bandits had only about sixty rifles in each gang and these weapons were in a bad state of repair. See Mao Zedong, "The Struggle in Jinggang Mountain," 22. Ouyang Hui notes that, despite this lack of weaponry, the two bandit kings, Yuan Wencai and Wang Zuo, could survive because they knew the secrets of the mountains and forests and built strongholds suited to the particular geography of this region. Ouyang Hui, "The Two Wang Zuos's Period of Struggle," 42. Indeed, initially at least, the crucial difference between the Jinggang Mountain bandits and the Red Army probably rested on the possession of rifles. Together, Yuan and Wang's forces were said to number no more than four hundred bandits, but, then, Mao's forces were said to be only around seven hundred at the time of the Red Army's 1927 Sanwan reorganization (*Sanwan gaibian*)—Sanwan being the village near Jinggang Mountain where this meeting took place—and even after other forces joined them, there were possibly only a little more than one thousand soldiers. While these figures are unreliable and indeed vary greatly due to poor and limited empirical evidence and the fluctuating circumstances of war, one can at least gain from them some sense of the ratio of bandits to Red Army forces. For the figures on the Chinese Communist Party army, see Yu Boliu and Chen Gang, *The Complete History*, 57. Figures on Yuan Wencai's bandits are drawn from Cui Youfu, "How Mao Zedong Incorporated the Mountain Kings Yuan Wencai and Wang Zuo," 53, while figures on Wang Zuo's forces are drawn from data in Kuang Sheng and Liu Xiaonong, *The Heroic Pair of Jinggang*, 208.

38 Cui Youfu, "How Mao Zedong Incorporated the Mountain Kings Yuan Wencai and Wang Zuo," 53.

39 Douglas, foreword to *The Gift*, vii–xviii.

40 In distinguishing between mainstream social values and the *jianghu*, Wang Xuetai outlines two key elements of the *jianghu* code: "The society of the *jianghu*

Halfway up the slopes of Jinggang Mountain at Double Horse Rock (*Shuangmashi*), Mao met the bandit king Wang Zuo. More rifles were given, as was a counter gift and an invitation: "Let me take you up the mountain," said Wang Zuo.[41] With that, Mao climbed the slopes of Jinggang Mountain and entered into the *jianghu* world, into the language of *chundian* and into a political realm based on a gift-like economy of affective flows that would bring forth a telluric connection. When the communists and bandits joined forces and killed Wang's deadliest enemy, the counterrevolutionary bandit and tyrant Yin Daoyi, their connection turned from friendship into the blood bond of "brotherhood."[42] The forging of a blood relationship between the bandit king and the Party enabled the partisans to enter into libidinal, excessive, and incalculable social bonds that flowed within the bandit pack. If the *jianghu* bandits learned revolutionary discipline, the Communist Party learned another affective dialect in the language of the war machine.

The Telluric

There is a strange, almost uncanny resemblance between the ancient Chinese art of the *jianghu* and the war machine of Gilles Deleuze and Félix Guattari. Caveats and care aside, one might be tempted to say that the *jianghu* was to

---

lays great stress on repaying debts of kindness [*bao'en*] and on accepting those who have the same destiny as them." Wang Xuetai, *Water Margin*, 40. According to Cui Youfu, Yuan Wencai had always stressed the idea of *yiqi*, or a spirit of righteousness. Hence, Yuan Wencai responded to Mao's gift by giving him six hundred silver coins. Cui Youfu, "How Mao Zedong Incorporated the Mountain Kings Yuan Wencai and Wang Zuo," 52.

41 Quoted by Cui, who also suggests five thousand *jin* of grain—enough to provide Mao Zedong's entire army with provisions—were given. See Cui Youfu, "How Mao Zedong Incorporated the Mountain Kings Yuan Wencai and Wang Zuo," 52.

42 The Party learned that the thing that turned Wang Zuo's heart to stone was the name Yin Daoyi. Surrounding Jinggang Mountain on all sides were Wang Zuo's enemies, who went by the name of the Four Elements Butchers (*Sida tufu*). These four armed gangs were led by Yin Daoyi, who was also the chief of militia for the seven counties that made up Jinggang Mountain. Wang had fought and lost repeatedly at the hands of Yin Daoyi. Moreover, Yin had also murdered Wang's niece. There was a debt of blood that the Party would help Wang repay. Wang Zuo then submitted to the discipline of the Party, and his band joined Mao Zedong's communist forces. Cui Youfu, "How Mao Zedong Incorporated the Mountain Kings Yuan Wencai and Wang Zuo," 54.

the traditional Chinese normative Confucian order what the war machine was to the Deleuzian and Guattarian rendition of the state. The symbiotic relationship established between the "flow," or *liu*, of this spirit of rivers and lakes, or *jianghu yiqi*, and the "stability" or *wen* of Confucian orthodox society finds echo in the words of Deleuze and Guattari who speak of the nomadic playing off the sedentary. Rhizomatic in form, telluric in nature, *jianghu*, as the name (rivers and lakes) implies, constitutes a series of ephemeral flows that pool together to achieve a collective spirit. In the case of *jianghu*, the bonding agent that made things "stick" as a commitment was the notion of "brotherhood." Despite, or maybe because of, its strongly masculinist nature, this brotherly love was invested with "strange and terrifying powers" that would turn the *jianghu* into a war machine.[43]

Here was a war machine populated by sorcerers,[44] artisans,[45] actors, the founders of guilds,[46] wandering knights errant,[47] bandits, and martial artists;

43 "A secret society always acts in society as a war machine" (Deleuze and Guattari, *A Thousand Plateaus*, 317), and *jianghu* is nothing if not a secretion of the Chinese secret society. Wang Li, "Reflections on the Spirit of *Jianghu*."

44 "Sorcerers have always held the anomalous position, at the edge of the fields or woods. They haunt the fringes. They are at the borderline of the village, or between villages." Deleuze and Guattari, *A Thousand Plateaus*, 271. "After the Han dynasty, Taoism as a religion rose in prominence so the shaman went into those institutions of the Tao and became Taoists and later spiritual adepts. As they entered the world of the common people, they roamed and became all kinds of *jianghu* masters." Liu Yanwu, *Tracing the Sources*, 2.

45 "The artisan is . . . the one who follows the flow of matter . . . *the itinerant, the ambulant*," and, "The first and primary itinerant is the artisan." Deleuze and Guattari, *A Thousand Plateaus*, 452, 454. It is said that people of various trades (*wuhang bazuo*) joined the *jianghu*. Liu Yanwu, *Tracing the Sources*, 1.

46 Specialized artisans who follow the flow and form into collective bodies, secret societies, guilds, and journeymen's associations. Deleuze and Guattari, *A Thousand Plateaus*, 494. Wang Xuetai, in discussing the formation of the *jianghu* in the Song dynasty, notes that unlike the medieval European city, China's dynastic cities offered no guild protection. Those who migrated into the Chinese city were excluded, and this became a key factor in the formation of the *jianghu*. See Wang Xuetai, *The Water Margin*, 27.

47 "The war machine was the invention of the nomad." Deleuze and Guattari, *A Thousand Plateaus*, 460. On the centrality of the wandering knights-errant to the *jianghu* literary tradition, see Liu, *The Chinese Knight-Errant*.

the nomadic people of the smooth space,[48] the dispossessed, people whose very sense of being would be defined not just by exclusion but by their shared sense of a (mental and physical) hiding place.[49] It was based on the forging of life-defining bonds of blood that were so powerful that sworn brothers would kill to defend them. This is not quite the condition of the political, but it does edge it toward one of the key (Schmittian) conditions that enables it to form. It helps it form because it shifts the ground away from the private realm of consanguineous attachments and disputations toward a form that mimics this consanguineous bond but makes it open to anyone and therefore more public.[50] As it edges away from biologically based familial bonds toward an associational "brotherhood," it simultaneously edges toward a more Schmittian idea about the publicness and nonfamilial nature of the (political) enemy.[51]

Jianghu is a war machine straddling this mental and material landscape to give form—an ur-form—to a constellation of forces enabling the establishment of a political surface of emergence. *Jianghu* is a form of group inclusion via social exclusion and nonfilial brotherhoods born of sworn oaths (*baibazi jieyi*) rather than pre-given birthrights. *Jianghu* establishes a blood connection that exists not in consanguinity but in a willingness for blood to be spilled in the defense of bonds of loyalty, self-sacrifice, and *yiqi*. *Yiqi*, it should be noted, is the pooling of these flows.

48 "The primary determination of the nomad is to occupy and hold a smooth space." Deleuze and Guattari, *A Thousand Plateaus*, 452. "One of the meanings of *jianghu* is 'everywhere' [*sifang gedi*]." Liu Yanwu, *Tracing the Sources*, 1.

49 The idea of a hiding place (*yinju changsuo*) was central to any understanding of the *jianghu*. See Liu Yanwu, *Tracing the Sources*, 1.

50 At the same time, the *jianghu* is a "pack." And like any "pack," it is still tied back to family, even if, as in this case, it is invented. For the argument about the pack being tied to family, see Deleuze and Guattari, *A Thousand Plateaus*, 272.

51 In the realm of the political, Schmitt tells us, the enemy is "the other, the stranger." See Schmitt, *The Concept of the Political*, 27. At the same time Schmitt tells us that the enemy is brother. Schmitt, *Ex Captivitate Salus*, 89–99, quoted in Müller, *A Dangerous Mind*, 55. If the transition from clan to *jianghu*, and then to the Communist Party, covers the shift from (familial) brother to (public) comrade, the power of the "enemy within" discourse in early Chinese communist discourse helps us appreciate the deep enmity felt toward the brother-enemy. See Dutton, *Policing Chinese Politics*, 23–71.

Yiqi, as the authoritative *Ciyuan* notes, covers both "a spirit of righteousness," or *gangzheng zhi qi*, and a "spirit of devotion and filiality," or *zhong xiao zhi qi*.[52] Here, then, is the righteousness of the rebel wedded to filiality without a father and a form of devotion without a king. Yet still it forges bonds so strong that "the pack" would willingly sacrifice their own lives for these bonds of friendship (*wei pengyou liang leichadao*).[53] These values produced brothers who were born of a shared sense of being "other" but who were not quite the opposite of the stable and static world of the traditional Confucian order through which they flowed. Wang Xuetai explains how, for the *jianghu*, there was, in fact, the superficial appearance of many shared values with Confucian orthodoxy but this, in many ways, masked another *jianghu* conjuring trick. He demonstrates this through language.

Take the compound *zhongyi*, in which *zhong* means devotion and *yi* is righteousness. This is a concept important to both the Confucian scholar and the *jianghu* rebel, for it demonstrates the importance of *yi*, or righteousness, within both the Confucian and *jianghu* lexicons. Despite this, each gave to the notion of *yi* a different emphasis. While the Confucian *yi* is the *yi* of *renyi*, meaning benevolence and righteousness, the *yi* of the *jianghu* emphasizes the fraternal aspect of *yi* and ties that to the idea of a heroic gathering for a righteous uprising called *juyi*.[54] Here, in the term *juyi*, the concept of *yi* is ignited in a tidal bore of intensity, and it is in *The Book of Propriety* that this aspect of *yi* is made clear: "The concentrated spirit [*qi*, which blows between heaven and earth,] begins in the southwest and flourishes in the northwest. This is the *qi* that represents the most commanding severity of heaven and earth—the *qi* of righteous justice or *yiqi*."[55]

As this "concentrated spirit" (*qi*) of righteous justice flows into the compound *yiqi*, it turns the conventional moral categories of normative society

52 Commercial Press, *Ciyuan*, vol. 3, p. 2497.

53 In exploring martial arts as a type of Confucianized chivalry (*Yi zhong Ruhua le de "xiayi" gainian*), Bai Tian*yin* notes the importance of the spirit of brotherhood of the "great rivers" (*jianghu yiqi*). See Bai Tianyin, "A General Discussion," 129.

54 See Wang Xuetai, *The Water Margin*, 214.

55 "The book of propriety: the Meaning of the Drinking Festivities in the Districts." Quoted in Wang Li, "Reflections on the Spirit of *Jianghu*," 40.

into a battle cry for justice against norms corrupted.[56] Yet *jianghu* righteousness (*jianghu dayi*) neither constituted nor cleaved toward a clear and unequivocal form that would stand against the orthodoxy of the state.[57] Indeed, the *jianghu* did not really stand against the state as much as shy away from it, skip around it, flirt with it, and, sometimes, just sometimes, seduce or be seduced by it. Yet it is just this sort of ambivalence that paradoxically enabled it to remain hidden within the mainstream.

Such bonds would remain subterranean currents within the traditional familialism (*jiazu zhuyi*) of orthodox Confucian society just as they would remain hidden within a notion of comradeship within Maoism.[58] Becoming

56 One of the key radical Maoist criticisms of the *jianghu* was that their cry for justice against norms corrupted did not go far enough because it still accepted the norms. The radical Maoist writer Xu Jixu, for example, argued that the political backwardness and limit of the *jianghu* was reflected in the fact that it saw injustice as simply a corruption of traditional norms rather than regarding the whole dynastic system as being rotten. This criticism by radical Maoists in 1975 was part of a political campaign criticizing the classic novel *The Water Margin*. In many ways, Xu Jixu's words only echo a statement by Mao Zedong, who once said, "*The Water Margin* only opposes corrupt officials, it doesn't oppose the emperor." Repeated like a mantra during the 1970s campaign against *The Water Margin*, this slogan of Mao's was a frontispiece feature of the "Sayings of Chairman Mao" in the journal *Study and Criticism*. Ma Tao says that this was a statement of Mao made during the enlarged meeting of the politburo in December 1973. For more details on this, see the section "Coda: The Anti–Water Margin Campaign" in chapter 14. Xu Jixu quotes Mao in his 1975 article critiquing *The Water Margin*; see Xu Jixu, "What Is There to Praise? What Is There to Oppose?," 44.

57 Wang Xuetai, *The Water Margin*, 40.

58 On this last point, Huang Jie sees it very differently. Employing what philosophers would call the law of the excluded middle, Huang Jie draws an absolute and clear distinction between the Party and the *jianghu*, largely on the basis of the transformation of terms being outlined above. In an article written to differentiate the Communist Party from any connection to the *jianghu*, Huang Jie argues that the attitude toward this tradition was a key difference between the Communist Party and their Nationalist Party enemies. Where the Nationalist Party was tolerant, Huang Jie argues, the communists were not:

> The Chinese Communist Party was the only political unit capable of really cutting off the traditional culture of rivers and lakes [*jianghu*]. . . . The Communist Party used the loftiest of dreams to enable them to enter the peoples' hearts, used a collectivist spirit to destroy the feudal clan system [*Zongfa*

Maoist meant bringing something of this bandit spirit into the revolutionary "pack," not because of but (in part) despite its criminality.[59] It meant holding on to the telluric spirit of righteousness, or *yiqi*, even if that righteousness was now pronounced "class struggle." Through class struggle, the strength of the brotherly bond would be channeled into the category of "comrade." This unconscious fusion of the *jianghu* spirit and Party spirit, a fusion that begins in the Jinggang mountains, took place despite the criticisms of city-based Party leaders and the killing of Wang Zuo and Yuan Wencai.[60] Despite all this, the bandit pack would infect the Party with their iconoclastic rustic spirit just as the Party would politicize the spirit of the *jianghu* "pack," injecting into it the binary colors of class struggle.[61] "Becoming Maoist," then, begins with

---

> *zhidu*], and used comradely relations to replace *jianghu*-style relations. It also used Party principles to replace the spirit of *jianghu* and Party character to temper and clean out a *jianghu* atmosphere and *jianghu* habits. It thereby maintained, from start to finish, a high-handed attitude to any expression of *jianghu* culture within the Party. (Huang Jie, "How the Communist Party Transcended *Jianghu* Culture," 12, 27)

59 There is an important caveat here. While the Chinese Communist Party wanted an ideological transformation of former bandits, in terms of their actual practices, the rusticating Party also required former bandits to use their criminal skills to "expropriate from the expropriators" and secure the silver that the Party needed to forge the coin and finance the operations of the communist base camps.

60 The criticism of Mao Zedong's lenient treatment of bandits in the remote rural base camp by the Party leadership in far-off Shanghai and Moscow was noted earlier, as were the deaths, at the hands of the Communist Party, of Yuan Wencai and Wang Zuo. While Mao would fall into line with the Party line on the explanation for their deaths, Mao was nevertheless away when this occurred. For more details on their deaths, see note 26 in chapter 2 of this work. See also, Zhang Xudong, "The Two Heroes of Jinggang Mountain," 40–41, esp. note 168.

61 The use of "pack" is a very shorthand and somewhat elliptical reference to Deleuze and Guattari, who begin with the concept of the pack and the idea of "becoming animal." Even a cursory glance at the conditions enabling the formation of the pack and this process of becoming—not filiation, not consanguinity, but contagion—helps plot a path from the filiation of the Chinese lineage group to the faux consanguinity of the *jianghu* and onto the infectious intensity of Mao's telluric partisanship. This channeling of affective energy has been dealt with at length, but for details of the pack "becoming animal," see Deleuze and Guattari, *A Thousand Plateaus*, 264ff.

the politicization of the *jianghu*, just as it constituted a localized example of a newly emerging and very Chinese version of the political Dasein.

The pack that joined the Party became the Party's coin makers. They secured the silver and stamped the *gong* character on the face of the coin, for only they had the skills, connections, and technology to do this. Party leaders had demanded that mint workers be as pure as the Gong coins being minted, so it was said that only the most "loyal [*zhongcheng*] and reliable [*kekao*] of personnel were to be chosen."[62] To this end, Wang Zuo drew people from the only group he knew to be both loyal and reliable and have the requisite skills and experience to mint the coins. He would, in other words, draw from the *jianghu*.[63] Whether these bandits became "loyal and reliable" comrades or remained "loyal and reliable" sworn brothers matters little. What matters is that as comrade or as blood brother, they would channel and direct affective energy flows toward a point of political intensity. Affectivity, as an "effectuation of a power of the pack that throws self into upheaval and makes it reel,"[64] flowed from leader to the led as Mao Zedong, Zhu De, Chen Yi, and other Party leaders visited the workers at this first Red Army mint and bestowed on them the title of "Producers of the Worker-Peasant Soviet's own coinage."[65] These counterfeiters, who had once been part of the *jianghu* bandit pack, had joined a Party that would ennoble them. This, in turn, would help electrify the pack. As affective energy flowed between leader and led, the question was whether this was the flow of the *jianghu* spirit or a newfound knowledge of Marxism-Leninism that gave this energy its intensity? Whatever the cause, like an acupuncture needle that reveals a symptom, this reeling and the out-

62 On the loyalty and reliability of the recruited, see Liang Jie, "On Knowledge of the 'Gong' Coin," 46.

63 In May 1928, Wang Zuo—a Central Xiang-Gan Border Region Special Committee member and deputy commander of the thirty-second regiment of the 4th Red Army Regimental—was put in charge of the mint. From the accounts of Li and others, it is clear that he used his *jianghu* network to set this mint up. See Li Zengwen, "Paying Homage at the Relics," 66–67.

64 Deleuze and Guattari, *A Thousand Plateaus*, 265. Affective energy might surface as emotion or feeling, but their flow operates at a deeper level than their surface appearance. As such, where and how affective flows are channeled and then gain expression lies at the heart of the question of political.

65 Liang Jie, "On Knowledge of the 'Gong' Coin," 46.

burst of emotion it occasioned are signs of the affective flow central to the question of the political, for without this flow, there could be no intensity.

Political Intensity

This is not how Carl Schmitt imagines political intensity. Far from being part of an affective flow, intensity comes from enmity felt toward a public enemy in the friend/enemy dyadic structure.[66] Schmitt doesn't explain how intensity comes into being, only how it functions. In Schmitt's concept, intensity seems to operate through friction, for the greater the degree of intensity, the more the fractious dyadic core of the political is revealed. It is the enmity felt toward a public enemy that fuels this intensity and makes the political visible.[67]

It is a public enemy despite the fact that the political always involves the private realm as it "grasps man wholly,"[68] even though, as an intensity, it is always felt existentially but as *hostis* not *inimicusm*.[69] Such intensity felt so deeply toward a public enemy leads into a paradox. This enemy is the stranger; it is "the other," yet paradoxically, the enemy is also the brother-friend.[70] The high degree of animus felt in the private and autochthonous

66 According to Jan-Werner Müller, Schmitt originally believed that "an autonomous sphere of collective life" was the basis of the concept of the political, but after Leo Strauss's criticisms, which pointed to the primacy of the enemy in Schmitt's formulation of the political, Schmitt abandons his earlier belief in community and opted instead for a concept focusing on enmity. For a summary of this transition and the conclusions arrived at by Schmitt, see Müller, *A Dangerous Mind*, 32–33. See also Schmitt, *The Concept of the Political*, 26.

67 To validate this use of a public enemy, Schmitt somewhat simplistically quotes Focellini approvingly: "A public enemy is one with whom we are at war publicly. . . . In this respect he differs from a private enemy. He is a person with whom we have private quarrels. They may also be distinguished as follows: a private enemy is a person who hates us, whereas a public enemy is a person who fights against us." Schmitt, *The Concept of the Political*, 29n9.

68 Meier, *The Lesson of Carl Schmitt*, 38.

69 Schmitt, *The Concept of the Political*, 28.

70 For an account of the enemy as other and as stranger, see Schmitt, *The Concept of the Political*, 27. For the enemy as brother, see Schmitt, *Ex Captivitate Salus*, 89–99, quoted in Müller, *A Dangerous Mind*, 55. On friendship and Schmitt, see Derrida, *Politics of Friendship*, 16. While on Derrida, note the question mark he places

realm is replicated in relation to an enemy in the public realm. Rendered as a real threat to one's existential world or one's innermost desires, this enemy becomes "our own question as a figure."[71] How does this flow of intense, existentially felt affective energy cross from the intimate and private realm into the figure of a public enemy? Once rendered, not as part of an insurmountable binary division (the public/private divide) but more fluidly, like *yin/yang*, the route taken by affective flows that generates the political form becomes clearer.[72] "Brother"-friend-stranger-enemy becomes a means by which to plot a trajectory not of "real" people but of "real" affective energy flows. These energy flows surface as emotions and feelings and can be channeled in a particular direction either by the enmity felt toward a public enemy or by the bond felt toward an intimate "friend."

In tracing this flow of affective energy through the "moments" of "brother"-friend-stranger-enemy, we cross from the private realm into the public domain. In China, and for the rusticating Chinese Communist Party, the encounter with the *jianghu* was part of this transition. This is because the intensity built up around the depth of feeling that is built into the consanguinity of the lineage group or clan was transferred to the faux consanguinity of the "brother" in the *jianghu* relation and this, then, became the "stickiness" that attached itself to an intense sense of comradeship within the Commu-

behind the gendering of the Schmittian political divide. Of Schmitt, he says, "It seems to me that Schmitt never speaks of the sister," for there is, in Schmitt's work, "not a woman in sight" (Derrida, *Politics of Friendship*, 149). Sisters, he continues, "if there are any, are a species of the genus brother" (155). Derrida then goes on to suggest that "Schmitt puts gender under house arrest" (158). How far can one take this argument that is registered in passing in Derrida's *Politics of Friendship*? While Schmitt's own gender politics are clear here, it is a position that might be accentuated by the fact that the political, if built on the concept of a potentially violent binary of friend and enemy, is invariably gendered male. By refocusing on affective energy flows, does that open a channel for gender fluidity, if not the figure of the woman? On Derrida's reference to Schmitt and gender, see Derrida, *Politics of Friendship*, 149–58.

71 Here I draw on an oft-repeated statement of Schmitt, coined by his friend Theodor Däubler. Däubler wrote, "The enemy is our own question as a figure. And he will hunt us, and we him, to the same end." Theodor Däubler, "Sang an Palermo," quoted in Meier, *The Lesson of Carl Schmitt*, 1.

72 For a different approach tying brother-enemy to brother-friend, see Derrida, *Politics of Friendship*, 148.

nist Party.[73] Within the *jianghu*, consanguine bonds of blood were replaced by blood oaths and pledges that were little more than mimetically configured reimaginings of lineage-based bloodlines and kinship relations.[74]

Different from the legal contract, these sorts of pledges remained tied by various ethereal and heartfelt bonds to the affective realm, even though they were something of a decoupling of the familial and autochthonous relations. Different from kinship but still tied by blood, no longer limited to place but still carrying within them the shared telluric cultural understandings of the soil, the *jianghu* bondings generated the affective energy that only filiation could otherwise offer. The *jianghu* spirit, then, gave to Maoism this form of telluric intensity.

With *jianghu*, the private bloodline is overwritten by a public blood oath, while affective flows surface as the patriarchal love of the nonconsanguineous "brother."[75] Here are conditions that open onto the potential for the carriage of intensity from the private into the public, political realm. According to Heinrich Meier, for Schmitt, the friend/enemy distinction is "an unshakable, fixed point from and toward which a network of graded intensity pervades and orders the whole."[76] For Schmitt, then, the focus is on that static, unshakable fixed point of friend and enemy, yet the power that enables that fixed point to be registered as political is itself fluid.[77]

73 As noted earlier, this idea of "stickiness" is drawn from the work of Sara Ahmed, who traces it in relation to other political forms the subject takes. It examines how certain emotions "stick" to particular extreme political forms. For details, see Ahmed, "Affective Economies."

74 This is why the oath is, according to Heinrich Meier, a good touchstone of the political character of a community. See Meier, *The Lesson of Carl Schmitt*, 36.

75 For details on a bond that does not imply filiation and a multiplicity without the unity of an ancestor, see Deleuze and Guattari, *A Thousand Plateaus*, 266.

76 Meier, *The Lesson of Carl Schmitt*, 34.

77 If Schmitt's Catholicism led him to recognize the power of intensity (Jerusalem), his training as a jurist led him to the "fixed point" (Athens). Institutional forms and juridical concepts, such as sovereignty, become the focal point of his work. The centrality of the concept of representation in Schmitt's thinking should not be underestimated, and this comes out most clearly in some of his earlier works written (in 1923) before he developed the concept of the political. Simona Draghici, in her introduction to Schmitt's essay "The Idea of Representation," suggests that this concept was so important to him that he not only wrote about it but also took

This is not an argument to deny the central importance of Schmitt's binary coding of the political, but rather to regard those "fixed points" of Schmitt's analysis (friend/enemy) as being more like stars in the night sky offering their own gravitational pull. Modes of being political orbit around it, as do affective energy flows. Technologies are used to engage with, channel, bend, harness, avoid, or even transform intensities. Maoism, however, weaponizes this flow through its use of "telluric" technologies. For Maoism, the question circles around what technologies can be brought into an assemblage to channel affective energy flows such that they are brought to the surface as political intensities. Intensity, as a directed, affective flow of energy, can no more define the political than it can be limited to the realm of the political. Unlike the friend/enemy distinction that is always tied to this concept, the political has no special purchase on, or monopoly over, the innumerable possibilities opened up as a result of the channeling of affective flows. Energy flows are always too disparate, too ethereal, and too heterogeneous to be confined to the one realm. Put simply, flows flow.

As an agglutination of affective elements, flows can manifest in a variety of intense emotional states that are sometimes private and sometimes not. What the machinery of the political binary does is to establish a channel whereby these energy flows can either be pointed toward or away from an affectively based emergence of intensity. While this affective flow cannot define the political, the political cannot be defined without it. If one wants to capture the rhythm of the dyadic political heartbeat, attempt to direct the pulsating flow of energy such that this dyadic heart continues to pump intensity into "the people,"[78] or even reach that point of political clarity whereby

---

on a PhD student to research the question further. See Draghici, introduction to *The Idea of Representation*, 23.

78 The energy flows, of course, go beyond the political, and political energy, in turn, goes beyond any single political cause. As Schmitt notes, "If a people no longer possesses the energy or will to maintain itself in the sphere of politics, the latter will not thereby vanish from the world. Only weak people will disappear." Note the role of energy or will in relation to the question of the political here. Weak people disappear, but the energy flow continues, albeit in a dissipated form. As it flows, the political has the potential to seize on opportunities to funnel affective excess energy into a new body politic through different channels or by combining different intersecting energy flows. Intensity, therefore, always remains an ever-present possibility, so flows always have the potential to produce "a people." Without this funneled fluidity, that which cannot "vanish from the world" (i.e.,

the intrinsic dyadic form of the political is revealed, then the question of affective flows cannot be ignored.

Schmitt does not ignore intensity but chooses instead to focus more on the concrete, existential, and legal forms that the political takes.[79] The focus tends to be on the state, on sovereignty, on the law and its exception, and on the public enemy. In terms of intensity, however, Schmitt notes that the historical embodiment of that was the figure of the partisan and among the partisans, its greatest exponent was Mao Zedong.[80] Why Mao? Because Mao, more than even Lenin, Schmitt writes, pushed the notion of partisanship to its limit.[81] Moreover, he notes that it was the telluric quality of that partisanship that made this all possible. It was because of Mao's "telluric partisanship" that the originally defensive, yet intensely felt sense of place became wedded to the non-place of global revolutionary analysis, he concludes.[82]

Like a magical act of transmogrification, this idea of telluric partisanship took the local and static (the telluric) and made it global and mobile (the partisan). Mao Zedong was able to do this, says Schmitt, by weaving the abstract enmity of the Marxist class analysis into the figure of a real concrete enemy facing China. Schmitt's explanation of Mao's ability to unify the global and the telluric through the wedding of class, race, and national enmity, however, does not adequately or fully explain the flow of affective energy into a form of political intensity. If, however, we begin by examining the historical and cultural development of Maoism in relation to the operation of Maoist technologies that draw all affective energies toward a unified

---

the people), would. The friend/enemy distinction is the technology of this funneling process that keeps "the people" alive. Quotes used here are from Schmitt, *The Concept of the Political*, 53.

79 On this, Derrida writes, "If the political is to exist, one must know who everyone is, who is a friend and who is an enemy, and this knowing is not in the mode of theoretical knowledge but in one of a *practical identification*. . . . For this reason . . . much effort must be exerted—vain effort—to find an intuition and a concept adequate to the concrete." Derrida, *Politics of Friendship*, 116–17.

80 "The greatest practitioner of contemporary revolutionary war became its most famous theoretician: Mao Tse-tung," wrote Schmitt in 1963. See Schmitt, *The Theory of the Partisan*, 55.

81 Schmitt, *The Theory of the Partisan*, 59.

82 Schmitt, *The Theory of the Partisan*, 58.

political intensity through Mao's "one big concept," then the way in which the telluric nature of the Chinese socialist experiment intensifies the political becomes clearer. To examine that, we must move from examining the early rural experiments of the revolution to the early days of the revolution. Here we can see how, after 1949, this same rusticated style of thought begins to infect the operations of the state. Thus, beneath any manifest claims being made about scientific socialism, there was a subterranean knowledge form being channeled and harnessed within Maoism. It would end up driving an affective, revolutionary-based spirit that would infect the world of scientific socialism. It would produce a life animated by the political manifesting in a series of undercurrents within this new revolutionary state's language, economy, and security concerns.

14

Becoming Maoist II

LANGUAGE, ECONOMY, SECURITY

Language

The Chinese revolution promised a reworlding. In the early days, the people listened. Reflecting this, the new language of the Party became the language of the street. As city streets bustled to the new street-speak that the social critic Yang Dongping called the "voice of the Central Committee," the new government worked frantically to touch something deeper, more permanent, and more systematic in its language reform than the momentary buzz of a fashionable revolutionary phrase.[1] The Party and government would channel their energies into a national language reform campaign.

From 1951 through until 1977, a series of radical and dramatic linguistic reforms were introduced in China, transforming the script and the way

1 See Yang Dongping, *City Monsoon*, 262–76. Parts of this are translated in Dutton, *Streetlife China*, 165–69.

people spoke, wrote, read, and therefore thought, through the Chinese language. From the layout of texts (from vertical to horizontal and from right to left) through to the simplification of characters (from *fanti*, or traditional full form, to *jianti*, or simplified characters); from the implementation of a new system of romanization (pinyin) through to a renewed emphasis on standard spoken Chinese based on the Beijing accent—*putonghua*, or the "common language," as Mandarin Chinese was now called—the Communist Party's "top-down" reforms quite literally changed the formal "flow" of the Chinese language. While the language politics of the Central Committee led to these dramatic structural changes, it was in the momentary, quixotic, and unstructured linguistic infatuations of the street that the genealogy of the subterranean political flow would be revealed. These "infatuations" were not just evident in the use of more revolutionary phrases but also in the use of more rustic and more militaristic sets of expression.[2] What emerges is a revolutionary *chundian* based on the life of the telluric partisan.

Devoted young revolutionaries began to be called "straight rooted Red seedlings" (*genzheng miaohong*), and the search for revolutionary activists was being constantly referred to as going out and finding "good seedlings" (*hao miaozi*). This new rustic inflection in city-speak was accompanied by a new and sometimes more violent set of political expressions that largely emerged and then charted the course of post-1949 political campaigns. In times of militant action, Party secretaries became the squadron leaders in Party branches that were (linguistically) turned into "revolutionary fortresses" (*dang zuzhi shi geming de baolei*). From these fortresses came orders to "repulse the savage assaults of the right faction" (*jitui youpai changkuan jingong*), "counter-attack the savage assaults of the black line" (*fanji heixian de changkuang jingong*), and "violently open fire on the anti-Party and anti-socialist black line" (*xiang fandang, fanshehuizhuyi de heixian menglie kaihuo*), all in order to bring about a bucolic vision-image of communism (*hong cancan geming de tiandi*).[3]

2 Yang Dongping, speaking of city language, concludes, "What is notable and characteristic in all this is the large number of new vocabulary items that came from military terms. . . . Apart from this, there was also the penetration of language from the rural sector." Yang Dongping, *City Monsoon*, 262–76.

3 The idea of communism rendered in metaphor and translatable as "a brilliant Red revolutionary world" (*hong cancan geming de tiandi*) doesn't quite capture the bu-

Yang Dongping notes the fluidity of this new popular language as it ebbs and flows to the rhythm of the political campaign. He notes the way gender "disappears" as the ubiquitous term *comrade* comes into vogue, flattening out gender and sexual difference as it flattens out difference in a linguistic assertion of equality within the demotic. The early popularity of the term *comrade* (*tongzhi*)—literally meaning a shared will—is a linguistic assertion of the "one big concept" in the realm of affective connections and borders on other linguistic shifts taking place on the street.

After the revolution, affective familial terms predominated. Neighbors and friends became aunties, uncles, and older sisters. Even the model communist Lei Feng would speak of the Party as being like his loving mother.[4] In this context, the extension of the filiation beyond kin reveals the shadows of a faux consanguinity inherent in the lingering presence of the brother-friend/brother-enemy structure. Here, politics (the machinery of government) and the affective political flow merge into the violence of the political campaign but also into almost innocent and innocuous forms—in the greeting of the neighbor, or the hailing of a friend. Here are political symptoms below the threshold of the political. It is here, through this linguistic slip into consanguinity, that we discover the moment when the paradoxical figure of the non-agonal brother makes a reappearance but this time, it is alongside elder sisters and aunties who no longer take the *jianghu* name "brother" but the Party name "comrade."[5]

These inflections in language were telltale signs of the sometimes perverse and quite often unconscious affective afterlife of "telluric partisanship" in the postrevolutionary Chinese lifeworld. They were also the surface expressions of a series of morphological social transformations that were reinforcing this form of "telluricism" by reorganizing the Chinese city lifeworld. These linguistic phenomena therefore might appear as momentary, faddish,

colic quality of the phrasing any more than the translation of the last word in this phrase, *tiandi*, as simply "earth" doesn't capture its cosmological significance. In Chinese *tiandi* literally means "the unity of heaven and earth" as in the phrase of Zhuangzi, *tiandi heyi*.

4 Indeed, the orphan Lei Feng famously wrote an article saying as much. See Lei Feng, "After Liberation."

5 See chapter 13, note 19, which details the use of familial terms within the Communist Party in the prerevolution period.

Figure 14.1. Red tourists: A busload of bank workers, dressed as Red Army soldiers, go to a short management course at Jinggang Mountain, May 24, 2014. Appearances can be deceptive. Photo by the author.

quaint, and isolated, but their appearance on the street shows the power of the "one big concept" in the early days of the People's Republic. They are the linguistic surfacing of a deeper and more heartfelt reworlding that was taking place and that still bore a telluric heart, albeit one that now pumped to a revolutionary beat.

Where scientific socialism would share a notion of modernity with the Crystal Palace, reflected in words like *objectivity*, *scientist*, and *rationality*, the Chinese partisan war of liberation produced beneath this surface of rationality another world of rustic and revolutionary slogans, phrases, and terms that would often intertwine with familial demotic expressions. Where the Crystal Palace and scientific socialism were abstractions from nature and built on technology to achieve this artificial environment, these telluric tendencies within Maoism pushed the idea of local solutions and affective connections, and these helped carry the potentiality for violent class struggle. The result was an unconscious telluricism feeding into everything, even the planned economy.

Despite Party public pronouncements that would speak principally in the language of scientific planning, there were still telltale signs of the telluric-indigenous knowledge bank lurking in the shadows and producing variations within. This demotic, familial language from below reflected another side of the affective political intensity being produced. Together, these affective tendencies would run into, cut through, work within, and sometimes work against the scientific, rational, and systematic language of planning. The result was that within the body of scientific socialist planning there lurked a shadow economy. This shadow economy of affective flows was smuggled into the positivistic and utopian economy of numbers and, ironically, helped create the appearance of the centralized planning model working as promised. Yet while appearances were deceptive, they were also crucially important. The scientific centralized planners of socialism, all the way back to Alexander Bogdanov's tektology, had thought this economy of numbers, after all, would bring about abundance and it is Bogdanov, as he reaches for the Red Star of communism, who would explain this to us.

“Now I have seen the machines and the workers,” I said, “but I have no idea whatever of how production is organized, and I wonder whether you could tell me something about that?”

Instead of answering, the engineer took us to a small, cubical building. . . . Their black walls were covered with rows of shiny white signs showing tables of production statistics. I knew the Martian language well enough to be able to decipher them. On the first of them, which was marked with the number one, was the following:

“The machine-building industry has a surplus of 968, 757 man-hours daily, of which 11,325 hours are skilled labor. The surplus at this factory is 753 hours, of which 29 hours are of skilled labor.

There is no labor shortage in the following industries: agriculture, chemicals, excavations, mining . . .” and so on, in a long alphabetical list of various branches of industry.

Table number two read:

“The clothing industry has a shortage of 392,685 man-hours daily, of which 21,380 hours require experienced repairmen for special machines and 7,852 hours require organization experts.”

“The footwear industry lacks 79,360 hours, of which . . .” and so on.

“The Institute of Statistics—3,078 hours . . .” and so on.

“But how does the central apparatus arrive at its figures on surpluses and shortages?”

“The Institute of Statistics has agencies everywhere which keep track of the flow of goods into and out of stockpiles and monitors the production of all enterprises and the changes in work forces. In that way, it can calculate what and how much must be produced for any given period and the number of man-hours required for the task. The Institute then computes the difference between the existing and the desired situation for each vocational area and communicates the result to all places of employment. Equilibrium is soon established by a stream of volunteers.”

“In other words your statistics work almost automatically—they are calculations pure and simple?”

“No, not really. . . .”[6]

6 Bogdanov, *Red Star*, 65–67.

In Bogdanov's science fiction novel *Red Star*, life on Mars is imagined as a communist utopia, a heaven of numbers. Martians, being more advanced than earthlings, were obviously communists. From Bogdanov's descriptions of life on Mars, one can glean his views about life on Earth. If only life on Earth could flow the Martian way, toward a totally planned and scientific communist society, then everything would be fine. The central planning model that the Chinese inherited from the Soviet Union carried within it something of the birthmarks of this Martian tale.[7]

When the Chinese adopted the central planning model from the Soviet Union, they accepted that it was the most scientific, rational, and efficient model of economic organization and far superior to anything thrown up by the vagaries of the capitalist market. Planning was part of the socialists' claim to economic superiority, for it held out the promise of a world with little waste, near total calculation, and absolute efficiency. With little leakage, the flow of goods and services could be calculated almost perfectly. Yet behind this positivist vision of near-perfect efficiency lay a strong moral claim. Capitalism had freed labor only to commodify it as labor-power. Socialist planning was a mechanism for labor's decommodification.

First, the centrally planned labor allocation system (*fenpei tizhi*) decommodified labor-power by eliminating the labor market. Second, lifelong job tenure, or the "iron rice bowl" (*tiefanwan*), and job allocation effectively withdrew the right of management to hire and fire labor, thereby, potentially, extending workers' rights. Third, where market capitalism had alienated labor from the conditions of its existence by separating work from home and social life, the Chinese wanted to merge these, reorganizing production units into communities based on their new work unit or *danwei* system. Lastly, where the capitalist market was geared to the production of commodities that momentarily satiated the dispersed desires of the consumer, the command economy refocused production back on what it deemed were use-values. Phantasmagorical desires would no longer be focused on the commodity realm but would instead, through the category of enemy, be driven into the zone of the political.

In gradually eradicating wage differentials, abandoning the use of hiring and firing for the disciplining of labor, and then promoting production through tapping into the fantasy of political sacrifice, the conditions for the

7 Dominique Lecourt points to the lingering influence of Bogdanovism in Soviet discourse under Stalin. See Lecourt, *Proletarian Science?*, 137–62.

political intensification of affective flows were achieved by transforming the dynamic heart of the planned economy into a politicized gift economy.

While the socialist textbooks might write of how history would sweep away the vagaries of the market with a scientific, transparent, calculable, and efficient system of planning, the operation of this "economy" told a different story. The subterranean flow of affect is brought to the surface by a systemic reliance on calls for self-reliance and self-sacrifice. The appearance of calculability, transparency, and efficiency promised by the theory ultimately and paradoxically came to rely on the opaque, affective, and sacrificial to keep up its appearance. Production and the political campaigns both relied on this form of "gift economy" within the system. This gift economy of the political would drive economic production. At a manifest level, however, this gift economy of the political remained invisible, for all that appeared publicly were numbers and a calculative central plan. Even the lowest-level units of urban economic production and calculation—the work unit, or *danwei*—reinforced the appearance of scientific precision through numbers.

The term *danwei* literally means "single unit." Its origins lay in the placing of Buddhist prayer mats, such that one mat equaled one place, while one place equaled one monk or one *danwei*.[8] In more contemporary times, however, it came into common usage not as a religious term but as a unit of mathematical calculation whereby it was described as being a "meter, a gram, a second and so forth."[9] Its use by planners to name the base-level units of Chinese urban life and economic production extends the calculative rather than religious meaning of the term and extends it into the realm of economic planning. It reveals the calculative unconscious of the socialist

8 The earliest definition of *danwei* comes from Buddhism and indicates how measurement might have come about. From the *Dictionary of Chinese Buddhist Terms* (*Foguang da cidian*) is the following: "Units of measurement regarding time, length and weight abound in Buddhist classic texts. In the lives of monks, every seat/mat on which a monk meditated had the name of the monk written on it, and therefore it was given the name *danwei*" (translated as "singular seat") (*chi xiu xinggui riyong guifan yue: "hun zhongming, xuxian gui danwei zuochan"*). See "*danwei*" in Zhou He et al., *Mandarin Dictionary*, 3rd ed.

9 While He Xinghan says this current usage "has broken through the limitations imposed by the standard dictionary definition," I would argue that it has interpolated this meaning into its form such that it simultaneously functioned for planners as a mode of measurement and for community members as a spatial ordering of social (but faux) consanguinity. See He Xinghan, "People in the Work Unit," 157.

economic planner. Indeed, it would be no exaggeration to say that, for these economic planners, the sum total of all work units constituted the aggregate picture of the Chinese urban economy.[10] While the rhetoric of scientific, socialist planning created the surface appearance of calculability, it was an appearance radically undercut by the social restructuring of life taking place on the ground. This social restructuring led to the urban populations being allocated work units and, as a result, creating the conditions for a socialist-style, Maussian gift economy.

Behind large compound walls that demarcated their area of jurisdiction, work units established a labyrinth of shops, hospitals, schools, workers' apartments, mass-line organizations, entertainment and sports venues, as well as administration centers and factories.[11] Much like a rural village, the work unit turned the urban population into discrete communities that blurred the lines between life, work, and politics. This blurring of life, work, politics, the law, and morality was a precondition not just of socialism but also of a gift economy.[12]

As work units grew in size and importance, the cities that housed them were transformed into clusterings of self-contained industrial and administrative villages. This merging of life and work within the work unit took place at the same time as changes to the economic order of things. From the early 1950s onward, along with the "iron rice bowl" came a strong egalitarian push to compress wage differentials. This led to a gradual decoupling of material incentives from individual work effort.[13] Rather than dealing with the problem of scarce resources through higher prices, the government introduced

10 Such calculations are not without some basis; as David Bray points out, by 1957 something like 90 percent of the entire urban population were members of a work unit. See Bray, *Social Space and Governance in Urban China*, 94.

11 See Zhang Jie and Wang Tao, "Housing Development in the Socialist Planned Economy," 118.

12 Mauss, *The Gift*, 5.

13 While work units were reducing wage differentials in urban areas, the agricultural sector was undergoing a steady increase in the size of its collective units of calculation used for remuneration in that sector. As these units increased in size—from mutual aid teams of the early 1950s, through to the communes of the Great Leap Forward—the individual's contribution to net output became less significant and less recognizable. This decoupling of individual effort from individual reward had only one potential and highly political exception, which was when the work effort

ration coupons allocated through the work units. In summary, work units withdrew conventional "economic" disciplinary levers but compensated for this loss of economic control by merging work and life, thereby creating the conditions for "noneconomic" incentives to dominate.[14] Left without conventional economic levers to discipline labor and deliver on production quotas, managers had few options other than to try to tap into the workers' political energy. That always involved moving beyond calculable outcomes and entering into some form of affectively based persuasion.

The code of giving and receiving and the obligation to reciprocate, which were the basis of the Maussian gift economy, thereby became the unconscious, opaque driver of an economy of affective flows that proved crucial to the productivity and political dynamism of the work-unit system. Indeed, the social connections and reciprocity that the gift economy demanded—and which is, in China, (often pejoratively) referred to as *guanxi*—became the bonding mechanism of the work-unit "pack" just as it had been a key bonding device of the *jianghu* pack.[15]

As a bonding mechanism that is a prelude to the formation of a "pack," the sometimes particularistic and utilitarian nature of *guanxi* gives way to a more affective and intense expression that, as we have seen, can form the basis of blood oaths of loyalty. This form of *guanxi* takes us beyond the tri-

---

was so outstanding that the worker became a political model. Such was the case with figures like "Iron Man Wang" (*Wang Tieren*) of Dazhai.

14 In terms of the history of the work unit, it should be noted that this argument simplifies the situation for the sake of clarity. It should also be noted that while individual differences within the work unit diminished there were, nevertheless, other hierarchies that did emerge because of things like the forms of ownership of the work units. There is little space here to detail the differences, but basically there were two types of ownership: state owned and collectively owned. State-owned work units were, relatively speaking, richer and more prestigious than their collectively owned counterparts. This had a significant effect on the quality of life and led to a form of competition developing between work units. For details on this competition in relation to housing, see Zhang Jie and Wang Tao, "Housing Development in the Socialist Planned Economy," 118. For details on how these differences affected everyday life, see Dutton, *Streetlife China*.

15 Mayfair Yang has convincingly argued that *guanxi* and the gift economy share more than a passing resemblance. For her seminal work on the subject, see Yang, *Gifts, Favors, and Banquets*.

partite need to give, receive, and reciprocate and leads us into what Maurice Godelier once described as the "famous fourth obligation" of Mauss.[16] That is to say, it opens to a gift that pertains "to the soul" and an exchange that takes place "in the sight of the gods."[17] It is a gift that turns on the "giving of part of oneself."[18] In this gift economy, the act of labor takes on a new and special meaning. Labor-power was now no longer purely an economic category but one pertaining to matters of commitment.[19] Under this sign, work-unit members joined the war machine to fight nature, struggle against class enemies, and combat economic shortage. The material goods produced under the sign of a planned economy were, in this respect, by-products of this affective system of a political struggle for production. This system produced energy by harnessing a complex, opaque admixture of flows, turning energy into feelings of commitment. Maoist technologies and structures channeled this through the faux consanguineous relation of work units, thus driving it into the very heart of the Chinese economy. In government, Maoism interpolated and habituated the intensity drawn from indigenous telluric, partisan techniques into the rhythmic surges of politics that characterized the Maoist political campaigns. Techniques developed and adapted for survival and war were being turned into a more general mentality that dominated government.

Within that frame of thought, the work unit became a nodal point of reassembly, realignment, and redrafting. Transformed into a component part of another larger machine-assemblage (the socialist state), work units would come to promote the central plan through reliance on affective flows. Essentially, the planned economy masked a reliance on this form of gift economy. In the absence of material incentives, it was the flow of symbolic capital (affectivity/*guanxi*) that would encourage workers to work. Two intertwined economies running in tandem, working in unison and operating from top (the abstraction of the central plan) to the very bottom (the operation of the work unit), to create the appearance of scientific calculation and planning but relying on the politicized, opaque operations of the gift economy within

16 Godelier, *The Enigma of the Gift*, 13.

17 Mauss, *The Gift*, 12, 14.

18 The words are Mauss's. See Mauss, *The Gift*, 12.

19 Mauss says, "In this system of ideas, one gives away what is in reality a part of one's nature and substance, while to receive something is to receive a part of someone's spiritual essence." Mauss, *The Gift*, 12.

base-level work units to create that appearance. Indeed, as one burrows even deeper into the work unit, beyond the personnel section and into an individual personnel file (*renshi dang'an*; see figure 14.2), one finds this paradoxical duality built even into the biopolitical operations at the micro-level of the Chinese state's data collection.[20]

Security

The personnel file was a key document of the work unit. For central planners it was designed to calculate and specify the human resources available to them in all urban areas.[21] Every work unit contained a personnel section,

20 This argument relates principally to the internal economy of the work unit and is therefore a simplification of the situation for the sake of clarity. Work-unit solidarity was not always built under the flag of commitment, and indeed other forms and expressions of the gift economy in practice changed over time, as did the degree of political intensity. The ubiquity of this form of economy, however, is evidenced by the fact that it operates not only within the work unit but also between work units. Here, one could point to the emergence very early on of an inter-*danwei* barter system. Emerging in place of the market allocation system, this barter trade between work units reveals the way the gift insinuated itself into other flows (from one work unit to the other) and thereby spread an alternative economy outside the logic but nevertheless within the folds of the central plan. In times of austerity, particularly around the early 1950s, work-unit leaders were still required to provide the socialist provision their workers expected and would suffer politically for failure to do so. With the government's allocation of materials given over to the production process rather than to social provision, work-unit bosses took to overstating their work unit's raw material needs in order to barter those goods with other work units, which were all doing the same with their surplus stock. On the question of how scarce resources led to the "gift" of the socialist provision and the formation of a black market, see Lu Duanfang, *Remaking Chinese Urban Form*, 93–94.

21 Peasants didn't have personnel files, work-unit files, or personal family household registers because the management of the rural sector was relatively simple and would ultimately fit into the Confucian ideal of "no neglecting of the land, no itinerants" (*wukuang tu, wu youmin*). In the People's Republic of China until economic reform, unless a peasant joined the army or went to university, they stayed in the commune where their collective household registers were held. This system existed until 1983 when the commune system was abolished and replaced by township governments and to a gradual loosening of these tight controls. On the

Figure 14.2. Cover of a cadre personnel file. Photo by the author.

every personnel section a dossier and copy, and every dossier and copy was tied back to an individual work-unit member.[22] This dossier would shadow the work-unit member's life. Within the work unit, with no labor market to direct the distribution of labor-power and no right to discipline workers through standard economic means, the personnel file became an essential technology of central planning for the regulation, disciplining, and allocation of human resources in an appropriate and efficient manner. At this level, the personnel file system could have been a technology straight out of the manuals of Bogdanov's Martian communists. Indeed, the Chinese would use it, as the Martians had used statistics in *Red Star*, to create the appearance of precise calculations when it came to labor allocation and productivity. In this base-level regime of economic calculation, the personnel file was supposedly centered on the work-unit member's skills, qualifications, and experience. At the same time, it was also the key document by which to discipline labor, assess competencies, and examine histories. Wherever one went, so, too, went one's file. Its omnipotence meant that it came to be "an important basis upon which to examine, understand, and select those people who are of use."[23] Yet what remained opaque, just as it had earlier in Marx's writings on the question of value,[24] was the fuller meaning of the word "use."

Confucian ideal, see Wang Xuetai, *The Water Margin*, 43. On the files, see Zhong Shuxiao, *The Handbook of Personnel Work in an Organization*, 242.

22 Personnel files were limited to three types: one for workers, one for students, and one for cadres. Cadre files were usually the longest but all three carried much the same type of information, which included résumés, autobiographical material, personal materials, appraisals and evaluations, education qualifications, documents, and reports on any investigations undertaken as well as material on entering the Party and the Party Youth League, awards and medals, as well as materials on punishments and penalties. The differences lay in the detail. For further details on the management organization and function of personnel files, see Tianjin City Archival Bureau, *A Handbook on Dossier Work*, 133–34.

23 Zhu Xinxia, *A Concise Dictionary*, 327.

24 As noted earlier, Althusser suggested that Marx's mathematical calculation of surplus value renders labor-power as little more than a commodity. See Althusser, "Crisis of Marxism," 219. However, Althusser also contends that this, in some ways, masks the surplus value that lies beyond the mathematically calculated use of labor-power.

To open a file is to open a life story. It is a reference book not just in terms of a person's economic skills, qualifications, and experience but also in relation to their class background and politics.[25] Just as class background and politics were spreading into all areas of life so, too, were they spreading a particular logic into every corner of the person's file, producing a symptomatic reading of all social relations through the vector of class. Relatives, friends, workmates, and any other connections were drawn in. While not quite a lineage record following a bloodline, the file's use of class and political inheritances produced a contiguous line of assessment that would still be inherited, leading one scholar to call it class racism because lives were determined through that paradigm.[26]

So it was with the personnel file of one Ms. Deng Ming (1933–1982).[27] Life for her was lived in a twilight zone of class "miscegenation." She lived between two different class designations that had been inherited from her parents. Like political typifications, her parents fell on either side of the friend/enemy divide, one being almost a member of the five Red categories, while the other was definitely one of the five black categories.[28] The bloodline from her father caused the problems.

During the early part of the "campaign to suppress counter-revolutionaries" (1950–1953), her father had been arrested, tried, and, along with thirty-one other counterrevolutionaries, executed. His execution left a black mark on the family name, but more importantly, it left a stain on their collective files. "Her father was a counter-revolutionary but he is dead," the 1958 county cadre investigation team would report in a short, handwritten sheet titled "investigative comments" and inserted into Ms. Deng's file. On the mother's side, things were slightly better. Her mother had been an ordinary member of the Nationalist Party but had no "debts of blood" (*xuezhai*) or any family-owned land.

25 Tianjin City Archival Bureau, *A Handbook on Dossier Work*, 134, notes how all this changes during the early days of economic reform.

26 Lee Haiyan, *The Stranger and the Chinese Moral Imagination*, 198–242. See also Lee Haiyan, "Class Feeling"; Yi Xiaocuo, "Blood Lineage."

27 This is not the woman's real name and, while the information given in this section on Deng's file is accurate, many of the details have been omitted or changed to ensure anonymity. This is at the request of family members.

28 The five black categories were the landlord, rich peasant, counterrevolutionary, bad element, and Rightist. The five Red categories were the revolutionary cadre, worker, poor and lower peasant, family of martyrs, and family of the military.

In addition, since the revolution, the mother had worked in a series of menial jobs, leading to an initial assessment of Deng Ming's mother and her family as part of the "urban poor."[29] Between a father from the exploiting classes and a mother connecting her to the "urban poor," Ms. Deng lived a life in flux.

"She does not belong to one of our investigated targets," the investigative committee concluded in 1958.[30] The fact that they had even looked at her file at all was a legacy of the political indeterminacy of her status. This indeterminacy came from a 1954 report inserted into her dossier by "Investigator Peng" that read, "Based on our current audit, the member lived at home since she was young from late 1937 to early 1949. She finished primary, junior, and high schools . . . and didn't join any anti-revolutionary organizations. However, her ideology could have been influenced by the fact that her father was a Nationalist Party member and executed and her mother was also a member of the Nationalist Party. Nevertheless, the current materials cannot prove one way or the other as to whether this has been an influence upon her."[31] Only constant testing could determine that.[32]

While her father's crimes left a stain, the family's impoverished circumstances, their lack of land,[33] and the mother's menial employment—"she made her living by peddling food and homemade mosquito repellents"[34]—turned Ms. Deng Ming's position into a political anomaly, for she could be given no clear class designation: "No official classification of class was

29 "Other Questions in Need of Explanation," in the personnel dossier of Deng Ming (henceforth PDDM).

30 "Investigation Comments," in PDDM. From the file it is clear that her father had been a member of the Nationalist Party, had allegedly been active in the "reactionary and feudal" *Qingbang* or Green Gang, and had briefly and, rather unwisely, taken the position of director on the local Nationalist Party Education Board just before the communist takeover.

31 "Conclusion of Cadre's Political History Investigation" (April 4, 1954), in PDDM.

32 "The essential," says Lenin, is not institutional, organizational, or legal, but found "in the selection of personnel and in checking performance." See Lenin, "Notes for a Speech on March 27, 1922," 573–74.

33 "Family status (class origin): The family has not possessed any estates or farmland since the grandfather's generation," in "Other Questions in Need of Explanation" (September 9, 1968), in PDDM.

34 "Other Questions in Need of Explanation," in PDDM.

ever given," she would plaintively claim in one of her many confessional statements.[35] So it was that she came to live between the two poles of the political, working hard to distance herself from her father while emphasizing the poverty-ridden status of her mother. The ambivalent class status proved to be an ongoing curse, for if the political was reawakened in any moment of intensity, so too was the counterrevolutionary legacy of her father. Here, then, was a life lived on a knife edge.[36]

Handwritten confessions by Ms. Deng joined the comments of investigators and the complaints and compliments of workmates and bosses. All these documents, reports, confessions, and intimate details, all the betrayals, the connections, the assessments: all would be gathered into her file awaiting "use." An ordinary female cadre with a less than ordinary life, caught in a class contradiction and haunted by the figure of the father. The historic crimes of the father would be visited on the son. When Deng Ming's brother was arrested for brawling during the Cultural Revolution, their father's past once again came to dominate the decisions to send him to reform through labor and to monitor other family members.[37] As a family, they were politically vulnerable and, therefore, more than most, they had to display their loyalty and devotion.

So it was that the young Ms. Deng, then just seventeen, volunteered to carry out work for the "culture and propaganda team" of her hometown. She would take part in the "purging of reactionaries" campaign and put on revolutionary performances in street theater close to her home. By 1950, she was seconded into an amateur drama troupe and, in this capacity, went around neighboring towns and villages performing revolutionary plays and songs. On one such occasion in 1950, while on the back of a truck singing revolutionary songs with other troupe members, Ms. Deng discovered the fate of her father. As the truck moved toward its destination, it went down a narrow

35 "Other Questions in Need of Explanation," in PDDM.

36 From the "working staff registration form" (*gongzuo dengjibiao*), September 16, 1968, in PDDM. The form features two columns titled "Economic situation before and after liberation (pre and post land reform)" in which the negative side of this bifurcated assessment is given: "Pre-liberation: Supported by parents with their income as teachers from birth until August 1945. Led a life of the exploiting class, sucking the working classes 'blood and tears' from September 1945 to the dawn of liberation."

37 PDDM.

alley on the walls of which were posters of criminals who had been executed. On one such poster, a large red cross cut through the middle of her father's name signified execution. Despite the shock, Deng would not speak of her pain but would instead sing her pain via revolutionary songs.[38] To survive, she would forsake her father, and in her dossier her personal repudiation is found. Her words read, "On the very day of his execution, I . . . gave a revolutionary performance before other comrades. . . . I chose the people's political standpoint and when my father was executed, I did not shed a tear."[39]

"She could not shed a tear," her sister would later tell me, "for she was under constant surveillance and was, herself, all too aware of the fact that one tear shed by her could easily lead to many more for her family." Filiality to the father was publicly replaced by a public display of a higher-order calling.

"To determine devotion, look to practice" (*zhong bu zhong, kanxingdong*), the Cultural Revolution Maoists repeatedly stated, as practice became the nodal point of all political assessments.[40] The personnel file was a technology of this practice-based politics. The file would plot a life that, by the time of the Cultural Revolution, seemed to have become little more than a veritable timetable of devotional revolutionary practices and celebrations that also functioned as disciplinary testing sites.

It was a world in which every day began with "morning instructions" (*zaoqingshi*) and concluded with "evening reports" (*wanhuibao*).[41] In between, one would dress, speak, and live the world of a Maoist becoming.[42] Panegyric ceremonies framed the day in much the same way as Maoism framed thought, turning every gesture and every word into a moment of

38 Additional insights and a counternarrative to the official account of her life come from details gleaned in a series of interviews undertaken with Deng's mother and sister (interview, Chengdu, June 2004) and with her best friend (interview, Beijing, 1997). Thanks to Li Shaorong and Zhao Fengshan, who aided this process.

39 Deng's official response is registered in the file itself: namely, category one, 3, in PDDM.

40 Or, in the words of Søren Kierkegaard, "it is the individual's task to divest himself of the determinant view of interiority that is incommensurable with the exterior." Kierkegaard, *Fear and Trembling*, 97.

41 Wang Yi, "The Growth of All Things," 132.

42 Refer to glossary A, "Terms and Concepts," for the term *becoming*.

Figure 14.3. Mao Zedong: Sign of devotion, *zhong* (忠). The character zhong appears on either side of the face of Mao on a plaque from early 1969. Photo by the author.

potential, inspection, assessment, and discipline. All things became subject to a symptomatic class-based reading. Such symptomatic readings that began to spell out the word "enemy" were potentially highly productive in a system driven by the friend/enemy distinction. Indeed, in broadening the field of class struggle so that it stretched from formal politics right through to the everyday biopolitical, the disciplinary regimes were, in fact, a means of channeling affective energy toward an intense revolutionary (re)action. They were experiments in maintaining political intensity beyond the moment and directing it into fields that were conventionally not thought of as political. In this respect, the disciplinary component of this type of regime tells only part of the story.

Mao's words, chanted, repeated, memorized endlessly, and, finally, and most importantly, believed in were not just a means of disciplining but also a way of politically intensifying.[43] These practices led to the expenditure of surplus energy in a politically productive fashion that worked to produce politically directed excess. Mao's intensity fueled a politicized world in which every object related to Mao became a sign of potential devotion and every action a means of expressing that devotion. From statues of Mao[44] through to the Mao badges,[45] Mao covered everything. Even the purchasing of items took on an aura of its own. In the Cultural Revolution, for example, one did not "buy a Mao badge" (*mai xiangzhang*), for that would be insufficiently devout. One would, instead, *qing*, or "request," the badge (*qing xiangzhang*).[46] To *qing* was to "beseech" (*qing, qiuye*) or to "beg" (*qing, qiye*),[47] and these words, drawn from a Buddhist lexicon relating to objects that held a sacred worth,[48] carried within them the Maussian fourth obligation to give part of oneself, part of one's soul. In other words, they connected the material act of acquisition with an intimate affective economy of commitment, devotion, and sacrifice. The Mao badge carried within it a secular version of the "aura

43 This would lead to the cult of Mao. For the most detailed study of that to date, see Leese, *Mao Cult*.

44 On the Mao statues, even Mao himself was scornful. On July 5, 1967, he said, "This whole enterprise is a waste of human resources, with no profit and a lot of harm and, if we don't stop, then we will create a wasteful wind. Can you please discuss this at the enlarged meeting of the Polit bureau and issue instructions to have it halted?" Cited by Chang Ping, "What Is the Tradition behind the Mao Zedong Statues?," 12.

45 On the excesses of Mao badge production, it has been estimated that between 1966 and 1971, no fewer than two billion badges were produced, sporting well over ten thousand different motifs of the Chairman. Wang Yi, "The Growth of All Things," 133. Another source claims that, up until 1969, something like 4.8 billion badges were minted. Zhou Jihou, *The Mystery of the Mao Badge*, 71. For another reading of the Mao badge, see Schrift, *Biography of a Chairman Mao Badge*.

46 Zhou Jihou, *The Mystery of the Mao Badge*, 40–41.

47 Jiang Renjie, *Explanatory Notes*, vol. 1, 456.

48 Chao Feng, *Cultural Revolution Dictionary*, 157.

of the sacred,"[49] and the wearing of this badge, the carrying of the Little Red Book, and the repeated chanting of slogans all aided the "one big concept" that Cai spoke of in relation to the *Rent Collection Courtyard* exhibition.

The "one big concept" used technology to tap into multiple senses, producing tears in the eye, lumps in the throat, or a taste in the mouth. This was the way the political moved beyond thought into action, and this was also the way the political would begin to "touch people to their very souls" (*chuji renmin linghun de dageming*).[50] Through the affective dimensions of this "one big concept," the Maoist Red Guard would be carried into the heterogeneous realm of "useless" expenditure. It was a recognition of this realm being tied not just to Mao badges, but to the entire panoply of Maoist political technologies that excited Julia Kristeva.

More profoundly than other Marxisms, she once wrote, Maoism was utterly dependent on a type of Bataillian "immediate and personal experience" that could lead, via class struggle, beyond rational calculation and into the inner experience of the heterogeneous world of exuberance. Thus, in bringing back to Marxism an "active subject," Maoism, more than any other creed, consciously worked to produce intensities by creating a space for "heterogeneous excess." This fluid "site of passage" was, she claimed, "a non-site where opposite tendencies struggle."[51] This "site of passage," the so-called nonsite of struggle, was where drives, desires, and needs revealed themselves to be as much a part of the world of class struggle as they were of "affective (parental, love) relations."[52]

Like Schmitt, who was able to pinpoint the power of Maoism as emanating from its "telluric partisan" tradition, the perspicacious element in Kristeva's analysis shows how Maoist political power emanated from a channeling of affective energies via class struggle. Yet neither Schmitt nor Kristeva were

49 Richman, *Reading Georges Bataille*, 35–36. It is worth noting that the sacred in Bataille's understanding of the term is drawn from Durkheim and offers a mere approximation of what he would label as something that was part of the heterogeneous realm. See Surya, *Georges Bataille*, 177.

50 This was used as the opening gambit of the sixteen-point circular of August 8, 1966, and published on the front page of the *People's Daily* the next day. See *People's Daily* [*Renmin Ribao*] 《人民日报》, August 9, 1966, 1.

51 Kristeva, "Bataille, Experience and Practice," 258–59.

52 Kristeva, "Bataille, Experience and Practice," 260.

fully able to appreciate the specific historic-cultural elements that produced this fluid form of telluricism and nonconsanguineous form of kinship. That came via the world of the *jianghu* but came with a different *jianghu* ethic that now tied righteousness to class struggle. That understanding was then turned into a political distinction at the very end of the Cultural Revolution and at the end of radical Maoist experimentation with affective energy flows.

Coda: The Anti–*Water Margin* Campaign

In 1974, wedged between a mass campaign against Lin Biao and Confucius and another calling for an all-round dictatorship of the proletariat was a third, oft-forgotten, mass-based nationwide political campaign. This campaign was launched against that manifesto of *jianghu* rebellious virtues, the Ming dynasty novel, *The Water Margin*. The campaign against the novel had as its leitmotif the words of Mao Zedong, who pointed to the political limits of the famous novel: "*The Water Margin* only opposes corrupt officials, it doesn't oppose the emperor."[53] With these words, a campaign began against a novel that, it was claimed, had lionized the roles of those within the rebel ranks who "opposed the peasant revolution and promoted a reactionary capitulationalist political line." Because they had sought an imperial amnesty rather than a revolutionary outcome, the rebel leaders of the novel were labelled capitulationalists by the Maoist radicals.[54] This then tied them to certain figures within the Chinese Communist Party. Thus, this campaign, like the campaign against Lin Biao and Confucius that opened before it, was tied to a specific political purge taking place within the Party at this time,[55]

53 For one example, see Xu Jixu, "What Is There to Praise, What Is There to Oppose?," 44.

54 Xu Jixu, "What Is There to Praise, What Is There to Oppose?," 45.

55 This specific purge around which this campaign developed was that of Deng Xiaoping. In mid-1975, Deng Xiaoping had been brought back into the leadership to initiate a series of reforms to aid economic recovery. He was then accused by radicals within the Party of capitulationalism. This was the rather pointed context within which the campaign against *The Water Margin* developed. Western commentators, employing techniques drawn from "Kremlinology," overwhelmingly focused on the realpolitik aspect of what was, for them, simply a purge with an obscure smokescreen used to legitimize the radical action. For one of the best approaches to this campaign that canvasses this view but then raises some important

and again, like the campaign against Lin Biao and Confucius, the historical component of the movement was no mere smokescreen.[56] From this campaign, key theoretical differences between Maoism and the *jianghu* spirit were also being made clearer.

Literature from this campaign argued that, while Marxism had always fought for the revolutionary overthrow of the entire system, the *jianghu* rebel army of *The Water Margin* was divided on this question. This division revealed the political weaknesses of the *jianghu* spirit. In place of the bonds of brotherhood, this campaign claimed, rebels needed a class analysis. Indeed, it was through their class analysis of the novel, they insisted, that the real revolutionaries of *The Water Margin* could be distinguished from capitulationalists.[57] For the radical Maoists, the affectivity of the *jianghu* obscures rather than illuminates the bonds of revolution. It was this particular form of symptomatic reading of the novel based on a class analysis that turned literary critique into a political purge. If Deng Xiaoping was the campaign's political target, his literary equivalent in the novel itself was the leader of the Liang Mountain rebels in *The Water Margin*, Song Jiang.

Song Jiang, it was suggested, was a public enemy.[58] Song Jiang had spoken of the need for the unity of nation (*yitong tianxia*) even over brotherhood, stressing the need to always follow heavenly decrees (*titian xingdao*) rather than the way of rebellion. Moreover, Song Jiang had long argued for, and long sought, an imperial amnesty for the Liang Mountain rebels rather than attempting the revolutionary overthrow of the dynastic order.[59] This "capitulationalist" policy of Song Jiang revealed his political nature. Just as the name Liu Wencai had earlier became synonymous with the term *landlordism* after the success of the *Rent Collection Courtyard* exhibition, so, too, Song Jiang came to stand in as a type of "typification" for the crime of capitula-

---

questions around the uses of history and mythology, see Fitzgerald, "Continuity and Discontinuity."

56 For an analysis of how the anti–Lin Biao and anti-Confucius campaign was part of a general rethinking of the state, for example, see Dutton, *Policing Chinese Politics*, 233–36.

57 Xu Jixu, "What Is There to Praise, What Is There to Oppose?," 44.

58 Xu Jixu, "What Is There to Praise, What Is There to Oppose?," 44.

59 Mu Yin, "How Are We to Assess Song Jiang?"

tionalism.[60] In contrast, characters in the novel, who by their acts of disruption could be said to have refused to compromise, be they Chao Gai,[61] Wu Yong,[62] the Ruan brothers,[63] or Li Kui,[64] were all regarded as revolutionaries. Thus, their every wanton and audacious act of rebellious destruction was, in this reading, a sign of their revolutionary dissatisfaction with the prevailing order.[65] Only those who rebelled were the true outlaws of the marsh, it was claimed.[66] Read through the vector of class struggle, the pages of this classic

60 Mu Yin, "How Are We to Assess Song Jiang?," 44.

61 Du Xuncheng, "On Chao Gai."

62 Zhang Shiming and Wan Shaoyuan, "Thinking about Resourceful Star (*Wu Yong*)."

63 Chen Dakang, "On the Three Ruan Brothers."

64 Chen Dakang, after explaining that the people who were forced to go to Liang Mountain were from all classes and went there with all sorts of dubious motives, quickly added that there were also revolutionaries with appropriate class backgrounds among them. Chen states, "Then there were those who after years of labor or simply by birth were from poor peasant households, for example, Li Kui, or those who were born poor fishermen, like the Ruan brothers." Chen Dakang, "On the Three Ruan Brothers," 15.

65 Campaign documents are written in a propagandistic and dogmatic fashion, but they also demonstrate an intimate knowledge of the text. Adding intentionality to the actions of characters, focusing on the class characteristics of each important character, and attributing political motives to their actions based on these characteristics required an intimate knowledge of the text. Reinterpreting sections of the text that dealt with certain "excesses" or revelry or criminality, the anti–*Water Margin* campaign found them to be full of revolutionary intent. One of the most famous incidents they interpreted in this way related to a group of the Liang Mountain bandits who stole expensive wine that was to be given to an envoy of the emperor as a peace offering. While, in the novel, this theft of wine was treated as loutish behavior by a small unruly group, the communist campaign literature interpretation focuses on their expressed hatred of the government officials as they stole and drank the wine. This, it was claimed, was an act full of revolutionary intentionality. In other words, the very things that could be dismissed as peripheral, without serious meaning or with criminal intent, were suddenly catapulted into an important role and given new meaning in this campaign literature. As perverse as this might sound, it was the result of a close reading and textual possibilities but always with a political sting in the tale.

66 On how these rebel figures within the *jianghu* were the real outlaws of the marsh, see Xu Jixu, "What Is There to Praise, What Is There to Oppose?," 44. *Outlaws of*

novel open onto a critique of the politics of the novel, of the characters, and of aspects of the *jianghu* spirit. This critique of the *jianghu*, however, is different to contemporary Chinese sociological and criminological critiques that attack the lumpen ways of *jianghu* members, their criminal activities, and their immoral excesses.[67] Rather than offering these sorts of criticisms, the critique of the *jianghu* being mounted in this campaign attacks the *jianghu* spirit because it overrides class differences. It does this by putting friendship and brotherhood above all else,[68] and this privileging of the blood brother, it is said, can be traced back to their spirit of righteousness, or *yiqi*.[69]

As was earlier noted, there is a paradox within the *yi* of the spirit of righteousness, *yiqi*. This spirit of righteousness (*yiqi*) sustains both the Confucian *yi*, of *renyi*, or benevolence, and also a radical alternative form with the idea of *juyi* (meaning a righteous rebellious gathering and uprising). Within the *jianghu* spirit of *yi* or *yiqi* this divided understanding authorized and sustained what the 1975 campaign literature called a "rebel program" within the ranks of Liang Mountain bandits.[70] "A peasant revolutionary war buried within the pages of feudal society" was how the Maoist literature described

the Marsh is, in fact, one possible translation of the title of this novel. Known in Chinese as *Shuihuzhuan*, this title proved difficult to translate and gave rise to various English-language titles. Sydney Shapiro, for example, chose the title *Outlaws of the Marsh* while Pearl Buck gave her 1933 translation of the novel the title *All Men Are Brothers*. The most widely used translation for this title, however, is the most literal, *The Water Margin*, and it is this that has been adopted throughout this text.

67 For an example of this contemporary view of the *jianghu*, see Yu Yang, *Chinese Jianghu*.

68 An example of this sort of critique comes from Du Xuncheng, who claims that the failures of revolutionaries like Chao Gai were because they put too much faith in friendship. See Du Xuncheng, "On Chao Gai," 9, 19. In Du Xuncheng's article, the critique of the *jianghu*'s limitations is implicit.

69 Zhai Qing, "Comment on Capitulationalism in *The Water Margin*," 8.

70 Du Xuncheng insisted that this "rebel program was summed up in just eight characters—'forged as one in the struggle for righteousness' [*jieli tongxin, gongju dayi*]—and one slogan—'gathered in the virtuous cause of righteousness, or *judayi*;'" both of which clearly presuppose a very specific form of *yiqi*. Yet as Du goes on to note, "For the vast majority of peasants, this was the pathway to revolution and rebellion." See Du Xuncheng, "On Chao Gai," 19.

Liang Mountain.[71] It was, for the Maoists, a civil war within the *jianghu* spirit. It was a war between Liang Mountain and Jinggang Mountain and between a society built on the back of the sworn oath of brothers (*baibazi jieyi*) and one based on revolutionary comradeship (*geming qingyi*).[72] Clearer lines needed to be drawn, both theoretically and on the ground.

So it was that in the middle of this campaign to criticize *The Water Margin* (and implicitly the *jianghu* spirit), the Chinese Ministry of Finance and the Chinese People's Bank dispatched a research team to Jinggang Mountain to carry out investigations into the financing of this earliest of communist base camps. In the course of their investigations they discovered that the Red Army had produced its own coin. Up until this point, however, the coin produced at the Jinggang Mountain mint had only ever been referred to as an indigenous or telluric coin (*tuban huabiao*).[73]

Such counterfeit indigenous coins had long been the stock and trade of rural *jianghu* bandit gangs and, as we have already seen, the communists would use the skills and techniques of former *jianghu* bandits to produce their own coinage in the mint of Jinggang Mountain. The question they would face, however, was how to empirically and concretely demonstrate that their focus on class struggle led to a separation of them from the *jianghu* brotherhood spirit? What better way to flag this class-based distinction than to chisel onto the first coin of the Chinese communist movement a Chinese character that could, in shorthand, represent the leading class in any socialist class

71 See Yan Yi, "Some Opinions," 66.

72 The 1975 campaign focused its attack on the idea of intense "brotherly" bonding. Du Xuncheng's article on why Chao Gai failed to more directly open up a two-line struggle against Song Jiang, the capitulationist leader of the Liang Mountain rebels, leads to one of the few times the term *jianghu* is directly mentioned in this campaign literature. When *jianghu* is mentioned, however, it is invariably used to signal a political limitation. Du writes, "Chao Gai was limited to the idea of the spirit of *jianghu*, so when he opened the two-line struggle with Song Jiang, he didn't express enough resoluteness." See Du Xuncheng, " On Chao Gai," 21.

73 Wu Manping writes that the Red Army at Jinggang Mountain had referred to this type of coin as the "indigenous or telluric coin" (*tuban huabiao*). See Wu Manping, "Markings on the Jinggang Mountain Silver Dollar," 43. In terms of the task force, it is Liang Jie (in "On Knowledge of the 'Gong' Coin," 44) who notes its makeup, although he does not mention any connection between it and the 1975 anti–*Water Margin* campaign.

struggle, the worker (*gong*)? The marking of the coin with the *gong* character on it was not so much a way of establishing a communist currency as a way of separating brotherhoods from worker-comrades.

Can this 1975 discovery and then naming of the "Gong" coin by a centrally dispatched research team be separated from the nationwide campaign denouncing aspects of the *jianghu* in 1975? Was it by chance that the discovery and naming of the coin seems closely aligned with the prevailing political campaign against *The Water Margin*, or was the centrally dispatched research team conjuring up a *jianghu* trick of its own? To name a coin through a chop mark that spelled out the word "worker" in 1975 helped establish the revolutionary credentials of the coin makers of 1928 at a time when there was an ongoing nationwide political campaign designed to separate commitment to the Party from the *jianghu* spirit. Yet, in their attempt to separate the Party from the *jianghu* spirit, a connection is revealed. The coin, with the character for "worker" carved on it, sheds light on the accommodation the communists of Jinggang Mountain made with the *jianghu*. Their spirit of rebellion was smuggled into the Party through this burst of telluric energy and knowledge, which enabled the coin to be forged and the revolution to be fought with telluric intensity.

The coin helps reveal how the *jianghu* spirit surreptitiously entered into the realm of the Chinese political. This politicalized *jianghu* spirit merges technique and knowledge—knowledge that was grounded, indigenous, telluric, and affective—with Marxism-Leninism, to feed into the highly specific process of "becoming Maoist." Channeling *yiqi* into political intensity, turning brotherly bonds into class comrades, and turning bandit forgeries into revolutionary currencies offer examples of the way in which the Chinese Communist Party used the *jianghu* tactics and techniques to harness telluric energy in the name of revolution.

Whether we turn to *Rent Collection Courtyard*, the Mao badge, or the gift economy within the work unit or we simply focus on the Gong coin, what we are examining are a series of technologies, practices, and machinery designed to channel energy into an intense, political form. This, then, was Maoism's attempt to harness "effervescence."[74] Here were apparatuses of capture work-

74 Allan Stoekl claims Bataille translates "excess energy" into an "effervescence," which he then calls "the subversive violence of the masses, the baseness of their refusal to enter into boring discussions." See Stoekl, introduction to *Visions of Excess*, xviii. See also Bataille, *The Accursed Share*, 10.

ing not so much to strengthen the state, as much as to strengthen and extend the war machine within the state.[75] This form of Maoism was a war machine driving a state. The machinery of state was rewired (by political campaigns), reassembled (as "revolutionary"), and refocused on myriad experiments, devices, and technologies designed to intensify affective currents and turn them political. Here, then, was an assemblage not just flagging the Maoist political but, through that highly specific cultural form, revealing more generally a very different mode of being political. It is a mode of being political revealed more in the poetic than the purely rational and, as we will conclude, more as a stroke order rather than an ordering of words.

75 Deleuze and Guattari, *A Thousand Plateaus*, 392.

PART 6

Strokes, Not Words

15

Calligraphy

Poetic words, drawn from the calligraphy in figure 15.1, Carl Schmitt believed, equip us with what we need to understand how Mao Zedong's partisanship was able to bind together the indigenous power of the telluric and the global intensity of revolution.[1] Written by Mao in 1935 during the Long March on his ascent to power, this poem, called "Kunlun,"[2] was said, by Schmitt, to offer the following revealing verse:

1 Schmitt points this out in *The Theory of the Partisan*, 59.

2 The poem was written by Mao during the epic Long March, and it dreamed of a time when peace would prevail. Based on the mythic Kunlun Mountain from Chinese folklore, Kunlun was a place of the imagination. It touched the heavens and was home to magical creatures and plants. In later Chinese traditions, it became renowned as the home of Taoist immortals.

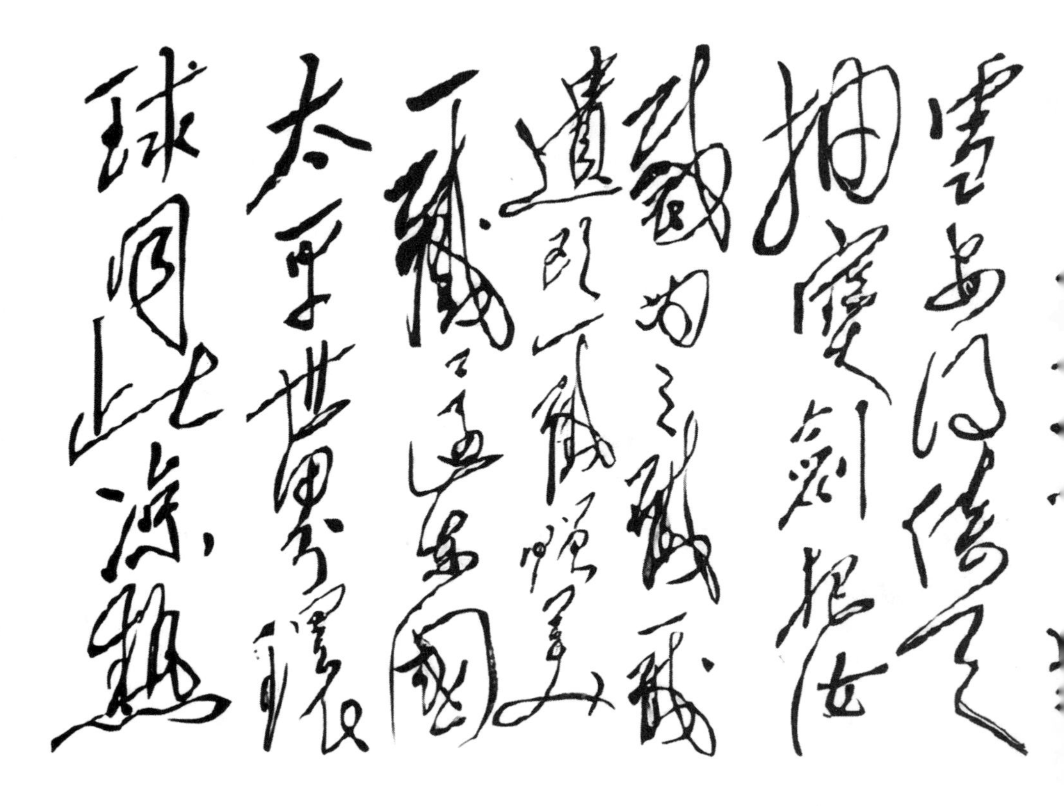

Figure 15.1. "Kunlun," by Mao Zedong. The calligraphy and Chinese script are sourced from Mao Tse-tung (Zedong), "Mao Zedong's Poems: Niannujiao—'Kunlun.'" The English translation is from Schmitt, *The Theory of the Partisan*, 59.

安得倚天抽宝剑,
If I could stand above the heavens, I would draw my Sword
　　把汝裁为三截
And cut you into three parts;
　　一截遗欧,
One piece for Europe,
　　一截赠美,
One piece for America,
　　一截还东国,

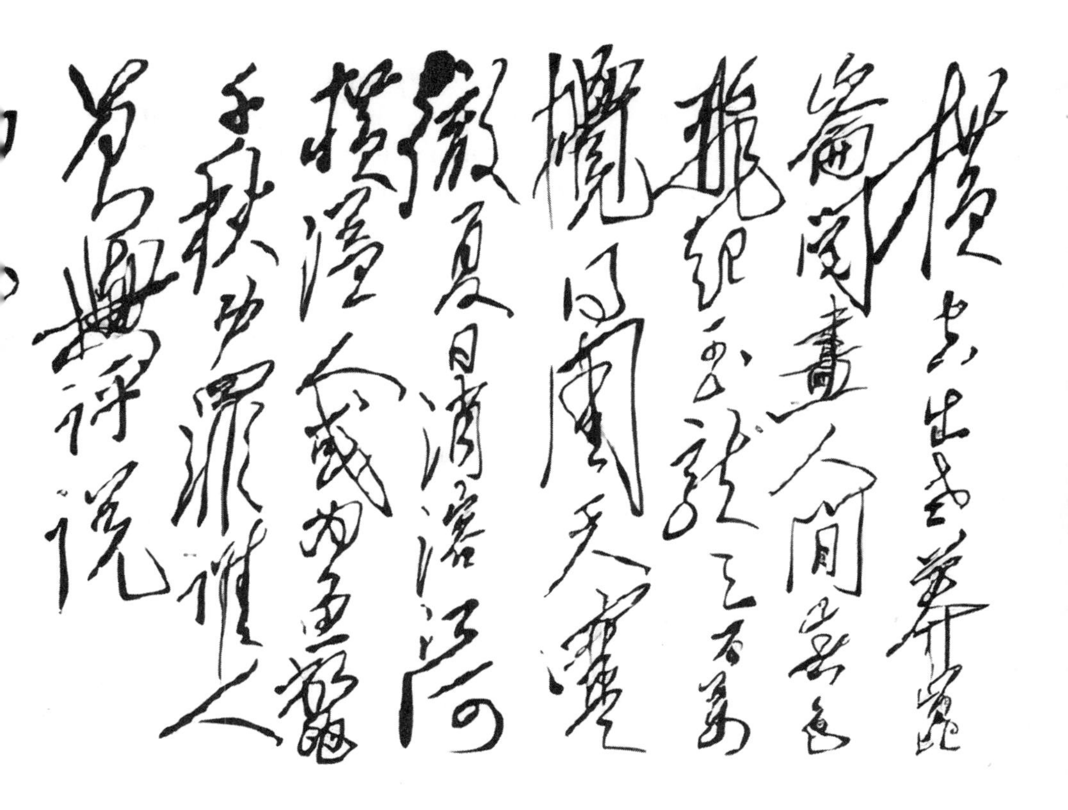

One piece for China,*[3]
太平世界，环球同此凉热.
then peace would rule the world.

From this stanza, Schmitt would discern a new nomos of the earth, bringing three forms of enmity together as one in the nationalism of Mao's future

3 China*: The reason for the asterisk (and deliberate mistranslation above) is a discrepancy between versions of this poem. In earlier versions, "One piece for China" was "One piece for eastern (Asian) countries." The discrepancy lies in the fact that Mao is said to have changed the original 1935 wording in 1963. For the change of wording, see Ingalls, *Dragon in Ambush*, 339. For Ingalls, "Kunlun" is "very likely the most rhetorically elegant authoritarian manifesto . . . in world literature" (347), and through a close reading of the poems in the context of Chinese political, cultural, and literary traditions, she claims to sense Mao's global ambitions. On this, see Ingalls, *Dragon in Ambush*, 325–50.

revolutionary nation-state.[4] Mao would tie racial enmity against white colonial rule (one piece for Europe) to the class hostility toward the capitalist bourgeoisie (one piece for America) and then bind these both to a nationalist enmity the Chinese felt toward the Japanese (one piece for China). These three forms of enmity would be homologized into one big concept, namely, Mao's telluric partisanship.[5] Yet the poetic words that Schmitt believed revealed so much of Mao's telluric partisan nature tell only part of the story.[6] Brushstrokes tell the rest. If the words of the poem point to the nationalism of a future revolutionary nation-state, the brushstrokes point back to an elite art form that uses affective means to speak beyond words.

Brushstrokes point back to an ancient Chinese aesthetic that regarded calligraphy, poetry, and painting as the three perfections (*shi, shu, hua, sanjue*) but, within this formulation, regarded calligraphy as the "supreme art."[7] While classical Chinese poetry, like its Western counterpart, obtained its poetic effect through rhyme and meter, in the Chinese tradition, this constitutes only one part of the poetic form. The other element was delivered through the brush. Calligraphy therefore opens onto an entirely different and unique art form that, in Chinese, is called *shufa*. In *shufa*, meaning is conveyed not just by beautiful words but also by the brushstroke. For Richard Kraus, the con-

4 For Ingalls, however, the poem is not about the nation-state but instead flags Mao's personal global ambitions. For her, Mao, while brilliant, was a ruthless, traditional authoritarian despot, caring only for power and nothing else. This aspect of Mao is revealed, Ingalls suggests, through an examination of Mao's use of language in poetry. The argument, however, discounts the fact that if there were any global ambitions of Mao Zedong in either 1935 or in 1963 they were always couched in terms of the global revolutionary ambition of a world communist movement, not as personal ambition. Ingalls's reading of certain textual intensifications through things like choice of characters in the poem, however, is far more interesting than the simplistic conclusions she draws about Mao's politics. On her wider analysis of Mao's politics through "Kunlun" and other poems, see Ingalls, *Dragon in Ambush*, 325–50.

5 Schmitt, *The Theory of the Partisan*, 59.

6 Bataille notes that poetry offers a door to the unknown: "Poetry is despite everything the restricted part—linked to the realm of words." See Bataille, *Inner Experience*.

7 Leys, *The Hall of Uselessness*, 295.

sequences of this were significant. Where, in the West, script would become a pathway to art and literature, in China, "the art lay in the writing itself."[8] In other words, *shufa* constitutes a uniquely Chinese art of doing: a visual art form in which aesthetic expression, while never separate from the words on the page, is not carried by words alone. Instead, it emerges in and through the suppleness and strength of the brushwork, in the elisions, spaces, and rhythms created between and within characters, and by the spatial relationships these markings establish between ink and paper. In this way, *shufa* is of much more significance than Western calligraphy, which ultimately remains tied to its etymological roots as "beautiful writing."[9]

Like the "decalcomaniacs" that Raymond Loewy decried in relation to early machine design, Western calligraphy offered no more than a means of decorating and illustrating the written word. Unlike its Chinese counterpart, Western calligraphy did not attempt to bring out another layer of meaning but was, instead, a decorative art form. Being decorative more than contemplative, it was parasitically attached to the text, adorning letters rather than adding a depth of meaning. *Shufa*, on the other hand, far from merely adorning text, is alive with other activity and meaning.[10] As a result, it produces, as Jean François Billeter notes, an art of movement,[11] through a technology that demands spontaneity.[12] Despite this, it is also highly disciplined.

8 Kraus, *Brushes with Power*, 37.

9 Calligraphy comes from the classical Greek word *kalligraphia*, wherein *kallos* means beauty, and *graphein*, writing.

10 Jean François Billeter explains how Chinese calligraphy is far from being a static, fixed compositional form. Some works, he notes, will have an unbalanced character compensating for another unbalanced character next to it, thereby forming an "unstable equilibrium." Other works have such distance between characters that they appear like the night sky, while other styles are so dense with characters that they resemble a rainforest. Text and writing offer up yet another site of such interplay. Whatever form the calligraphy takes, however, they are all and always instances of energy circulating. See Billeter, *The Chinese Art of Writing*, 92–93.

11 Billeter, *The Chinese Art of Writing*, 11.

12 "The technology of calligraphy demands spontaneity: water-based ink on tissue paper does not forgive errors or permit second thoughts." Kraus, *Brushes with Power*, 27.

Running across all the different styles of Chinese calligraphy is a strict stroke order and a variety of brush techniques that must be mastered and adhered to. Once mastered, the "creative upsurge" and the "forces arising from the depths of being" are then channeled, captured, and recorded by this art of calligraphy.[13] In traditional Chinese cosmology, "forces arising from the depths of being" are vital energies that, as we know, are called *qi*. Chinese calligraphy is, then, concerned with the channeling of *qi*, or vital energy. In this regard, Chinese calligraphy goes well beyond the beautification of letters and words, offering a far more complex and intimate relationship with text and affective textual meaning than Western calligraphy. Indeed, in one particular style of calligraphy, the pictographs are rendered so abstract, dynamic, and intense that characters can become almost impossible to recognize, thus making textual translation of any poetic content, even for an aficionado, turn into a form of contemplation.[14] That particular style, known as the wild grass cursive style, or *kuangcao*, was the one favored by Mao Zedong. Indeed, so distinctive was his own wild grass cursive style that, in Mainland China at least, it became a style in its own right, called the "Mao style," or *Maoti*.[15] Mao employed this distinctive cursive style in the writing of the poem "Kunlun."

The added layer of complexity produced by grass-style calligraphy demonstrates an art form that, far from purely illustrating or decorating the text or even conveying meaning, focuses instead on an entirely different way of framing perception and apprehending textual meaning. It points to a dimension unexplored by Schmitt as he uncovers Mao's nomos of the earth.[16]

13 Billeter, *The Chinese Art of Writing*, 11.

14 Billeter, in fact, argues that the cursive style of calligraphy is so complex that "to be able to read it, you must have some experience of writing it." Billeter, *The Chinese Art of Writing*, 79.

15 In the People's Republic of China, and unlike the post–Cultural Revolution assessment of Mao's political legacy, the views on his calligraphy have largely remained unchanged. Indeed, there is even an active and official "Mao-style" calligraphy association. For details of this association, see China-maoxie (The Art of Writing Chinese Mao Calligraphy), "Carrying Forward Mao-Style Calligraphic Art as an Inherited Artform of China." Michelle Wong, writing in Hong Kong's *South China Morning Post*, even suggests that Xi Jinping mimics Mao's signature style! See Wong, "Out of Character?"

16 There is a paradox in Mao using this particular art form and in it being treated as a legitimate cultural inheritance. As should be clear from the above, calligraphy

Moreover, it also lies outside Western metaphysics, which, as Derrida has detailed, turns on the written word as a sign of voicing.

From Aristotle and the Greeks, right through to Hegel's privileging of the alphabet, Derrida notes,[17] writing had been taken to clothe sound just as speech clothed thought.[18] Writing was, then, the "speaking" of script. Such acts opened onto the interiority of the subject and their sense of Being while simultaneously functioning as a utensil that verbalized and "spoke outwardly" but as concrete marking.[19] Founded on speech acts that were then transcribed into a phonetically based alphabet, this Western logocentric form, Hegel claimed, had a certain mental reflexivity that the languages of the hieroglyph lacked. Yet this claim of mental reflexivity is based on a privileging of the spoken over the written and on conveying meaning rather than emotion. In other words, it is based on a mind-body split absent from traditional Chinese metaphysics. *Shufa* offers a concrete form through which we contemplate the possibility of another way of being outside the logocentric privileging of the spoken and the mind-body split.[20]

Simon Leys suggests that while the Bible might begin with "the word," Chinese cosmologies arguably begin with script.[21] This is because the origins of the Chinese character lie in the mystical divination that pictographs created on oracle bones sometime in the Shang dynasty (1556–1046 BC).[22] It

---

is an elitist "high" art form and would usually be attacked in the Maoist period as one of the "Four Olds." Instead, it adorns buildings, statues, and steles, not to mention being on the masthead of the most prominent revolutionary newspapers and magazines, and is the frontispiece of important works. For further details, see Yen Yuehping, *Calligraphy and Power in Contemporary Chinese Society.*

17 Derrida, *Of Grammatology*, 97.

18 Derrida, *Of Grammatology*, 35

19 Derrida, *Of Grammatology*, 34.

20 According to Billeter, it establishes a very different relationship to the body from that of the Western mind-body split. See Billeter, *The Chinese Art of Writing*, 203–4.

21 Simon Leys suggests that while the Saint John's Gospel might open with the words "In the beginning there was the word," in Chinese calligraphy, it could be argued that "in the beginning there was the script." Leys, *The Hall of Uselessness*, 307.

22 Xie Jianhua, *The Vigor and Grace of Chinese Calligraphy*, 7–8.

is said that they were created by the king's diviners who marked characters onto turtle shells and cattle bones, heating them until they cracked and this then gave them an indication of heaven's will.[23] From these divinely inspired characters came a language form that centered on characters conveying meaning without the need for oral or audio unity.[24] The writing of such sacred scripts would later develop into an elite art form in which the calligrapher gained something of the sacred aura associated with divine characters. Chinese calligraphy therefore became a key element in elite notions of self-cultivation.[25] This made *shufa* quite different from Western calligraphy and the Chinese calligrapher quite different from the Western scribe. Indeed, even in bodily comportment, the Chinese calligrapher was different, writing not at the steady methodical pace of Western calligraphers but through an "attack" upon a page in which the brush lingers, leaps, stops, and sets forth again in a series of movements across the paper. "Bodily performance" rather than the movement of the hand produced a form of writing that tilted meaning away from "voicing" or even from the meaning of words, but what it captured was the flare and vibrancy of the gesture.[26]

Shufa is, then, an art of movement channeling the flow of vital energy from the body onto paper or silk and, from there, into other human bodies. It is life revealed by the flow of vital energy, or *qi*.[27] Infusing things with life, then affecting the human spirit (*qi zhi jiaogan huayu le shengming*) by bringing energy (*qi*), form (*xing*), spirit (*shen*), and melody (*yue*) into

23 Kraus, *Brushes with Power*, 4. One character that was said to come from this source was *qi*. According to Zheng Li, "The character *qi* was first written as an inscription on an oracle bone and on ancient bronze ware." See Zheng Li, *On Zhuangzi's Aesthetics*, 117.

24 Leys, *The Hall of Uselessness*, 307. The fact that spoken Cantonese is incomprehensible to a Mandarin speaker and vice versa, for example, is the result of this privileging of script over "voicing." The privileging of the scriptural form enables innumerable dialects.

25 Xie Jianhua notes how calligraphy constituted the very basis of traditional education. See Xie Jianhua, *The Vigor and Grace of Chinese Calligraphy*, 9.

26 For details of the perfect comportment while writing Chinese characters with the brush, see Xie Jianhua, *The Vigor and Grace of Chinese Calligraphy*, 11.

27 For a fuller explanation of this distinction see Billeter, *The Art of Chinese Writing*, 204–5.

one body: this brings to the fore an understanding that under heaven (*tongtianxia yiqi er*), *qi* gives breath to all living things, to the ten thousand things (*qihuayu wanwu*).[28] Without the involvement of vital energy, "form would have no form, and spirit would have no spirit, but form/spirit would instead divide into two extremities."[29] By not falling into this mind/body-form/spirit binary division, what is revealed is the flow of life itself.[30]

Closer to classical Chinese painting than to poetry,[31] Chinese calligraphy reveals its meaning through affective means in a series of sensuous yet disciplined and structured "performances" that leave their trace through the lines, dots, streaks, strokes, and spaces on the page. This becomes particularly apparent in the wild grass cursive style Billeter refers to as a "genre apart"![32]

Unlike other genres, this "wild grass cursive style," or *kuangcao* style, of Chinese calligraphy, is less concerned with conveying the written meaning than giving "infinite freedom" in the way one could "connect strokes, compose and abbreviate characters, and arrange the whole text."[33] In Mao's writing, it gains a distinctive vibrancy and dynamism that is expressed through the lines, dots, streaks, strokes, and spaces that appear to almost capture flow stilled into a character form yet still appearing to be in motion. Indeed, in Mao's writing, the intensity is such that lines seem to spill from the brush onto the page like a raging torrent. These lines, dots, streaks, strokes, blotches, and spaces, while encapsulating the movement of the poem, also record the

28 Zheng Li, *On Zhuangzi's Aesthetics*, 119.

29 There are multiple ways of understanding this Taoist-inspired flow of vital energy—from Mengzi's "abundant *qi*" (*chongshi zhi qi*) through to Guanzi's "essential *qi*" (*jingqi*)—but it is in the work of the philosopher Zhuangzi that this movement of vital energy leads to form (*xing*), energy (*qi*), spirit (*shen*), and melody (*yue*) being brought into one body, leading Zheng Li to conclude that "in discussions about the form-spirit [*xingshen*] relationship, to speak of the closely connected and vitally important category of *qi* is inevitable." Zheng Li, *On Zhuangzi's Aesthetics*, 117.

30 When Derrida writes "what non-phonetic writing betrays is life itself," he could be writing about the practice of Chinese calligraphy, for it is more than an act of writing: it is a performance. See Derrida, *Of Grammatology*, 25.

31 Billeter, *The Chinese Art of Writing*, 206.

32 Billeter, *The Chinese Art of Writing*, 77.

33 Da Zheng, "Chinese Calligraphy and the Cultural Revolution," 189–91.

flow of energy as it moves from the body to the brush and onto paper until it finally spills off the page as it did in Mao's (1957) poem "Reply to Li Shu-yi—to the Tune of *Tieh Lien Htua*" (see figure 16.1 in the next chapter).[34] Mao's wild, chaotic calligraphy attracted criticism, and much like graphologists who would claim psychological insight through an understanding of someone's handwriting, so, too, Mao's calligraphy was said to show his state of mind.[35]

Richard Curt Klaus once called Mao's calligraphy "eccentrically puissant."[36] Yen Yuehping agreed, finding this style "attractive" but adding that it carried within it a "murderous air" (*dai shaqi*).[37] Da Zheng called *Maoti*, or the Mao style, a "self-centered" style of calligraphy that excluded the masses.[38] Indeed, for him, "Mao was now an Odysseus on a voyage, free to enjoy the Sirens' songs,

34 The image is drawn from New China Publishing House *Mao Images*, 165–66. A translation of the poem can be found at Marxists Internet Archive, https://www.marxists.org/reference/archive/mao/selected-works/poems/poems24.htm, accessed June 1, 2020. Note that the phonetic translation used at Marxists Internet Archive is not pinyin, the most recognized form of character translation into phonetic script, and it should have read, "Reply to Li Shuyi—to the Tune of *Dielianhua*."

35 There is, in fact, an old Chinese aphorism that Richard Curt Klaus recalls, which suggests that through calligraphy the Chinese character reveals a human's moral character (*ziruqiren*). Kraus concludes, "The assumption that calligraphy reveals the person permeates Chinese life." Kraus, *Brushes with Power*, 45.

36 Kraus mentions this while explaining the widespread use of Mao's calligraphy on newspaper and journal mastheads, on university gates, and as the frontispieces of significant books. See Kraus, *Brushes with Power*, 12. As Da Zheng notes, it became a common practice for people to join together various bits of Mao's handwriting and rearrange them to make up new titles and, in some instances, stylistically problematic slogans or banners. For an example, see Da Zheng, "Chinese Calligraphy and the Cultural Revolution," 188.

37 Yen Yuehping, *Calligraphy and Power in Contemporary Chinese Society*, 29.

38 For Da Zheng, the wild grass cursive script of Mao was self-centered because "as an artistic expression of his personal emotions, [it] was not obliged to observe the mass's need for an easy recognition of the content." Da Zheng, "Chinese Calligraphy and the Cultural Revolution," 191. This stands in contrast to the "Big Character Posters" of the Cultural Revolution, which conveyed clear messages more often than not in the highly regimented and disciplined "Regular style" of calligraphy. Da Zheng, "Chinese Calligraphy and the Cultural Revolution," 192. For Da Zheng, this proved that the masses, unlike Mao, were straitjacketed by politics rather than liberated by it. Da Zheng, "Chinese Calligraphy and the Cultural Revolution," 195.

while the whole society had their ears plugged and followed his command."[39] For Leys, Mao's brushstrokes also revealed egotism, but for him it was "egotism, to the point of arrogance, if not extravagance." As Leys wrote, Mao's famously wild and exuberant brushstrokes showed "a contempt for technical requirements," and his style "disregards the formal discipline of the brush."[40] Thus, while many Chinese regarded and, in fact, still regard Mao's calligraphy as exceptional, for Leys, it was simply vulgar. As we will recall from an earlier chapter, however, Georges Bataille had an answer to the question of vulgarity.[41]

Bataille brought some ancient coins with images of a horse on them to the table.[42] One of the coins was geometrical and Athenian. Bataille labeled this image "The Academic Horse.[43] The other coins were from Gaul and appeared to be little more than cheap, ugly, imitations of the beautiful Athenian original. In comparing the two sets of coins, however, Bataille would show how the very vulgarity and aggressive ugliness of the horses on the surface of the coins from Gaul would paralyze the idealistic classicism of the ancient Greeks. As we will recall, the coins from Gaul produced a dislocation and disruption to the academic horse, producing, in Bataille's view, "successions of revolutions that have lasted without end, beating and frothy like a wave on a stormy day, within a limited time frame."[44] The rhythmic pulsations of Bataille's mind's-eye are in tune with Mao's notion of "continuous revolution," or *jixu geming*, whereby "one revolution must follow another," must

39 Da Zheng, "Chinese Calligraphy and the Cultural Revolution," 195.

40 Leys, *The Hall of Uselessness*, 184.

41 This rebuke of beauty and lauding of the vulgar came in a series of articles in Bataille's journal *Documents*. The first of these articles, titled "The Academic Horse," was published in April 1929, but it was followed by a string of other articles praising the grotesque in place of the marvelous, leading Bataille's biographer, Michel Surya, to write, "The tone was set. *Documents* would be the abscess burst each month from surrealism." Despite this, he goes on to note that "in the fifteen issues of *Documents* he did not once cite the name of André Breton." See Surya, *Georges Bataille*, 120–22.

42 For fuller details of the coins that Bataille discussed in "The Academic Horse," see the section "Ill-Disciplined Numismatics" in chapter 2.

43 This, in fact, was the name of the article in the April 1929 issue of *Documents*. See Bataille, "The Academic Horse," 238. See also chapter 2 for more details.

44 Bataille, "The Academic Horse."

be spontaneous, and "strike while the iron is hot."[45] If we can indeed psychologize on the basis of calligraphy, could we not, then, say that far from dismissing Mao's calligraphy as vulgar, might it not be better to examine this as an example of the tidal bore of an intense energy flow?[46]

Throwing balance to the wind, Mao would, in part, join the Gauls as they destroyed the geometric quality that made the "academic horse" such an object of aesthetic veneration, but Mao would do so through the disciplining of an intensity carried in a series of revolutionary strokes. It was this intensity that would drag words, lines, and characters off the page. As they left the page and entered life, the wild flourishes seemed to capture, in the mind's-eye, the power of affective energy being transformed into a form that would power the brushstrokes of revolution.[47]

In the cosmogony of ancient China, the flow of *qi* ran through everything.[48] It would feature in traditional Chinese medical remedies and understandings of the body but it would equally be recognized as being carried through breath into the sound of a lute, or into the movement of dancers or

45 Mao Zedong, "Speech at the Supreme State Conference," 94. For further details of continuous revolution, see glossary A, "Terms and Concepts."

46 Here, it might be useful to mention Louis Marin's work on the dual life of kings and its relationship to Mao before completely accepting this use of calligraphy as a means of developing a psychological profile and, from there, mounting ad hominem attacks. For Marin, the king lived two lives: one as a mortal being; the other, engraved on plaques, statues, and medallions. Mao's calligraphy is part of this second life. His distinctive calligraphy and the ubiquitous Little Red Book, Mao badge, and Mao statue were part of Mao's second life, and it is this that is of diagnostic value in understanding not Mao the man, but the Maoist revolution. For details of this distinction made in relation to Louis XIV, see Marin, *Food for Thought*, 12–14.

47 Stuart Schram recognizes the Taoist-inspired notion of fluidity in Mao's thought when he links Mao's thoughts on the "correct rhythm of production" to "the dialectics of Taoism," which he claims are nothing other than the "rhythm of nature." See Schram, *Mao Tse-tung Unrehearsed*, 27.

48 As noted at the beginning, city gates would open and close to its rhythm; it would lead to the organization of space and fashion the land. It guided the use of geomancy's tools and techniques just as it guided the brush in the hand of the calligrapher, the word in the head of the poet, and the needle in the hand of the Chinese doctor. On the city, see Yi Ding, Yu Lu, and Hong Yong, *Geomancy and Selections from the Built Environment*. On calligraphy, see Zheng Li, *On Zhuangzi's Aesthetics*. On acupuncture, see Sivin, *Traditional Medicine in Contemporary China*.

into the punch the martial artist would pack.[49] The power of this bodily energy was being harnessed in Mao's calligraphy, just as collectively it was being harnessed in his revolution. *Qi* powered the brush of Mao such that his writing style became a kind of calligraphic torrent. These brushstrokes of telluric partisanship opened onto the potentially wild waywardness of the *jianghu* and pointed to novel elements crucial to an understanding not just of Maoism but also of the telluric element, and not just of the political but of a politics of energy flow. Whatever "vulgarity" there may be in Mao's calligraphy,[50] whatever the specifics of the telluric engagement he was involved in, it is through this uniquely intense, dynamic, and vibrant engagement with a calligraphic art form that spills off the page that one is drawn into the spirit of revolutionary change. To trace and appreciate this as a dialect in the language of the political not only requires recognizing other dialects, but also going beyond language and beyond the question of a logocentric "voicing." Instead of focusing on voicing, language, or even the Chinese characters themselves, we will instead follow the lines, dots, streaks, strokes, blotches, and spaces that apprehend life and move into another dimension. This requires a move not just from Chinese calligraphy to painting, but to a form of painting that gives the lines, dots, streaks, strokes, blotches, and spaces their own self-sufficiency.[51] That form of painting comes to the fore with Jackson Pollock.

Like a Pollock canvas, Mao's "art" runs off the page and flows into life—albeit in a very different direction to the one Pollock's work came from and would foreshadow. They are, therefore, ships in the night that, nevertheless, share the kinship of a turbulent sea. They both open onto lines of flight navigated by gestures, dots, streaks, brushstrokes, and blotches that signpost the flow of life itself.

49 Such efficacy and propensity is, according to François Jullien, a "potential born of disposition" and captured by the character *shi* that first emerges in military strategy. Jullien, *The Propensity of Things*, 27. The translator of Sun Tzu's *Art of War*, John Minford, explains it thus: "It is a philosophy of maximum effect through minimum expenditure of energy. It is the effortless gliding movement of the *taiji* practitioner, the soft but irresistible force of a brushstroke from a master calligrapher." Minford, introduction to *The Art of War*, xxvii.

50 Mao, in fact, never referred to his writings as *shufa*, yet his distinctive use of the brush, not to mention the popularization of his style, suggests otherwise. For this and other insights into Mao's style and the politics of revolution, see Schram, *Mao Tse-tung Unrehearsed*, 185–201.

51 Kaprow, *Essays on the Blurring of Art and Life*, 2–3.

16

Spilling Off the Page

In the calligraphy by Mao (figure 16.1), lines run off the page just as they do in the artwork by Joe Fig of Jackson Pollock (figure 16.2). In Fig's work, Pollock is captured jumping into his own work to add new lines, strokes, blotches, and dots. Pollock was becoming part of the work—"when I am in my painting, I don't know what I am doing," he once said.[1] In jumping in, he transformed the painting into a borderline act of ritual.[2] All around his feet were lines, dots, streaks, and blotches trailing off into a jumble of paint cans producing a "different" kind of bodily encounter. Pollock spreads the canvas across the floor. There is no overview. Pollock is "in it." The density of lines, dots, streaks, and blotches increases as paint spreads across the canvas. As

1 Quoted in Kaprow, *Essays on the Blurring of Art and Life*, 157.

2 "With the huge canvas placed upon the floor, thus making it difficult for the artist to see the whole or any extended section of 'parts,' Pollock could truthfully say that he was 'in' his work." Kaprow, *Essays on the Blurring of Art and Life*, 4.

it gains velocity, it increasingly explodes into a cacophony of forms. Living in the absence of marked zones, his work offers no beginning, no middle, and no end. As Pollock jumps into the picture, his work jumps off the canvas and, if Allan Kaprow is to be believed, straight into life itself. And while Pollock would not take that fateful leap off the canvas, Kaprow did.[3] Kaprow would cross a line that Pollock wouldn't by moving the work off the canvas and into everyday life. According to Alan W. Moore, for Kaprow, Pollock's work pointed in a direction that seemed "ready to break into the world beyond the canvas—out of the realm of illusion and abstract idealism into the world of the everyday."[4] Pollock's lines, drips, strokes, and drops formed an almost autonomous "dance of the dripping" and took his work beyond formalism, becoming a sign, to use Kaprow's words, of "the effect of energies in the state of becoming."[5] The effect of energy, rendered as a state of becoming, would move off the canvas into life and into what Kaprow came to call a "Happening." It was, as we have seen, the effects of energy, as a state of becoming, that moved the political into everyday life in Maoist China also. It did this by adopting artistic techniques and performance methods that bore at least some resemblance to Kaprow's "Happenings," as noted in passing by Roland Barthes.[6]

In the spring of 1974, at the height of the anti–Lin Biao/anti-Confucius campaign, or the *PiLin, PiKong* campaign, and against a backdrop of pro-Maoist enthusiasm in Western leftist circles, five important French intellectuals

3 Here I am being both polemical, and as Moore points out "a little simple," but my point is not to offer a picture of art history but to join some dots. To be fair, there were many artists working around this and similar themes at this time. For just one critique of such a Kaprow-centric approach, see A. Moore, "A Brief Genealogy of Social Sculpture."

4 Moore, author's note in "A Brief Genealogy of Social Sculpture."

5 Kaprow, *Essays on the Blurring of Art and Life*, 157.

6 This is not the only point of comparison between the Maoist campaign and the "Happening." Their pedagogical and philosophical kinship are both also loosely tied back to the work of John Dewey and, while this is not the place to pursue this linkage, it does open onto an important overlapping influence on both. For those interested in pursuing this link, Jeff Kelley notes Dewey's profound influence on Kaprow (see Kelley, introduction to *Essays on the Blurring of Art and Life*, xi–xxvi), in much the same way as Niu Xiaodong shows the influence of Dewey on Mao's pedagogy. See Niu Xiaodong, "Mao Zedong and John Dewey."

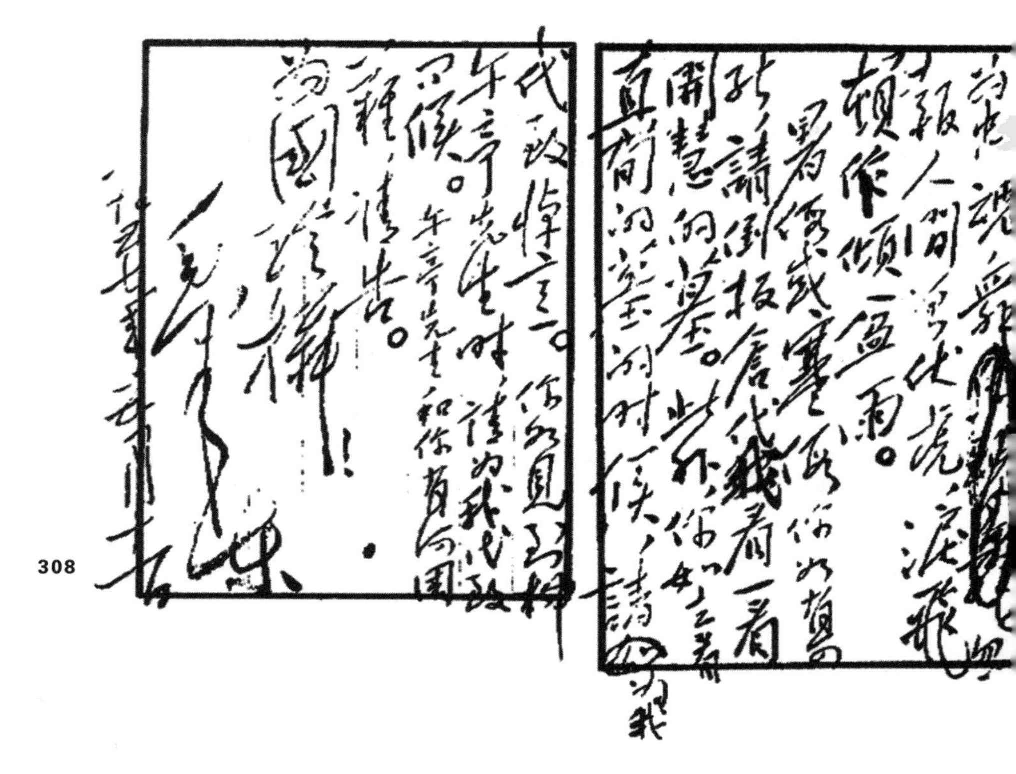

Figure 16.1. Mao Tse-tung (Zedong), “Reply to Li Shuyi—to the Tune of *Dielianhua*.” In New China Publishing House, *Mao Images*, 165–66.

from the journal *Tel Quel* visited China. One of them was Roland Barthes.[7] Like an ironic Engineer Menni in Bogdanov’s *Red Star*, Barthes cynically offered numbers in his account of Chinese socialism: “Irrigation works. 550 electric pumps . . . Transports: 110 lorries, 770 carriages = 11,000 families = 47,000 persons,” etc.[8] At the same time, he also saw something beyond cen-

7 The other members of the delegation were Julia Kristeva, Philippe Sollers, Marcelin Pleynet, and François Wahl.

8 See Barthes, *Travels in China*, 10–11. Barthes’s view of China was different to the pro-Mao, pro-China positions of both Julia Kristeva and Philippe Sollers. Barthes claimed to be neither for nor against, nor even neutral. In terms of China, this led Simon Leys, a very anti-Mao Sinologist, to suggest he was offering up little more than “lukewarm water from a tiny spigot.” Leys, *The Hall of Uselessness*, 376. Leys’s

tral planning and production numbers when he wrote of the campaign to criticize Lin Biao and Confucius. He said, "Its very name chimes like a merry little bell and the campaign is split into invented games: a caricature, a poem, a sketch performed by children, in the course of which a little girl with a made-up face will assail, between two ballets, the ghost of Lin Piao: The political Text . . . engenders these minor 'happenings.'"[9] Is Barthes's reference to "happenings" purely by chance?

While Maoist campaigns, like Happenings, employed a series of ad hoc and loosely scripted performative techniques to move bodies beyond the purely rational and cognitive and into affective encounters, they would nev-

---

cynicism and moral opprobrium at the fact that Barthes didn't condemn the regime may have gotten the better of him. See Stafford, "Roland Barthes's *Travels in China*."

9 Quoted in O'Meara, "Barthes and Antonioni in China," 279.

Figure 16.2. Joe Fig, *Jackson Pollock*, 2008. Mixed media, 8 × 21 × 17.5 in. Accessed June 30, 2020, at https://www.joefig.com/historical?lightbox=dataItem-iqn31bp81. Courtesy of Joe Fig.

ertheless speak of very different encounters. A Happening was a nondirectional art form, while Maoist campaigns and the ensemble of technology they required pointed in only one direction. While the Maoist campaign worked toward total political identification, Happenings worked with estrangement to develop a sense of the "suchness" of things.[10] Both were an encounter with the everyday, but where Happenings worked with self-produced experiences

10 Jon Erickson writes of the "suchness" of things as being "a nonrational, nongrasping acceptance of 'things as they are,' a distancing of object and events from the categorizing processes of meaning." J. Erickson, "The Spectacle of the Anti-Spectacle," 37.

fantasizing about unspecified mythical contexts,[11] the Maoist political campaigns drew individual experiences into collective activity. From primary school children doing the "Quotations of Chairman Mao gymnastics" (*Mao zhuxi yulucao*) to adults doing the devotion dance (*zhongziwu*), song, dance, and performance were tied back into traditional quotidian practices, collectively referred to as *yangsheng*, or "nurturing life practices."[12]

Like Chinese calligraphy, *yangsheng* practices are forms of individual self-cultivation, but unlike that elite art form, *yangsheng* is demotic. Moreover, unlike calligraphy, it is not "one thing" but rather a clustering of activities that could be said to nurture life. Like Chinese calligraphy, these practices are tied by a telluric thread back to questions of the channeling and harnessing of vital energy, or *qi*. Often collectively undertaken, *yangsheng* practices included calisthenics, the singing of songs, and the performance of public collective dance routines.[13] Could one not think of the mass singing that raised revolutionary spirits or the revolutionary dance performances that demonstrated devotion to the Chairman as being not only uplifting of

11 Much like Russian Constructivism and Dadaism that preceded Happenings and Situationism that came later, at a very general and abstract level, all employed various devices of "estrangement" in order to produce their own sense of "suchness." Suchness, however, was far more individualistic than the politically driven and collectively based movements it is being compared to here. They are linked by their desires to reach into what has been called, following Bataille, the heterogenous realm. While there were many shared ideas and techniques, there is also a massive political difference perhaps best expressed in the response of the Situationist International to Kaprow's Happenings. For the leading Situationist, Guy Debord, Kaprow's approach was politically suspect and, with shades of the Breton/Bataille debate, Debord contrasted the extreme state of dissolution to which the spectacle was pushed in Kaprow's Happenings, with the "foundation of material and spiritual richness" on which Situationist actions were performed. See J. Erickson, "The Spectacle of the Anti-Spectacle," 50.

12 The translation of *yangsheng* as a nurturing of life and the descriptions of practices undertaken in its name are all drawn from the work of Farquhar and Zhang, *Ten Thousand Things*.

13 Calisthenics, Farquhar and Zhang point out, was a mandated part of the day in the Maoist work units (*Ten Thousand Things*, 309). This is not to say individual activities such as walking (67), eating, or even crocheting cannot be part of *yangsheng*; it is just that so many of their practices are also collective.

individual spirit[14] but also collectivizing, weaponizing, and thereby intensifying that spirit? Was it not through these subtle, less visible telluric techniques that Maoism attempted to learn to "speak" and develop an affective language of the political? It has been an altogether different language of affect spoken from the West.

While Maoism attempted to use intensity to transform the singular "I" of the subject into the collective revolutionary "we" of the unified political cause, capitalism used desire to transform the collective "we" into the desiring "I" of the consumer. Disciplined through market veridiction, capitalism increasingly employed the phantasmagorical element of the commodity to bring this energy into its orbit. This fantasy element ensured that the momentary but fashionable trending item was constantly and quickly replaced by the next "hot"-ticket item—whether this be a "thing" or an event, be it your favorite band or football team. Even in the latter examples, the almost *yangsheng* techniques of collectivizing and uplifting the spirit are evident in the shared song or football chant. However, unlike political ends, in the stadiums, when spirits soar, profits are maximized. The result, as has long been noted, was new but always the same. This quality of the commodity form was locked into the fundamental operations of the market-based growth cycle. That element of market capitalism has never fundamentally changed. What has changed, however, is the development of technologies to enhance, uncover, and channel desire in the virtual realm.

In this realm, machine learning, facial-recognition technology, and algorithmically predictive marketing systems emerged as key devices of market growth and, as a result, as major growth markets. The use of big data to frame marketing campaigns is, paradoxically, to turn the telluric Maoist mass-line into a virtual assembly line of affective energy channeling.[15] Predictive adver-

14 Often involving mass street dancing, or exercise routines, one "model" *yangsheng* practitioner told Farquhar that *yangsheng*, for him, was the singing of revolutionary songs in unison with others. "The first time I went [to the People's Choral Group] and heard so many older people singing at the top of their lungs, I felt an upsurge of emotion, and tears came to my eyes." Farquhar and Zhang, *Ten Thousand Things*, 71.

15 Mao said, "Take the ideas of the masses (scattered and unsystematic ideas) and concentrate them (through study turn them into concentrated and systematic ideas), then go to the masses and propagate and explain these ideas until the masses embrace them as their own." Mao Tse-tung, "Some Questions concerning

tising doesn't just push a product: it helps transform the subject into a desiring subject who makes the "rational" choices and buys the product based on their desires and/or fears. With every purchase and every click, the consumer becomes ever more knowable. As they become knowable, they also become suggestable and pliable. Yet as they become increasingly enmeshed in this online-based interaction, new opportunities and new tactical spaces open up. As facial recognition and other machine learning technologies develop, there will, inevitably, be a clash with demands to protect privacy, freedom, and democracy. Big data that is "crunched" and triangulated with behavioral tendencies increasingly feeds back into policy decision-making processes, raising questions that go to the very heart of representative democracy.[16] This might be some way off, but a business model that enabled the internet to grow and become ubiquitous has produced a set of interrelated technologies that will inevitably lead to it "jumping species" out of marketing and into governmental policy. In this way, processes of market veridiction will guide the growth of new political approaches.

Maoism attempted to break this market cycle with a political spiral of its own. It produced a cyclical rhythm through Mao's theory of "continuous revolution" (*jixu geming*) wherein one political campaign pulsated into another and then another. This rhythmic, pulsating, often violent political process proved exhausting and polarizing, but, in its failure, we must nevertheless still recognize the first and very tentative appearance of a new type of political machinery being engaged with. It is one that offered a radically different way of channeling energy to the now globally hegemonic form that grew out of the Crystal Palace.

Methods of Leadership," 119. For a longer quotation of this passage, see *mass-line* in my glossary A, "Terms and Concepts."

16 While post-COVID China seems to have abandoned its attempt to implement it nationwide, the Chinese social credit system nevertheless points the way in this regard. Designed to assess trustworthiness by analyzing "big data," this system can discipline for "quality" but could also be used, like predictive marketing, to frame policy. Moreover, according to Drew Donnelly, a survey of Chinese people by Free University, Berlin, found that around 80 percent of respondents approved of this system, which, if true, shows a very high degree of acceptance of machine-driven approaches to social control in China. For an introduction to the Chinese social credit system, particularly with regard to the policing of (foreign) companies, see Donnelly, "China Social Credit System Explained."

Why Maoism and the Crystal Palace are important is that both constitute points at which various forms, devices, and machinery of energy transformation and use come into view. Both initiate attempts to create machinery to elongate, direct, and productively redeploy the heterogenous, pulsating energy that I have called here the affective flow. As technical solutions to these momentary energy outbreaks, Maoism and the Crystal Palace offer radically different solutions to the channeling of energy into collective sensibilities. Thus, rather than being about structure or agency, it was the degree and direction of this movement or flow of energy calculated in relation to the binary of friend and enemy that would become central to this approach to politics. What becomes important to examine are the strategies and tactics "we" employ—irrespective of who that "we" might be—to either harness, dispel, get around, or get away from that all-powerful friend/enemy divide. It is the story of how we have come to live these journeys as though they were the only possible journeys. To look at the possibility of another journey will, hopefully, open the way to thinking more broadly about ways of being in this world and how things could, in fact, be organized differently.

AFTER*WORDS*

INTENSITY AS LINE OF FLIGHT

Like Cai Guo-Qiang's 2006 installation, *Head On*, Deleuze and Guattari tie wolves to intensity and intensity to swarming, swarming to "wolfing," and "wolfing" to the pack. The wolf is a pack (*A Thousand Plateaus*, 35), they tell us, and a pack is an intensity (37). It is a reterritorialized intensity (36), a multiplicity, but simultaneously, like Cai Guo-Qiang's wolves, it can become a line of flight. Cai's wolves smash into an invisible wall with spectacular aesthetic intensity, just as the lines of flight of this work have hit that cathartic point where abstract and intangible affective flows are transformed into political intensities.

RCC: THREE LAYERS OF AN INTENSITY MACHINE

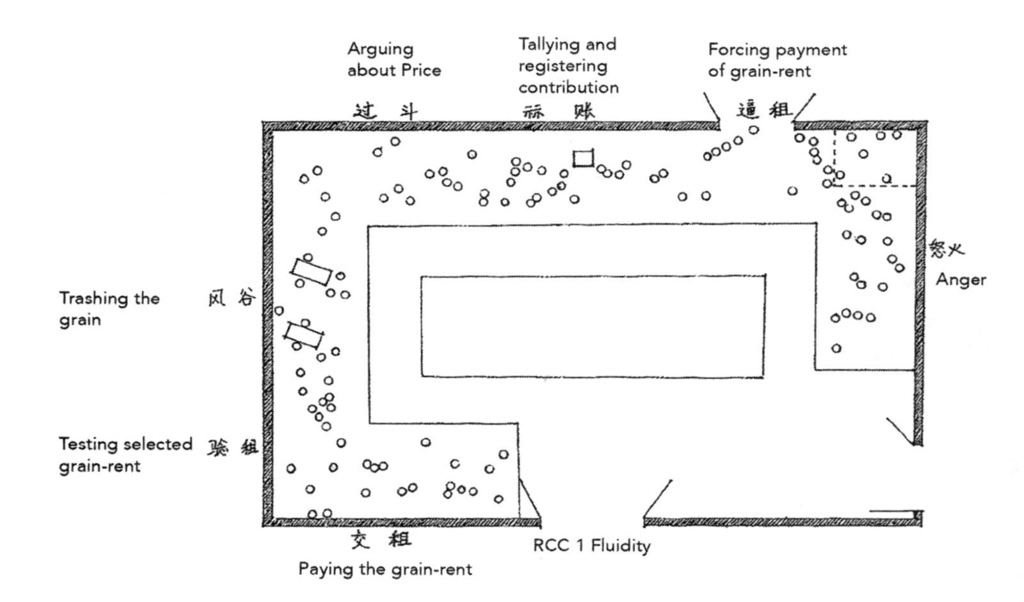

RCC 1: Fluidity

Small dots map out a movement that clusters, then thins, before clustering again in a process of contraction and expansion. Choreographed along lines that trace the exploitative, rural rent-collection process, the small dots follow a path of contraction and expansion that correlates with moments of "collection" (*jiaozu*), "inspection"(*yanzu*), "dehusking" (*fenggu*), and "checking" (*guodou*) of the peasants' grain. If the "settling of accounts" (*suanzhang*) followed by the "forced payments" (*bizu*) are the feudal political consequences of this economic system, the gathering clouds of "revolt" (*nuhuo*) are its political consequences.

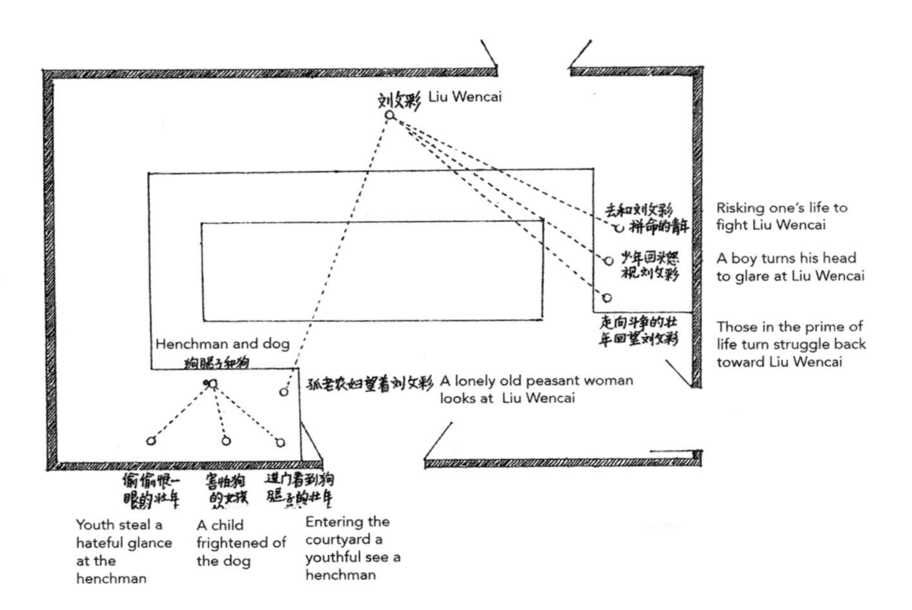

RCC 2: The Concrete Political

To follow the dotted lines of sight of the landlord (Liu Wencai) is to trace the contours of power both in the courtyard and in the country. While one dotted line traces Liu glancing over at his henchmen harassing the downtrodden, there are, simultaneously, three dotted lines leading to a focus on the fermenting youth rebellion. Here, the fluid dots become teenagers (*xiaonian*), young adults (*qingnian*), and those in the prime of life (*zhuangnian*). Youth would lead this rebellion against landlordism just as they would come to take the lead in the early stages of the Cultural Revolution.

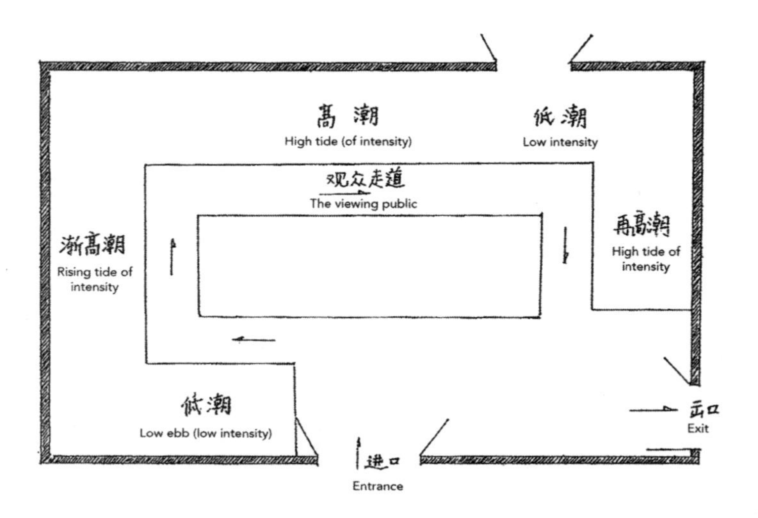

RCC 3: Power

The pulsating affective flow is charted, channeled, and choreographed with these dots in mind. In this diagram, the courtyard is transformed into a series of affective surges rising and diminishing but heading toward the formation of a political intensity. This path is what the viewing public will accompany as they follow the dots toward a revolutionary swarming. As the existentially felt exploitation grows, there is an ever-increasing high tide of antagonism (*gaochao*). Transformed into political intensity, this energy then both feeds the cathartic machinelike power of the RCC as well as being produced by it.

TELLURIC KNOWLEDGES

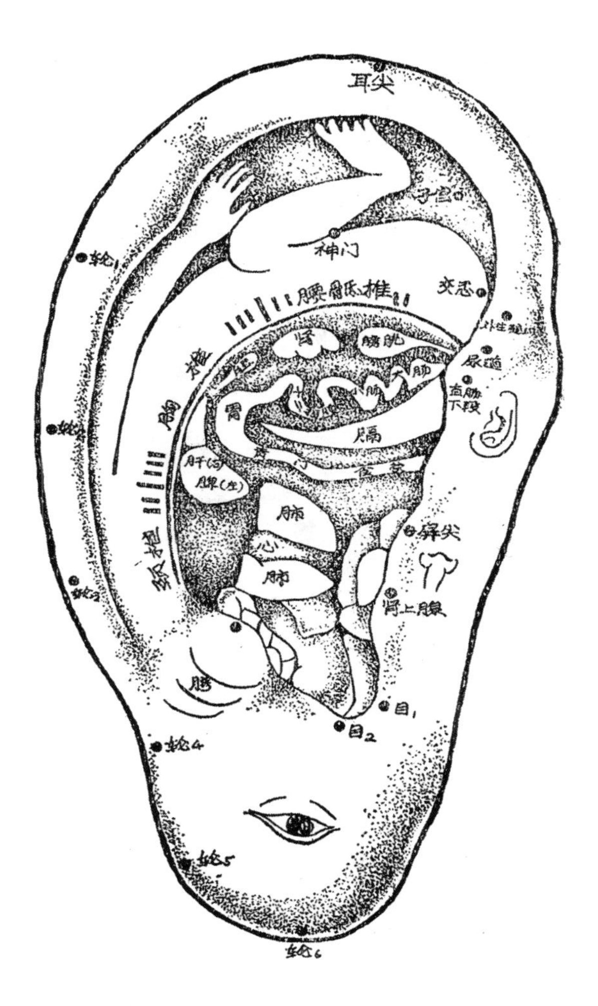

Telluric Knowledges 1

If the Red Army hospital at Jinggang Mountain shows the early effects of this indigenous knowledge encounter with modern Western medical sensibilities that would eventually lead to the hybrid knowledge form, traditional Chinese medicine, the construction of a Red Army mint would reveal another effect of indigenous knowledge on communist practices and thought. This time, it would be an encounter leading directly into the realm of the political. Work around the mint would lead Maoism "up the mountain," not in order to collect herbal remedies but instead to collect an altogether different form of telluric remedy.

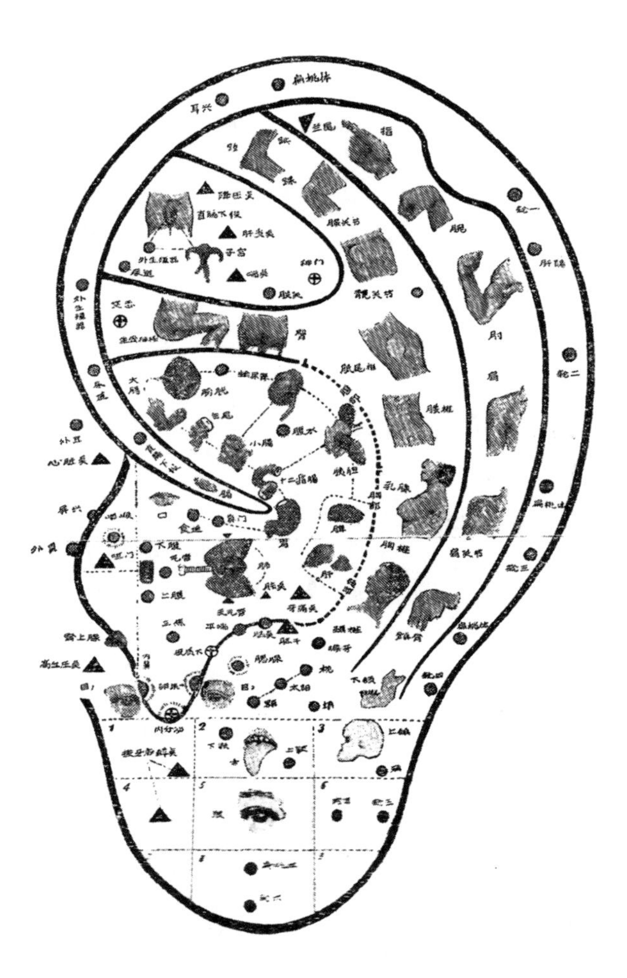

Telluric Knowledges 2

"When you insert the needle, observe the arrival of 'vital energies' [*qi*]. This arrival is formless, it is heralded by no signal and is almost untraceable. It is like a flock of birds passing. When there is an abundance of *qi* it is as rich as a field of grain. When *qi* passes, it is as if the bird's wings have fluttered yet no one is left to capture the form." Cui Xiaoli, *Huangdi Neijing*, 95.

Telluric Knowledges 3

Centering on the political, it was the Sirens' Song of modernism that Maoism would listen to, but would do so with hybridized telluric ears.

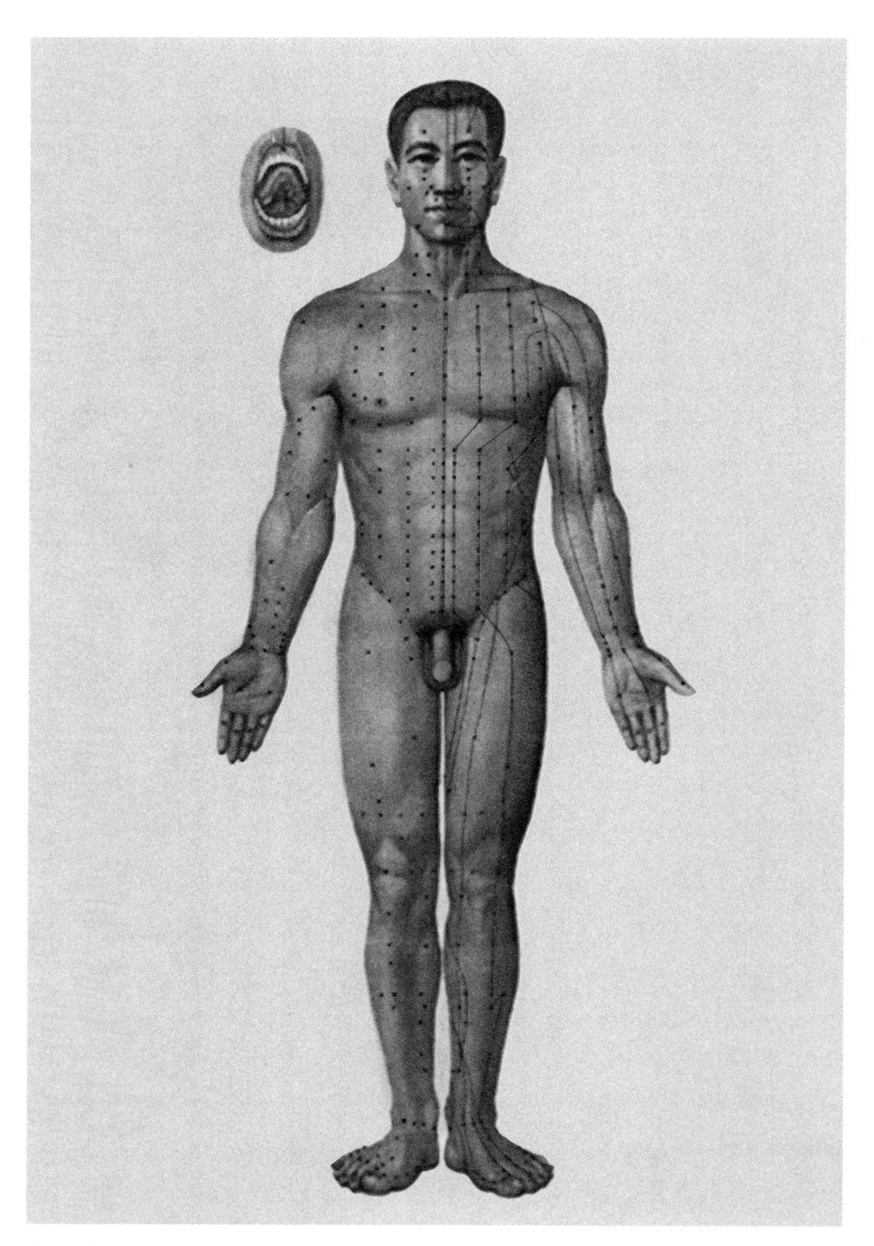

Telluric Knowledges 4

Think how this chart works to divide the body through meridians and acupoints. To quote an earlier passage in this volume, "Strange names compound the esoteric quality of meridians and acupoints (Hundred Meetings, Yin Metropolis, Purple Palace, for example). These conform to another world of understanding bodily functions. Now

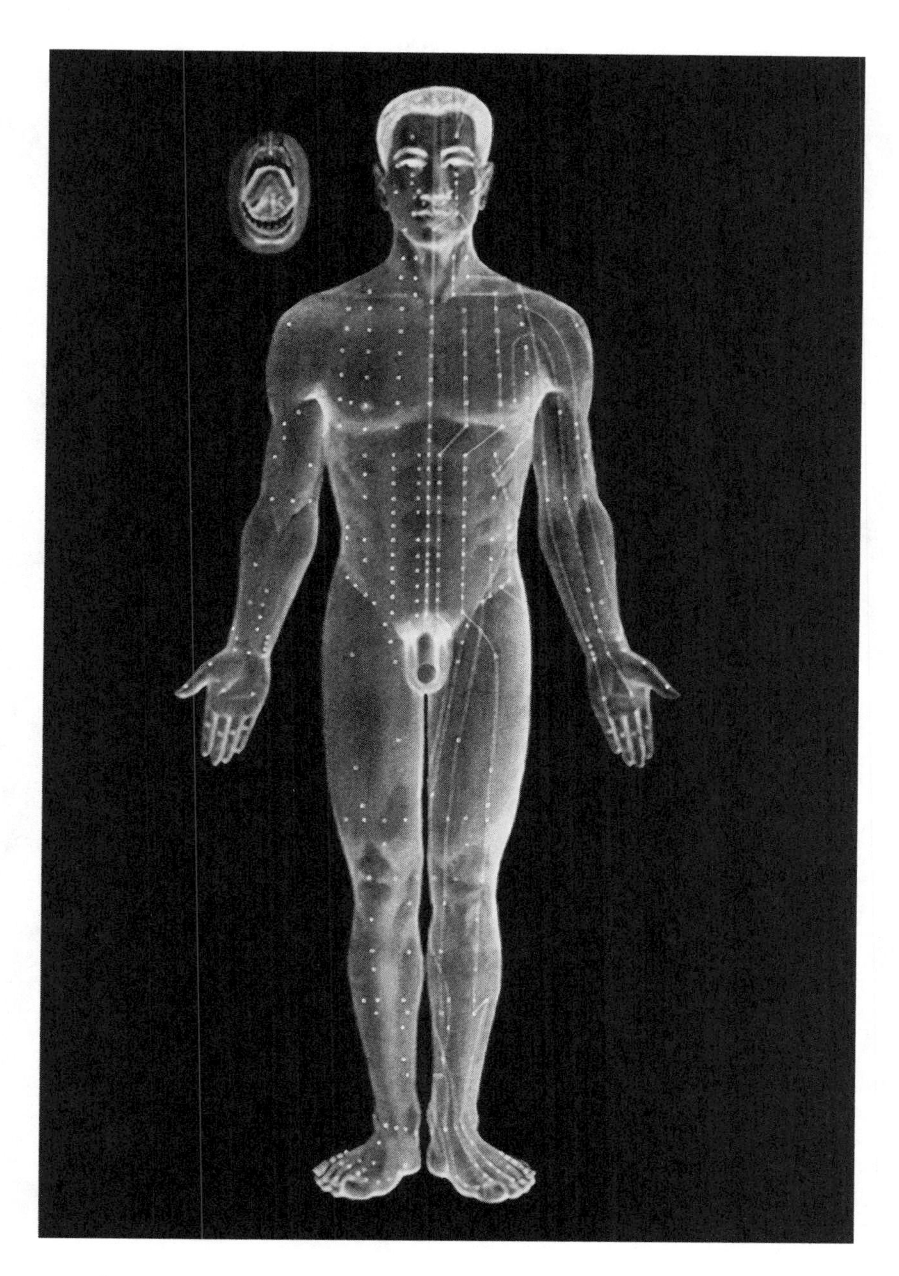

move from the legitimacy of that specialist knowledge form to a 'dialect' or 'slang' still operating within this same, seemingly nonlogocentric Chinese-language system, but so 'telluric,' so earthy, and so 'illegitimate' that it would remain as incomprehensible to the Chinese scholar-officials of Borges's imagination as it would to a traditional Chinese doctor." See this volume, "Chinese Curios," chap. 1, p. 47.

CONSTRUCTIONS

Constructions 1

“There can be no construction without destruction.” (Mao Zedong)

“In every era the attempt must be made anew to wrest tradition away from a conformism that is about to overpower it.” Benjamin, “Theses on the Philosophy of History,” 247.

停车场
信息服务中心
老成都照片馆
日军馆
伪军馆
中心广场
信息服务中心
停车场
川军馆

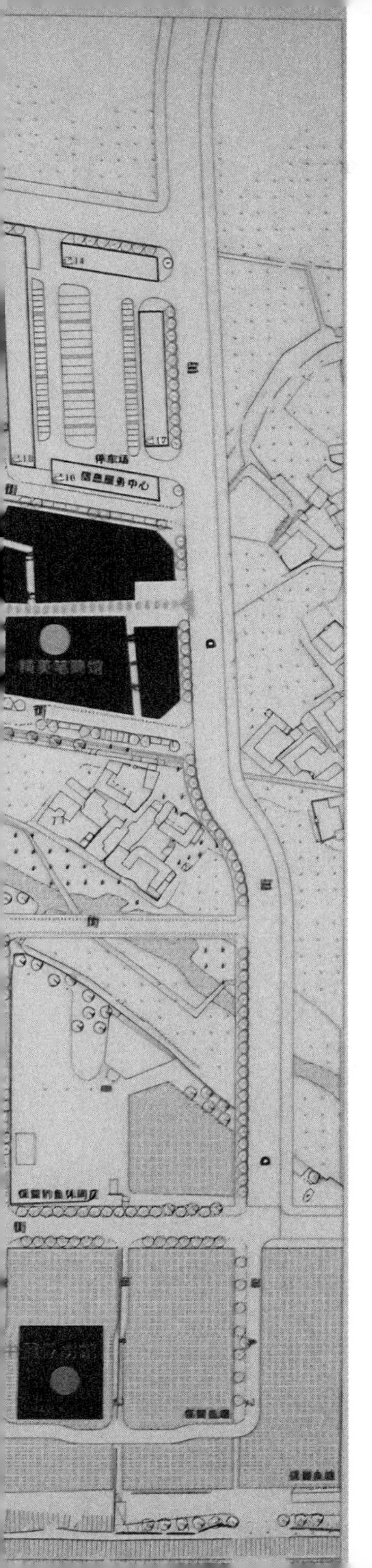

Constructions 2: Phantasmagoric Nostalgia

"And just as the alchemist, with his *base* wish to make gold, experiments with chemicals in which the planets and elements combine to form images of spiritual man, so did the collector, while satisfying the base wish for possession, undertake the exploration of an art in whose creations the productive forces and the masses combine to form images of historical man." Benjamin, *One-Way Street and Other Writings*, 386.

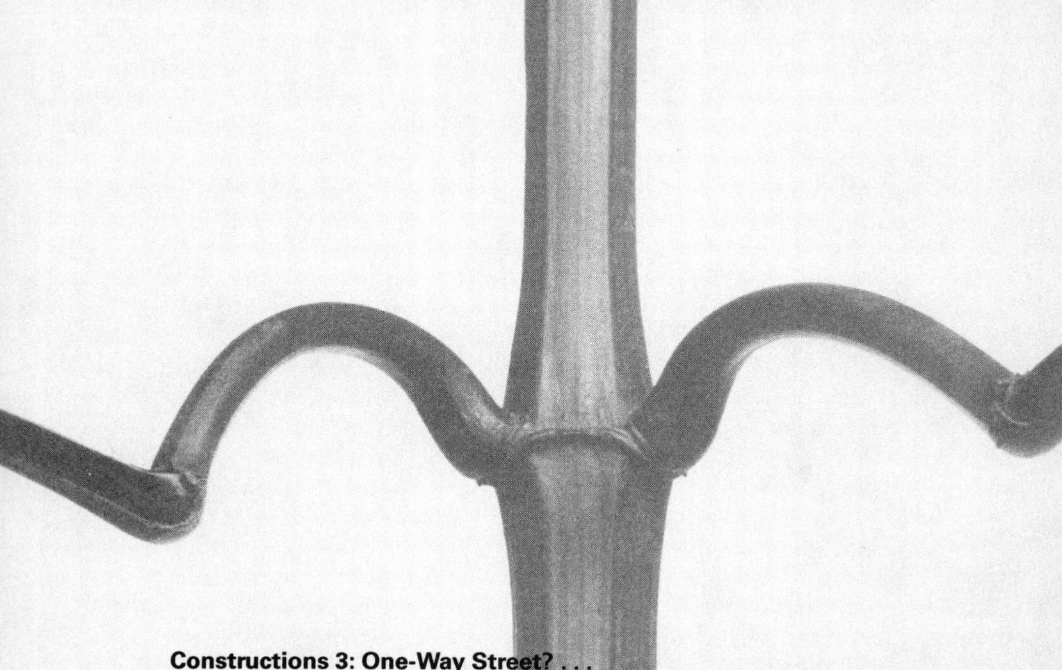

Constructions 3: One-Way Street? . . .

My partner told me a story about the Bobohizan of her Kadazan people. Her aunt had been the last woman in her family to be chosen by the spirits to take on this key role of spiritual bridge between the Kadazan tribes and spirits. Having become a devout Roman Catholic, however, her mind was made up. She refused. With this refusal and a simple shrug, many Kadazans suspected the days of the Bobohizan were numbered. In one touching, final Bobohizan ceremony, "a ritual held once every two years to strengthen and reinforce the working relationship between the spirits and the people," the Bobohizan communicated this to the spirits: "We told them that they could attend weddings and amuse themselves but they must not disturb any people. . . . We bade farewell to the spirits on behalf of the family who will probably never meet them again in this world" (Hurst, "Momohizan," 12). And, with this, the ancient world of the Bobohizan disappeared from this household, leaving behind those few material traces that would end up as artifacts in a museum, or ethnographic or historical stories like this one. As the Bobohizan recedes, the world of market veridiction encroaches . . . rice fields flourish because of chemical fertilizers and machinery, rather than the approval of the spirits; and what remains is whatever the trinketization of tourism can revive, rather than a world in which the spirits can speak. If only the gods of market veridiction would recognize that its days were numbered and it must now depart and do so, without a fuss, in order to save what it had created.

NUMBERS UP?

It's time to recognize the power of market veridiction in terms of political quietism and economic growth. At the same time is it time to ask, what is the cost of this struggle against nature? We know the market has an alchemic way of producing desire, and we also know that through such alchemy, technologies of capitalist and colonial exploitation gave power to the slave trade, imperialism, and colonialism. We also know it is a growth machine that will be the death of us all. How can we begin to recalculate?

$$f + e + 气 = P$$

Where P = the political, f = friend, e = enemy, and 气 = the affective energy that flows between, away from, parallel to, around, or toward f/e. That simple? As even the Martians made clear: "No, not really."

GLOSSARY A

TERMS AND CONCEPTS

affect; affective energy flows

Irreducible to personal feelings or characteristics, affective energy manifests in experiential states that involve a discharge of energy, leading to their crystallization in, and augmentation or diminution of, emotions and bodily capacities to act. Affect, therefore, involves one state of Being, moving and transforming into another. This transformative effect requires movement and energy; hence, affect is a flow of energy.[1]

area studies

Area studies could be understood as an institutionalized interdiscipline governing the organization and enunciative sites of knowledge forms based on concrete geographic regions or areas rather than on theoretical and abstract conceptual forms.

becoming

A term drawn from Gilles Deleuze and Félix Guattari, referring to the scattered relationships that precede the emergence of identities that then become units of representation. Affects, they note, are becomings.[2]

1 This understanding of affect draws on a reading of Gilles Deleuze and Félix Guattari, wherein affect is "the active discharge of emotion" and a weapon that alters a bodily capacity to act. See Deleuze and Guattari, *A Thousand Plateaus*, 441.

2 Deleuze and Guattari, *A Thousand Plateaus*, 283.

***chundian* (春点)**
This lexicon contains over forty thousand or fifty thousand Chinese characters. *Chundian* is the vocabulary of the *jianghu* (江湖).

commodity form
Tied to market value, the commodity is an "exchangeable" made up of a phantasmagorical element that merges with use-value to create a form. This phantasmagoric element works to produce and promote (material) desire, producing effects that have gradually come to "world" our world in crucial ways.

"continuous revolution" (*jixu geming*; 继续革命)
A concept drawn from Mao Zedong that suggests, as an a priori, the idea that history was reversible and that class struggle becomes more intense as socialism develops. Based on these understandings (that separate Mao from Stalinist historiography), continuous revolution developed the idea of a rhythmic, pulsating process in which one political campaign would follow another.

dépense
Drawn from Georges Bataille's notion of a general economy, the term *dépense*, meaning "expenditure" in French, is given an extended meaning that takes it well beyond the "restricted" economy to a more expansive focus on the need and desire we have, as humans, to expend.

energy flows
The energy focused on in this work is affective and can be registered only by its manifest effects. These effects enable the tracking of its movement politically, either toward an eruption as an intensity, or dissipated and turned into other forms, such as material desire. Energy flows are promiscuous in that they can lead "anywhere" and are channeled by means that may or may not appear "designed" for that purpose. Such channeling technologies can range from formal institutions and allegiances through to fads and coincidences but, no matter how these are manifest and brought into an assemblage, they form the surface "symptoms" that allow us to follow the flow and diagnose its political nature.

***fengshui* (风水)**
A form of geomancy drawn from Taoist practices and concerned with the laws governing the spatial arrangement and orientation of things in relation to the flow of vital energy (see *qi*). These favorable or unfavorable effects then determine the siting, orientation, and design of buildings.

general economy
In Georges Bataille's work, the idea of a general economy stands in contrast to what he calls the "restricted economy" of the mainstream. Unlike the restricted economy, which is organized around scarcity, money, and rationality, a general economy is organized around excess energy and the need to expend, which includes everything from money to bodily substances.

gift economy
The gift economy (of the political) is drawn from the work of Marcel Mauss. In Mauss's concept, gift economies, which he claims were operative in what he calls "archaic" societies, predate the restricted-market economies of the contemporary period. The focus on the gift economy, here, however, centers on its powerful affective dimensions within socialist planning. It turns on the fourth obligation, which involves more than just giving, receiving, and reciprocating. It can also involve the giving of part of thyself.

"going up the mountain" (*shangshan sixiang*; 上山思想)
A term that comes out of the early work of Mao Zedong during the rustication phase of the Chinese Communist Party. Empirically, it came from the need to physically escape and hide from a superior army. More importantly, here the use of the term is extended to reveal a *jianghu* spirit within this style of thought. The expression used by Mao, "going up the mountain," could be thought of as shorthand for the classical expression "forced to go to Liang Mountain" (*bishang Liangshan*; 逼上梁山), which over time became an oft-used phrase (or *chengyu*; 成语) in China. This latter expression comes from one of China's classic novels, *The Water Margin*. Written in the Ming dynasty about the life of rebels in the Song, it is the first text to popularize and lionize the demotic elements within the *jianghu*.

homogeneous/heterogeneous

The homogeneous/heterogeneous distinction is one used by Georges Bataille, with the former being the world of commensurable elements that have an awareness of commensurability while the latter are elements that cannot be assimilated. See *tendential homogeneity*.

haecceities

A term used by Gilles Deleuze and Félix Guattari that refers to the singularities that generate affect but cannot be comprehended by the economy of individual, species, and genus. Haecceities relate to individuation that is not part of an object or person but of an event, such as wind, river, day, and so forth.

human anxiety

Human anxiety is distinguished by Martin Heidegger from fear. Fear is directed at something, while anxiety is that which "makes manifest in Dasein its *Being towards* its own most potentiality-for-Being—that is, it is *Being-free for* the freedom of choosing itself and taking hold of itself."[3]

***jianghu* (江湖)**

"*Jianghu*" literally translates into English as "rivers and lakes," and as this combination implies, the *jianghu* is a series of ephemeral flows that pool together to achieve, as a collective, a sense of kinship. Organizationally modeled on traditional lineage group structures, the *jianghu* is strongly patriarchal, investing in the idea through a form of faux consanguinity that all men are brothers and tied by bonds that go beyond calculation. The *jianghu* is, therefore, a source of some ambivalence in Chinese writing, romanticized in Chinese kung fu movies and knight-errant literature but the bane of police and criminologist reports.

***juyi* (聚义), or *judayi* (聚大义)**

Juyi, or *judayi*, are righteous gatherings usually associated with an armed or violent uprising against oppression. It is the description that the *jianghu* gave to their own heroic collective action.

***liu* (流)**

Literally meaning "to flow." See also *wen* (稳).

3 See Heidegger, *Being and Time*, 232.

market veridiction

A term from the work of Michel Foucault. Foucault explains market veridiction as "the formation of a natural price that enables us to falsify and verify governmental practice when, on the basis of these elements, we examine what government does, the measures it takes, and the rules it imposes. . . . By a site of veridiction, I mean a site of verification-falsification for governmental practice." In this text, it is used alongside Edward Said's idea of a "style of thought" to suggest it has permeated all aspects of human life.[4] Modern markets' distribution of commodities relies on a system of market veridiction and it is this that has spread the logic of the market as a "style of thought" to the point whereby it is now all-pervasive, pulling virtually everything into the realm of the homogeneous. See *homogeneous/heterogeneous*.

Maoism

Maoism is often portrayed as a series of traits that include a reliance on the poor peasant, the "mass-line," and widespread social mobilization.[5] That is to say, Maoism is not the description of "the man"; nor is it shorthand for what the Chinese Communist Party currently calls Marxism, Leninism, or Mao Zedong thought. Rather, Maoism, as used here, points to a series of ideas registered through policies, traits, tendencies, and practices that, when cherry-picked from Chinese revolutionary history, helps reveal the importance of telluric political intensities within the emergence of the modern Chinese political. This concept of Maoism employed here is partial and designed to highlight certain traits and tendencies rather than establish a "Truth," and in so doing, it downplays countervailing attachments to scientism, positivism, and modernism and largely ignores any ethical claims made about the good or evil nature of the man, the regime, or the practices.

mass-line

Mao Zedong: "'From the masses to the masses.' This means: take the ideas of the masses (scattered and unsystematic ideas) and concentrate them (through study turn them into concentrated and systematic ideas), then go to the masses and propagate and explain these ideas until the masses embrace them as their own, hold fast to them and translate them into action, and test

4 See Foucault, *The Birth of Biopolitics*, 32. See also Said, *Orientalism*.

5 Strauss, *State Formation in China and Taiwan*, 87.

the correctness of these ideas in such action. Then, once again, concentrate ideas from the masses and, once again, go to the masses so that the ideas are persevered in and carried through. And so on, over and over again, in an endless spiral, with the ideas becoming more correct, more vital and richer each time. Such is the Marxist theory of knowledge."[6]

modern market

Key factors that differentiate the modern market from its own multiple past histories are the increasing spread of its rationality in the development of the system by market veridiction. This rationality is accompanied by the growing recognition of the importance of the phantasmagoric element in the growth of the entire system.

***Neijing* (内径), or *Huangdi Neijing* (黄帝内经)**

The classic text of traditional Chinese medicine, known in English as *The Yellow Emperor's Classic of Internal Medicine.*

"one big concept"

The "one big concept" is a context-specific, culturally embedded political form that focuses on drawing all affective connections toward a single point of political intensity. Working to engage all senses, this über-concept uses a series of techniques and culturally embedded objects and forms to draw affective elements momentarily together around an extreme antagonism that then is designed to function as a moment of political transformation.

political Dasein

The political Dasein is one particular expression of the Dasein because Being is an issue for it. Dasein exists, writes Martin Heidegger, and does so whether taking hold of or neglecting that fact. It is political, however, for those who regard existence not just as an issue but as a profoundly felt issue that gains expression politically. For those who feel it strongly, it can be life itself wagered for a collective cause. This, then, is a key element in what is being called here "political Dasein."

6 Mao Tse-tung (Zedong), "Some Questions concerning Methods of Leadership," 119.

qi (氣/气), or vital energy

The ancient Chinese philosopher Zhuangzi once stated that vital energy, or *qi*, gave rise to spirit and this highlights an affective dimension of this concept.[7] Vital energy is said to manifest in all things, but it is formless and ineffable and its movement is cyclical but determined by the play of an array of contextual, temporal, and spatial factors. In proffering a more fluid notion of the political energized by affective flows, the formlessness and ineffability, coupled with the fluid nature of vital energy, furnish us with a set of conceptual and practical examples that share something of a kinship with the flow of the political. Like the traditional Chinese doctor's use of acupuncture to modulate the flow of vital energy though the body so, too, the political body finds form in the channeling and harnessing of affective energy.

subsumption

A Marxist term used to demonstrate the transformation to economic life brought on by capitalist penetration. Where it is purely extractive, it is called "formal subsumption," but where it changes the relations of production, it is called "real subsumption." Hence, peasants growing their own produce in a traditional way and then selling it on a capitalist market is an example of formal subsumption, whereas labor employed in a factory setting and subject to the discipline of labor would constitute an example of real subsumption.

Taylorism

Often referred to as "scientific management," Frederick Taylor's system was the precursor to Fordism, introducing new techniques to streamline factory production, raise output, and famously simplify tasks such that even a gorilla could do them, thus producing the conditions for factory-line assembly and a massive increase in the alienation of labor.

tektology

"Tektology" comes from the Greek word *tektron*, meaning "builder," and was used by Alexander Bogdanov (1873–1928) to describe a general science of organization that would privilege organizational forms over property or production relations.[8]

7 Zheng Li, *On Zhuangzi's Aesthetics*, 120.

8 Bogdanov, *Essays in Tektology*, 19.

telluric

A word from the Latin *tellus*, meaning the "earth." The telluric means the earth, soil, territory, and the often-intense human attachments, feelings, and actions that come with these. Even under the code of modernism, the relationship with the telluric continues to manifest in radically different ways.

tendential homogeneity

This is part of the heterogenous/homogeneous binary play at work in Georges Bataille's more political work.[9] Production is the basis of social homogeneity, Bataille claims, and this rests on tendential homogeneity, which is the tendency toward a world dominated by a restricted field of calculation based on science, reason, and technology.

thymos

An ancient Greek term used by Fukuyama to indicate "spiritedness."[10]

torrent method / *xiefa* (泻法)

A term from acupuncture indicating a needle technique designed to draw a strong reaction so as to release a torrent that has been building up. It was a method first mentioned in the classic *Neijing* but also found its way into the new methods that Maoist traditional Chinese medicine developed in acupuncture.

war machine

Heterogeneous in form and function, the war machine was, as Gilles Deleuze and Félix Guattari wrote, "the invention of the nomad."[11] Indeed, for them, the war machine is the nomadic playing off the sedentary. If fluid versus sedentary is one play-off, the war machine / state relation is another. While a war machine can be captured by the state it is, in terms of its structure, its

9 The homogeneous/heterogeneous division that led Bataille to become interested in all heterogeneous forms was, in some ways, the backbone of his political position and important in his argument with Simone Weil. See Surya, *Georges Bataille*, 170–73.

10 Fukuyama, *The End of History and the Last Man*, 162–65.

11 Deleuze and Guattari, *A Thousand Plateaus*, 460.

objective, and its use of technology, operating in a relation of exteriority to the state.

***wen* (稳)**
While in Chinese the term *wen* means calm and stable, it carries within this meaning a sense of stasis. This latter element authorizes the contrast being made between it and the term *liu* (流), meaning flow.

whatever singularities
Drawn from the work of Giorgio Agamben, whatever singularities are recognized as having some kind of autonomous ethical value. "Singularities" are unique and cannot be reduced to a measurement or representation, while "whatever" relates to those who have an autonomous, ethical value.

wolfing
This term from the work of Gilles Deleuze and Félix Guattari is about the nature of the wolf pack. The term is designed to capture the dynamic, organized intensity of the pack.

***wuxing* (五行)**
Within Taoist cosmogony, water, fire, wood, metal, and earth form a cyclical relationship called *wuxing*. These five cycles are conceptually more like phases than concrete forms, yet these phases share the qualities of the five forms of water, fire, wood, metal, and earth.

***xieqi* (邪气)**
Xieqi is a heteropathic energy, as opposed to *zhengqi* (正气).

***yi* (义)**
A term meaning "righteousness." *Yi* works with the idea of energy to produce the compound *yiqi* (义气), which is translated as "the spirit of righteousness."

***zhengqi* (正气)**
This is one of the basic categories of traditional Chinese medicine. *Zhengqi* is said to be a form of energy that has the ability to counter the heterotopic energy of *xieqi*, which violates the body's normal processes. Nathan

Sivin calls *zhengqi* "orthopathic" in that it maintains and renews these processes.[12]

***Zhouli* (周礼)**
One of the classic texts of ancient China.

12 See Sivin, *Traditional Medicine in Contemporary China*, 49, for details.

GLOSSARY B

CHINESE TERMS, NAMES, TITLES, WORDS, AND PHRASES

***an*; 安; peace**

Anren; 安仁

A small town in Sichuan Province where Liu Wencai's Manor House Museum, housing the *Rent Collection Courtyard* and the Jianchuan Museum Cluster, is located

***baibazi jieyi*; 拜把子结义; sworn brotherhood**

A term popularized in the Chinese classics *The Tale of Three Kingdoms* and *The Water Margin* meaning "to become a brother with a different surname." The term *jieyi* (结义) reinforces the meaning of sworn brothers with a common purpose in life. The term is used to signify and instill a lifelong bond to a group.

***baihui*; 百会; "hundred meetings"**

An acupoint on the dorsal midpoint dealing with dizziness, headaches, numbness, apoplexy, rectal and anal prolapse, and uterine prolapse

***Baizuitu*; 《百罪图》; "The Display of 100 Crimes"**

A series of small statuettes in Liu Wencai's Manor House Museum, Anren, China, that details his alleged crimes

Ba Jin; 巴金
A famous Chinese author

***bao'en*; 报恩; "debt of kindness"**
This term is made up of two characters, with the first, *bao* (报), meaning either to repay or to wreak revenge and the the latter character, *en* (恩), meaning gratitude. Together the characters mean "to repay a debt in excess of any original favor bestowed."

***bishang Liangshan*; 逼上梁山; "forced to go to Liang Mountain"**
An expression drawn from *The Water Margin* that has entered contemporary parlance, meaning "to flee to safety"

***bizu*; 逼租; forced payments of rent**
A section of the *Rent Collection Courtyard* exhibition in which the landlord, Liu Wencai, forced the peasants to pay in-kind for the use of his land

***buliu zhen*; 不留针; "Don't leave the [acupunctural] needle in too long."**
Technical advice on needle use offered as part of the Maoist new medical methods. It was part of a series of techniques that brought these methods into alignment with the general political slogan of the time that encouraged "better, faster, and more economical production." For the latter, see the *duo kaui haosheng* (多快好省) glossary entry.

Cao Rong; 曹嵘
Head of the Jinggang Mountain Red Army hospital

***chao*; 潮; tide, current, upsurge**

***chedi fouding*; 彻底否定; completely repudiate**
An expression used in relation to the Cultural Revolution after the fall of the Maoist radicals.

***chenlieguan*; 陈列馆; display site, exhibition hall**

***chi tian chuang*; 吃天窗; to eat from a heavenly window**
A colorful metaphor from *jianghu* slang meaning to steal (from the top pocket of a shirt). See the *chundian* (春典) glossary entry.

***chi xiu xinggui riyong guifan yue: "hun zhongming, xuxian gui danwei zuochan"*; 敕修清规日用轨范曰："昏钟鸣，须先归单位坐禅"; "the revised official edict: 'When the bell rings at dusk, return to the unit and meditate'"**
Units of measurement regarding time, length, and weight abound in Buddhist classic texts. In the lives of monks, every seat/mat on which a monk meditated had the name of the monk written on it, and therefore it was given the name *danwei*. (*Danwei* is literally translated as "singular seat.") For the very different modern use of this term, see the glossary entry *danwei* (单位), meaning work unit, below.

***chongshi zhi qi*; 充实之气; "abundant" *qi*, or vital energy**
A description of vital energy drawn from the Confucian philosopher Mencius

***chongyajia*; 冲压架; press, or vice**

***chouhen*; 仇恨; enmity**

***chouzidian*; 臭子点; a "stinker"**
Jianghu slang, or *chundian*, for a bad person. See the *chundian* (春典) glossary entry.

***chuji renmin linghun de dageming*; 触及人民灵魂的大革命; "a great revolution that will touch people to their very soul"**
A slogan by Mao Zedong from the beginning of the Chinese Cultural Revolution

***chundian*; 春典**
An untranslatable term designating the lexicon, or language, of the *jianghu*

***dai shaqi*; 带杀气; murderous intent**

***dang zuzhi shi geming de baolei*; 党组织是革命的堡垒; "The Party organization is a revolutionary fortress."**
A Chinese communist expression used during radical periods

***danwei*; 单位; work unit**
In the Mao period, every enterprise, school, and organization in urban China was described as a work unit.

***daosheng yi, yisheng er, ersheng san, sanshengwanwu. Wanwu fuyin er baoyang, chongqi yiwei he*; 道生一, 一生二, 二生三, 三生萬物。萬物負陰而抱陽, 沖氣以為和。**
A saying that can be translated as "The Tao originates in One. One produces Two [*yin* and *yang*]. Two produces Three. Three produces ten thousand things [all things]. All things depart from *yin* and gradually embrace *yang*. They harmonize while developing."

***dengxiang* (*shi*); 灯箱式; lamp-case or light-box style**
A form of illuminated display used within the manor house of the landlord Liu Wencai

***diaoyang*; 吊羊; "fishing"**
In this volume, a *jianghu* slang term for an opportunity to make money.

***dousi pixiu*; 斗私, 批修; "Struggle against self, criticize revisionism."**
A slogan from the Cultural Revolution era

***duo*; 多; greater/more**

***duo kuai hao sheng*; 多快好省; greater, faster, better, more economical**
A Communist Party slogan for production that is "greater, faster, better, [and] more economical"

***er'ke*; 耳壳; auricle**
A healthy auricular (耳壳) is like an inverted fetus in a womb, according to the new medical methods.

Falungong; **法轮功**
A *qigong* organization established in China in the 1990s but banned by the end of the decade

fandi, fanxue de zhanchang; **反帝反修的战场**; **"Battlefield against imperialism and revisionism"**
A Communist Party slogan from the Cultural Revolution era

Fan Jianchuan; **樊建川**
The owner and creator of the Jianchuan Museum Cluster in Anren

fanji heixian de changkuang jingong; **反击黑线的猖狂进攻**; **"Counterattack the savage assaults of the black line."**
A Communist Party slogan from the Cultural Revolution era

fankang; **反抗**; **resistance**

***fanti*[*zi*]**; **繁体[字]**; **traditional Chinese characters**
Fanti is shorthand for *fantizi*, referring to traditional or full-form Chinese characters.

fenggu; **风谷**; **dehusking the grain**
In this volume, the section of the *Rent Collection Courtyard* exhibition in which the grain is dehusked

fengshui; **风水**
A form of geomancy

fenpei tizhi; **分配体制**; **labor allocation system**
As there was no labor market in the time of Mao Zedong in China, jobs were allocated to workers.

Foguang da cidian; **《佛光大辞典》**; ***A Dictionary of Chinese Buddhist Terms***

fushu kuangjia; **附属框架**; **auxiliary framework or structure**
An expression from the work of Wang Min'an, who writes of the family household spatial order as auxiliary to its moral order prior to economic reform

gangzheng zhi qi; 刚正之气; **a spirit of righteousness**
According to the authoritative etymological dictionary *Ciyuan* 《词源》, the code of brotherhood—or *yiqi* (义气)—contains this "upright and honest" (*gangzheng*; 刚正) spirit or energy, *qi* (气).

gaochao; 高潮; **high tide**
A metaphor used during the pre-reform period usually used in relation to revolutionary actions

geming qingyi; 革命情义; **revolutionary sentiment of comradeship**

genzheng miaohong; 根正苗红; **straight-rooted Red seedlings**
A metaphor meaning a true believer

Gong; 工; **work**

The literal meaning is "work," but when used in the context of the communist coin, it is shorthand for "worker."

"Gong" zibi; '工'字币; **work coin**
The earliest currency of the Chinese Communist Party, from the base camp on Jinggang Mountain

gongzuo dengjibiao; 工作登记表; **"work registration form"**
A section within the *renshi dang'an*, or personnel file

Gongzuozhong xuexi, xuexizhong gongzuo; 工作中学习, 学习中工作; **"Learn at work and work at learning."**
An expression used by one of the classically trained sculptors working on the *Rent Collection Courtyard* statues as a way of saying they were learning from traditional Chinese sculptors

guanxi; 关系 关系; **networks, connections, relations**

Guanzi; 管子
A major Chinese philosopher usually associated with the (authoritarian) Chinese Legalist school of thought

Gugong; 故宫; Forbidden City (Imperial Palace)
Built between 1406 and 1420 and located in the Chinese capital, Beijing, it was the winter residence of the emperors from the Ming dynasty onward.

***gui*; 轨; track or pathway**

***guodou*; 过斗; checking the grain**
A section of the *Rent Collection Courtyard* exhibition depicting the landlord's henchmen checking the quality and quantity of grain

***Haining Xianzhi*; 《海寧縣志》; "Gazetteer of Haining County"**
A historical record written in 1733 and cited in this volume

***hao*; 好; good, or better**

***hao miaozi*; 好苗子; good seedlings**

***haoyong doulang*; 好勇斗浪; brave, courageous fighters**

***hen*; 恨; hate, or hatred**

***Hexie shehui*; 和谐社会; harmonious society**
A term rooted in Confucianism and revived in recent times by the former general secretary of the Communist Party of China, Hu Jintao, to stress the need for social stability

***hong cancan geming de tiandi*; 红灿灿革命的天地; "the bright Red world of revolution"**
A phrase used in the Mao period that captured the bucolic image of China's communist future

***Hongjun yiyuan*; 红军医院; Red Army hospital (in the town of Jinggangshan)**

***Hongse xuchang*; 红色圩场; Red market**
A market set up in the town of Jinggangshan, where the Communist Party established its first rural base camp

***hongsijun sanshi'ertuan futuanzhang*; 红四军三十二团 副团长; deputy regiment commander of the 32nd regiment of the 4th army**

Huangdi Neijing; 皇帝内经》; *The Yellow Emperor's Classic of Internal Medicine*
Sometimes referred to in this volume by the abbreviated form Neijing《内经》, this text can be thought of as the bible of traditional Chinese medicine.

Huang Huaju; 黄华菊
A communist former bandit

***hundai zaidi*; 昏倒在地; falling to the ground, fainting**

***huo*; 火; fire**

***huodian*; 火点; "moneyed patron"**
A word used by *jianghu* members as part of their *chundian* slang

***jianghu*; 江湖**
Literally translated, the term means "rivers and lakes," but in the cultural context of China, the term refers to a (patriarchal) "righteous" sworn brotherhood that lives outside of society and has an ambivalent relationship with it.

***jianghu dayi*; 江湖大义; *jianghu* righteousness**
The ethos said to traditionally drive the *jianghu* gangs; similar in spirit to the ethos of Robin Hood's merry men

***jianghu yiqi*; 江湖义气; *jianghu* spirit**
As with *jianghu dayi, jianghu yiqi* is a spirit that asserts a righteousness despite being on the wrong side of the law.

***jianti*[*zi*]; 简体[字]; simplified Chinese characters**
Jianti is shorthand for *jiantizi*, meaning simplified Chinese characters.

***jiaozu*; 交租; pay rent**
A section of the *Rent Collection Courtyard* exhibition depicting the collection of grain in payment for land rent

***jiazu zhuyi*; 家族主义; familialism**
Familialism in China is based on Confucian values and reifies a patrilineal patriarchy.

***jiebai xiongdi*; 结拜兄弟; sworn brotherhood**
The bonding of very close friends that is nonconsanguineous but borne of a shared commitment to one another

***jiefu jipin, chubao anmin*; 劫富济贫,除暴安民; "stealing from the rich, aiding the poor; eradicating violence and giving peace to the people"**
A slogan from Wang Zuo's gang, demonstrating values similar to the legend of Robin Hood in the West

***jieji jiaoyude ketang*; 阶级教育的课堂; a classroom for class education**

***jieli tongxin, gongju dayi*; 竭力同心, 共聚大义; "forged as one in the struggle for righteousness"**
Maoist radicals, in their campaign against the classical novel *The Water Margin*, claimed that this eight-character phrase summed up the rebel program.

***jijiao*; 犄角; horns**

***jin*; 金; metal/gold**

***jin*; 斤; catty**
A unit of measurement, equivalent to 0.6 kilograms.

***jingqi*; 精氣; "essential *qi*"**
Guanzi's conception of essential vital energy regards *qi* as being the origin of all things.

***jitui youpai changkuan jingong*; 击退右派猖狂进攻; "Repulse the savage assaults of the rightists."**
A Communist Party slogan that became increasingly part of everyday parlance soon after the revolution in 1949

***jixu geming*; 继续革命; "continuous revolution"**
A Maoist concept that partially broke with the Stalinist linear stagiest history by suggesting the revolution could fall back a stage and that class struggle intensifies rather than diminishes as the revolution moves forward

***judayi*; 聚大义; "gathered in the virtuous cause of righteousness"**
"Righteous gatherings" that took place when mustering the troops for battle.

***junxiechang*; 军械厂; munitions factory**

***juyi*; 聚义; righteous uprising**
A mustering similar in meaning to *judayi* (聚大义) above

***kekao*; 可靠; reliable**

***kuai*; 快; faster**

***kuangcao*; 狂草; wild grass**
Used in this volume to point to a Chinese calligraphy style

"Kunlun"; 《昆仑》
A poem by Mao Zedong

***laogeng*; 老庚**
An untranslatable term used in southern China that is usually related to men, meaning a very close relation

Leng Yueying; 冷月英
Better known as Leng Mama, or Mother Leng, she was alleged to be the only surviving victim of Liu Wencai's water dungeon (*shuilao*).

***lingyu*; 零余; zero surplus**
Used in this volume to mean "worthless"

***liu*; 流; flow, to flow**

***liumang*; 流氓; hoodlum**

Long Taicheng; 隆太成
One of the original sculptors on the *Rent Collection Courtyard* exhibition

***luanbadian*; 銮把点; gambler**
Chundian slang for "gambler" and whose literal meaning is "small tinkling bells"

***luanshi xiaoxiong*; 乱世枭雄; heroes in troubled times**
A term that is often the basis of *jianghu* mythology

***mai xiangzhang*; 买像章; to buy a Mao badge**
A phraseology prohibited during the Cultural Revolution in China

***mangliu*; 盲流; itinerant or vagrant**
A term used for a bandit or vagrant but literally meaning "to flow blindly"

***Maoti*; 毛体; Mao-style calligraphy**
While Mao Zedong was renowned for his wild grass (*kuangcao*; 狂草) style, his was so distinctive that it became known as Mao-style calligraphy.

***Mao zhuxi yulucao*; 《毛主席语录操》; "Quotations of Chairman Mao gymnastics"**
During the Cultural Revolution, the Second Artillery art troupe in Beijing used freehand gymnastics movements set to music and to the rhythm and sound of Chairman Mao's quotations. These became known as "Quotations of Chairman Mao gymnastics" and spread nationwide.

***mu*; 木; wood**

Nan Dou; 南斗; "Southern Compass"
Wang Zuo's *chundian* name

***niezi*; 镊子; tweezers**

Ninggangxian, Maoping; 宁冈县,茅坪; Maoping in Ninggan County
The location of the first Red Army hospital

***nuhuo*; 怒火; revolt**

***ouxiang*; 偶像; idol**

***Panlong shudian*; 攀龙书店; Panlong Bookshop**
This shop was converted into the Red Army hospital in October 1927.

***PiLin, PiKong* [*yundong*]; 批林批孔(运动); campaign to criticize Lin Biao and Confucius**
Beginning in 1973, a political campaign launched against Mao's chosen successor, Lin Biao, who was accused of being analogous to Confucius.

***posijiu*; 破四旧; "Smash the Four Olds."**
Launched in the early days of the Cultural Revolution, Red Guards set about smashing old customs, old culture, old habits, and old ideas as part of their fervent revolutionary action.

***putonghua*; 普通话; "common language"**
Literally meaning "common language," this term is more widely known in the West as Mandarin or Mandarin Chinese.

***qi*; 气 /氣; vital energy**
Qi, or vital energy, is central to Taoist cosmology and is a life force that flows through everything.

Qian Liu; 錢鏐
A Chinese king (852–932)

***qianwan buyao wangji jieji douzheng*; 千万不要忘记阶级斗争; "Never forget class struggle."**
A famous Maoist slogan from the days of the Cultural Revolution

***qianyan zhendi*; 前沿阵地; advanced command post**

***qibu chengsheng*; 泣不成声; "can't hold back the tears"**
A term used to describe peasants' reaction upon viewing the *Rent Collection Courtyard* exhibition

***qifen*; 气氛; spirit**

***qihuayu wanwu*; 气化育万物; “*Qi* gives breath to the ten thousand things.”**
A saying meaning that *qi* gives rise to everything

***qingnian*; 青年; young adults**

***qing, qiuye*; 请, 求也; beseech**
A classical Chinese expression drawn from Buddhism that related to ways of addressing the sacred

***qing, qiye*; 请,乞也; beg**
A classical Chinese expression drawn from Buddhism that related to ways of addressing the sacred

***qing xiangzhang*; 请像章; to “request” a badge**
An acceptable phraseology for obtaining a Mao badge during the Cultural Revolution in China

***qi zhi jiaogan huayu le shengming*; 气之交感化育了生命; “infusing things with life,” affecting the human spirit**
A phrase is used in discussing the role of vital energy, or *qi*, which is central to Taoist philosophy but in the polytheistic belief systems of ancient China is found in all of its belief systems

***qunqing jifen*; 群情激奋; mass feelings of excitement**

***quxueshao*; 取穴少; “inserting the needle less”**
A term of technical advice on needle use offered as part of the Maoist new medical methods. It was part of a series of techniques that brought these methods into alignment with the general political slogan of the time that encouraged “better, faster, and more economical production.” For the latter slogan, see the entry for *duo kuai hao sheng* (多快好省).

***ren*; 仁; benevolence**

renshi dang'an; 人事档案; **personnel file**
In Mao's China, every Chinese person, other than the peasants, had a personnel file that accompanied them throughout their life. Held by the personnel section of the work unit, it had both an economic and a political use.

renyi; 仁义; **benevolence and righteousness**
An important moral and ethical concept within the thought of Confucius and Mencius

rongyin'ou; 溶银瓯; **cooling vat**
Vats used for dissolving silver in the making of coins at the Red Army mint

Sancha Gongshe; 三岔公社; **Three-Fork Commune**
The commune where the classically trained sculptors from the Sichuan Academy of Arts working on the *Rent Collection Courtyard* statues were sent to learn from the peasants

Sanwan gaibian; 三湾改编; **Sanwan reorganization**
A series of reforms within the Red Army undertaken by Mao Zedong in 1927 that would pave the way for the future Maoist transformation of the Communist Party

shan dawang; 山大王; **king of the mountaintop**
A term used for Wang Zuo, a former bandit whose gang occupied the upper reaches of Jinggang Mountain and who was important in the work of the Red Army mint

shangshan sixiang; 上山思想; **"going up the mountain ideology"**
An ideology that involved turning away from the focus on cities and relying on telluric peasant/indigenous solutions to the problems the communists faced

shanzilidui, buting diaoqian, baobu luokeshao; 擅自离队、不听调遣、包庇罗克绍; **"leaving one's post without permission, ignoring dispatches, and looking after one's own people"**
These terms are some of the key accusations used by elements within the Red Army to denounce the former bandit Yuan Wencai.

***shen*; 神; spirit**

***sheng*; 省; economical**

***shenquan*; 神全; completeness of spirit**
For the ancient Taoist philosopher Zhuangzi, *qi*, or vital energy, in its movement at both form and affect, turns humans into the carriers of the completeness of spirit (神全) that is bound together in a living form.

***shi*; 势; propensity**

***shi, shu, hua, sanju*; 诗书画三绝; "poetry, calligraphy, and painting: the three perfections"**
The three perfections were interlinking art forms that all channeled vital energy, or *qi*.

Shuangmashi; 双马石; Double Horse Rock
A landmark on Jinggang Mountain so named because of its two large stones that, overlapping together, looked like two horses from a distance

***shufa*; 书法; Chinese calligraphy**

***shui*; 水; water**

Shuihuzhuan*;《水浒传》; *The Water Margin
The most common English translation of the Ming dynasty novel, sometimes translated as *All Men Are Brothers* or *Outlaws of the Marsh*

***shuilao*; 水牢; water dungeon**
A major exhibit in the revolutionary renovation of Liu Wencai's manor house, though later found to be a fabrication

***shuimazi*; 水码子**
An untranslatable term meaning "poor person" in the *jianghu's chundian* vocabulary

***Sida tufu*; 四大屠夫; Four Elements Butchers**
A gang; enemies of Wang Zuo

***sifang gedi*; 四方各地; everywhere**

Song Jiang; 宋江
A legendary leader of *The Water Margin* rebels

***suanzhang*; 算账; settling of accounts**
A section of the *Rent Collection Courtyard* exhibition depicting the collection of grain as payment for land rent

***tiandi*; 天地;**
Heaven and earth; the universe

***tiandi heyi*; 天地合一**
A standard phrase used in classical Chinese meaning unity of heaven and earth

***tiandi yanning zhiqi, shiyu xinan er shengyu xibei. Ci tiandi zhi zunyanqi ye, ci tiandizhi yiqi ye*; "天地严凝之气, 始于西南而盛于西北。此天地之尊严气也, 此天地之义气也."**
A quotation from *The Book of Rites: Meaning of the Drinking Festivity* (《礼记·乡饮酒义》) meaning, "The concentrated spirit [*qi*] [that blows between] heaven and earth begins in the southwest and flourishes in the northwest. This is the *qi* that represents the most commanding severity of heaven and earth—the *qi* of righteous justice, or *yiqi*."

***tian panzi*; 舔盘子; "lick the plate"**
Jianghu chundian slang meaning "fellatio"

***tiaokan'er*; 调侃儿; ridicule**
Chundian slang meaning quick-witted ridicule

***tiefanwan*; 铁饭碗; "iron rice bowl"**
A term describing a Mao-era welfare provision in which one could not be sacked from one's employment

***Titian xingdao*; 替天行道; "Follow the way of heaven."**
To follow heavenly decrees meant accepting the existing order and was an oft-used expression of Song Jiang, the leader of the bandits in the classical novel *The Water Margin*. It is one of the expressions Song Jiang used that the radical Maoists claimed showed he was a capitulationist.

***tongku shisheng*; 痛苦失声; "crying so much they lost their voices"**
This, it was claimed, was how peasants reacted when they first viewed the *Rent Collection Courtyard* exhibition.

***tongtianxia yiqi er, qihuayu wanwu*; 通天下一气耳, 气化育万物**
A saying that means "Vital energy, or *qi*, gives breath to all living things (the ten thousand things)."

***tongzhi*; 同志; comrade**

***tu*; 土; the earth, the soil, terra, indigenous, the telluric**

***tuban huabiao*; 土版花边; indigenous or telluric coinage**
A generic term for counterfeit coins made with rustic methods

Wang Zuo; 王佐
A communist former bandit

***wanhuibao*; 晚汇报; evening reports**
In the Cultural Revolution, one had evening reports and morning instructions. Both of which were designed to show loyalty to Chairman Mao.

***wanshi xianshizhuyi*; 玩世现实主义; cynical realism**
A Chinese art movement in the latter part of the twentieth century

***wei pengyou liang leichadao*; 为朋友两肋插刀; a willingness to do anything to help friends**
A sense of commitment to a friend (or in this case, a "brother") that is central to the *jianghu* ethos

***wen*; 稳; static or stable**

***wuhang bazuo*; 五行八作; "five professions and eight workshops"**
An expression meaning people of various trades and professsions

***wukuang tu, wu youmin*; 无旷土, 无游民; "no neglecting of the land, no itinerants"**
An aspect of the Confucian value system in which peasants should remain on the land to ensure social harmony and stability

Wumaodang; 五毛党; the 50 Cent Army
A sarcastic, derogatory nickname for pro-China commentators prior to 2010 indicating that internet commentators would earn fifty cents for each pro-government post they made

***wuxing*; 五行; five phases**
A Doaist-inspired, ancient Chinese cyclical cosmology of traveling through the five phases of wood, earth, fire, water, and metal

***wuyi fujia*; 无以复加; absurd in the extreme**

Wu Yong; 吴用
A character in *The Water Margin* who, in some translations, is known as "Resourceful Star," was in the Maoist campaign, said to hold a revolutionary line

***xiang fandang, fanshehuizhuyi de heixian menglie kaihuo*; 向反党, 反社会主义的黑线猛烈开火; "violently open fire on the anti-Party and anti-socialist black line"**
A slogan that was prominent in the Cultural Revolution in China

***xiaonian*; 小年; teenager**

***xiefa*; 泻法; the torrent method**
In acupuncture, a suggested technique of needle use by the Maoist new medical methods designed to release a heteropathic torrent

Xie Guanlong; 谢官龙
The brother of a counterfeiter who started the Red Army mint on Jinggang Mountain

Xie Huolong; 谢火龙
A counterfeiter who started the Red Army mint on Jinggang Mountain

***xieqi*; 邪气; heteropathic energy**
A term drawn from traditional Chinese medicine (TCM) to indicate negative energy

***xin*; 心; heart**
In Chinese philosophy, the heart is not an organ and is tied to the mind.

***xing*; 形; form**

***xingshen*; 形神; form-spirit**

***xingti baoshen*; 形体保神; "The form envelops the spirit."**

***xingxunshi*; 刑讯室; torture chamber**
In this volume, the term refers to a room created after the revolutionary renovation of Liu Wencai's manor house. The torture chamber, along with the water dungeon, became one of the site's major exhibits.

***xinsheng shiwu*; 新生事物; "new socialist things"**
A term that refers to new revolutionary things created during the Chinese Cultural Revolution

Xuan San; 选三
Yuan Wencai's *chundian* name

***xuezhai*; 血债; debt of blood**
In this volume, blood debts are one of the means by which to strengthen *jianghu* connections.

***yangban*; 样板; model**
The model is the most politically advanced ideal type made famous during the Cultural Revolution by the revolutionary model operas.

***yangsheng*; 养生; nurturing life practices**
An array of practices and exercises that are thought to extend and enrich life

***yanzu*; 验租; inspection of grain**
A section of the *Rent Collection Courtyard* exhibition in which the peasant offers payment to the landlord for the renting of their land

***yegong haolong*; 叶公好龙; "Mr. Ye loves dragons."**
Literally meaning "Mr. Ye loves dragons," this classical expression is similar to the English expression "Be careful what you wish for."

***yi*; 义; righteousness**

Yin Daoyi; 尹道一
A local tyrant of Jinggang Mountain

***yindu*; 阴都; Yin Metropolis**
An acupoint close to the navel that regulates *qi*, strengthens the spleen, and promotes digestion and is of value in treating gastric problems and upper abdominal pain

***yinju changsuo*; 隐居场所; hiding place**

***yinju shanlin, dunji jianghu*; 隐居山林, 遁迹江湖; "Live in the mountains and forests, escape in the rivers and lakes."**
Meaning, "Be part of the *jianghu*."

***yinshuachang*; 印刷厂; print shop**

yin/yang; 阴/阳
A concept from Taoism of opposite yet interconnected forces

***yiqi*; 义气; spirit of loyalty, code of brotherhood**
In this volume, *yiqi* is used to designate an affectively based spirit that binds two people tightly together.

***yitong tianxia*; 一统天下; unity under heaven; unity of nation**
A classical dynastic concept

***yizhuan yiwa, yicao yimu*; 一砖一瓦, 一草一木; "Every brick, tile, blade of grass, and stick of wood"**
An aspect of the claim that everything is part of the "one big concept" of Mao Zedong thought

***yi zhong Ruhua le de "xiayi" gainian*; 一种儒化了的"侠义" 概念; "a Confucian-based concept of 'chivalry'"**
A concept of chivalry at the heart of the *jianghu* ethos, almost despite its basis in Confucianism

Yuan Wencai; 袁文才
A communist former bandit

***yue*; 韵; melody/music**

***yuoxia*; 游侠; knight-errant**
A chivalrous martial arts expert

***zaobichang*; 造币厂; mint**
The mint created by the communists in Jinggangshan

***zaoqingshi*; 早请示; morning instructions**
In the Cultural Revolution, one had morning instructions and evening reports. Both of which were designed to show loyalty to Chairman Mao.

Zhao Fazhong; 赵发仲
A Communist Party chief at the Jinggang Mountain Red Army hospital

Zhao Shutong; 赵树同
One of the leading sculptors of the *Rent Collection Courtyard*

Zhejiang Chao; 《浙江潮》; ***The Tide of Zhejiang***
An anti-Qing newspaper from Zhejiang Province

zhengqi; **正气; orthopathic *qi***
A term drawn from traditional Chinese Medicine (TCM) to indicate positive *qi*, or vital energy

zhi'an ermu; 治安耳目; **security eyes and ears**
Meaning police informants

Zhijian Daogang; 直箭道巷; Straight Arrow Lane
A street name in Hangzhou commemorating an event that took place during the reign of King Qian Liu (錢鏐, 852–932) when arrows were fired into the sea to avert a tidal bore

zhong; 忠; **loyalty/devotion**

zhong bu zhong, kanxingdong; 忠不忠, 看行动; **"To determine devotion or loyalty, look at one's actions."**
A slogan during the Cultural Revolution designed to highlight the primacy of practice over theory

zhongcheng; 忠诚; **loyal**

zhong xiao zhi qi; 忠孝之气; **spirit of devotion and filiality**
In classical China, devotion to the emperor and filiality toward the family were the cornerstones of the patriarchal system, and the homologization of them is summed up in this expression.

zhongyangdian; 忠样点; **"loyalty points"**
Chundian slang meaning good, loyal types (of people)

zhongyang xiang ganbianjie tewei weiyuan; 中央湘赣边界特委委员; **member of the Xiang (Hunan)-Gan (Jiangxi) Border Region Special (Defense) Committee**
A committee that was part of the Red Army formed after the Communist Party of China proclaimed the Central Soviet Republic in 1931

***zhongyi*; 忠义; loyalty and righteousness**
Two key concepts in the traditional patriarchal order of China

***zhongziwu*; 忠字舞; devotion dance**

Zhouli*; 《周礼》; *Rites of Zhou
One of three ancient ritual texts of the classics of Confucianism despite its Legalist tendencies

***zhuangnian*; 壮年; prime of life**
In China, a reference to people typically between the ages of thirty and forty

***zifaxing*; 自发性; spontaneity**

***zigong*; 紫宫; Purple Palace**
Located on the upper chest, this acupoint regulates vital energy to alleviate coughing and can treat asthma, bronchitis, tonsillitis, and pains in the gullet.

***ziruqiren*; 字如其人; "Characters reveal a human's character."**
Meaning a person's moral character is revealed in their calligraphy

***zongfa zhidu*; 宗法制度; feudal clan system**
A system in the historiography of the Communist Party that was said to dominate dynastic China

Zuo Jiagui; 邹甲贵
A landlord whose house became the Red Army mint

BIBLIOGRAPHY

Interviews

All interviews by Michael Dutton.

Cai Guo-Qiang. Interview in New York, March 24, 2010.
Deng Ming's best friend. Interview in Beijing, September 1997.
Deng Ming's mother and sister. Interview in Chengdu, June 2004.
Fan Jianchuan. Interview in Anren, October 2004.
Liu Jiakun. Interview in Chengdu, December 2008.
Long Taicheng. Interview in Chongqing, August 21, 2011.
Peasants. Interview in Anren, October 2004.
Peasant tourists. Interviews in Anren, July 2010.
Mr. Wu. Interview in Anren, August 18, 2011.
Zhao Shutong. Interview in Chengdu, August 17, 2011.

Publications and Other Media

Aarsleff, Hans. *From Locke to Saussure: Essays on the Study of Language and Intellectual History*. Minneapolis: University of Minnesota Press, 1982.

Adorno, Theodor W. *The Culture Industry: Selected Essays on Mass Culture*. Edited by Jay M. Bernstein. London: Routledge, 1991.

Adorno, Theodor W. *The Jargon of Authenticity*. Translated by Knut Tarnowski and Frederic Will. Evanston, IL: Northwestern University Press, 1973.

Adorno, Theodor W., and Max Horkheimer. *Dialectic of Enlightenment*. Translated by John Cumming. London: Verso, 1979.

Agamben, Giorgio. *The Coming Community*. Translated by Michael Hardt. Minneapolis: University of Minnesota Press, 1993.

Agamben, Giorgio. *Homo Sacer: Sovereignty and Bare Life*. Translated by Daniel Heller-Roazen. Stanford, CA: Stanford University Press, 1998.

Ahmed, Sara. "Affective Economies." *Social Text* 22, no. 2 (2004): 117–39.

Ahmed, Sara. *The Cultural Politics of Emotion*. Edinburgh: Edinburgh University Press, 2004.

Allert, Tilman. *The Hitler Salute: On the Meaning of a Gesture*. Translated by Jefferson Chase. New York: Metropolitan, 2008.

Althusser, Louis. "Crisis of Marxism." Translated by Grahame Lock. *Marxism Today*, no. 227 (July 1978): 215–27.

Althusser, Louis. *For Marx*. London: Verso, 1977.

Amadae, S. M. *Rationalizing Capitalist Democracy: The Cold War Origins of Rational Choice Liberalism*. Chicago: University of Chicago Press, 2003.

Anderson, Norman D. *Ferris Wheels: An Illustrated History*. Bowling Green, OH: Bowling Green State University Popular Press, 1992.

Anusaite, Vilma. "Welcome to Stalin World!" ABC News, September 12, 2007. https://abcnews.go.com/International/story?id=3591453&page=1.

Arditi, Benjamin. "On the Political: Schmitt contra Schmitt." *Telos*, no. 142 (Spring 2008): 7–28.

Arendt, Hannah. *The Human Condition*. Chicago: University of Chicago Press, 1958.

Associated Press. "City of London Corporation Wants 'Spy Bins' Ditched." *Guardian*, August 12, 2013. http://www.theguardian.com/world/2013/aug/12/city-london-corporation-spy-bins.

Atkin, Nicolas. "Hong Kong Protests Embrace Bruce Lee but Reject Jackie Chan in Tale of Two Martial Arts Heroes." *South China Morning Post*, June 29, 2019. https://www.scmp.com/sport/martial-arts/kung-fu/article/3016609/hong-kong-protests-embrace-bruce-lee-reject-jackie-chan.

Auerbach, Jeffrey. *The Great Exhibition of 1851: A Nation on Display*. New Haven, CT: Yale University Press, 1999.

Averill, Stephen C. *Revolution in the Highlands: China's Jinggang Mountain Base Area*. New York: Rowman and Littlefield, 2003.

Baar, A. "The Funnel Is Dead, Long Live the Loop." *Digiday*, July 25, 2013. http://digiday.com/sponsored/mediamathbcthe-funnel-is-dead-long-live-the-loop/.

Bah, Abu B. "Racial Profiling and the War on Terror: Changing Trends and Perspectives." *Ethnic Studies Review* 29, no. 1 (2006): 76–100. https://scholarscompass.vcu.edu/cgi/viewcontent.cgi?article=1250&context=esr.

Bai Tianyin. "A General Discussion of the Chivalry of the Martial Arts." [In Chinese.] *New West*, no. 6 (2011): 129. [白天寅, "中国武侠精神浅论"《新西部》(第六卷), 2011, 129.]

Ba Jin. *Random Thoughts*. [In Chinese.] Vol. 5. Hong Kong: Joint Publishing, 1986. [巴金,《随想录》(第五卷) 三联书店,香港, 1986.]

Bakken, Børge. *The Exemplary Society*. Oxford: Oxford University Press, 2000.

Ball, James. "NSA's Prism Surveillance Program: How It Works and What It Can Do." *Guardian*, June 8, 2013. http://www.theguardian.com/world/2013/jun/08/nsa-prism-server-collection-facebook-google.

Ball, James, Julian Borger, and Glenn Greenwald. "Revealed: How US and UK Spy Agencies Defeat Internet Privacy and Security." *Guardian*, September 6, 2013. http://www.theguardian.com/world/2013/sep/05/nsa-gchq-encryption-codes-security.

Ball, Philip. "Life's Lessons in Design." *Nature*, no. 409 (January 18, 2001): 413–16. https://www.nature.com/articles/35053198#citeas.

Bamford, James. "Shady Companies with Ties to Israel Wiretap the U.S. for the NSA." *Wired*, April 3, 2012. http://www.wired.com/threatlevel/2012/04/shady-companies-nsa/.

Barmé, Geremie R. *Shades of Mao: The Posthumous Cult of the Great Leader*. New York: M. E. Sharpe, 1996.

Barmé, Geremie R. "The Tide of Revolution—Zhejiang Chao." *China Heritage Quarterly*, no. 28 (2011): 1–13.

Barmé, Geremie R. "Toward a New Sinology." CSAA *Newsletter*, no. 31 (2005): 4–9.

Barthes, Roland. *The Eiffel Tower and Other Mythologies*. Translated by Richard Howard. Berkeley: University of California Press, 1997.

Barthes, Roland. *Travels in China*. Edited by Anne Herschberg Pierrot. Translated by Andrew Brown. Cambridge: Polity, 2012.

Bataille, Georges. "The Academic Horse." In *Undercover Surrealism: Georges Bataille and Documents*, edited by Dawn Ades and Simon Baker, 236–39. Translated by Krzysztof Fijalkowski and Michael Richardson. Cambridge, MA: MIT Press, 2006.

Bataille, Georges. *The Accursed Share: An Essay on General Consumption*. Vol. 1, *Consumption*. Translated by Robert Hurley. New York: Zone, 1988.

Bataille, Georges. "A Critique of the Foundation of the Hegelian Dialectic." In *Visions of Excess, Selected Writings, 1927–1939*, edited by Allan Stoekl, 105–16. Minneapolis: University of Minnesota Press, 1996.

Bataille, Georges. "Hegel, Death and Sacrifice." Translated by Jonathan Strauss. *Yale French Studies*, no. 78 (1990): 9–28. https://necrocenenecrolandscaping.files.wordpress.com/2018/01/bataille_hegel-death-and-sacrifice.pdf.

Bataille, Georges. *Inner Experience*. Translated by Leslie Anne Boldt. Albany: State University of New York Press, 1988.

Bataille, Georges. "The Notion of Expenditure." In *Visions of Excess, Selected Writings, 1927–1939*, edited by Allan Stoekl, translated by Allan Stoekl, with Carl R. Lovitt and Donald M. Leslie, Jr., 116–30. Minneapolis: University of Minnesota Press, 1996.

Bataille, Georges. "The Psychological Structure of Fascism." In *Visions of Excess, Selected Writings, 1927–1939*, edited by Allan Stoekl, translated by Allan Stoekl, with Carl R. Lovitt and Donald M. Leslie, Jr., 137–61. Minneapolis: University of Minnesota Press. 1996.

Bataille, Georges, Roger Caillois, Denis de Rougemont, Georges Duthuit, Rene M. Guastella, Pierre Klossowski, Alexandre Kojève, Michel Leiris, Anatole Lewitsky, Hans Mayer, and Jean Paulhan. *College of Sociology (1937–39)*. Edited by Denis Hollier. Translated by Betsy Wing. Minneapolis: University of Minnesota Press, 1988.

Baudrillard, Jean. *Simulacra and Simulation*. Translated by Sheila Faria Glaser. Ann Arbor: University of Michigan Press, 1994.

Beijing Agriculture. "Remembering the Two Heroes of Jinggang: Yuan Wencai and Wang Zuo." Mid-June 2011, 40–44. ["忆井冈双雄袁文才, 王佐"《北京农业》, 6 月中旬刊 2011, 40–44.]

Beijing Youth Daily (《北京青年报》). "Beautiful Writings Give Birth to Evil Flowers" ("妙笔生出恶之花"), July 5, 2004.

Beaver, Patrick. *The Crystal Palace*. West Sussex: Phillimore and Company, 2001.

Beckett, Samuel. *Proust and Three Dialogues—Samuel Beckett and Georges Duthuit*. London: John Calder, 1965.

Bellis, Mary. "Circus and Theme Park Innovations." Inventors (website). Accessed November 7, 2023. https://theinventors.org/library/inventors/blrollercoaster.htm.

Bellis, Mary. "The History of Theme Park Inventions." ThoughtCo. Last updated January 16, 2020. https://www.thoughtco.com/the-history-of-theme-park-inventions-1992556.

Benjamin, Walter. *The Arcades Project*. Edited by Rolf Tiedemann. Translated by Howard Eiland and Kevin McLaughlin. Cambridge, MA: Belknap Press of Harvard University Press, 1999.

Benjamin, Walter. *One-Way Street and Other Writings*. Translated by Edmund Jephcott and Kingsley Shorter. London: Verso, 1979.

Benjamin, Walter. "Theological-Political Fragment." In *Walter Benjamin, Selected Writings*, vol. 3, *1935–1938*, edited by Howard Eiland and Michael W. Jennings, translated by Edmund Jephcott, Howard Eiland, et al., 305–6. Cambridge, MA: Belknap Press of Harvard University Press, 2002.

Benjamin, Walter. "Theses on the Philosophy of History." In *Illuminations*, edited by Hannah Arendt, 245–55. Translated by Harry Zohn. London: Fontana, 1992.

Benton, Gregor. *Mountain Fires: The Red Army's Three-Year War in Southern China*. Berkeley: University of California Press, 1992.

Berger, J. "Art and Revolution." *AD*, no. 7 (1970): 66–67.

Billeter, Jean François. *The Chinese Art of Writing*. Translated by Jean-Marie Clarke and Michael Taylor. New York: Rizzoli, 1990.

Binti Hamzah, Fairoza Amira, Cher Lau, Hafez Nazri, Dominic Vincent Ligot, Guanhua Lee, Cheng Liang Tan, Mohammad Khursani, et al. "CoronaTracker: Worldwide COVID-19 Outbreak Data Analysis and Prediction." *Bulletin of the World Health Organisation*. March 19, 2020. https://inspem.upm.edu.my/upload/dokumen/2020050411400620-255695.pdf.

Bodmer, Frederick. *The Loom of Language*. London: George Allen and Unwin, 1944.

Bogdanov, Alexander A. *Essays in Tektology: The General Science of Organization*. Translated by George Gorelik. Seaside, CA: Intersystems, 1984.

Bogdanov, Alexander A. *Red Star: The First Bolshevik Utopia*. Translated by Charles Rouge. Bloomington: Indiana University Press, 1984.

Böger, Astrid. "Envisioning Progress at Chicago's White City." In *Space in America: Theory, History, Culture*, edited by Klaus Benesch and Kerstin Schmidt, 265–84. Amsterdam: Rodopi, 2005.

Bolotin, Norman, and Christine Laing. *The World's Columbian Exposition: The Chicago World Fair of 1893*. Champaign: University of Illinois Press, 1992.

Bossio, Diana. "Be Alert, Not Alarmed: Governmental Communication of Risk in an Era of Insecurity." Paper presented at the annual meeting of the Australian and New Zealand Communication Association, Christchurch, New Zealand, July 4–7, 2005. Available at https://www.researchgate.net/publication/228455937_Be_alert_not_alarmed_Governmental_communication_of_risk_in_an_era_of_insecurity.

Bourdieu, Pierre. "Public Opinion Does Not Exist." In *Communication and Class Struggle*, edited by Armand Mattelart and Seth Siegelaub, 124–30. New York: International General, 1979.

Boym, Svetlana. *Architecture of the Off-Modern*. New York: Princeton Architectural Press, 2008.

Boym, Svetlana. *The Future of Nostalgia*. New York: Basic Books, 2001.

Boym, Svetlana. "Tatlin, or, Ruinophilia." *Cabinet*, no. 28 (Winter 2007–2008). http://cabinetmagazine.org/issues/28/boym2.php.

Bracken, Christopher. *The Potlatch Papers: A Colonial Case Study*. Chicago: University of Chicago Press, 1997.

Bradsher, Keith. "China Enacting a High-Tech Plan to Track People." *New York Times*, August 12, 2007. http://www.nytimes.com/2007/08/12/business/worldbusiness/12security.html.

Bragg, Melvyn. *The Adventure of English: The Biography of a Language*. London: Hodder and Stoughton, 2004.

Bray, David. *Social Space and Governance in Urban China: The Danwei System from Origins to Reform*. Stanford, CA: Stanford University Press, 2005.

Bredekamp, Horst. "From Walter Benjamin to Carl Schmitt via Thomas Hobbes." Translated by Melissa Thorson Hause and Jackson Bond. *Critical Inquiry*, no. 25 (Winter 1999): 247–66.

Brenkman, John. "Introduction to Georges Bataille, *The Psychological Structure of Fascism*." *New German Critique*, no. 16 (Winter 1979): 59–63.

Breton, André. "Second Manifesto of Surrealism, 1929." *Matteson Art*. Accessed July 20, 2020. http://www.mattesonart.com/1111111111111111111111111new-page.aspx.

Brogan, J. V. "A Mirror of Enlightenment: The Rational Choice Debates." *Review of Politics*, no. 4 (Fall 1996): 793–806.

Brown, Wendy. *States of Injury: Power and Freedom in Late Modernity*. Princeton, NJ: Princeton University Press, 1995.

Brown, Wendy. *Undoing the Demos: Neoliberalism's Stealth Revolution*. New York: Zone, 2017.

Buber, Martin. *I and Thou*. Translated by Walter Kaufmann. New York: Touchstone, 1970.

Buchholz, Katharina. "The Most Surveilled Cities in the World." *Statista*, August 23, 2021. https://www.statista.com/chart/19256/the-most-surveilled-cities-in-the-world/.

Burkeman, Oliver. "Obama Administration Says Goodbye to 'War on Terror.'" *Guardian*, March 25, 2009. http://www.theguardian.com/world/2009/mar/25/obama-war-terror-overseas-contingency-operations.

Butler, Judith. *Gender Trouble: Feminism and the Subversion of Identity*. London: Routledge Classics, 2006.

Cadwalladr, Carole, and Emma Graham-Harrison. "How Cambridge Analytica Turned Facebook 'Likes' into a Lucrative Political Tool." *Guardian*, March 17, 2018. https://www.theguardian.com/technology/2018/mar/17/facebook-cambridge-analytica-kogan-data-algorithm.

Caillois, Roger. "Festival." In *The College of Sociology: 1937–1939*, edited by Denis Hollier and translated by Betsy Wing, 279–303. Minneapolis: University of Minnesota Press, 1988.

Campbell, Duncan, Oliver Wright, James Cusick, and Kim Sengupta. "Exclusive: UK's Secret Mid-East Internet Surveillance Base Is Revealed in Edward Snowden Leaks." *Independent*, August 23, 2013. http://www.independent.co.uk/news/uk/politics/exclusive-uks-secret-mideast-internet-surveillance-base-is-revealed-in-edward-snowden-leaks-8781082.html.

Chang Ping. "What Is the Tradition behind the Mao Zedong Statues?" [In Chinese.] *Educational Age* (2009): 12. [长平, "毛泽东塑像是 什么传统,"《时代教育》2009, 12.]

Channel 4 News. "FactCheck: How Many CCTV Cameras?" June 18, 2008. https://www.channel4.com/news/articles/society/factcheck%2Bhow%2Bmany%2Bcctv%2Bcameras/2291167.html.

Chao Feng. *Cultural Revolution Dictionary*. [In Chinese.] Hong Kong: Hong Kong Dragon, 1993. [巢 峰,《文化大革命词典》, 港龙出版社, 香港, 1993.]

Charity Watch. "'Not So' Great Nonprofits." Last modified January 4, 2012. http://www.charitywatch.org/tips.html.

Chen Dakang. "On the Three Ruan Brothers." [In Chinese.] *Study and Criticism*, no. 9 (1975) : 15–18. [陈大康, "论阮氏三兄弟"《学习与批判》. (第九卷), 1975, 15–18]

Cheung, Catherine, Rob Law, and Ada Lo. "The Survival of Hotels during Disaster: A Case Study of Hong Kong in 2003." *Asia Pacific Journal of Tourism Research*, no. 11 (February 2, 2007): 65–80. https://www.tandfonline.com/doi/abs/10.1080/10941660500500733.

Chicago History Museum. "Ferris Wheel, Standard of Business by the Week." Chicago: Chicago History Museum, 1983. Accessed July 20, 2019, at Google Arts and Culture. https://artsandculture.google.com/story/a-wheel-with-a-view-chicago-history-museum/JAVhbfL84qm6LQ?hl=en.

China-maoxie (The Art of Writing Chinese Mao Calligraphy). "Carrying Forward Mao-Style Calligraphic Art as an Inherited Artform of China." [In Chinese, "弘扬毛体书法艺术 传承中华民族文化."] China-maoxie website. Accessed June 3, 2020. http://www.china-maoxie.com.cn/index.php.

Christie, Nils. *Crime Control as Industry*. London: Routledge, 1993.

Chung Hua-Min and Arthur C. Miller. *Madame Mao: A Profile of Chiang Ch'ing*. Hong Kong: Union Research Centre, 1968.

Clark, Paul. *The Chinese Cultural Revolution: A History*. Cambridge: Cambridge University Press, 2008.

Claudin-Urondo, Carmen. *Lenin and the Cultural Revolution*. Translated by Brian Pearce. Sussex: Harvester, 1977.

Coderre, Laurence. *Newborn Socialist Things: Materiality in Maoist China*. Durham, NC: Duke University Press, 2021.

Colquhoun, Kate. *The Busiest Man in England: Life of Joseph Paxton, Gardener, Architect, Victorian Visionary*. Biddleford, ME: Godine, 2003.

Commercial Press, *Ciyuan*. [In Chinese.] Vol. 3. Beijing: Commercial Press, 1979. [《辞源》(第三卷), 商务印书馆 , 北京 1979.]

A Compilation of Materials on Following the Command of Mao Zedong Thought with New Medical Methods. [In Chinese.] Beijing: Beijing Municipal Health Bureau Leading Group, Beijing Second Medical College Revolutionary Committee, February 1969. [《毛泽东思想统帅新医疗法资料汇编》北京市卫生局领导小组北京 第二医学院革委会, 二月, 1969.]

Connolly, Kate. "Merkel Wins Narrow Victory over Social Democrat Rival in Preelection TV Clash." *Guardian*, September 2, 2013. http://www.theguardian.com/world/2013/sep/02/merkel-wins-hustings-debate.

Craig, David. *The Great Charity Scandal: What Really Happens to the Billions We Give to Good Causes*? Bournemouth, UK: Original Books, 2015.

Crane, Sam. "Cai Guo-Qiang: Taoist?" *Useless Tree*, March 5, 2008. http://uselesstree.typepad.com/useless_tree/2008/03/cai-guo-qiang-t.html.

Crawford, Neta C., and Catherine Lutz. "Human Cost of Post-911 Wars: Direct War Deaths in Major War Zones." Providence, RI: Watson Institute for International and Public Affairs, Brown University. November 13, 2019. https://watson.brown.edu/costsofwar/figures/2019/direct-war-death-toll-2001-801000.

Cruyl, Lieven. *Prospectus Turris Babylonicae* (engraving and etching). In *Turris Babel*, by Athanasius Kircher, 40. Amersterdam: Janssonio-Waesbergiana, 1679. Available at https://digi.ub.uni-heidelberg.de/diglit/kircher1679/0059. Last modified November 28, 2009.

Cui Xiaoli, ed. *Huangdi Neijing* [*The Yellow Emperor's Classic of Internal Medicine*]. [In Chinese.] Beijing: China Textile, 2012. [催晓丽:编译。《黄帝内经》中国纺织出版社, 北京, 2012.]

Cui Youfu. "How Mao Zedong Incorporated the Mountain Kings Yuan Wencai and Wang Zuo." [In Chinese.] *Historical Monthly*, no. 3 (2010): 52–54 [崔有富, "毛毛泽东是怎样收编 山大王袁文才 和王佐"《文史月月刊》(第03期), 2010, 52–54.]

Damisch, Hubert. "L'Autre 'Ich,' L'Autriche-Austria, or the Desire for the Void: Toward a Tomb for Adolf Loos." Translated by John Savage. *Grey Room*, no. 1 (2000): 26–41.

Dapiran, Antony. "'Be Water!' Seven Tactics That Are Winning Hong Kong's Democracy Revolution." *New Statesman*, August 1, 2019. https://www.newstatesman.com/world/2019/08/be-water-seven-tactics-are-winning-hong-kongs-democracy-revolution.

Davies, Gloria. "Homo Dissensum Significans: Or the Perils of Taking a Stand in China." *Social Text* 29, no. 2 (2011): 38–40.

Da Zheng. "Chinese Calligraphy and the Cultural Revolution." *Journal of Popular Culture* 28, no. 2 (Fall 1994): 185–201.

de Certeau, Michel. *Practices of Everyday Life*. Translated by Steven Rendall. Berkeley: University of California Press, 1984.

Delehaye, Hippolyte. *The Legends of the Saints*. Translated by Donald Attwater. New York: Fordham University Press, 1962.

Deleuze, Gilles. "Gilles Deleuze, Lecture Transcripts on Spinoza's Concept of *Affect*." Translated by Emilie and Julien Deleuze. Accessed June 19, 2018. https://www.gold.ac.uk/media/images-by-section/departments/research-centres-and-units/research-centres/centre-for-invention-and-social-process/deleuze_spinoza_affect.pdf.

Deleuze, Gilles, and Félix Guattari. *A Thousand Plateaus*. Vol. 2 of *Capitalism and Schizophrenia*. Translated by Brian Massumi. New York: Continuum, 2004.

Denton, K. A. "Can Private Museums Offer Space for Alternative History? The Red Era Series at the Jianchuan Museum Cluster." In *Popular Memories of the Mao Era: From Critical Debate to Reassessing History*, edited by S. Veg, 80–113. Hong Kong: Hong Kong University Press, 2019.

Derrida, Jacques. *The Gift of Death*. Translated by David Wills. Chicago: University of Chicago Press, 1995.

Derrida, Jacques. *Of Grammatology*. Translated by Gayatri Spivak. Baltimore: Johns Hopkins University Press, 1974.

Derrida, Jacques. *Politics of Friendship*. Translated by George Collins. London: Verso, 1997.

de Waal, Alex. "War on Disease Is a Self-Fulfilling Prophecy." *Foreign Policy*, June 13, 2021. https://foreignpolicy.com/2021/06/13/war-on-disease-is-a-self-fulfilling-prophecy.

Donnelly, Drew. "China Social Credit System Explained—What Is It and How Does It Work?" Horizons website. Last modified September 28, 2023. https://nhglobalpartners.com/chinas-social-credit-system-explained/.

Dorrian, Mark. "Cityscape with Ferris Wheel, Chicago, 1893." In *Urban Space and Cityscapes*, edited by Christoph Lindner, 17–37. London: Routledge, 2006.

Douglas, Mary. Foreword to *The Gift: The Form and Reason for Exchange in Archaic Societies*, by Marcel Mauss, translated by W. D. Halls, ix–xxiii. London: Routledge, 1990.

Draghici, S. Introduction to *The Idea of Representation*, by Carl Schmitt, 7–25. Washington, DC: Plutarch, 1988.

Drum, Kevin. "The Disposition Matrix." *Mother Jones*, October 25, 2012. http://www.motherjones.com/kevin-drum/2012/10/disposition-matrix.

Dupré, John, and Daniel J. Nicholson. "A Manifesto for a Processual Philosophy of Biology." In *Everything Flows: Towards a Processual Philosophy of Biology*, edited by John Dupré and Daniel J. Nicholson, 3–45. Oxford: Oxford University Press, 2018.

Dutton, Michael. "Lead Us Not into Translation: Notes toward a Theoretical Foundation for Asian Studies." *Nepantla: Views from South* 3, no. 3 (2002): 495–537.

Dutton, Michael. "'Mango Mao' Infections of the Sacred." *Public Culture* 16, no. 2 (2004): 169–71.

Dutton, Michael. "911: The After-Life of Colonial Governmentality." *Postcolonial Studies* 12, no. 3 (2009): 303–14. https://doi.org/10.1080/13688790903232393.

Dutton, Michael. *Policing Chinese Politics: A History*. Durham, NC: Duke University Press, 2005.

Dutton, Michael. *Streetlife China*. Cambridge: Cambridge University Press, 1998.

Du Xuncheng. "On Chao Gai." [In Chinese.] *Study and Criticism*, no. 10 (1975): 9, 19–21, 48–51. [杜恂诚, "论晁盖,"《学习与批判》(第十号), 1975, 9, 19–21, 48–51.]

Eco, Umberto. *The Search for the Perfect Language*. Translated by James Fentress. Oxford: Blackwell, 1995.

Economist. "The Baghdad Boom." March 25, 2004. https://www.economist.com/britain/2004/03/25/the-baghdad-boom.

Elias, Norbert. "The Quest for Excitement in Leisure." In *The Norbert Elias Reader*, edited by Johan Goudsblom and Stephen Mennell, 96–103. Oxford: Basil Blackwell, 1998.

Elias, Norbert, and Eric Dunning. *The Quest for Excitement: Sport and Leisure in the Civilising Process*. Oxford: Basil Blackwell, 1986.

Ellsworth, Chelsea. "What Donald Trump Learnt from Business." *Raconteur*, August 22, 2018. https://www.raconteur.net/business-innovation/trump-learnt-business.

Elvin, Mark, and Su Ninghu. "Man against the Sea: Natural and Anthropogenic Factors in the Changing Morphology of Hangzhou Bay, circa 1000–1800." *Environment and History* 1, no. 1 (1995): 3–54.

Erickson, Britta. "The *Rent Collection Courtyard*, Past and Present." In *Art in Turmoil: The Chinese Cultural Revolution 1966–1976*, edited by Richard King, 121–35. Vancouver: University of British Columbia Press, 2010.

Erickson, Jon. "The Spectacle of the Anti-spectacle: Happenings and the Situationist International." *Discourse* 14, no. 2 (1992): 36–58.

Explore PA History. "Ferris Wheel Inventor Historical Marker." Accessed June 3, 2011. http://explorepahistory.com/hmarker.php?markerId=1-A-35D.

Farquhar, Judith, and Qicheng Zhang. *Ten Thousand Things: Nurturing Life in Contemporary Beijing*. New York: Zone, 2012.

Fay, Charles Ryle. *Palace of Industry: A Study of the Great Exhibition and Its Fruits*. Cambridge: Cambridge University Press, 1951.

Feeney, Katherine. "Being a Porn Star Ain't What It Used to Be." *Brisbane Times*, March 4, 2010. http://www.brisbanetimes.com.au/entertainment/your-brisbane/being-a-porn-star-aint-what-it-used-to-be-20100303-pj5m.html.

Feuchtwang, Stephan. "François Jullien's Landscape, Site Selection, and Pattern Recognition." *Theory, Culture & Society* 40, no 4–5 (July 2023): 115–29. https://doi.org/10.1177/02632764221147663.

Fig, Joe. *Jackson Pollock* [Mixed media], 2008. Retrieved from https://www.joefig.com/historical?lightbox=dataItem-iqn31bp81.

Fitzgerald, John. "Continuity and Discontinuity: The Case of *The Water Margin* Mythology." *Modern China*, no. 12 (July 3, 1986): 361–400.

Fitzgerald, John. "The New Sinology and the End of History." CSAA *Newsletter*, no. 32 (2005): 13–18.

Forbes, Peter. "Building on Nature." *Nature* 425, no. 241 (September 18, 2003). https://www.nature.com/articles/425241b#citeas.

Ford, Henry, with Samuel Crowther. *My Life and Work: Henry Ford Autobiography*. Garden City, NY: Doubleday, Page, 1922.

Forty, Adrian. "Introduction to the Art of Forgetting." In *Material Culture: Critical Concepts in the Social Sciences*, edited by Victor Buchli, 181–95. London: Routledge, 2004.

Foster, John Bellamy. "Marx's Theory of Metabolic Rift: Classical Foundations for Environmental Sociology." *American Journal of Sociology*, no. 105 (1999): 366–405.

Foucault, Michel. *The Birth of Biopolitics: Lectures at the Collège de France, 1978–79*. Edited by Michel Senellart. Translated by Graham Burchell. London: Palgrave Macmillan, 2008.

Foucault, Michel. *Discipline and Punish: The Birth of the Prison*. Translated by Alan Sheridan. London: Penguin, 1978.

Foucault, Michel. "Governmentality." In *The Foucault Effect: Studies in Governmentality*, edited by Graham Burchell and Colin Gordon, 87–104. Chicago: University of Chicago Press, 1991.

Foucault, Michel. *The History of Sexuality, Part One*. Translated by Robert Hurley. New York: Vintage, 1980.

Foucault, Michel. *The Order of Things: An Archeology of the Human Sciences*. Translated by Alan Sheridan. New York: Vintage, 1970.

Foucault, Michel. *Society Must Be Defended: Lectures at the College de France; 1975–76*. Edited by Mauro Bertani and Alessandro Fontana. Translated by David Macey. New York: Picador, 2003.

French, Howard W. "Scenes from a Nightmare: A Shrine to the Maoist Chaos." *New York Times*, May 29, 2005. http://www.nytimes.com/2005/05/29/international/asia/29museum.html.

French, R. Antony. *Plans, Pragmatism, and People: The Legacy of Soviet Planning for Today's Cities*. Pittsburgh: University of Pittsburgh Press, 1995.

Freshwater, Ed. "COVID 19: Why We Need to Ditch the Military Terms." *Nursing Standard*. April 17, 2020. https://rcni.com/nursing-standard/opinion/comment/covid-19-why-we-need-to-ditch-military-terms-160071.

Freud, Sigmund. *Jokes and Their Relation to the Unconscious*. Vol. 6. Edited by A. Richards. Translated by James Stachey. Middlesex, UK: Penguin, 1976.

Freud, Sigmund. "Psychopathology of Everyday Life." In *The Basic Writings of Sigmund Freud*, edited and translated by Abraham Arden Brill, 35–152. New York: Random House, 1997.

Freud, Sigmund. "The Uncanny." In *The Standard Edition of the Complete Psychological Works of Sigmund Freud*, vol. 17, edited and translated by James Strachey, 217–52. London: Hogarth, 1919.

Fukuyama, Francis. *The End of History and the Last Man*. Middlesex, UK: Penguin, 1992.

Furner, James. "Marx's Sketch of Communist Society in *The German Ideology* and the Problems of Occupational Confinement and Occupational Identity." *Philosophy and Social Criticism* 37, no. 2 (2011). https://doi.org/10.1177/0191453710387071.

Gao Wei. *Random Notes on Beijing City*. Beijing: Xueyuan Publishing House, 2007. 高巍,《漫话北京城》学苑出版社出, 2007.

Gibney, Frank Jr., and Belinda Luscombe. "The Redesigning of America." *Time*, June 26, 2000. https://content.time.com/time/world/article/0,8599,2050262,00.html.
Gilman, Nils. *Mandarins of the Future: Modernization Theory in Cold War America*. Baltimore: Johns Hopkins University Press, 2007.
Givenchy advertisement. Accessed September 12, 2000. https://www.adforum.com/creative-work/ad/player/5687/video-surveillance/givenchy-oblique.
Godelier, Maurice. *The Enigma of the Gift*. Translated by Nora Scott. Chicago: University of Chicago Press, 1999.
Gorman, Carma, ed. *The Industrial Design Reader*. New York: Allworth, 2003.
Goux, Jean-Joseph. "General Economics and Postmodern Capitalism." Translated by Kathryn Ascheim and Rhonda Garelick. *Yale French Studies*, no. 78 (1990): 206–24.
Great Exhibition of the Works of Industry of All Nations (1851, London). *Reports by the Juries on the Subjects in the Thirty Classes into Which the Exhibition Was Divided*. London: William Clowes, 1852. Accessed June 15, 2005. https://doi.org/10.5479/sil.464343.39088012405411.
Greenwald, Glenn, and Ewen MacAskill. "Boundless Informant: The NSA's Secret Tool to Track Global Surveillance Data." *Guardian*, June 11, 2013. https://www.theguardian.com/world/2013/jun/08/nsa-boundless-informant-global-datamining.

Gross, Daniel M. *The Secret History of Emotion—from Aristotle's Rhetoric to the Modern Brain Science*. Chicago: University of Chicago Press, 2006.
Groys, Boris. *The Communist Postscript*. Translated by Thomas H. Ford. London: Verso, 2009.
Groys, Boris. *The Total Art of Stalinism: Avant-Garde, Aesthetic Dictatorship, and Beyond*. Translated by Charles Rougle. London: Verso, 2011.
Guanzi. "Water and Earth." In *Guanzi: Political Economic and Philosophical Essays from Early China*, vol. 2, edited and translated by W. Allyn Rickett, 98–107. Princeton, NJ: Princeton University Press, 1998.
Hall, D. Elden. *A Condensed History of the Origination, Rise, Progress and Completion of the "Great Exhibition of the Industry of all Nations."* New York: Redfield, 1852. https://www.loc.gov/item/07015705/.
Hannam, Peter, and Susan V. Lawrence. "Solving a Chinese Puzzle: Lin Biao's Final Days and Death, after Two Decades of Intrigue." *US News and World Report*, January 23, 1994. Archived October 23, 2012, at Archive.org. https://web.archive.org/web/20121023032235/http://www.usnews.com/usnews/news/articles/940131/archive_012336.htm.
Harding, Luke. "Edward Snowden: US Government Spied on Human Rights Workers." *Guardian*, April 8, 2014. http://www.theguardian.com/world/2014/apr/08/edwards-snowden-us-government-spied-human-rights-workers.
Hardt, Michael, and Antonio Negri. *Empire*. Cambridge, MA: Harvard University Press, 2000.
Harman, Graham. *Immaterialism: Objects and Social Theory*. Cambridge: Polity, 2016.
Harney, Stefano, and Fred Moten. *The Undercommons: Fugitive Planning and Black Study*. New York: Minor Compositions, 2013.

Harootunian, Harry. *Marx after Marx: History and Time in the Expansion of Capitalism*. New York: Columbia University Press, 2015.

Harper, Justin. "Coronavirus: Missouri Sues Chinese Government over Virus Handling." BBC News, April 22, 2020. https://www.bbc.co.uk/news/business-52364797.

Hauffe, Thomas. *Design: A Concise History*. London: Laurence King, 1998.

Hebei Art Press. *The Public Sculptures of "Rent Collection Courtyard."* [In Chinese.] Hebei: Art Press, 2000. [《收租院群雕》, 河北美术出版社, 河北, 2000.]

Hedrick-Wong, Yuwa. "Trump's Attack on China Could Ruin His Re-election Bid." *Forbes*, May 16, 2020. https://www.forbes.com/sites/yuwahedrickwong/2020/05/16/trumps-attack-on-china-could-ruin-his-re-election-bid/#956bfeb323ce.

Hegel, Georg Wilhelm Friedrich. *Phenomenology of Spirit*. Translated by Arnold V. Miller. Oxford: Oxford University Press, 1977.

Heidegger, Martin. *Being and Time*. Translated by John Macquarrie and Edward Robinson. Oxford: Blackwell, 1962.

Heidegger, Martin. *The Principle of Reason*. Translated by Reginald Lilly. Bloomington: Indiana University Press, 1991.

Heidegger, Martin. "What Is Metaphysics?" In *Basic Writings*, edited by D. F. Krell, 89–110. New York: HarperCollins, 1993.

Heilmann, Sebastian, and Elizabeth Perry. *Mao's Invisible Hand: The Political Foundations of Adaptive Governance in China*. Cambridge, MA: Harvard University Press, 2011.

Hempel, Jessi. "Social Media Made the Arab Spring, but Couldn't Save It." *Wired*, January 26, 2016. https://www.wired.com/2016/01/social-media-made-the-arab-spring-but-couldnt-save-it/.

Hensher, Philip. "Philip Hensher: The State Wants to Know What You're Up To. But Why Do We Let It?" *Independent*, November 17, 2011. http://www.independent.co.uk/voices/commentators/philip-hensher/philip-hensher-the-state-wants-to-know-what-youre-up-to-but-why-do-we-let-it-6263187.html.

Hern, Alex. "Cambridge Analytica: How Did It Turn 'Clicks' into Votes?" *Guardian*, May 6, 2018. https://www.theguardian.com/news/2018/may/06/cambridge-analytica-how-turn-clicks-into-votes-christopher-wylie.

He Xiaowen. "Jinggangshan's Silver 'Gong' Coin." [In Chinese.] *Old Friend*, 3, no. 14 (2015). [何小文, "井冈山'工'字银元"《老友》(第三卷, 第十四号), 2015.]

He Xinghan. "People in the Work Unit." [In Chinese.] In *People and Prose*, edited by Shao Yanxiang and Lin Xianzhi, 157–66. Guangzhou: Huachen Publishing House, 1993. [賀星寒, "人在单位中," 邵燕祥 & 林贤治,《散文与人》华晨 出版社 广州市, 1993.]

Hix, John. *The Green House*. London: Phaidon, 1974.

Ho, Denise Y., and Jie Li. "From Landlord Manor to Red Memorabilia: Reincarnations of a Chinese Museum Town." *Modern China* 42, no. 1 (2016): 3–37.

Holland, Gary. "Why 999 for an Emergency?" BBC News. May 13, 2010. http://news.bbc.co.uk/local/london/hi/people_and_places/history/newsid_8675000/8675199.stm.

Hollier, Denis. *Against Architecture: The Writings of George Bataille*. Translated by Betsy Wing. Cambridge, MA: MIT Press, 1998.

Howard, Michael. "For God, King and Country." *National Interest*, September 2, 2008. https://nationalinterest.org/article/for-god-king-and-country-2845.

Huang Jie. "How the Communist Party Transcended *Jianghu* Culture." [In Chinese.] *Realistic*, no. 12 (2011): 25–28. [黄杰, "中国共产党如何超越江湖文化"《唯实》(第十二号), 2011, 25–28.]

Hunter, Ian. *Culture and Government: The Emergence of Literary Education*. London: Macmillan, 1998.

Hu Ping. *The Thought Remolding Campaign of the Chinese Communist Party-State*. Edited by Philip F. Williams. Edited and translated by Yenna Wu. Amsterdam: Amsterdam University Press, 2012.

Hurst, Dominic. "Momohisan: The Gathering of the Spirits." *Mystical Borneo* 5, no. 4 (2000): 6–12.

Ingalls, Jeremy. *Dragon in Ambush: The Art of War in the Poems of Mao Zedong*. Edited by Allen Wittenborn. Lanham, MD: Lexington, 2013.

Jacobs, Katrien, Marije Janssen, and Matteo Pasquinelli, eds. *C'Lick Me: A Netporn Studies Reader*. Amsterdam: Institute of Network Cultures, 2007.

Jay, Robert. "Taller Than Eiffel's Tower: The London and Chicago Tower Projects, 1889–1894." *Journal of the Society of Architectural Historians* 46, no. 2 (1987): 145–56.

Jiang Renjie. *Explanatory Notes*. [In Chinese.] Vol. 1. Shanghai: Shanghai Ancient Books, 1996. [蒋人杰,《说文解字集注(上)》, 上海古籍出版社 上海市, 1996.]

Jones, Katie. "How COVID-19 Has Impacted Media Consumption, by Generation." *Visual Capitalist*, April 7, 2020. https://www.visualcapitalist.com/media-consumption-covid-19/.

Jullien, François. *The Propensity of Things*. Translated by Janet Lloyd. New York: Zone, 1999.

Kaprow, Allan. *Essays on the Blurring of Art and Life*. Edited by Jeff Kelley. Berkeley: University of California Press, 1993.

Kaprow, Allan. "The Legacy of Jason Pollock (1958)." In *Essays on the Blurring of Art and Life*, edited by Jeff Kelley, 1–9. Berkeley: University of California Press, 1993. https://doi.org/10.1525/9780520930841-005.

Kelley, Jeff. Introduction to *Essays on the Blurring of Art and Life*, by Allan Kaprow, xi–xxvi. Berkeley: University of California Press, 1993.

Kern, Stephen. *The Culture of Time and Space 1880–1918*. Cambridge, MA: Harvard University Press, 1983.

Kierkegaard, Søren. *Fear and Trembling*. Middlesex, UK: Penguin, 1985.

King, Gary. "How Censorship in China Allows Government Criticism but Silences Collective Expression." Presentation at the Data, Society and Inference Seminar, Fung Institute for Engineering Leadership, May 2, 2013. YouTube video, 1:20:03. https://www.youtube.com/watch?v=hybtm4Fp1jc.

King, Gary, Jennifer Pan, and Margaret E. Roberts. "How Censorship in China Allows Government Criticism but Silences Collective Expression." *American Political Science Review* 107, no. 2 (2013): 326–43.

King, Gary, Jennifer Pan, and Margaret E. Roberts. "Reverse-Engineering Censorship in China: Randomized Experimentation and Participant Observation." *Science* 345, no. 6199 (August 22, 2014): 891–901.

King, Magda. *A Guide to Heidegger's Being and Time*. Edited by John Llewelyn. Albany: State University of New York Press, 2001.

King, Ritchie S. "How 5 Security Technologies Fared after 9/11." *IEEE Spectrum*, August 30, 2011. https://spectrum.ieee.org/biomedical/devices/how-5-security-technologies-fared-after-911.

Kiss, Kenneth. *The Crystal Palace Museum: Pocket Profiles No. 3; The World's First*. London: Trustees of the Crystal Palace Museum, 2007.

Kline, Ryan, and Zack Martin. "ID Industry Fighting Big Brother Image." *SecureIDNews*, July 14, 2008. https://www.secureidnews.com/news-item/id-industry-fighting-big-brother-image/.

Knight, Nick. "Mao Zedong's 'On Contradiction': An Annotated Translation of the Preliberation Text." Griffith Asian Papers 3. Brisbane: Griffith University, 1981.

Kobler, John. "The Great Packager." *Life* 26, no. 18 (May 2, 1949): 110–12, 114, 116, 119–20, 122. Accessed May 3, 2005, at Google Books. https://books.google.com/books?id=hk4EAAAAMBAJ&pg=PA110&source=gbs_toc_r&cad=2.

Kohlmaier, Georg, and Barna von Sartory. *Houses of Glass: A Nineteenth Century Building Type*. Translated by John C. Harvey. Cambridge, MA: MIT Press, 1991.

Kojève, Alexandre. *Introduction to the Reading of Hegel: Lectures on the Phenomenology of the Spirit*. Translated by James H. Nichols, Jr. Ithaca, NY: Cornell University Press, 1980.

Koolhaas, Rem. *Delirious New York*. New York: Random House, 1994.

Kouwenhoven, John Atlee. *Half a Truth Is Better Than None: Some Unsystematic Conjectures about Art, Disorder and American Experience*. Chicago: University of Chicago Press, 1982.

Kraus, Robert Curt. *Brushes with Power*. Berkeley: University of California Press, 1991.

Kristeva, Julia. "Bataille, Experience and Practice." In *On Bataille: Critical Essays*, edited and translated by Leslie-Ann Bolt-Irons, 237–64. Albany: State University of New York Press, 1995.

Kuang Sheng and Liu Xiaonong. *The Heroic Pair of Jinggang—Yuan Wencai, Wang Zuo Zhuan*. [In Chinese.] Nanchang: Jiangxi People's Press, 2006. [匡胜, 刘晓农 ,《井冈双雄— 袁文才, 王佐传》, 江西人民出版社, 南昌, 2006.]

Leapman, Michael. *The World for a Shilling*. London: Headline, 2002.

Lecourt, Dominique. *Proletarian Science? The Case of Lysenko*. Translated by Ben Brewster. London: New Left, 1977.

Lee, Bruce. "Bruce Lee Be as Water My Friend." YouTube video, 0:38 (posted by Terry Lee McBride). Accessed December 3, 2019. https://www.youtube.com/watch?v=cJMwBwFj5nQ.

Lee Haiyan. "Class Feeling." In *Afterlives of Chinese Communism: Political Concepts from Mao to Xi*, edited by Christian Sorace, Ivan Franceschini, and Nicholas Loubere, 23–28. Acton, Australia: Australian National University Press and Verso, 2019.

Lee Haiyan. “The Enemy Within: The Fabling of the Water Dungeon, Rent Collection Courtyard, and Socialist Undead.” Paper presented at In the Heat of the Sun: The Production of Legitimacy in Mao’s China, Fairbank Center Workshop, Harvard University, April 7, 2007.

Lee Haiyan. *Revolution of the Heart: A Genealogy of Love in China 1900–1950*. Stanford, CA: Stanford University Press, 2007.

Lee Haiyan. *The Stranger and the Chinese Moral Imagination*. Stanford, CA: Stanford University Press, 2014.

Leese, Daniel. *Mao Cult: Rhetoric and Ritual in China’s Cultural Revolution*. Cambridge: Cambridge University Press, 2011.

Lei Feng. [In Chinese.] “After Liberation I Had a Family and My Mother Was in Fact the Party.” Chinaleifeng.com. [雷锋 “解放后我有了家,我的母亲就是党”《中国雷锋网》.] Accessed March 25, 2024. https://www.chinaleifeng.com/content/2019/11/12/6198368.html.

Lei, Sean Hsiang-Lin. “How Did Chinese Medicine Become Experiential? The Political Epistemology of Jingyan.” *Positions* 10, no. 2 (2002): 333–64.

Lenin, Vladimir Ilyich. “‘Left-Wing’ Communism—an Infantile Disorder.” In *Collected Works*, vol. 31, edited and translated by Julius Katzer, 17–118. Moscow: Progress, 1966.

Lenin, Vladimir Ilyich. “Notes for a Speech on March 27, 1922.” In *Collected Works*, vol. 36, edited by Yuri Sdobnikov and translated by Andrew Rothstein, 571–75. Moscow: Progress, 1966.

Lenin, Vladimir Ilyich. “State and Revolution.” In *Collected Works*, vol. 25, edited and translated by Stepan Apresyan and Jim Riordan, 385–539. Moscow: Progress, 1964.

Levine, Yasha. “Google’s Earth: How the Tech Giant Is Helping the State Spy on Us.” *Guardian*, December 20, 2018. https://www.theguardian.com/news/2018/dec/20/googles-earth-how-the-tech-giant-is-helping-the-state-spy-on-us.

Leys, Simon. *The Chairman’s New Clothes*. London: St. Martin’s, 1971.

Leys, Simon. *Chinese Shadow*. Middlesex, UK: Penguin, 1976.

Leys, Simon. *The Hall of Uselessness: Collected Essays*. New York: NYRB Classics, 2011.

Li, Jeff. “Hong Kong-China Extradition Plans Explained.” BBC News, December 13, 2019. bbc.co.uk/news/world-asia-china-47810723.

Li, Katherine, and Mike Ives. “Fueling the Hong Kong Protests: A World of Pop-Culture Memes.” *New York Times*, August 2, 2019. https://www.nytimes.com/2019/08/02/world/asia/hong-kong-protests-memes.html.

Lian Kuoru. *The Miscellany of Jianghu*. [In Chinese.] Beijing: Contemporary Chinese Press, 2007. [连阔如,《江湖行当》当代中国出版社, 北京, 2007.]

Liang Jie. “On Knowledge of the ‘Gong’ Coin.” [In Chinese.] *Money*, no. 100, January 2008, 44–49. [梁洁, “对井冈山‘工’字银元的认识,”《钱币》(第一百号)一月, 2008, 44–49.]

Li Jiakui, Ju Qizhi, and Li Zhenwu. “The Jinggangshan Five-Point Star ‘Gong’ Silver Dollar.” [In Chinese.] *Anhui Money* 1, no. 55 (2006): 6. [李家奎, 鞠起志, 李 振武 “井冈山五角星‘工’字银元”《安徽钱币》(一, 第五十五号), 2006, 6.]

Li Shaoyan. “Learning from the Sculptural Workers.” [In Chinese.] *Art Research*, November 6, 1965, 3–5. [李少言 “向雕塑工作者学习”《美术》六月, 1965, 3–5.]

Li Shiqiao. *Understanding the Chinese City*. London: Sage, 2014.

Lissitzky, El. *Russia: Architecture of World Revolution*. Translated by Eric Dluhosch. Cambridge, MA: MIT Press, 1970.

Littlewood, Anne. "Cyberporn and Moral Panic: An Evaluation of Press Reactions to Pornography on the Internet." *Library and Information Research* 27, no. 86 (Summer 2003): 8–18. http://www.lirg.org.uk/lir/pdf/article86a.pdf.

Liu, James J. Y. *The Chinese Knight-Errant*. London: Routledge and Kegan, 1967.

Liu Qun. "The Silver Dollar 'Gong' Coin of Jinggangshan." [In Chinese.] Jibi Online (website). December 10, 2003. http://bbs.jibi.net/TopicOther.asp?t=5&BoardID=20&id=5182. [柳群, "井冈山'工'字银元,"《Jibi Online》十号, 十二月, 2003.]

Liu Shanhong. "Big Data—Statistics and Facts." *Statista*, October 1, 2019. Archived June 13, 2020, at Archive.org. https://web.archive.org/web/20200613121137/https://www.statista.com/topics/1464/big-data/.

Liu Yanwu. *A Compendium of Slang and Hidden Language*. Beijing: Public Security University Publishing House, 1992. [刘彦武《俚语和隐语汇编》公安大学出版社, 北京, 1992.]

Liu Yanwu. *Tracing the Sources of the Secret Language of Chinese Jianghu*. [In Chinese.] Beijing: China Social Sciences Press, 2003. [刘延武,《中国江湖隐语溯源》, 中国社会科学 北京, 2003.]

Li Zengwen. "Paying Homage at the Relics of the Red Army Mint." [In Chinese.] *Hebei Finances*, no. 8 (2007): 66–77. [李增仁, "拜谒红军造币厂遗址,"《河北金融》(第八号), 2007, 66–77.]

Li Zhisui. *The Private Life of Chairman Mao: The Memoirs of Mao's Private Physician*. New York: Random House, 1994.

Loewy, Raymond. F. *Industrial Design*. London: Duckworth, 2002.

Loewy, Raymond F. *Never Leave Well Enough Alone*. Baltimore: Johns Hopkins University Press, 2002.

Loewy, Raymond (the Estate of). "About Raymond Loewy." Raymond Loewy, the Official Site. Accessed July 17, 2020. https://www.raymondloewy.com/about/biography/.

Loos, Adolf. "Ornament and Crime." In *Ornament and Crime: Selected Essays*, edited by Adolf Loos and translated by Michael Mitchell, 167–76. Riverside, CA: Ariadne, 1998.

Lu Duanfang. *Remaking Chinese Urban Form: Modernity, Scarcity and Space, 1949–2005*. London: Routledge, 2011.

Lynton, Norbert. *Tatlin's Tower: Monument to Revolution*. New Haven, CT: Yale University Press, 2009.

Maass, Peter. "How Laura Poitras Helped Snowden Spill His Secrets." *New York Times*, August 18, 2013. https://archive.nytimes.com/www.nytimes.com/2013/08/18/magazine/laura-poitras-snowden.html.

MacAskill, Ewen. "NSA Paid Millions to Cover Prism Compliance Costs for Tech Companies." *Guardian*, August 23, 2013. http://www.theguardian.com/world/2013/aug/23/nsa-prism-costs-tech-companies-paid.

Maine, Henry Sumner. *Ancient Law: Its Connection with the Early History of Society and Its Relation to Modern Ideas*. Gloucester, MA: P. Smith, 1970.

Makinen, Julie. "China Museum Builder Lets History Speak." *Los Angeles Times*, November 7, 2012. https://www.latimes.com/world/la-xpm-2012-nov-07-la-fg-china-museums-20121108-story.html.

Mao Tse-tung (Zedong). "Analysis of the Classes in Chinese Society." In *Selected Works of Mao Tse-tung*, vol. 1, pp. 13–23. Peking: Foreign Languages Press, 1975.

Mao Tse-tung (Zedong). "China's Red Political Power; Why Can It Exist?" [In Chinese.] In *The Military Writings of Mao Zedong*, vol. 1, pp. 11–18. Beijing: Military Science Press and Central Documents Press, 1993. [毛泽东, "中国的红色政权为什么能够存在?"《毛泽东军事文集》(第一卷), 军事科学出版社和中央文献出版社, 北京, 1993, 11–18.]

Mao Tse-tung (Zedong). "The Hunan Autumn Harvest Rising Needs Military Help, 1927." [In Chinese.] In *The Military Writings of Mao Zedong*, vol. 1, p. 7. Beijing: Military Science Press and Central Documents Press, 1993. [毛泽东, "湖南秋收暴动要有军队帮助"《毛泽东军事文集》(第一卷), 军事科学出版社和中央文献出版社, 北京, 1993, 7.]

Mao Tse-tung (Zedong). "Mao Zedong's Poems: Niannujiao—'Kunlun.'" [In Chinese.] Accessed July 9, 2024, at the Chinese Studies Network (website). http://sino.newdu.com/m/view.php?aid=21070.

Mao Tse-tung (Zedong). "On Contradiction." In *Selected Works of Mao Tse-tung*, vol. 1, pp. 311–46. Peking: Foreign Languages Press, 1975.

Mao Tse-tung (Zedong). "On Protracted War." In *Selected Works of Mao Tse-tung*, vol. 2, pp. 113–94. Peking: Foreign Languages Press, 1975.

Mao Tse-tung (Zedong). "Reply to Li Shu-yi—to the Tune of *Tieh Lien Htua* [*Dielianhua*]." May 11, 1957. Last modified 2007 at Marxists Internet Archive. https://www.marxists.org/reference/archive/mao/selected-works/poems/poems24.htm.

Mao Tse-tung (Zedong). "Sayings of Chairman Mao." In *Study and Criticism*, no. 9, 1975, frontispiece. [毛泽东。"毛泽东语录,"《学习与批评》9:1975.] Accessed February 13, 2024. https://www.bannedthought.net/China/Magazines/StudyAndCriticism/1975/StudyAndCriticism-1975-09-OCR-sm.pdf

Mao Tse-tung (Zedong). "Some Questions concerning Methods of Leadership." In *Selected Works of Mao Tse-tung*, vol. 3, pp. 117–23. Peking: Foreign Languages Press, 1975.

Mao Tse-tung (Zedong). "Speech at the Emergency Central Committee Meeting." [In Chinese.] In *The Military Writings of Mao Zedong*, vol. 1, pp. 1–3. Beijing: Military Science Press and Central Documents Press, 1993. [毛泽东, "在中央紧急会议上发言"《毛泽东军事文集》(第一卷), 军事科学出版社和中央文献出版社, 北京, 1993, 1–3.]

Mao Tse-tung (Zedong). "Speech at the Supreme State Conference (Excerpts)." In *Mao Tse-tung Unrehearsed: Talks and Letters, 1956–71*, edited by Stuart Schram and translated by John Chinnery and Tieyun, 91–96. London: Pelican, 1974.

Mao Tse-tung (Zedong). "The Struggle on Jinggang Mountain (25 January 1928)." [In Chinese.] In *The Military Writings of Mao Zedong*, vol. 1, pp. 21–50. Beijing: Military Science Press and Central Documents Press, 1993. [毛泽东, "井冈山的斗争 (二十五号, 一月, 一九二十八年)"《毛泽东军事文集》(第一卷), 军事科学出版社和中央文献出版社, 北京, 1993, 21–50.]

Maranzani, Barbara. "7 Things You May Not Know about the 1893 Chicago World's Fair." History.com. Updated May 16, 2023. http://www.history.com/news/7-things-you-may-not-know-about-the-1893-chicago-worlds-fair.

Marin, Louis. *Food for Thought*. Translated by Mette Hjort. Baltimore: Johns Hopkins University Press, 1989.

Marin, Louis. *Portrait of a King*. Translated by Martha M. Houle. Minneapolis: University of Minnesota Press, 1988.

Marinetti, Fillipo Tommaso. "1909: The Foundation and Manifesto of Futurism." In *The Industrial Design Reader*, edited by Carma Gorman, 70–74. New York: Allworth, 2003.

Markus, Thomas A. *Buildings and Power: Freedom and Control in the Origin of Modern Building Types*. London: Routledge, 1993.

Marr, Bernard. "Why Companies Turn to Digital Marketing to Survive COVID-19." *Forbes*, March 20, 2020. https://www.forbes.com/sites/bernardmarr/2020/03/20/why-companies-turn-to-digital-marketing-to-survive-covid-19/#357f08fc2425.

Martin, Brian G. *The Shanghai Green Gang: Politics and Organized Crime, 1919–1937*. Berkeley: University of California Press, 1996.

Martin, Theodore. *The Life of His Royal Highness the Prince Consort*. Vol. 2. London: Smith, Elder, 1876.

Marx, Karl. *Capital*. Vol. 1. Translated by Ben Fowkes. Middlesex, UK: Penguin, 1976.

Marx, Karl. *Capital*. Vol. 2. Translated by David Fernbach. Middlesex, UK: Penguin, 1978.

Marx, Karl. "The Eighteenth Brumaire of Louis Bonaparte." In *Karl Marx: Political Writings*, vol. 2, *Surveys from Exile*, edited and translated by David Fernbach. Middlesex, UK: Penguin, 1973.

Marx, Karl, and Friedrich Engels. "The German Ideology." In *Selected Works*, vol. 1, pp. 16–79. Moscow: Progress, 1977.

Massumi, Brian. "The Autonomy of Affect." *Cultural Critique* no. 31 (1995): 83–109.

Massumi, Brian. *A User's Guide to Capitalism and Schizophrenia*. Cambridge, MA: MIT Press, 1992.

Mataconis, Doug. "The Never Ending War on Terror." *Outside the Beltway*, October 24, 2012. http://www.outsidethebeltway.com/the-never-ending-war-on-terror/.

Ma Tao, "The Inside Story of Mao Zedong's 1975 Commentary on *The Water Margin*." In *Studies from the Commune Digital Library*. ["1975 年毛泽东 评《水浒》内幕"《学习公社数字图书馆》.] Accessed February 13, 2024. http://library.ttcdw.com/libary/zhengzhililunsuyang/ddls/2017-05-03/131761.html.

Matejka, Ladislav, and I. R. Titunik. Translator's note to *Marxism and the Philosophy of Language*, by V. N. Volosinov, translated by Ladislav Matejka and I. R. Titunik, 1–6. Cambridge, MA: Harvard University Press, 1998.

Matsakis, Louise. "How the West Got China's Social Credit System Wrong." *Wired*, July 29, 2019. https://www.wired.com/story/china-social-credit-score-system/.

Mauss, Marcel. *The Gift: The Form and Reason for Exchange in Archaic Societies*. Translated by W. D. Halls. London: Routledge, 1993.

Meehan, Patrick. "Ferris Wheel in the 1893 Chicago World's Fair." *Hyde Park Historical Society Newsletter* 22, no. 1/2 (Spring 2000). Accessed November 10, 2023. https://

www.hydeparkhistory.org/blog/2015/04/27/ferris-wheel-in-the-1893-chicago-worlds-fair?rq=treffman.

Meier, Heinrich. *The Lesson of Carl Schmitt: Four Chapters on the Distinction between Political Theology and Political Philosophy*. Translated by Marcus Brainard. Chicago: University of Chicago Press, 1998.

Merridale, Catherine. "All Wood and Dreams; Taitlin's Tower: Monument to Revolution." *Literary Review*, no. 367. Last modified July 2009. https://literaryreview.co.uk/all-wood-and-dreams.

Miller, Greg. "Plan for Hunting Terrorists Signals U.S. Intends to Keep Adding Names to Kill Lists." *Washington Post*, October 23, 2012. https://www.washingtonpost.com/world/national-security/plan-for-hunting-terrorists-signals-us-intends-to-keep-adding-names-to-kill-lists/2012/10/23/4789b2ae-18b3-11e2-a55c-39408fbe6a4b_story.html.

Minford, John. Introduction to *The Art of War*, by Sun Tzu, xi–xxxv. Translated by John Minford. New York: Penguin, 2003.

Ming Hong. "The Manor House of the Liu Family and the *Rent Collection Courtyard*, Today and Tomorrow." [In Chinese.] *Cultural History Monthly* 11, no. 52 (2004): 51–55. [明红, "刘氏庄园与《收租院》之今昔)"《文史月刊》(第十一期, 第五十五号), 2004, 51–55.]

Mitchell, Jon. "How Google Search Really Works." ReadWrite. Updated February 29, 2012. https://readwrite.com/2012/02/29/interview_changing_engines_mid-flight_qa_with_goog/#awesm=%7EoiNkM4tAX3xhbP.

Mitchell, Timothy. *Colonising Egypt*. New York: Cambridge University Press, 1988.

Moore, Alan. W. "A Brief Genealogy of Social Sculpture." Accessed June 30, 2020. http://www.joaap.org/webonly/moore.htm.

Moore, Keith. "Dial 999: 75 Years of Emergency Phone Calls." BBC News, June 30, 2012. https://www.bbc.co.uk/news/magazine-18520121.

Mouffe, Chantal. *The Return of the Political*. London: Verso, 1993.

Müller, Jan-Werner. *A Dangerous Mind: Carl Schmitt in Post-war European Thought*. New Haven, CT: Yale University Press, 2003.

Mu Yin. "How Are We to Assess Song Jiang?" [In Chinese.] *Study and Criticism*, no. 4 (1974): 44–46. [木印 "怎样评价宋江?"《学习于批判》(第四号), 1974, 44–46.]

National Archives. "Vietnam War U.S. Military Fatal Casualty Statistics." Last reviewed August 23, 2022. https://www.archives.gov/research/military/vietnam-war/casualty-statistics.

Naughton, John. "Why NSA's War on Terror Is More Than Just a 'Neat' Hacking Game." *Guardian*, November 9, 2013. http://www.theguardian.com/world/2013/nov/10/nsa-war-on-terror-neat-hacking-game.

New China Publishing House. *Mao Images*. [In Chinese.] Beijing: New China Publishing House, 1993. [《毛泽东画册》新华出版社, 北京, 1993.]

Nietzsche, Friedrich Wilhelm. *The Gay Science*. Bk. 4. Translated by Walter Kaufmann. New York: Vintage, 1974.

Nietzsche, Friedrich Wilhelm. *Thus Spoke Zarathustra*. Translated by R. J. Hollingdale. London: Penguin, 2003.

Nietzsche, Friedrich Wilhelm. *Twilight of the Idols*. Translated by Duncan Large. Oxford: Oxford University Press, 1998.

Nithyanand, Rishab. "The Evolution of Cryptographic Protocols in Electronic Passports." ResearchGate, May 27, 2015. https://www.researchgate.net/publication/266875822_The_Evolution_of_Cryptographic_Protocols_in_Electronic_Passports.

Niu Xiaodong. "Mao Zedong and John Dewey: A Comparison of Educational Thought." *Journal of Educational Thought* 29, no. 2 (August 1995): 129–47.

Noelle-Neumann, Elisabeth. "The Spiral of Silence: Public Opinion, Our Social Skin." In *A First Look at Communication Theory*, edited by Em Griffin, 372–82. New York: McGill-Hill, 2009.

Olender, Maurice. *The Languages of Paradise: Race, Religion, and Philology in the Nineteenth Century*. Translated by Arthur Goldhammer. Cambridge, MA: Harvard University Press, 1992.

O'Meara, Lucy. "Barthes and Antonioni in China." *Textual Practice* 30, no. 2 (2016): 267–86.

Ouyang Hui. "The Two Wang Zuos's Period of Struggle in Jinggang Mountain." [In Chinese.] *Party History*, no. 7 (2010): 41–43. [欧阳慧. "井冈山斗争时期的两个王佐." 《党史纵横》(第七号), 2010, 41–43.]

Ouyang Zongshu. *Chinese Genealogies*. [In Chinese.] Beijing: Xinhua Publishing House, 1992. [欧阳宗书,《中国家谱》, 新华出版社, 北京, 1992.]

Palmer, Abram Smythe. *Folk-Etymology: A Dictionary of Verbal Corruptions or Words Perverted in Form or Meaning, by False Derivation or Mistaken Analogy*, s.v. "Hiccough." New York: Henry Holt, 1890.

Palmer, David A. *Qigong Fever: Body, Science and Utopia in China*. London: Hurst, 2007.

Pashukanis, Evgeny Bronislavovich. *Law and Marxism: A General Theory*. Edited by Chris Arthur. Translated by Barbara Einthorn. London: Ink, 1978.

Pashukanis, Evgeny Bronislavovich. *Selected Writings on Marxism and Law*. Edited by Piers Bierne and Robert S. Sharlet. London: Academic Press, 1978.

Pearlman, Ellen. "Cai Guo-Qiang with Ellen Pearlman." *Brooklyn Rail*, April 4, 2008. http://brooklynrail.org/2008/04/art/cai-guo-qiang-with-ellen-pearlman.

People's Daily. "A Great Revolution That Will Touch People to Their Very Souls." [In Chinese.] June 2, 1966. ["触及人民灵魂的大革命."《人民日报》二号, 六月, 1966.]

People's Daily. "*Rent Collection Courtyard*—the Clay Sculptures of the Landlord Manor House Exhibition Hall of Dayi, Sichuan." [In Chinese.] November 27, 1965. ["《收租院》— 四川大邑地主庄园陈列馆泥塑群像"《人民日报》二十七号, 1965.]

Personnel dossier of Deng Ming (PDDM). [In Chinese.] N.d. Beijing, unpublished internal document. [《人事档案》.]

People's Daily Online. "Nineteen Sixty-Two: Mao Zedong Coined the Slogan 'Never Forget Class Struggle.'" [In Chinese.] September 27, 2009. Archived November 23, 2012, at Archive.org. https://web.archive.org/web/20121123155013/http://www.jiaodong.net/special/system/2009/09/27/010644159.shtml. ["1962年：毛泽东提出'千万不要忘记阶级斗争'."《人民网》北京, 二十七号, 九月, 2009.]

Petrova, Evgeniya, ed. *Malevich: Artist and Theoretician*. Translated by Sharon McKee. Paris: Flammarion, 1990.

Pettinger, Lynne. "Brand Culture and Branded Workers: Service Work and Aesthetic Labour in Fashion Retail." *Consumption, Markets, and Culture* 7, no. 2 (2004): 165–84.

Philips, Deborah. *Fairground Attractions: A Genealogy of the Pleasure Ground*. London: Bloomsbury Academic, 2012.

Poorhashemi, Abbas. "Can China Be Sued under International Law for COVID-19?" *Jurist*, May 21, 2020. https://www.jurist.org/commentary/2020/05/abbas-poorhashemi-lawsuits-china-covid19/.

Porkett, Manfred. *The Theoretical Foundations of Chinese Medicine*. Cambridge, MA: MIT Press, 1974.

Prince Consort Albert. "Speech at the Banquet Given at the Mansion House." In *The Principal Speeches and Addresses of His Royal Highness, the Prince Consort*, edited by A. Helps, 109–14. London: John Murray, 1862.

Qiu Jin. *The Culture of Power: The Lin Biao Incident*. Stanford, CA: Stanford University Press, 1999.

Qu Yanwu. *The Mysterious World of Gangster Jianghu Jargon*. Beijing: Jiuzhou Publishing House, 2023. [曲彦斌，《江湖隐语行话的神秘世界》九州出版社出版的图书, 北京, 2023.]

Quartz. "Two Different Museums in China about the Cultural Revolution Show Very Different Versions of History." Qz.com, May 16, 2016. https://qz.com/684836/two-museums-in-china-about-the-cultural-revolution-show-very-different-versions-of-history/.

Radojev, Hugh. "Coronavirus: Multichannel Retailers' Online Sales Soar in Lockdown." *Retail Week*, May 14, 2020. https://www.retail-week.com/technology/coronavirus-multichannel-retailers-online-sales-soar-in-lockdown/7034853.article.

Rancière, Jacques. *The Politics of Aesthetics*. Translated by Gabriel Rockhill. London: Continuum, 2004.

Ranger, Steve. "What Is the IoT? Everything You Need to Know about the Internet of Things Right Now." ZDNet, February 3, 2020. https://www.zdnet.com/article/what-is-the-internet-of-things-everything-you-need-to-know-about-the-iot-right-now.

Rao, P. Ramachandra. "Biomimetics." *Sadhana* no. 28 (June/August 2003): 657–76.

Richman, Michele H. *Reading Georges Bataille: Beyond the Gift*. Baltimore: Johns Hopkins University Press, 1982.

Rider, Alex. "An Introduction to the Early History of Ear Acupuncture." *International Business Times*, September 14, 2009. http://www.ibtimes.com/introduction-early-history-ear-acupuncture-183775.

Rifkin, Jeremy. *Beyond Beef: The Rise and Fall of the Cattle Culture*. New York: Penguin, 1993.

Robertson, Nic. "How Robot Drones Revolutionized the Face of Warfare." CNN, July 27, 2009. http://edition.cnn.com/2009/WORLD/americas/07/23/wus.warfare.remote.uav/.

Rodchenko, Aleksandr. *Experiments for the Future: Diaries, Essays, Letters and Other Writings*. Edited by Alexander N. Levrentiev. New York: Museum of Modern Art, 2005.

Rose, Julie K. “Welcome to the Fair.” World’s Columbian Exhibition: Idea, Experience, Aftermath. Last modified August 1, 1996. http://xroads.virginia.edu/~MA96/WCE/introduction.html.

Rose, Ken. New foreword to *The Yellow Emperor’s Classic of Internal Medicine*, translated by Ilza Veith, v–ix. Berkeley: University of California Press, 2002.

Roth, Andrew, Stephanie Kirchgaessner, Daniel Boffey, Oliver Holmes, and Helen Davidson. “Growth in Surveillance May Be Hard to Scale Back after Pandemic, Experts Say.” *Guardian*, April 14, 2020. https://www.theguardian.com/world/2020/apr/14/growth-in-surveillance-may-be-hard-to-scale-back-after-coronavirus-pandemic-experts-say.

Rushe, Dominic. “Apple Insists It Did Not Work with NSA to Create iPhone Backdoor Program.” *Guardian*, December 31, 2013. http://www.theguardian.com/technology/2013/dec/31/apple-nsa-backdoor-iphone-program.

Said, Edward. *Orientalism*. New York: Pantheon, 1978.

Salmon, Y., and Nicolas Zdanowicz. “Net, Sex and Rock ’n’ Roll! Les potentialités d’un outil comme internet et son influence sur la sexualité des adolescents.” *Sexologies* 16, no. 1 (March 2007): 43–52.

Sanger, David E., and Nicole Perlroth. “NSA Breached Chinese Servers Seen as Security Threat.” *New York Times*, March 22, 2014. http://www.nytimes.com/2014/03/23/world/asia/nsa-breached-chinese-servers-seen-as-spy-peril.html.

Schivelbusch, Wolfgang. *Disenchanted Night: The Industrialization of Light in the Nineteenth Century*. Translated by Angela Davies. Berkeley: University of California Press, 1988.

Schleifer, Theodore. “The Once-Hot Robotics Startup Anki Is Shutting Down after Raising More Than $200 Million.” Vox, April 29, 2019. https://www.vox.com/2019/4/29/18522966/anki-robot-cozmo-staff-layoffs-robotics-toys-boris-sofman.

Schmitt, Carl. *The Concept of the Political*. Translated by J. H. Lomax. Chicago: University of Chicago, 1996.

Schmitt, Carl. *The Idea of Representation*. Translated by E. M. Cobb. Washington, DC: Plutarch, 1988.

Schmitt, Carl. *Political Romanticism*. Translated by Guy Oakes. Cambridge, MA: MIT Press, 1986.

Schmitt, Carl. *Political Theology*. Translated by George Schwab. Chicago: University of Chicago Press, 2005.

Schmitt, Carl. *The Theory of the Partisan: Intermediate Commentary on the Concept of the Political*. Translated by G. L. Ulmen. New York: Telos, 2007.

Schneier, Bruce. “What We Don’t Know about Spying on Citizens: Scarier Than What We Know.” *Atlantic*, June 6, 2013. http://www.theatlantic.com/politics/archive/2013/06/what-we-dont-know-about-spying-on-citizens-scarier-than-what-we-know/276607.

Schnock, Frieder, and Renata Stih. *Bus Stop: Project for a Holocaust Museum in Berlin, 2005*. Accessed June 10, 2020. http://www.stih-schnock.de/bus-stop.html.

Schram, Stuart R., ed. *Mao Tse-tung Unrehearsed: Talks and Letters, 1956–71*. London: Pelican, 1974.

Schram, Stuart R. Introduction to *Mao's Road to Power*, vol. 3, *From Jinggangshan to the Establishment of the Jiangxi Soviets, July 1927–December 1930*, xxi–lxv. New York: M. E. Sharpe, 1995.

Schram, Stuart R., and Nancy J. Hodes, eds. *Mao's Road to Power*. Vol. 2, *Revolutionary Writings, 1912–1949*. New York: M. E. Sharpe, 1994.

Schram, Stuart R., and Nancy J. Hodes, eds. *Mao's Road to Power*. Vol. 3, *From Jinggangshan to the Establishment of the Jiangxi Soviets, July 1927–December 1930*. New York: M. E. Sharpe, 1995.

Schrift, Melissa. *Biography of a Chairman Mao Badge: The Creation and Mass Consumption of a Personality Cult*. New Brunswick, NJ: Rutgers University Press, 2001.

Schroyer, Trent. Foreword to *The Jargon of Authenticity*, by Theodor W. Adorno, translated by Knut Tarnowski and Frederic Will, vii–xvii. Evanston, IL: Northwestern University Press, 1973.

Schulz, Matthias. "'Red Tourism' Is Golden for Chinese Economy." *Spiegel*, March 28, 2013. http://www.spiegel.de/international/zeitgeist/the-growth-of-red-tourism-in-communist-china-a-891353.html.

Schwarcz, Vera. *Bridge across Broken Time: Chinese and Jewish Cultural Memory*. New Haven, CT: Yale University Press, 1998.

Seibt, Johanna. "The Myth of Substance and the Fallacy of Misplaced Concreteness." *Acta Analytica*, no. 15 (1996): 119–39.

Seibt, Johanna. "Ontological Tools for the Process Turn in Biology: Some Basic Notions of General Process Theory." In *Everything Flows: Towards a Processual Philosophy of Biology*, edited by John Dupré and Daniel J. Nicholson, 113–36. Oxford: Oxford University Press, 2018.

Shalikashvili, John M., and Hugh Shelton. "The Latest National Security Threat: Obesity." *Washington Post*, April 30, 2010. http://www.washingtonpost.com/wp-dyn/content/article/2010/04/29/ar2010042903669.html.

Shklovsky, Viktor. *Knights Move*. Translated by Richard Sheldon. Dallas: Dalkey Archive, 2005.

Sivin, Nathan. *Traditional Medicine in Contemporary China*. Ann Arbor: University of Michigan Center for Chinese Studies, 1987.

Sloterdijk, Peter. *In the World Interior of Capital: Toward a Philosophical Theory of Globalisation*. Translated by Wieland Hoban. Cambridge: Polity, 2013.

Smith, Adam. *An Inquiry into the Nature and Causes of the Wealth of Nations*. Edited by R. H. Campbell and A. S. Skinner. Indianapolis: LibertyClassics, 1981. http://files.libertyfund.org/files/220/0141-02_Bk.pdf.

Snow, Edgar. *Red Star over China*. London: Left Book Club, 1937.

Snyder, Laura J. "William Whewell." In *The Stanford Encyclopedia of Philosophy* (Spring 2022), edited by Edward N. Zalta. Last modified September 22, 2017. https://plato.stanford.edu/archives/spr2019/entries/whewell/.

Sochor, Zenovia A. *Revolution and Culture: The Bogdanov-Lenin Controversy*. Ithaca, NY: Cornell University Press, 1988.

Sofman, Boris. "Anki DRIVE." YouTube video, 4:29 (posted by Digital Dream Labs). July 23, 2014. https://www.youtube.com/watch?v=u9xcpSBQJJw.

Spillane, James. "From Edison to Internet: A History of Video Surveillance." Business-2Community. Updated September 2, 2022. http://www.business2community.com/tech-gadgets/from-edison-to-internet-a-history-of-video-surveillance-0578308.

Spinoza, Benedict de. *The Ethics*. Translated by R. H. M. Elwes. Project Gutenberg ebook. Updated December 11, 2017. http://www.gutenberg.org/files/3800/3800-h/3800-h.htm.

Spivak, Gayatri. Translator's preface to *Of Grammatology*, by Jacques Derrida, lxxxii. Baltimore: Johns Hopkins University Press, 1974.

Stafford, Andy. "Roland Barthes's *Travels in China*: Writing a Diary of Dissidence within Dissidence." *Textual Practice* 30, no. 2 (2016): 290.

Stedeler, Eckart. "Der Stein des Anstoßes-Ein denkmal für deserteure." [In German.] In *Verewigt und Vergessen Kriegsdenkmäler, Mahnmale und Gedenksteine in Göttingen*, edited by C. Gottschalk, 134–40. Göttingen: Volker Schmerse Text und Bildgestaltung, 1992.

Stein, Judith E. "Sins of Omission: Fred Wilson's Mining the Museum." *Art in America* (October 2003): 110–15.

Stein, Lise. "Sour Cherries of Freedom (Säure Kirschen der Freiheit)." *Göttinger Tageblatt*, August 31, 1990.

Stewart, Susan. *On Longing: Narratives of the Miniature, the Gigantic, the Souvenir, the Collection*. Durham, NC: Duke University Press, 1993.

Stoekl, Allan. Introduction to *Visions of Excess, Selected Writings, 1927–1939*, by George Bataille, edited by Allan Stoekl, ix–xxv. Minnesota: University of Minnesota Press, 1996.

Stoler, Ann L. *Race and the Education of Desire: Foucault's History of Sexuality and the Colonial Order of Things*. Durham, NC: Duke University Press, 1995.

Strauss, Julia C. *State Formation in China and Taiwan: Bureaucracy, Campaign, and Performance*. Cambridge: Cambridge University Press, 2019.

Strauss, Leo. "Jerusalem and Athens: Some Preliminary Reflections." In *Leo Strauss Studies in Platonic Political Philosophy*, edited by Thomas Lee Pangle, 147–73. Chicago: University of Chicago Press, 1983.

Strauss, Leo. "Notes on Carl Schmitt: The Concept of the Political." In *The Concept of the Political*, by Carl Schmitt, translated by J. H. Lomax, 81–108. Chicago: University of Chicago Press, 1996.

Strauss, Leo. "Progress or Return? The Contemporary Crisis in Western Civilization." *Modern Judaism* 1, no. 1 (1981): 17–45.

Stuchka, Pyotr Ivanovich. *Selected Writings in Soviet Law and Marxism*. Edited by Robert Sharlet and Piers Bierne. Translated by Peter B. Maggs. New York: M. E. Sharpe, 1988.

Sun-tzu. *The Art of War*. Translated by John Minford. New York: Penguin, 2003.

Surya, Michel. *Georges Bataille: An Intellectual Biography*. Translated by Krzysztof Fijalkowski and Michael Richardson. London: Verso, 2002.

Swedberg, Richard. "Civil Courage (*Zivilcourage*): The Case of Knut Wicksell." *Theory and Society* 28, no. 501 (1999): 501–28.

Tafuri, Manfredo. *The Sphere and the Labyrinth: Avant-gardes and Architecture from Piranesi to the 1970s*. Translated by Pellegrino d'Acierno and Robert Connolly. Cambridge, MA: MIT Press, 1987.

Taipei Times. "Hong Kong Hotel Is Eliminating Memories of SARS." February 23, 2004. http://www.taipeitimes.com/News/world/archives/2004/02/23/2003099824.

Tallis, John. *Tallis's History and Description of the Crystal Palace and the Exhibition of the World's Industry in 1851*. London: John Tallis, 1852.

Taussig, Michael. *Walter Benjamin's Grave*. Chicago: University of Chicago Press, 2006.

Taylor, Kim. *Chinese Medicine in Early Communist China, 1945–1963*. London: Routledge, 2005.

Taylor, Petroc. "Big Data and Business Analytics Revenue Worldwide, 2015–2022." *Statista*. Last modified August 26, 2022. https://www.statista.com/statistics/551501/worldwide-big-data-business-analytics-revenue.

Teng Yong. "A Viewpoint on Friendship in Personal Relations." [In Chinese.] *Political Work*, October 2009, 46–47. [滕勇,"论人际关系中的友谊观,"《政工学刊》, 十月, 2009, 10, 46–47.]

Tharoor, Ishaan. "Why Was the Biggest Protest in World History Ignored?" *Time*, February 15, 2013. http://world.time.com/2013/02/15/viewpoint-why-was-the-biggest-protest-in-world-history-ignored/.

Theobald, Mark. "Count Alexis de Sakhnoffsky (b. November 12, 1901–d. April 29, 1964)." Coachbuilt.com. Last modified 2012. http://www.coachbuilt.com/des/d/desakhnoffsky/desakhnoffsky.htm.

Tianjin City Archival Bureau. *A Handbook on Dossier Work*. [In Chinese.] Tianjin: Dossier Publishing House, 1988. [天津市档案局 1988《档案工作手册》档案出版社, 天津.] Accessed March 25, 2019. https://baike.baidu.com/item/档案工作手册/23792893.

Tianjin City Archival Bureau. *A Handbook on Dossier Work*. [In Chinese.] Tianjin: Dossier Publishing House, 1988. [天津市档案局.《档案工作手册》档案出版社, 天津.]

Todorov, Vladislav. *Red Square, Black Square*. Albany: State University of New York Press, 1995.

"The 2001 Ig Noble Prize Winners." In *Annals of Improbable Research* 8, no. 1 (January/February 2002): 8. https://www.improbable.com/ig/miscellaneous/ig-2001-winners.html.

V., Daniel [pseud.]. *Belshazzar's Feast in Its Application to the Great Exhibition*. London: Houlston and Stoneman, 1851.

Vincent, Julian. "Biomimetic Patterns in Architectural Design." *Architectural Design* 79, no. 6 (2009): 72–81.

Volosinov, Valentin Nikolaevich. *Marxism and the Philosophy of Language*. Translated by Ladislav Matejka and I. R. Titunik. Cambridge, MA: Harvard University Press, 1998.

Von Clausewitz, Carl. "Art of War or Science of War." In *On War*, edited by Michael Howard and Peter Paret, 148–51. Translated by Michael Howard and Peter Paret. Princeton, NJ: Princeton University Press, 1976.

Von Moos, Stanislaus, and Margaret Sobiesky. "Le Corbusier and Loos." *Assemblage*, no. 4 (1987): 25–37. https://doi.org/10.2307/3171033.

Wang Guanyi. "Looking Back on the *Rent Collection Courtyard*." [In Chinese.] *Sculpture Magazine*, no. 1 (1996): 38. [王官乙, "回首《收租院》,"《雕塑》, (第一号), 1996, 38.]

Wang Hua and Wang Li, eds. *The Jianchuan Museum Cluster—China: Anren Township*. [In Chinese.] Jianchuan Real Estate Co., n.d. [《建川博物馆聚落– 中国, 安仁镇》(王华与王蕾编辑), 四川安仁镇建川文化产业有限公司, 成都 n.d.]

Wang Li. "Reflections on the Spirit of *Jianghu* in Organizations with a Criminal Nature." [In Chinese.] *Journal of the Southwest University* 36, no. 2 (March 2010): 40–46. [汪力," 论江湖义气在黑社会性质组织中的影响."《西南大学学报》(第三十六卷, 第二二号) 三月, 2010, 月, 40–46.]

Wang Luxiang (producer) and Xia Jun (director). *River Elegy* [In Chinese,《河殇》.] China: CCTV, 1988. YouTube video, 58:00 (posted April 24, 2012, by Tetley Bildungsroman). https://www.youtube.com/watch?v=39j4ViRxcS8.

Wang Min'an. *Domestic Spaces in Post-Mao China: On Electronic Household Appliances*. [In Chinese.] Translated by Shaobo Xie. Oxford: Routledge, 2018. [汪民安,《论家用电 器》河南大学出版社, 河南, 2015.]

Wang Xuetai. *The Water Margin, Jianghu—Another Thread through Which to Understand Chinese Society*. [In Chinese.] Xian: Sha'anxi People's Press, 2011. [王学泰.《水浒一江湖— 理解中国社会的另一条线索》陕西人民出版社, 西安 2011.]

Wang Yi. "The Growth of All Things Relies on the Sun and Primitive Worship." [In Chinese.] In *The Great Cultural Revolution: Historical Facts and Research*, edited by Liu Qingfeng, 128–36. Hong Kong: Chinese University Press, 1996. [王毅. 万物生长靠太阳" 与原始崇拜,"《文化大革命:事实与研究》, 刘青峰 (编) 中文大学出版社 香港, 1996, 128–36.]

Wang Zhi'an. *The Heavens Thundered at the Peak of Poetic Perfection*. [In Chinese.] Chengdu, Sichuan: Tiandi Publishing House, 2001. [王治安,《轰天绝唱》, 天地出版社, 四川, 2001.]

Wang Zhi'an, Wang Fei, and Wang Shao. *The Secrets of the Manor*. [In Chinese.] Chengdu: Sichuan Publishing Group, 2003. [王治安, 王飞, 王晓,《莊園秘聞》四川出版社, 成都, 2003.]

Wang Zilin. *The Geomancy of the Imperial City*. [In Chinese.] Beijing: Forbidden City Press, 2011. [王子林,《皇城风水》, 紫禁城出版社, 北京, 2009.]

Weber, Max. *Economy and Society*. Vol. 2. Edited by Guenther Roth and Claus Wittich. Berkeley: University of California Press, 2013.

Weber, Max. *The Protestant Ethic and the Spirit of Capitalism*. Translated by Talcott Parsons. London: Unwin, 1985.

Wedell-Wedellsborg, Anne. "Contextualizing Cai Guo-Qiang." *Kontur*, no. 20 (2010): 9–18. http://kontur.au.dk/fileadmin/www.kontur.au.dk/Kontur_20/Microsoft_Word_-_vam-wedell_mod2.pdf.

Wiggershaus, Rolf. *The Frankfurt School: Its History, Theories, and Political Significance*. Translated by Michael Robertson. Cambridge, MA: MIT Press, 1998.

Wilson, Daniel. *The Archaeology and Prehistoric Annals of Scotland*. Edinburgh: Sutherland and Knox, 1851. Archived March 12, 2009, at Archive.org. https://archive.org/details/archaeologyprehioowils.

Wilson, Daniel. *Prehistoric Man: Researches into the Origin of Civilisation in the Old and the New World*. Vol. 1. Cambridge: Macmillan, 1862. Archived October 9, 2008, at Archive.org. https://archive.org/embed/prehistoricmanro6wilsgoog.

Wilson, Valerie Plame, and Joe Wilson. "The NSA's Metastasised Intelligence-Industrial Complex Is Ripe for Abuse." *Guardian*, June 23, 2013. https://www.theguardian.com/commentisfree/2013/jun/23/nsa-intelligence-industrial-complex-abuse.

Wired. "The Cambridge Analytica Story Explained: A Quick, but Thorough, Overview of the Controversy." March 21, 2018. https://www.wired.com/amp-stories/cambridge-analytica-explainer/.

Wittgenstein, Ludwig. *The Blue and Brown Books: Preliminary Studies for the "Philosophical Investigations."* Oxford: Blackwell, 1994.

Wittgenstein, Ludwig. *Philosophical Investigations*. Translated by Gertrude Elizabeth Margaret Anscombe. Oxford: Blackwell, 1993.

Wolf, Naomi. "The Coming Drone Attack on America." *Guardian*, December 21, 2012. http://www.theguardian.com/commentisfree/2012/dec/21/coming-drone-attack-america.

Wolin, Richard. *Walter Benjamin: An Aesthetic of Redemption*. Berkeley: University of California Press, 1994.

Wolkowitz, Carol. "The Working Body as a Sign: Historical Snapshot." In *Constructing Gendered Bodies*, edited by Katherine Backett-Milburn and Linda McKie, 85–103. Basingstoke, UK: Palgrave, 2001.

Wong, Michelle. "Out of Character? Xi Jinping Has a Mao Zedong–Style Signature." *South China Morning Post*, January 8, 2019. https://www.scmp.com/news/china/society/article/2181256/out-character-xi-jinping-has-mao-zedong-style-signature.

Wu Cheng'en. *Journey to the West*. 3 vols. Translated by William Francis Jenner. Beijing: Foreign Languages Press, 1984.

Wu Manping. "The Markings on the Jinggang Mountain Silver Dollar, Explored." [In Chinese.] *Chinese Money*, no. 102 (March 2006): 43–45. [吴满平, "井冈山 '工' 字银元戳记版式考证,"《中国钱币》, (第一百零二号) 三月, 2006, 43–45.]

Xia Mengshu. *Traveling in Jinggang Mountain*. [In Chinese.] Jinggang Mountain: Jinggang Mountain Tourism Series, 2000. [夏梦淑,《井冈山旅游》井冈山旅游丛书 井冈山, 2000.]

Xiao Shu. *The Big Landlord, Liu Wencai*. [In Chinese.] Guangdong: Guangdong People's Press, 2008. [笑蜀,《大地主刘文彩》广东人民出版社 广东, 2008.]

Xiao Shu. *The True Liu Wencai*. [In Chinese.] Xi'an: Shaanxi Normal University Publishing House, 1999. [笑蜀,《刘文彩真相》陕西师范大学出版社, 西安, 1999.]

Xie Jianhua. *The Vigor and Grace of Chinese Calligraphy*. [In Chinese.] Shenyang: Liaoning Ancient Books, 1995. [谢建华《笔走龙蛇的中国书法》辽宁古籍出版社 沈阳, 1995.]

Xin Guo. "Du Xiujing and the Jinggang Mountain 'Gong' Coin." [In Chinese.] *Old Dongquan Court*, no. 6 (2008): 84–85. [新国, "杜修经与井冈山'工'字银元,"《老董泉苑》(第六号) 2008, 84–85.]

Xinhuanet. "Public Security Ministry Notice concerning the Issuance of Second-Generation Identity Cards." [In Chinese, 公安部通报换发第二代居民身份证有关情况.] Xinhuanet, March 16, 2006. Archived March 5, 2016, at Archive.org, https://web.archive.org/web/20160305194249/http://news.xinhuanet.com:80/legal/2006-03/16/content_4309183.htm.

Xin Jiyuan. "The New Era: Facts and Fiction of Liu Wencai." [In Chinese, 新纪元:真假刘文彩.] *Epochtimes*, August 2, 2013. Archived September 14, 2014, at Archive.org, https://web.archive.org/web/20140914225459/http://jiengxien.blog.epochtimes.com/article/show?articleid=44789.

Xu Jixu. "'What Is There to Praise? What Is There to Oppose?' Commenting on the Essence of the Capitulationism in *The Water Margin*." [In Chinese.] *Study and Criticism*, no. 10 (1975): 44–48. [徐缉熙, "歌颂什么, 反对什么: 平《水浒》的 投降主义本质》,《学习与批判》10, 44–48.]

Yang, Mayfair Mei-hui. *Gifts, Favors, and Banquets: The Art of Social Relationships in China*. Ithaca, NY: Cornell University Press, 1994.

Yang Dongping. *City Monsoon; the Spiritual Culture of Beijing and Shanghai*. [In Chinese.] Beijing: Dongfang Publishing House, 1994. [杨东平,《城市季风:北京与上海文化精神》东方出版社, 北京, 1994.]

Yan Yi. "Some Opinions on the Struggle over the 'Line' within the Liang Mountain Peasant Army." [In Chinese.] *Study and Criticism* 5, no. 66 (1974): 63–68. [严己, (1974) "试论梁山农民军中的路线斗争"《学习于批判》五 (第六十六号), 1974, 63–68.]

Yen Yuehping. *Calligraphy and Power in Contemporary Chinese Society*. New York: Routledge, 2005.

Yi Ding, Yu Lu, and Hong Yong. *Geomancy and Selections from the Built Environment*. [In Chinese.] Taiwan: Arts Press, 1999. [一丁, 雨露 与 洪湧, (1999),《中國風水與建築選址》藝術家, 台湾, 1999.]

Yi Xiaocuo. "Blood Lineage." In *Afterlives of Chinese Communism*, edited by Christian Sorace, Ivan Franceschini, and Nicholas Loubere, 17–22. Acton: Australian National University Press and Verso, 2019.

Young, Paul. *Globalization and the Great Exhibition: The Victorian World Order*. Hampshire, UK: Palgrave Macmillan, 2009.

Young, Paul. "Mission Impossible: Globalization and the Great Exhibition." In *Britain, the Empire, and the World at the Great Exhibition of 1851*, edited by Jeffrey A. Auerbach and Peter H. Hoffenberg, 3–27. Aldershot, UK: Ashgate, 2008.

Yu Boliu and Chen Gang. *The Complete History of the Jinggang Mountain Revolutionary Base*. [In Chinese.] Nanchang: Jiangxi People's Press, 2007. [余伯流, 陈钢, (2007)《井冈山革命根据地 全史》江西人民出版社, 南昌 2007.]

Yu Shiquan. "My Views on the Silver Coins of Jinggang Mountain." [In Chinese.] *Anhui Money*, no. 4 (2008): 15n1. [余石泉, "井冈山银币之我见"《安徽钱币》, 第四期 2008, 15n1.]

Yu Yang. *Chinese Jianghu: The Chinese Origins of a Non-official System*. [In Chinese.] Beijing: Contemporary Chinese Press, 2006. [于阳.《中国江湖: 一个非正式制度在中国的起因》, 北京: 当代中国出版社, 2006.]

Zhai Qing. "Comment on Capitulationalism in *The Water Margin*." *Study and Criticism*, no. 9 (1975): 4–10. [翟青, "评《水浒》投降主义"《学习与批判》(第九号), 1975, 4–10.]

Zhang Jie and Wang Tao. "Housing Development in the Socialist Planned Economy from 1949 to 1978." In *Modern Urban Housing in China, 1840–2000*, edited by Lu Junhua, Peter G. Rowe, and Zhang Jie, 105–40. Munich: Prestel, Verlag, 2001.

Zhang Longxi. "The Myth of the Other: China in the Eyes of the West." *Critical Inquiry* 15, no. 1 (1988): 108–31.

Zhang Shiming and Wan Shaoyuan. "Thinking about Resourceful Star." *Study and Criticism*, no. 10 (1975): 48–51. [章智明, 完绍元, "试论吴用"《学习与批判》(第十号), 1975, 48–51.]

Zhang Xudong. "The Two Heroes of Jinggang Mountain: Yuan Wencai and Wang Zuo." [In Chinese.] *Party History Materials*, no. 9 (2007): 38–41. [张旭东, "井冈山双雄: 袁文才, 王佐"《党史博采》(第九号), 2007, 38–41.]

Zhang Youyun. "The Roots of the Changing Appreciation of the *Rent Collection Courtyard* in Popular Perceptions." [In Chinese.] *Art Research* (April 2005): 46–53 [张幼云, "论公众对泥塑《收租院》兴趣转向之主要根源,"《美术研究》, 四月, 2005, 46–53.]

Zheng Li. *On Zhuangzi's Aesthetics and Chinese Traditional Art*. [In Chinese.] Beijing: Commercial Press, 2012. [郑笠,《庄子美学与中古代画论》商务印书馆出版, 北京, 2012.]

Zheng Shigeng. *Zhuangzi's Theory of Qi*. [In Chinese.] Taipei: Taiwan Student Bookstore Press, 1993. [鄭世根,《莊子氣化論》臺灣學生書局印行, 台配, 1993.]

Zhong Shuxiao, ed. *The Handbook of Personnel Work in an Organization*. [In Chinese.] Wuhan: Hubei People's Press, 1986. [钟书, 撨《组织人事工作手册》, 湖北出版社 武汉, 1986.]

Zhou, Viola, and Alan Wong. "Be Water: The Bruce Lee Philosophy behind Hong Kong's Protests." *Inkstone*, August 6, 2019. https://www.inkstonenews.com/politics/hong-kong-protesters-get-inspirations-bruce-lee-kung-fu-strategy/article/3021622.

Zhou He et al., eds. *Mandarin Dictionary*. [In Chinese.] 3rd ed. Taipei: Wunan Books, 2004. [周何 (主编)《國語活用字典》五南圖書出版公司, 台配, 2004.]

Zhou Jihou. *The Mystery of the Mao Badge: The Ninth Wonder of the World*. [In Chinese.] Beijing: Beiyue, 1993. [周继厚,《毛泽东像 章之谜—世界九大奇迹》, 北岳出版社, 北京, 1993.]

Zhu Jianfei. *Chinese Spatial Strategies: Imperial Beijing 1420–1911*. London: Routledge, 2004.

Zhu Jianfei. "Empire of Signs of Empire: Scale and Statehood in Chinese Culture." *Harvard Design Magazine*, no. 38 (2014): 132–42.

Zhu Shengguo. "What Is Being Managed at the Cultural Revolution Museum?" [In Chinese.] *Qianlong*, April 22, 2004. http://review.qianlong.com/20060/2004/04/22/1260@2017265.htm. [朱胜国, "文革博物馆在'经营'什么?"]

Zhu Xinxia. *A Concise Dictionary of Librarianship, Information Technology, and Dossier Collection*. [In Chinese.] Tianjin: Nankai University Press, 1991. [朱新夏,《图书馆学情报学档案学简明辞典》, 天津: 南开大学出版社, 天津, 1991.]
Zmuda, Natalie. "Mastercard's Priceless Evolution: How the Brand Put a New Twist on Its 15-Year-Old Campaign." *Ad Age*, October 11, 2012. http://adage.com/article/special-report-ana-annual-meeting-2012/mastercard-s-priceless-evolution/237706/.
Zuboff, Shoshana. *The Age of Surveillance: The Fight for a Human Future at the New Frontier of Power*. London: Profile, 2019.

INDEX